Praise for Charles J. Sykes' *ProfScam*

"Mr. Sykes' vivid and occasionally eloquent exposé is sure to provoke howls of indignant rage in the academy. . . . But as a report from the front, *ProfScam* is an incisive and convincing indictment that deserves to be read by anyone concerned about the future of American higher education."
                    —*The New York Times Book Review*

"Stupendously provocative . . . *ProfScam* is an immensely important document, one that cuts to the heart of America's academic darkness and it deserves to be taken seriously by anyone who cares about our universities and worries about the future."
                    —Jonathan Yardley, *The Washington Post*

"[A] pugnacious, absorbing, funny, informative book. . . . Could Charles Sykes be the Ralph Nader of a coming academic reform movement? To the professors, such a movement will probably look like a horde of barbarians storming the gates of the Temple of Knowledge. But the mass of evidence chronicled by Sykes suggests that the barbarians are on the other side of the gates."
                    —*The Detroit News*

"There are few institutions more in need of a thorough debunking than American universities, and in *ProfScam* they have found it."
                    —*The Wall Street Journal*

"Any parent who is planning to spend big bucks to send a son or daughter to a big-name university should especially read *ProfScam*. . . . It should be required reading for anyone who wants to think or talk seriously about universities."
                    —Thomas Sowell, Syndicated Columnist

"Sykes demonstrates both his skill as an investigative reporter and as an essayist. His thesis—that the professoriate is responsible for inflicting terrible damage to our system of higher education—is well-documented and delineated in a clear, engaging and often humorous style. . . . *ProfScam* is a stunning and disturbing piece of work. One can only hope that it will be an influential one as well."
—*The California Review*

"An extraordinary book about higher education in America. . . . The thrill of Mr. Sykes's book resides in its relentless specificity."
—*National Review*

"This man is a truth teller, therefore he is shrill, obnoxious, abusive, aggressive, offensive, and absolutely right. . . . A first-rate analysis of a major national calamity—the end of the university as a suitable medium for educating our young people."
—*Chronicles*

"Sykes goes beyond the ivied walls and yields us a view of the university that combines wit with serious and important criticism."
—Robert Nisbet, Professor Emeritus,
Columbia University

"[*ProfScam*] tells us much more than Bloom does about the sickening tailspin into which American higher education has fallen, and he tells it in a brief, rapid-fire, and useful way."
—*Commentary*

"A valuable contribution to the continuing debate on what is wrong and right with higher education."
—*Modern Age*

"A passionate—at times marvelously witty—expression of love by one who learned from his professor-father that criticism can improve education by making professors better than they are."
—*Phi Kappa Phi Journal*

THE
HOLLOW
MEN

POLITICS AND CORRUPTION
IN HIGHER EDUCATION

Charles J. Sykes

Regnery Gateway
Washington, D.C.

Copyright © 1990 by Charles J. Sykes

Library of Congress Cataloging-in-Publication Data

Sykes, Charles J., 1954–
   The hollow men : politics and corruption in higher education / Charles J. Sykes.
   p.   cm.
   Includes bibliographical references.
   ISBN 0-89526-539-7 (alk. paper)
   1. Education, Higher—United States.   2. Universities and colleges—United States—Curricula.   3. Dartmouth College—Curricula.   I. Title.
LA227.3.S92   1990
378.73—dc20   90-36533
                                                                              CIP

Published in the United States by
Regnery Gateway
1130 17th Street, NW
Washington, DC 20036

Distributed to the trade by
National Book Network
4720-A Boston Way
Lanham, MD 20706

1990 printing
Printed on acid free paper
Manufactured in the United States of America
10   9   8   7   6   5   4   3   2   1

For Katherine B. Sykes

CONTENTS

PART III: WHAT IT MEANS

PREFACE

This book is about the triumph of ideology over ideas in American higher education: the fragmentation and incoherence of the curriculum; the nihilism that passes for the humanities; the politicization of both scholarship and the classroom; and the darkening shadow of intolerance and intimidation reflected in official attempts to limit free speech.

To understand the nature of this collapse, I have focused not merely on what is happening in the exotic realms of academic scholarship, but more specifically on how ideology has trickled down into the classroom and shaped the quality and content of the education that college students in 1990 receive. The first half of this book discusses the depth and extent of the crisis in higher education, while the second half discusses its impact on a single institution: Dartmouth College.

Why Dartmouth?

Certainly not because it is the most flagrant case (it is not), but because it is a microcosm of the changes in American colleges and universities over the last seventy years. Perhaps because of its size and its relative isolation, those issues tend to be writ larger at Dartmouth than other institutions. As a result of its apparently limitless capacity to indulge in internecine bloodlettings, Dartmouth has probably received more national attention in the past decade than any other single institution of higher learning. To its deep chagrin, it has become emblematic of the academic crisis of the 1980s and 1990s.

But it is also a paradox. Dartmouth remains one of the most prestigious institutions of higher education in the nation. It is ranked eighth—ahead of such schools as the University of Chicago, Columbia, Johns Hopkins, Georgetown, and the University of Michigan—in one widely distributed survey of major universities. Its student body is bright and ambitious; its faculty talented. At one time, Dartmouth was perhaps the premiere independent liberal arts college in the country and a leading light in the preservation of academic freedom. But those traditions only bring its current agony and confusion into sharper relief.

If a school of Dartmouth's traditions and obvious quality can fall so far, and so hard, what does that say of the virulence of the academic disease?

While there are those who are quick to attribute its quarrels and alarums to the presence of a provocative student newspaper, *The Dartmouth Review*, that explanation ignores the seriousness of the issues facing the College. Dartmouth, it seems, would rather talk about *The Dartmouth Review* than liberal education.

Even so, I was taken somewhat by surprise by the intensity of the divisions at Dartmouth. As I told one magazine interviewer, I sometimes felt as if I had been dropped into medieval Verona, in the middle of a feud that had been going on for generations between the Montagus and Capulets.

An incident that occurred during the writing of this book may shed some light on the atmosphere in Hanover. As a followup to *ProfScam: Professors and the Demise of Higher Education,** I began a study of the liberal arts curriculum and the politicization of the university. After I had begun work on that project, I was contacted by the Ernest Martin Hopkins Institute which asked me to study Dartmouth College's curriculum, an endeavor I undertook with a grant from the Institute. I have incorporated that study into this book.

I should add here that the Institute and its chairman, George Champion, were thoughtful, gracious, generous, and imposed no limits or preconditions of any sort on my work. This book does not necessarily

---

* Regnery Gateway, 1988

reflect the views of the Hopkins Institute and its conclusions should not be imputed to the Institute.

Dartmouth's attitude was rather different. Actually, it was extraordinary.

After the Hopkins Institute had shared its plans with the College, three members of the Dartmouth Board of Trustees, including chairman George Munroe, attended a board meeting of the Hopkins Institute in an attempt to induce the Institute to drop the study. They argued that a critical study could damage Dartmouth's public image and hurt its ability to raise money. To its eternal credit, the Hopkins Institute board refused to back off.

But this was only one aspect of Dartmouth's institutional aversion to criticism. Shortly before this meeting, another Dartmouth trustee wrote a memo to the College's president and the chairman of the board of trustees outlining a public relations blitz. The first item on the memo was the trustee's recommendation that Dartmouth "cut the ground out" from Charles Sykes. Unfortunately for the trustee, while he drafted the memorandum on an airplane he was seated next to an editor of *The Dartmouth Review*, who subsequently reported in some detail on the plan. This was somewhat inconvenient for the College inasmuch as the blitz was planned before a word of this book had been written.

I did not then and do not now take it personally. The trustees' attitude merely reflected an institutional tradition, a not-wanting-to-know-any-bad-news tradition that has played a crucial role in the story of the College. The long history of this abdication of responsibility—and the price Dartmouth has paid for it—will become apparent, I think, in the following chapters.

In any case, their feints and jabs posed no hindrance to the completion of my study, which would not, however, have been possible without the help of the many people who defied the trustees' displeasure and provided me with assistance, advice, and support. I am deeply grateful for the support (and persistence) of the Hopkins Institute, and for the assistance given me at Dartmouth by Dr. John Steel, Ruth LaBombard, Colin Campbell, Henry Terrie, William Smith, Donald Pease, Stuart Trembly, William Spengemann, John Rassias, Bill Grace, and many others who have to survive at Dartmouth and would rather I not mention them by name. I owe a special debt of gratitude to Jeffrey Hart for his many kindnesses.

I also want to make special mention of the invaluable assistance provided by my research assistant, Alvino Mario Fantini-Cespedes, a Dartmouth senior, who took time from his studies to track down much of the documentation for this book. His enthusiasm was a constant inspiration and a reminder of what the issues are ultimately all about; this book, after all, was written specifically with students like Alvino Mario in mind.

Every page of this book also reflects the influence of my editor at Regnery Gateway, Harry Crocker, who acted as an invaluable sounding board for me throughout the writing of this book. His sympathetic and insightful handling of the manuscript at every stage—from its earliest conception to its final draft—added immeasurably to whatever value it has.

And to my family, Diane, Sandy, Jay Benjamin, and Woody (our golden retriever), who have patiently endured it all, my thanks and love.

THE HOLLOW MEN

PROLOGUE: WINTER 1989

For the average American college student, higher education's most arduous test sometimes is simply having to choose from among all the delicacies that pass for a curriculum in the modern university. As they pick their way through four or five (and occasionally six) years of the academic shopping malls, the young scholars are tempted with options ranging from the "Sociology of Sociability" (the study of parties) at Vassar, to "Poets Who Sing" at Washington University, to the aggressively relevant "Rock 'n' Roll Is Here to Stay" at Brown. Every once in a while, they stumble upon the motherlode, like those lucky few who enrolled in "Applied Social Theory and Qualitative Research Methodology" at the University of North Carolina at Greensboro. Known affectionately as "Deadhead 101," its course materials consist of Grateful Dead cassettes and reviews of past shows. Students are required to attend Grateful Dead concerts to "observe the subculture that surrounds the band."

At Dartmouth College, the items on the curricular menu are somewhat more limited, but include such morsels as "Sport and Society," "The History of Clothing and the Psychology of Dress," and "TV: A Critical Approach."

3

But for the adventurous, there are more provocative choices. There is the burgeoning field of "victim studies," that offers such courses as "Women and Change in the Third World" and "Black Womanhood in Culture and Society," ("We will explore the nature, extent and consequences of the multiple discriminations of race, sex, and class . . . "). Although they lack the entertainment value of the genuine "guts" — courses that offer high grades for little or no intellectual exertion—they appeal to the undergraduates who have imbibed the school's incessant preachments on "diversity" and the need to reform students' sexist-racist-Eurocentric-patriarchal-phallocentric worldviews. They are also easy A's, if you say the right things on the exams. (They also fulfill Dartmouth's "non-Western" studies requirement.)

In the winter of 1989, some of Dartmouth's more open-minded students chose Women's Studies 22, "History and Theory of Feminism." For some it is a political statement. Others may be in search of elevated consciousness, while still others have more practical concerns. In the past it has been taught by some of the most prominent members of the Dartmouth College faculty. Moreover, it has become all but impossible to avoid feminist analysis and criticism in many courses in the humanities or the social sciences; in some courses it has become *de rigueur*. ("Didn't they write about anything except phallic images in the sixteenth century?" one freshman wonders.) Two faculty committees at Dartmouth have recommended that women's studies courses be made mandatory, and the course is one of the program's core offerings. For some students it is more or less a pre-emptive strike to take it now. In any case, it certainly beats having to wade through Aristotle.

On the first day of class, the syllabus is handed out, setting the course's agenda for the next ten weeks—an in-depth study of liberal feminism, Marxist feminism, existential feminism, radical feminism, socialist feminism, Freudianism and feminism, the nature of phallo-centrism and the "inseparability of gender, class, and race oppression."[1]

It all ends up with a session on "Where Do We Go From Here?" centered on an article titled "Postmodernism and Gender Relations in Feminist Theory" which more or less summarizes the intellectual experience of the past two and a half months.[2]

It also provides a glimpse into the sort of scholarship that now dominates the American academy.

In the article, Howard University professor Jane Flax argues that feminism "makes us skeptical about beliefs concerning truth, knowledge, power, the self, and language that are often taken for granted within and serve as legitimation for contemporary Western culture."

Among the beliefs that she sees thrown "into radical doubt" by deconstructionist postmodernist feminism are: "the existence of a stable coherent self. . . ."; the belief that "Reason and its 'science'—philosophy—can provide an objective, reliable, and universal foundation for knowledge"; that "the knowledge acquired from the right use of reason will be 'True' "; that "Reason itself has transcendental and universal qualities. . . ."; that "By grounding claims to authority in reason, the conflicts between truth, knowledge, and power can be overcome. . . ."; and finally that "Language is in some sense transparent. . . .[that] there is a correspondence between 'word' and 'thing'. . . ."

The author expands upon her insights into the new nihilism: "In fact, feminists, like postmodernists, have begun to suspect that *all such transcendant claims reflect and reify the experiences of a few persons—mostly white, Western males.*" [Emphasis added.]

Of course, if reason and truth are discarded as racist and sexist concepts, and if there is "no objective basis for distinguishing between true and false beliefs," then what we are left with, the author acknowledges, is a situation in which conflicts will be determined by "power alone." She admits that this poses "frightening" possibilities. But even having gazed into that abyss, she concludes that feminist theory demands the discarding of the anachronistic concepts of "person or knowledge" and indeed civilization itself.

"If we do our work well," she concludes, " 'reality' will appear even more unstable, complex, and disorderly than it does now. In this sense, perhaps Freud was right when he declared that women are the enemies of civilization."[3]

This deconstruction of science, language, reason, and the self comes at the end of a course in which Dartmouth students are led through the various stages of feminism's rise, including a discussion of the place of lesbian sadomasochists in the feminist movement as an oppressed "sexual minority"* and how "patriarchal ideology" is not only "a total

---

* Alison Jaggar, the author of *Feminist Politics and Human Nature*, one of the course's main texts, writes that those who advocate sadomasochism "argue that sadomasochism is concerned with fantasy rather than with reality, that the appearance of

system of domination," but also makes women into "sexual slaves" and "legitimizes rape."[4]

Students are assigned as required reading black lesbian feminist poet Audre Lorde's *Sister Outsider* and a collection of essays and poems by Third World feminists called *This Bridge Called My Back: Writings by Radical Women of Color*.

In *Sister Outsider*, Lorde describes her "black woman's anger" as a "molten pond at the core of me," and throughout the book she vents it on other radical and even (white) lesbian feminists with whom she has at various times fallen out. The book includes her generally sympathetic account of a visit to the Soviet Union, and an essay denouncing the savagery, "lies and distortions" surrounding the U.S. invasion of Grenada.[5]

This Bridge Called My Back echoes many of the same themes, but is far more direct. Although the specific readings are not designated in the syllabus, the book includes the Black Feminist Statement of the so-called Combahee River Collective (a Black feminist group in Boston), which declares: "We realize that the liberation of all oppressed peoples necessitates the destruction of the political economic system of capitalism and imperialism as well as patriarchy. We are socialists. . . ."[6]

Several pages later, a feminist named Pat Parker, who is identified as a black lesbian feminist poet and revolutionary, insists that "as anti-imperialists we must be prepared to destroy all imperialist governments," and explains that revolution, when it comes, "will not be neat or pretty or quick." Parker continues: "It is a long dirty process. We will be faced with decisions that are not easy. *We will have to consider the deaths of friends and family. We will be faced with the decisions of killing members of our own race*."[7] [Emphasis added.]

Alison Jaggar's *Feminist Politics and Human Nature*, the main text for Women's Studies 22, makes no pretense of scholarly objectivity. Her goal, she writes in her introduction, is not an attempt to clarify or describe feminist theory. "This book," she says, "is intended as a

---

violence may be illusory. They point out that both participants agree to engage in a sadomasochistic encounter and that, contrary to appearances, the masochist is actually in control because she can halt the encounter at any time. Sadomasochists are engaging in radical sexual exploration but, by condemning sadomasochism, 'The women's movement has become a moralistic force and it can contribute to the self-loathing and misery experienced by sexual minorities.' " (Jaggar, p. 275)

substantive contribution to feminist theory insofar as it argues for the superiority of one conception of women's liberation over all others. That one is socialist feminism."[8]

Her intent in writing the book is, in fact, the systematic consideration and refutation of non-Marxist approaches to feminism, while pushing a synthesis of radical feminism and traditional Marxism. She too has a radical theory of knowledge.

> The socialist feminist conception of women's standpoint specifies certain interpretations of verification and of usefulness. It asserts that knowledge is useful if it contributes to a practical reconstruction of the world in which women's interests are not subordinate to those of men.[9]

Thus, knowledge, Dartmouth students read, is "useful" only to the extent it supports the political line and advances the political goals of the movement. The class uses Jaggar's book *exclusively* in discussions of "The problems and the Politics of Liberal Feminisms," "Feminism and Traditional Marxism: Theory," "Feminism and Traditional Marxism: Critique," "Radical Feminisms: Theory," "Socialist Feminisms: Theory," and "Socialist Feminisms: Critique." No other readings are assigned for any of the above topics.

From Sandra Harding's *The Science Question in Feminism*, the class learns that science is deeply aligned with "sexist, racist, classist, and imperialist social projects."[10]

These masculinist obsessions, Harding insists, result in such distinctions as "objectivity vs. subjectivity . . . reason vs. the emotion, mind vs. body." Harding, who has visited Dartmouth as a guest lecturer, has in the past detected "rape and torture" metaphors in the early development of scientific methods; arguing that Newton's laws could as easily be described as "Newton's rape manual."[11]

She even sees male dominance reflected in the "master molecule" theory of DNA; the notion that forces act on objects; the emphasis on "struggle in evolution"; and even in concepts like mass and force.[12] In the preface to her book, Harding writes:

> The radical feminist position holds that the epistemologies, metaphysics, ethics, and politics of the dominant forms of science are androcentric and mutually supportive; that despite the deeply in-

grained Western cultural belief in science's intrinsic progressive-
ness, science today serves primarily regressive social tendencies;
and that the social structure of science, many of its applications and
technologies, its modes of defining research problems and design-
ing experiments, its ways of constructing and conferring meanings
are not only sexist but also racist, classist and culturally coercive.[13]

Harding advocates not merely a more progressive science, but a
thoroughly politicized science that would be directed by "morally and
politically emancipatory interests" apparently more or less in her own
image. As part of an effort to "reinvent" science, Harding calls for
continued refinement of theories of gender, the destruction of "the
dogmas of empiricism," and a good deal of "political struggle."[14]

All of this has not gone unchallenged. Harding's theories have been
subjected to a devastating critique by Margarita Levin, who teaches
philosophy at Yeshiva University in New York.

She has Harding in mind when she writes that "Many feminists who
write about science from a Marxist perspective seem wholly unin-
formed about science, and identify 'male' science with weapons and
strip-mining, all intended for use, as Harding writes, 'in the service of
sexist, racist, homophobic and classist projects.' "[15]

"No claim," writes Levin, "is judged too bizarrely reductive for
them to defend." In particular, she noted Harding's explicit endorsement
of the bizarre theory that because capitalism is characterized by the
unending movement of money, it was the source of Galileo's concept of
inertial motion, which, in turn, underlies Newtonian physics. Levin
dismisses Harding's theoretics as "embarrassing," empty, and "insub-
stantial."

But in Dartmouth's "History and Theory of Feminism," Harding's
book is required reading; Levin's critique is not. Nor is any other
alternative approach to the question included in the reading list. Nor are
the students provided any historical perspective that might cast some
light on previous attempts to develop political critiques of science,
including the notions of "Jewish physics," "Aryan science," and
"Lysenkoism." The only reading assigned for discussions on "Developing New Feminist Standpoint Epistemologies," "Justifying Feminist
Theory," and, "Problems, Valuable Tensions, and a New Unity of
Science," are the two books by Jaggar and Harding.[16]

What the students are confronted with is an extraordinarily ambitious attempt to dismantle Western culture and rewrite the theory of knowledge; clearly one of the headier intellectual exercises attempted in the modern academy. One would imagine such an effort presupposes familiarity with both the history of ideas and some exposure to the development of those ideas.

But given Dartmouth's curriculum the students involved in deconstructing Western civilization may never have read a single of the philosophers they are discrediting. In Women's Studies 22, not only is Margarita Levin not assigned, but neither is Plato, Aquinas, Locke, Bacon, Descartes, Spinoza, Aristotle, Copernicus, Kepler, or Galileo. They are reduced to dead, white, Western males.

They are deconstructed. But not read.

It would be comforting, of course, to dismiss the course as an anomaly. But it is not. Nor, in 1990, is it just Dartmouth or just women's studies.

PART I

ATTACK
ON
THE WEST

CHAPTER

I

THE CRISIS

*A passionate tumultuous age will overthrow everything, pull every-
thing down; but a revolutionary age that is at the same time
reflective and passionless leaves everything standing but cunningly
empties it of significance.*

—SOREN KIERKEGAARD

C. S. Lewis, who was himself an academic of long experience, once
noted that each age is invariably warned against "those vices of which it
is least in danger": cruel ages are put on their guard against the dangers
of sentimentality, "feckless and idle ones against Respectability, lech-
erous ones against Puritanism."[1]

So it is perhaps not surprising that in the late 1980s, an academic
leader of the stature of Dartmouth's President James Freedman would
direct his attention not to the threat of cultural illiteracy, but to the
menace of what he calls an "unqualified emphasis upon Western civilization" that "legitimates an assumption of European and American
cultural superiority." *There* lies the *real* danger, Freedman insists, because "that assumption is as damaging to our nation as it is menacing to
the world that our students will be compelled to understand and shape."[2]

One would imagine, listening to Freedman, that American universities are actively suppressing the cultures of other civilizations and
hastening to construct curriculums built around Western chauvinism.
And, indeed, if the average college was overrun by militant Aris-
totelians or dogmatic medievalists brandishing copies of the *Summa*

13

Theologica and chanting "Hey, hey, ho, ho, Eastern culture's got to go!" his admonition *might* have some merit.

But coming amid the riotous fragmentation of the humanities and the near eclipse of the intellectual legacy of the West in the curriculum, his comments are the very essence of paradox—like warning a binging drunkard of the perils of an unqualified emphasis on sobriety.

The incongruity of Freedman's warning was underlined by a survey sponsored by the National Endowment for the Humanities in 1989 that found that a majority of college *seniors* would *flunk* even a basic test on Western cultural and historical literacy: a quarter could not distinguish between the thoughts of Karl Marx and the United States Constitution (or the words of Winston Churchill from those of Joseph Stalin), 58 percent did not know Shakespeare wrote *The Tempest*, 42 percent could not place the Civil War in the correct half-century. A majority were unable to identify the Magna Carta, Reconstruction, or the Missouri Compromise, and were "clearly unfamiliar" with Jane Austen's *Pride and Prejudice*, Dostoevsky's *Crime and Punishment*, and Martin Luther King's "Letter from the Birmingham Jail."[3]

Of course, the knowledge of important dates and facts alone does not constitute a liberal education, and can even be dismissed as little more than a glorified game of "Trivial Pursuit." But the results hinted at a more profound gap in the curriculum of higher education, in which a student's exposure to intellectual history, philosophy, religion, literature, science, and mathematics is often a matter of pure chance.

It is certainly more important to understand the intellectual roots of the American Revolution than the dates of the various battles. But the evidence suggests that American college students know *neither*.

One recent graduate of Brown University, for example, tells of two friends (both American) who were majoring in Art History at the Ivy League school. "They were studying *The Last Supper* [the painting by Leonardo da Vinci]," she recalled. "And they asked me to explain what it was all about. They wanted to know, 'Why the supper?' 'How did all this come about?' 'What's an apostle, really?' They were just curious. They had no historical reference."[4] I have to admit that when I first heard this story, my initial reaction was disbelief. But when it comes to the magnitude of academic ignorance—even in the nation's most elite institutions—such skepticism is increasingly unwarranted.

The unfortunate reality is that to the average American college graduate both the literature and history of his culture are often *terra incognita*;

he is likely to have only the vaguest conception of Homer, Dante, Shakespeare, and the Founding Fathers, to say nothing of the Last Supper or its meaning. He will have little or no idea what it means to be a member of Western civilization except, perhaps, that his forefathers oppressed someone or another.

What then is the nature of the danger facing higher education? It is that *it is in the Western tradition* that we find the origins of democratic society, of the focus on individual worth and humanity dignity, and of aspirations for human freedom. It is the fountainhead of our language, our culture, our aesthetics, our religions, and our ethical systems. To lose that legacy through a curriculum of enforced cultural amnesia is to deconstruct an entire civilization. One would expect that its preservation would be the primary concern of the academy.

Instead, it is Freedman's warning against "legitimating" the assumption of the superiority of this tradition that typifies the *Zeitgeist* of American higher education at the beginning of the 1990s, which insists on cautioning against the very things of which it is least in peril.

There are no simple explanations for the disintegration of academia's humanistic traditions; blame can be laid on academic microspecialization, faculty self-interest, institutional greed, the American cult of credentialism, and student careerism. But the humanistic legacy of the West has also been pushed aside by the more insistent preoccupations of the new academy—many of them the legacy of the 1960s.

For those who lived through it, the campus revolution of the 1960s seemed in retrospect a phantasmagorical nightmare in which reasoned discourse, logic, and civility were reduced to what at times seemed one long shouted obscenity. Even at the time there was an air of unreality about higher education's almost weekly rituals of abasement when administrators and faculty members negotiated university contributions to Black Panther defense funds, fawned on student radicals who had shut down their institutions ("the best informed, the most intelligent, and the most idealistic [generation] this country has ever known")[5], and vied with one another in the speed with which they surrendered their most basic principles, from their control of the curriculum to tolerance for unpopular points of view.

No one viewing the wreckage of institutions and ideals could help but feel that the changes wrought by these mutilations were momentous. Surveying the academic landscape in 1969, Philosopher Sidney Hook had written, "It is not hard to predict that from the vantage point of the year 2000, if not earlier, the last decade in American education will appear as the most bizarre in its history."[6] He was horrified by what he saw as the "systematic politicization" of the university classroom, reflected in "biased reading lists and unscholarly assignments" and the use of classrooms by professors for the "propagation of political and other ideas that have no relation to the subject matter of their courses."

Twenty years later, he would write: "Since then, far from improving, the situation has worsened in that the violations of the academic ethic have become more widespread if less dramatic."[7]

The trend that had appalled Hook in the 1960s and that he was to see grow over the succeeding two decades was the wholesale rejection of the principle that scholarship should serve some end other than ideological proselytization. Traditionally, the self-restraint implicit in the ethics of the academy had been the foundation of academic freedom, which he described as "the right not to *teach* the truth but to *seek* truth. . . ."[8] At stake was the distinction between teaching and indoctrination; the abyss that separates the Socratic method from propaganda.

In the years since the final fires of the 1960s consumed themselves, the crisis of higher education has taken on forms that could then only have been dimly foreseen even by such a prescient pessimist as Hook: the institutionalization of intolerance by the university itself, including official limits on free speech; the dismemberment of the liberal arts canon under what amounts to a persistent campaign of affirmative action for ideas; an attack on the foundations of reason euphemized as an assault on the "patriarchical" and oppressive values of the West; and the rise of a trendy nihilism so thoroughgoing that one leading scholar has proclaimed our era the new "Dark Age of the Humanities,"[9] (surely a slander on the average self-respecting Visigoth).

Inevitably, the rise of a culture of cultural negation has decisively shaped the conditions of civility, tolerance, and intellectual integrity within higher education. Concepts like "pluralism" and "diversity" are central to the democratic philosophy of the West and to the liberal arts themselves. But stripped of their intellectual roots, they have been transformed into banners under which dour and brittle new orthodoxies are imposed on both scholarship and academic life and which are used to prescribe draconian limits on both free speech and the exchange of ideas. Both the moral and intellectual atmosphere are often shaped by the extraordinary promiscuity with which such emotionally charged terms as "racist" and "sexist" are wielded against heretics both real and imagined. As reason and civil discourse are submerged, their place has been taken by a therapeutic ethos, whose goal is not the clash of ideas, but the *curing* and *extirpation* of ideas now deemed not merely unacceptable, but beyond the pale of tolerated discourse.

The post-1960s transformation of higher education fed upon the academy's fragmentation, and its loss of its traditional shared sense of purpose: to produce inquiring, knowledgeable, thoughtful adults. For scholar Peter Shaw, the decline in intellectual discourse is a continuation of the war against the intellect itself, a triumph of commitment and right feeling over reason, characterized by "the willed suspension of the critical faculty." Hook believed the decisive event of the 1960s was the collapse of higher education's moral courage; for Shaw it was the surrender of the intellect to the passions that allowed intimidation to become respectable.

> The supine intellectual posture of the academics [of the 1980s] will be familiar to anyone who recalls the variety of the capitulations with which they greeted the student movement out of which deconstructionism grew. . . . The edifice had been shaken, and few were any longer confident about the solidity of its underpinnings.[10]

The extent of the dissolution of those underpinnings is reflected in the way that the basic terms of the debate have been torn loose from their traditional meaning. Where the liberal arts were once described by Robert Maynard Hutchins as freeing man "from the prison-house of his class, race, time, place, background, family, and even his nation," that definition has, in effect, been turned on its head, as both scholarship and curricula alike are focused on the ideological agenda encapsulated in the explicit emphasis on race, class, gender, and sexual orientation.

By rights, the issue of the intellectual integrity of the academy is not one that should divide right from left. But the abandonment of liberal learning by liberals—both their silent acquiescence and their active collaboration in its corruption—will surely be one of the most poignant ironies in intellectual history.

The essence of the traditional humanities curriculum, with its focus on the so-called Great Books, has been the participation in an ongoing, often raucous and contentious debate over the questions of life, death, love, power, democracy, God, man, and fate. The unsettling experience of reading classic works is that they force students to break out of their own mental prisons formed of fashion, prejudice, and the ubiquitous modern error that equates opinion with thought. The great books help students to recognize and challenge the sterile clichés of their generation. "To deprive students of this debate," warned William Bennett, "is to condemn them to improvise their ways of living in ignorance of their real options and the best arguments for each."[11] Philosopher Michael Oakeshott described the humanistic tradition of the West as encompassing "not only the lyre of Apollo but also the pipes of Pan, the call of the wild; not only the poet but also the physicist; not only the majestic metropolis of Augustinian theology but also the 'greenwood' of Franciscan Christianity."[12] It is, in fact, this diversity that is the essence of the Western liberal arts tradition. Authors as disparate as Tolstoy, Moliere, Goethe, Milton, and Dante engage their readers in a conversation that has been going on for centuries, enduring neither because of their race nor their sex. Liberal education pits theories of knowledge one against another and no dogma stands unchallenged.

In stark contrast, the politicized classroom—created in the name of the new official ideology of "diversity" —is dominated by a single ideological interpretation that often imposes the most rigid categories of analysis. In place of a perceptive, complex, and nuanced understanding of human experience, the ideological interpretation is absolute, dogmatic, and the essence of the rankest illiberalism imaginable. The product is often a curriculum as denuded of value as if it had, in fact, been created by a curriculum committee of Vandals with doctorates.

There are, of course, exceptions to these trends. There are still individuals and institutions that eloquently defend academic integrity and cultural sanity; but in the new order, their voices are often drowned out or simply ignored.

In the last two decades, the passionate and tumultuous age of the 1960s has been succeeded by the passionless deconstruction of scholarship. As Kierkegaard recognized a century ago, the most insidious subversion is that which leaves intact the structures and language of an institution, while stripping them of meaning. In this case, the meaning that has been lost is the rational moral purpose and hierarchy of values that underlie Western culture.

If the extent of the dissolution of higher learning remains largely unrecognized, it is because we continue to have its pale substitutes, lively effigies that often behave like—and claim the privileges of—the humanities, but which ultimately lack their reality.

II

THE POLITICIZATION OF ACADEMIA

Irving Howe quips that in the 1980s Marxists went to the universities "to die in comfort."[1] Indeed, deconstructing Emily Dickinson was not quite the same as storming the Winter Palace; nor was interrogating Jane Austen to determine whether her characters rejected the "regressive and patriarchal definition of love as conquest"[2] exactly paving the way for the revolution of the proletariate. But by 1990, many of the radicals of the 1960s had been transformed into the tenured gurus of American higher education.

One-time Berkeley activist Annette Kolodny, for example, had become the dean of the humanities faculty at the University of Arizona. "I see my scholarship," she told *U.S. News & World Report*, "as an extension of my political activism."[3]

An example of that scholarship was her book, *Lay of the Land*, in which Kolodny discusses the pastoral tradition in American literature and opens with a nostalgic reminiscence of the 1969 "battle for People's Park" at Berkeley, during which campus radicals sought to stop the university from paving over a small piece of ground near the campus. She describes the fate of the park as the "rape" of "a natural maternal realm," and thus "a mirror in which our society may see itself," and quotes a poem circulated at the time:

> The University must stop
> fucking with our land.
> The University must stop being a motherfucker.

Presumably as an example of extending her political activism to her analysis of poetry, Kolodny cites the poem as an example of the "American pastoral impulse."[4] Leon Trotsky, call your office. But a similar process of trivialization was at work in the social sciences. The increasingly technical and narrow focus of social science research in particular threatened to submerge ideology in number-crunching. As Carl Boggs, a Marxist academic himself, warned:

> Marxist theory . . . is in danger of evolving into a conservative ideology—the expression of a quasi-scientific world-view shaped by technocratic imperatives that looks quite different from a critical theory directed toward social transformation.[5]

In practice, this meant that radical scholars found themselves withdrawing from the very world they had set out to save. Increasingly, their discourse was directed not at the masses, or even at the broad educated left, but to other scholars who, like themselves, were specialists who spoke the rarefied language of academia. Worse than their anonymity as laborers in the mines of academic obscurantism was their failure to resuscitate the fading ideologies of the left or to use their positions to force or finesse any significant intellectual breakthroughs. Russell Jacoby described both the transformation and the scope of the left's failure:

> Intellectuals of the irrational, far-out, hang-loose 1960s matured into a more buttoned-up, professional and invisible group than did preceding intellectual generations. One thousand radical sociologists, but no C. Wright Mills; three hundred critical literary theorists, but no Edmund Wilson; scads of Marxist economists but no Paul Sweezy or Harry Braverman. Urban critics galore but no Lewis Mumford or Jane Jacobs.[6]

It was an ironic twist of fate. Instead of becoming a revolutionary vanguard, the academic revolutionaries had become case-studies in arrested development. But the mediocrity and, frequently, the irrelevance of radical scholarship has proved no impediment to its growing influence within a broad range of academic disciplines. "What has changed most since 1968," said one Columbia University professor in a 1988 interview, "has been the faculty, especially the junior faculty. They are the children of the 60's. They were marching then, but now political action takes place in the classroom, and in scholarly books dedicated to social change."[7]

Throughout the 1960s and 1970s, Marxists in particular played a crucial role in redefining the language and methodologies of literary studies, economics, political science, history, sociology, and anthropology, thus winning a legitimacy they had never previously enjoyed.

Equally as important was the institutionalization of the left within the formal structures of the universities themselves. Many of the radicals of the 1960s became the tenured faculty of the 1980s with control over the process of recruitment, promotion, and tenure. Ironically, tenure, which is claimed as the guarantor of the academy's freedom of thought is also the ultimate control mechanism.

There are no reliable figures indicating a pattern of conservatives being denied tenure. But even if such figures existed, they would be of minimal value because tenure is only the terminal point of the weeding-out process. It is not by any means the only mechanism for enforcing ideological conformity in academia. To the contrary, it is highly unlikely that anyone outside of the orthodox academic mainstream would survive the process long enough to even get close to being considered for admission into academia's sacred precincts. "As in the McCarthy period," historian C. Vann Woodward wrote, "there is no reckoning the number of books not written, research not done, and the standards, values and ideals besmirched or trashed."[8]

By the 1980s, the left had effectively ensconced itself in what Stephen Balch and Herbert London described as "a network of journals and professional organizations, university departments and academic programs."[9] In time, the system becomes self-perpetuating and self-replicating.

One measure of the progressive politicization of scholarship can be taken from an account in The New York Times of the 1989 convention of the Modern Language Association. Headlined, "Literary Critics Meet, and Find Politics Everywhere," the Times article noted the dominance of certain trends within the association, "trends with their roots in the political activism of the 1960s."

Sessions bristled with the fashionable jargon of political commitment, such as "patriarchal authority," "empowerment," "discourses in emancipation," "marginalized subjects," "the dominant order," "systems of stratification," and "culturally over-determined structures of seeing." Scholars who toiled over the ideological implications of humor, the *Times* noted, reflected "the tendency of literary critics to scrutinize just about everything for the political code that is embedded in it." Little escaped. Topics from medieval literature to Shakespeare to black film were discussed by the academic humanists "in terms of a frequently repeated quartet of terms—'race, gender, social class and sexuality.' "

Such was the mood of ideological conformity at the gathering that the group's new president, feminist Catharine Stimpson, could dismiss critics of the radicalization of the humanities as mere "gnats."[10]

A Despairing Shrug

The collapse of academic liberalism in the 1960s has left the enduring image of an establishment that watched itself rendered impotent and irrelevant by its own ideas made flesh.

The mandarins of the old liberal intelligentsia grew up in the 1920s and 1930s, imbibing from the modernist movement of that time a hostile view of the philistinism of American life. Though they maintained tenuous ties to the humanistic tradition, they often ended up indulging what Lionel Trilling called a "disenchantment . . . with culture itself"[11]—a disenchantment that made the standards of their disciplines indefensible because unimportant.

Vital and dynamic in opposition, liberal modernism had by the mid-1960s, Irving Howe noted, "acquired wrinkles and a paunch."[12] The paunch was not merely physical.

Not only had the adversary culture of liberal modernism been assimilated into the mainstream, it had become an establishment itself, a New Class that was in many ways as philistine as the culture it had arisen to critique. By the 1960s, Trilling noted, the openness of American society had led to "the socialization of the anti-social . . . the acculturation of the anti-cultural . . . the legitimation of the subversive."[13] Modernism was undone by the ease of its victory—bourgeois society had fled virtually at the first shot. But the adversary culture existed not as an alternative in any sense, but solely as a critique; it desperately needed a foil against which to define itself. The collapse of convention and the rush to embrace radical subjectivism and alienation as if they were commonplaces created an unexpected crisis for the old liberals. They had not really ever considered the fruit their ideas might bear.

For the liberal academic establishment, the shock of the 1960s came *not* from the resistance of the young to its adversarial ideas, but from the almost casual ease with which students absorbed them without any of the reservations, qualms, or understanding of the traditions being critiqued that had so preoccupied their elders. Trilling's students at Columbia eagerly leapt into the abyss of modernism, apparently unaware or unconcerned that there even *was* an abyss. More troubling was their impatience to see adversarial, modernist ideas transformed into action, whatever the cost.

"Everything that was speculatively implied in literature is being actualized in politics in social action," Trilling said in a 1969 interview. "No one ever thought that when these writers represented violence as interesting or beneficent they were really urging their readers to bloody actions. But now violence is proposed and justified on moral and psychological grounds."[14]

In the 1960s, ideas that had once been confined to the seminar and the obscurity of academic journals now found their way into the street theater of the new generation. Theodor Adorno's lament captured the pathetic complaint of the theoretician suddenly confronted with the realization of his own ideas. "When I made my theoretical model, I could not have guessed," he complained "that people would try to realize it with Molotov cocktails."[15] When Herbert Marcuse had written of the need for "instinctual liberation," he did not expect to see himself taken up on it by undergraduates on the College green in broad daylight.*

For the liberal intellectuals of the decade, the changes were both baffling and wrenching. Where the tradition of the radicals of the 1930s had been grounded in "dialectical toughness, rationalism, enlarged political consciousness and sharp moral conscience," they were now

---

* "I think it is the great sin of the intellectual," Trilling said in 1974, "that he never really tests his ideas by what it would mean to him if he were to undergo the experience that he is recommending."

challenged by their own intellectual progeny—but somehow horribly distorted. In place of their rigorous rationality, there was now, "a farrago of authoritarian, elitist, anarchistic and revolutionary doctrines randomly bound together by delusions of innocence and injections of amnesia."[16] The new revolutionists rejected not merely their elders' caution and their insistence on tolerance and process and academic integrity, but their lingering affinity to the West itself.

In their passionate commitment, some radicals saw the Vietnam War as an indictment of all of Western civilization. Ever at the forefront of radical fashions, Susan Sontag denounced the war as a product of the values of "Western 'Faustian' man, with his idealism, his magnificent art, his sense of intellectual adventure, his world-devouring energies for conquest." With more sentimentality than logic or historical accuracy, she counterpoised to that tradition a mythical image of the gentle East.[17]

The legacy of this repudiation of the West would not only be a lingering fascinating with the Third World (and a studied avoidance of acknowledging its brutality, its economic failure, and its vicious, and racist, tyrannies) but also a rejection of the Western tradition of the intellect, which Trilling traced to the ancient Greeks, "both in what might be called its aesthetic appreciation of mind, its admiration of the mental faculties almost for their own sake, apart from what practical ends they might achieve, and also in its assumption that mind can play a decisive part in the moral life of the individual person."[18]

The loss of that ideal was accompanied by the atrophy and disintegration of the liberal tradition itself; the displacement of the liberal values of Montaigne, Mill, and Arnold, by an ideology of self-indulgence, the lugubrious pieties of progressive clichés, and the suffocation of reason beneath ideology.[19] Perhaps most troubling of all for those veterans of the 1930s was the often covert but very real passion for totalitarianism implicit in the rejection of the intellect and the assault on the mind by the new revolutionists.

Hannah Arendt's critique in the *Origins of Totalitarianism* of the process of disintegration seemed to apply to the universities with special urgency.

> To yield to the process of disintegration has become an irresistible temptation, not only because it has assumed the spurious grandeur of "historical necessity," but also because everything outside it has begun to appear lifeless, bloodless, meaningless and unreal.[20]

The response of the liberals to this challenge was almost complete collapse and often eager collaboration. Their principles of tolerance and rigorous application of reason seemed pale and etiolated abstractions when compared to the emotionalism of the revolutionists' "right feelings." As the cycles of violence, both real and rhetorical, continued to rise, the liberal intellectuals' major contribution to the debate was their silent acquiescence. "They conceded," Peter Shaw has written, "that authority was by its nature coercive and that subjective impressions were as valuable as reasoned analysis. . . ."[21]

Although cowardice was clearly a prime ingredient in the collapse of liberalism, Trilling chose to emphasize another factor, which he called "fatigue." His confession marked an apologia of sorts for a generation of principled liberals of whom he was the outstanding exemplar. "Subjects and problems were presented in a way that made one's spirits fail," Trilling observed. "It wasn't that one was afraid to go into it, or afraid of being in opposition—I suppose I am speaking personally—but rather that in looking at the matter one's reaction was likely to be a despairing shrug."[22]

But Trilling also attributed this reticence to a more profound loss of confidence among academics which he linked to "their reluctance to formulate any coherent theory for higher education, to discover what its best purposes are, to try to realize them through the requirements of the curriculum."[23]

Into this void, the newly triumphant anarchists moved confidently.

DECONSTRUCTING ACADEMIA

The rhetoric of revolution soon disappeared from the public forum of the universities. But as it was rechanneled into the academic culture in more discreet ways, its destructive tendencies remained intact. Professor Louis Kampf spoke for the spirit of much of the new scholarship when he declared that exposing the underprivileged to the classics of Western art and literature was itself tantamount to an act of oppression because "high culture tends to reinforce the given alignments of power within society." Kampf denounced the very concept of culture as "rooted in class elitism."[24]

"The movement should have harassed the Lincoln Center from the beginning," he declared. "Not a performance should go by without disruption. The fountains should be dried with calcium chloride, the statuary pissed on, the walls smeared with shit." Less surprising than Kampf's cultural program was the degree to which it was legitimized by the academic community. In 1971, Kampf was the president of the Modern Language Association, the dominant academic organization for literary studies.[25]

In the nineteenth century, Matthew Arnold had looked to culture as the preserver of civilization. By the end of the 1980s, Arnold's views would have been derided if not violently rejected within the more advanced sectors of the American academy. Kampf's views were more or less conventional—and lucrative. Some of the richest Marxists in the nation, one academic quipped, could now be found in prestigious English Departments.[26] At Duke University, for instance, Professor Frederic Jameson boldly proclaimed his intention of creating a "Marxist intelligentsia," in part by vandalizing "pleasing, exciting and 'beautiful stories'," which are really instruments for "promoting acquiescence to, and even identification with, the relations of domination and subordination peculiar to the late-capitalist social order."

"Nothing can be more satisfying," Jameson declared, "for a Marxist teacher than to 'break' this fascination for students."[27]

By the early 1980s, Marxist scholar Bertell Ollman boasted that "A Marxist cultural revolution is taking place today in America's universities . . . fought chiefly with books and lectures." As evidence of the progress of the revolution he cited the fact that in the 1970s, four "Marxist-inspired" textbooks in American government had been published, while the most prestigious academic presses were turning out books on Marxism at an accelerating rate. By 1982, Ollman noted, there were more than 400 courses in Marxist philosophy in American universities, "whereas hardly any were given in the 1960s."[28]

But the real action had been within the mainstream of scholarship, where Marxism had made remarkable inroads. Ollman declared that Marxism had achieved notable gains in "practically every discipline" in some cases by coming to dominate the formal academic organizations. Two avowed Marxists—Eugene Genovese and William A. Williams— had been elected president of the Organization of American Historians.

"Paradoxically," Ollman noted, "few of the participants on either side are aware of the extent of this struggle or of the positions that have already changed hands. The general public knows even less. Yet, its initial results are evident throughout the academy."[29]

Marxist philosopher Antonio Gramsci had foreshadowed the social transformations and dislocations of the 1960s when he suggested that in modern society the most promising grounds for revolutionary activity rested not in economics—as Marxists had long insisted—but in culture.[30] The instruments were the ripening theories of structuralism, post-structuralism, semiotics, and deconstructionism emerging from academic leftists in France—professors who had won enthusiastic support from many participants in France's abortive 1968 student revolution. Marxist critic Terry Eagleton argued that deconstructionism was a direct product of the failure of the student revolution. "Unable to break the structures of state power," he writes, "post-structuralism found it possible, instead, to subvert the structures of language." The ultimate goal of the new approaches was an attack on what Roland Barthes called "coherent beliefs of any kind."[31]

Somewhat simplified, the new theories questioned the foundations of reason and language, arguing that a work of literature—or a "text" in the obligatory new jargon—was made up of words with no objective meaning, except as reflections of themselves. A narrative thus signifies nothing.*

Authority of all kinds—of the author, of history, of language, of reason—could now be attacked as "fascistic," "tyrannical," "imperialistic," and "hegemonic." If language is "duplicitous," as theorists like Jacques Derrida insisted, then it can be decoded and deconstructed to make whatever political point was desired. "A deconstructionist," Yale's J. Hillis Miller exulted gleefully, "is not a parasite but a parricide.

---

* Literary critic Rene Wellek has written of deconstructionism: "If literature has nothing to say about our minds and the cosmos, about love and death, about humanity in other times and other countries, literature loses its meanings. . . . The view that there is 'nothing outside of the text,' that every text refers or defers only to another text, ignores the fact that texts—political, juridical, religious, philosophical, and even imaginative and poetic—have actually shaped the lives of men and thus the course of history. Denying the self and minimizing the perpetual life of man, the theory deliberately refuses to acknowledge that the relation of mind and world is more basic than language. . . . In its extreme formulation, which looks for the abolition of man, denies the self, and sees language as a free-floating system of signs, the theory leads to total skepticism and ultimately to nihilism."

He is a bad son demolishing beyond hope of repair the machine of Western metaphysics."[32]

Although deconstructionism was theoretically politically ambiguous, Marxists like Jameson noted that in practice, "structuralist and post-structuralist theories acknowledged an explicit solidarity with left and socialist politics."[33]

One leading postmodernist scholar, Ihab Hassan, identified some of the major aspects of postmodernism as "indeterminacy," "fragmentation," and "decanonization," which included the "massive delegitimation" of all conventions of authority.

> Thus from the "death of god" to the "death of the author" and "death of the father," from the derision of authority to revision of the curriculum, we decanonize culture, demystify knowledge, deconstruct the languages of power, desire, deceit.

Hassan recognized the political implications of the new movement. Taken to their extreme the processes of derision and revision were profoundly subversive, "of which the most baleful example is the rampant terrorism of our time." But Hassan noted that other, "more benevolent" forms of subversion, including the push for minority rights and the "feminization of culture" also required the breakdown of traditional canons.[34]*

In disciplines like history, the new theories proved useful battering rams against the edifice of "fact," breaking down the notion of historical reality itself and rendering the past indeterminate. As traditional literary classics were dismissed as elitist, so too was traditional history, as the new historians insisted that comic books were equally as important as official papers and Mickey Mouse "more important to an understanding of the 1930s than Franklin Roosevelt."[35]

The catch, of course, was that sweeping away history was only a

---

* Actually Hassan's attitude toward the politicization of scholarship inherent in this sort of scholarship is notably ambiguous. "I confess," he writes, "to some distaste for ideological rage (the worst are now full of passionate intensity *and* lack all conviction) for the hectoring of both religious and secular dogmatists." Too often, politics is "An excuse to bully or shout in public, vengeance vindicating itself as justice and might pretending to be right . . . the place where history rehearses its nightmares . . . a deadly banality of being." Even so, he ultimately, acquiesces, saying that "we must all heed politics because it structures our theoretical consents, literary evasions. . . ."

means, not an end. Deconstruction was both less and more than it claimed to be. Strict limits were placed on the deconstruction of reality, because the whole point was to construct an alternative reality that was more politically correct, focusing on the new trinity of race, sex, and class. It took a shrewd critic like historian Gertrude Himmelfarb to notice the double-edged nature of the new fashions. "It is only by making the past indeterminate, making it a *tabula rasa*," she wrote, "that historians can impose upon the past their own determinacy . . . the past has to be deconstructed and constructed anew."[36]

In the study of literature, too, critic Peter Shaw noted, "the new theories rest on the belief that literary interpretation itself, if conducted in a certain way, can function as a politically revolutionary act."[37]

The University of Pennsylvania's Houston Baker won considerable notoriety when he declared in *The New York Times* that choosing between authors such as Virginia Woolf and Pearl Buck was "no different from choosing between a hoagy and a pizza," and that he had dedicated his career to the abolition of all traditional standards of literary value. But his comments placed him in the vanguard of academic trendiness—and politics. In place of the discarded standards of taste, Baker proposed his own theory of "supraliteracy," which he defined as "the committed scholar's 'vernacular' invasion and transcendence of fields of colonizing discourse in order to destroy whitemale [sic] hegemony. . . ."[38]

The new approaches meant that scholars could now dismember works of literature to discover their "hidden" ideological contradictions. But even if none were there, they could impose their own political interpretations anyway, because, they insisted, *all* writing was, at bottom, political. The most outrageous misreading—and even distortion—of works of literature was not only countenanced, it was virtually required. O, brave new world!

Duke's Jameson made no apologies for the politicization of literary studies. "The analysis of literary and cultural texts," he wrote, "and the tasks of cultural revolution in general, then, increasingly appear *as central, not secondary, to socialist political strategies*—necessary conditions for transforming the patterns of ideological closure and political passivity that are enforced in societies like ours, less by fear of the police than by fascination with the page or screen."[39] [Emphasis added.] The new theories had proven extraordinarily useful for the Marxist critics because they enabled them to avoid some of the cosmetic problems Marxism had experienced in the 1930s and 1940s, when American Marxist literary critics—most notably Mike Gold and Granville Hicks—hewed to a strict Zdhanovite line in their work.

That is to say they were Stalinist toadies. "Zdhanovite" refers to the humorless and sycophantic drone, A. A. Zdhanov, who as Stalin's Minister of Culture, was responsible for ensuring ideologically correct aesthetic standards. For the most part, his job among American Marxists was embarrassingly easy. In their enthusiasm, they had swiftly accommodated themselves to the doctrines of "socialist realism." But the first high summer of Marxist literary criticism was ultimately doomed, as much by its poor public relations as by Stalinism's fall from fashion. "This kind of criticism," Jameson later noted, "became an easy target against which later bourgeois literary criticism could retrospectively make telling points, conveniently equating Marxism with Stalinist party politics."[40]

But now, with the artillery of the French post-structuralists, Jameson wrote, "Marxism has managed to strengthen its hold in academic literary theory, becoming progressively more influential through a curious alliance with recent European theory. . . ."[41] Many of the familiar elements remained; Marxist critics still insisted on ideological purity and a slavish conformism to the dogma of dialectical materialism. Scholars like Jameson still checked in regularly with the stand-bys of the old regime, making suitably pious obeisance to the literary theories of L. Trotsky, V. Lenin, and F. Engels with a truly impressive frequency.

But Marxism now had new trappings. With their new partners, Marxist critics were able to resume their place in the academic festivities under far more decorous auspices than the blunt-edged Stalinism of their predecessors had ever allowed. A. A. Zdhanov had simply not been very presentable, and socialist realism didn't travel well. But Derrida, Foucault, and de Man not only provided a new terminology and set of theoretical weapons, they also provided *tone*.

The result was that even though Marxism as a political idea was in full retreat across the globe (at least outside of the Forbidden City and Albania), its variations and mutations became virtually the unchallenged orthodoxy of much of what passed for the academic humanities. In 1983, Hilton Kramer attended the annual meeting of the Modern Language Association. His account highlighted the advanced stage of politicization of the humanities and the degree to which Kampf's and Jameson's program of desecration had succeeded, albeit in more genteel and academically respectable ways.

> In the sessions we attended, it was more or less taken for granted that revolution on one or another Marxist model was a good thing. It is doubtful, of course, that everyone attending the MLA convention—or even, for that matter, these particular sessions—agreed with the Marxist views they were designed to propagate. Yet to the extent that political ideology was given official sanction in the centennial program, that ideology was largely Marxist or feminist or some radical combination of both. No other social or sexual views—except, of course, those deriving from the doctrinaire programs of male homosexuality—found their way into the convention's program. No one, moreover, seemed to regard all this as a particularly noteworthy phenomenon. In American academic life, this development now seems pretty much to be taken for granted.*

By the late 1980s, critic William Cain could not only declare that Marxist criticism has a "special status and is now the predominant subject and system of belief," but that its dominance is so complete that "No one *dares* to utter a liberal doctrine."[42] [Emphasis added.] One of the leaders in politicizing literary scholarship, Cain openly declared that his approach to literature was not based on such obsolete concepts as style, art, form, or beauty—but rather on political usefulness. While others began with gender, Cain believed that "race" is the "central problem" of modern society, and so grounds his teaching of literature in that agenda.[43] "I prefer myself to begin, as I have emphasized, with present political interests and to proceed from there to choose writers

---

* By the late 1980s the idea that the study of literature was a political act had become so institutionalized in *au courant* departments such as Yale's that it even affected the way literature students dressed. One Yalie told *The New York Times* that literature students wore black at Yale to "rebel against society and conformity." Another student was probably more typical, admitting that she chose to wear black "to fit in" with the "artsy or marginalized people who wore black and seemed to have the same political values." Another student discussing the black uniform explained that "It derives from Yale having deconstruction, a school of criticism designed to show contradictions in the supposed meanings of literary works." He equated that with black, which represents "the mystery behind the veil, hidden reality and the misunderstood antihero."

and texts which I can examine with students to develop and express these interests."

In other words, the process *begins* with political considerations and only then moves toward the selection of books, which are chosen not for any intrinsic value they might have, but specifically to "develop and express" Cain's pre-ordained ideological agenda. Such was the environment by the 1980s that Cain not only made no attempt to conceal his tactics, but proudly boasted of them.*

The politicization of scholarship has generated bizarre new permutations in the curriculum itself. At Syracuse University, for example, the English Department reorganized its major by subdividing its courses into three sections: historical, theoretical (with a heavy emphasis on deconstructionism), and political. "Political inquiries," the department explained, "assume that texts are bearers of political meaning. That is, they mediate power relations."[44] Henceforth, at Syracuse, English majors will be required to take courses from each of the three divisions. Under "politics," their choices include (bear in mind these are *literature* courses): "Studies in Ideology" ("advanced analysis of culture in terms of ideology"); "Studies in Canons" ("the politics of canon formation"); "Studies in Institutions" ("the role of institutions in mediating and determining cultural representations, political power, and knowledge"); "Studies in Race and Discourse" ("the cultural and discursive construction of race"); "Studies in Imperialism and Nationalism" ("cultural imperialism and resistance"); "Studies in Class, Culture, and the Power of Discourse" ("analysis of discourses of class as sites of power and resistance"); "Studies in Feminisms" ("the theories and practices of feminist discourses"); "Studies in Gender" ("sexual difference as a political construction"); "Studies in Sexualities" ("the politics of sexualities in specific cultural and textual contexts").[45]

After the new program was unveiled, one Syracuse professor was moved to remark on "the desire of the English department to teach

---

* It is unlikely that Lionel Trilling would have been surprised by the development of the new absolutism in the 1980s. Robert Scholes, an early guru of the new age, argued that it was politically progressive to devalue personal intention and individualism and traced the historic development of the new ideology from liberalism through existentialism and structuralism, towards what he described as a "politics of structure."

In the last years of his life Lionel Trilling took note of Scholes' position and his growing influence and remarked that the antipathy of his ideas toward individuality was the distinctive mark of Stalinism.

everything but English Literature."46* Unfortunately, Syracuse was not particularly unusual. It was merely somewhat more open about institutionalizing ideology in the place of literature as the focus of its programs.

Neither the size of an institution, its traditions, or its affiliation guarantees immunity from the pressures to politicize the curriculum. Thus, at prestigious Haverford, "an institution . . . committed to educational diversity," students are required to complete a course in non-Western cultures or on "the nature, history and workings of prejudice as exemplified among other things by the history and working of persecutions suffered by any collectivity because of religion, culture . . . or sexual orientation."47 Tiny Ursinus College in Pennsylvania "seeks to include the issues of race, class, and gender across the curriculum."48 At Carleton College, students must fulfill the "Recognition and Affirmation of Difference Requirement (RAD)"49—so called, presumably, because it is no longer enough to study the Third World, it is necessary to *affirm* it. Even venerable Williams College's curriculum has become loaded with courses such as "Bad, Mad and Imbruted Women," "The Female Prison: Convents and Brothels," and "Gender, Science and Technology."50

The presence of ideology, was, of course, not new. Ideology had never been absent from academia or academic scholarship. What *was* new was the radical shift in the understanding of academic ethics that inevitably grew out of the decision to create academic disciplines that were in actuality political movements.

These professional ethics, which guaranteed the free and open discussion of ideas, had been the foundation of academic freedom. These ethics demanded, according to historian Frederick Rudolph that "in the classroom the American professor used his professional competence and his scientific knowledge of the facts to present controversial questions in such a way that his own neutrality protected the students from indoctrination."51

Those principles were embodied in the American Association of University Professors' 1940 Statement of Principles on Academic Free-

---

* As an example of the prose of Syracuse's English professors, consider this passage from a memorandum explaining the new program: "The purpose of the new groups is not simply to collate existing courses, but to serve as sites for discussion of new modes of organizing our pedagogical interests, elaborating new sets of course offerings, and combining, collapsing or replacing existing ones."

dom and tenure. The AAUP drew a careful distinction between freedom of research, which was entitled to "full freedom," and classroom teaching, which required professional restraint. Professors, the AAUP declared, "should be careful not to introduce into [their] teaching controversial matter which has no relation to [their] subject. . . ." Faculty members "should at all times be accurate, should exercise appropriate restraint, should show respect for the opinions of others, and should make every effort to indicate that [they] are not institutional spokesmen."[52]

The decline of this ethic had especially fateful consequences for the liberal arts.

The paradox of the liberal arts is that they have a dual and contradictory function. They are the preservers of the traditions and intellectual inheritance of the West; but they are also subversive of many of those same values. But that tension has been held in balance—albeit often an uneasy one—by academia's ethical standards of restraint and tolerance as well as by its insistence on submitting questions of value to the rigorous inquiry of scholarship and reason. The Socratic method presupposes not merely the freedom of intellectual inquiry but also the validity of human reason to discover truth. All things are subject to question, not because there is no truth, or because it is unknowable, but precisely because the apprehension of truth is so vital and its pursuit requires the full effort of the human mind, untrammeled by dogma or ideology.

These traditions ensured both continuity and growth: continuity by guaranteeing that objective standards of judgment would be applied to new ideas and challenges to conventional wisdom; growth because those ideas that passed muster could be absorbed into the continuing dialogue of the liberal arts tradition.

By starting not with the questions, but with the answers, the politicization of academia has meant that much of what passes for scholarship is no longer a search for "truth," but rather an inquiry into political loyalties and ideological usefulness. Radical activist turned academic Annette Kolodny, for example, insists that works of criticism should be judged by criteria that ask: "What ends do these judgments serve and what conceptions of the world or ideological stances do they (even if unwittingly) help to perpetuate?"[53]

Leading critics like Rosalind Coward blithely adopted the language of totalitarianism by arguing that in order to be acceptable as a feminist writer one must pass an ideological test; feminist writing must reflect "a shared commitment to certain political aims and objectives." Coward goes even farther when she describes books being "interrogated" by readers to determine the degree of their political correctness.[54]

The hectoring tone of ideological purity has turned much of academic debate into a search for deviancy—witch-hunting, with traditional scholars often cast in the role of the witches. Such standards are decisive for the integrity of scholarship. Writes Peter Shaw: "Once loyalty and orthodoxy replace the ordinary standards of intellectual discourse, those who enforce the most Draconian standards tend to prevail."[55]

In academia today, the limits on discourse are Draconian indeed.

CHAPTER

III

THE OFFICIAL IDEOLOGY I:
FEMINISM

In the years since the 1960s, no change in the academy has approached the rise of academic feminism in magnitude. The triumph of feminism in the academy is largely a result of what James Nuechterlein has called "the feminization of the American left." With the decline of Marxism as a plausible doctrine and the assault on liberalism from the radical left during the 1960s, feminism has risen to become the prime critical vehicle of the left. By supplying a new vocabulary and innovative critiques of society, it has provided the left with a desperately needed infusion of personnel and ideas. While academic Marxism owes much of its new prestige and clout to its new structuralist guises, it is most in debt to its feminist reincarnation.*

---

* Writes Nancy Harstock, a well-known Marxist-feminist: "Others have argued that socialist feminism must be recognized as a definite tendency within Marxism generally; in contrast, I am suggesting that *because feminists have reinvented Marx's method, the women's movement can provide a model for the rest of the left in developing theory and strategy*." [Emphasis added.]

"For those on the Left," Nuechterlein noted, "it is in many ways the only game in town. Feminization provides a dynamic for left-wing thought that it would today otherwise lack."[1]

In 1990, it is the rare institution that lacks either a program or a department of women's studies. There are more than 530 separate programs, offering something in excess of 30,000 separate courses. Fifty separate "centers" are devoted to the study of women's issues.[2] But feminism's influence far exceeds its formal structures. It has become virtually an orthodoxy within many of the traditional academic disciplines themselves. At one recent convention of historians, no fewer than 21 panels focused on "the role of race, gender or sexual preference in history." Papers included "Sex, Gender and the Constitution," "Sodomy and Pederasty Among 19th Century Seafarers," "Science, Medicine and Gender," and "Black Women in the Workforce."[3]

Historian Gertrude Himmelfarb remarked that gender had become the center of virtually all of the new scholarship on history. "You can't do anything now without making reference to gender," she said. "You can't talk about the Austro-Hungarian Empire without talking about gender. . . . It used to be class. Now it's gender."[4]

The push to make gender studies mandatory throughout the curriculum has already made progress at some major schools. At Cornell, faculty are *required* to "be familiar with at least the broad outlines of feminist scholarship in their discipline." Rutgers University has created an Institute for Research on Women, which conducts two-week faculty workshops with state money. The project's leaders say they expect to eventually train faculty in every school in the state. Says Carol Smith, a feminist English professor who has directed the program, "We want them to go back, not just as individuals changing their courses, but to be a team that will go back and reform the basic curriculums of their schools."[5] At Colgate University in New York, the head of the women's studies program boasts that a new core curriculum "shows some impact of a feminist presence," and predicts that the addition of more feminists to the faculty will result in "long-range changes that will occur *regardless of the intention of the majority of the faculty*."[6] [Emphasis added.]

Even more than the ethnic studies courses that arose from the 1960s, the rise of academic feminism reflects both the extent and the depth of the shift in the values and ethics of higher education. Despite its scholarly trappings, women's studies has never shed its political roots. Even as it has moved into the universities it has continued to behave like a political movement. At a 1978 Women's Studies Conference, the keynote speaker addressed herself to "Breaking the Disciplines," arguing that "From a feminist perspective, knowledge has a normative social purpose—not the continuation of the world as we know it, but the transformation of that world. . . ." Her comments were echoed by another professor who declared bluntly, "Feminism, from my point of view, is an ideology designed to change society. The idea, after all, is not to describe the world but to change it. . . ."[7]

Nor was this inconsistent with the direction the movement as a whole was taking. The slogan that "the personal is the political" had effectively eliminated any area of life or scholarship in which political considerations were inappropriate or irrelevant. Feminist critics have been remarkably candid about their political agenda. Toril Moi, author of *Sexual/Textual Politics* acknowledges that "the principle objective of feminist criticism has always been political."[8]

University of California-Irvine Professor Leslie Rabine puts it even more directly: "The very nature of women's studies requires that its faculty not involve ourselves [sic] solely in the abstract theoretical side of the field but also engage politically in controversial issues. . . . Marxist-feminists cannot afford the false divisions between practice and theory. . . ."[9]

That commitment to political action is made explicit in *All the Women Are White, All the Blacks Are Men, But Some of Us Are Brave*, a textbook used by Dartmouth Professor Deborah King in her sociology course on "Black Womanhood in Culture and Society." In the book's introduction, the authors, Gloria Hull and Barbara Smith, proclaim "the *necessity* for Black women's studies to be feminist, radical and analytical," and warn against the temptation of black feminist academics to fall into the "trap" of academic respectability by muting their politics or their radicalism. Black feminist academics, they insist, must continue to reject "the modes of bankrupt white-male Western thought," and must teach and write in a way that will further their "liberation."

The blending of orthodox Marxism with feminism has, at times, been somewhat strained, but the attempt has made for interesting theoretical calisthenics. Marxists argue that all knowledge is based on class and that the working class's oppression "provides a basis for a view of reality that is more impartial than that of the ruling class and also more comprehensive." Marxist-feminist Alison Jaggar piggy-backs gender on top of class. For Jaggar, "women's experience of subordination puts them in a uniquely advantageous position for interpreting reality. . . ."[10]

As Jaggar notes, however, any theory of a special "women's standpoint" must be able to "explain why it is itself rejected by the vast majority of women." Jaggar declares that the "standpoint of women" cannot be discovered "through a series of women's existing beliefs and attitudes" under conditions of "male dominance" any more than "the standpoint of the proletariat [can be] discovered by surveying the beliefs and attitudes of workers under capitalism."[11] In other words, the will of women, like the will of the people, cannot be determined through bourgeois instruments such as elections, or surveys, or any of the other usual means of determining opinion in a democratic society.

The conclusion follows: obviously women need a vanguard revolutionary elite, just as the proletariat did to lead them to revolutionary consciousness.* In its Leninist formulation, this idea is discredited in every capital of Eastern Europe, Moscow not excepted. Miraculously, it is reborn in feminist academia and thus in the curriculum of many of America's elite universities.

Academic feminists did not arrive at such a radical consciousness immediately. At first, they confined their concerns to finding neglected women writers and suppressed classics that could be added to the "patriarchal" curriculum. This approach, however, ran into immediate difficulties. Despite the best efforts of the feminist restorers, such forgotten feminist classics simply did not exist, certainly not in the numbers required for a burgeoning academic movement. Some early feminists addressed this problem directly and with notable candor. Simone de Beauvoir frankly acknowledged the scarceness of great literature by women. "Why is it then that . . . there are so few that amount to much? And amongst those that are of some worth, why is it that so few are really first-rate?" She did not challenge the existence of artistic and literary standards, or the need for artists to pursue universal themes; she argued that the social milieu discouraged artistic endeavors by women. Artists, she said, make

---

* It is interesting to note that Jaggar's book, *Feminist Politics and Human Nature* was made possible in part by generous grants from the American Association of University Women and a fellowship from the National Endowment for the Humanities. As discussed in the Prologue, it is required reading in Dartmouth's women's studies program.

extreme demands of themselves, which alone allow the individual
to attain the greatest heights of achievement. For want of such
exacting standards, women lack the infinite patience which Buffon
described as the essence of genius. These qualities are denied
them not by virtue of any flaw in their nature, but by virtue of the
conditioning they have undergone.[12]

She was, in effect, echoing Virginia Woolf, who had also stressed the
social and economic limitations faced by women writers and who had
also explicitly rejected the idea of sex-based critical theories. "It is
fatal," she had warned, "for anyone who writes to think of their sex." It
was essential, Woolf insisted, for great artists to write "without hate,
without bitterness, without fear, without protest, without preaching."
According to Virginia Woolf, "The greatest writers lay no stress upon
sex one way or the other. The critic is not reminded as he reads them that
he belongs to the masculine or feminine gender."

But by the late 1980s, de Beauvoir's position had been decisively
rejected and Woolf's warnings ignored. Critic Toril Moi denounced de
Beauvoir for deviationism, including "a disturbing tendency to accept
dominant patriarchal definitions of arts and artists," and for her "pecu-
liarly Western individualism." Moi also denounced Beauvoir for her
seemingly reactionary belief that "great artists are always somehow
universal in their outlook on life and art."[13]

As late as 1977, American feminist critic Elaine Schowalter approached the question of neglected women writers from a perspective
that respected traditional aesthetic standards. Specifically, she cautioned
against the adoption of any theory of feminine sensibility that would
imply "a deep, basic, and inevitable difference between male and female
ways of perceiving the world." Within four years, however, she had
effectively reversed herself, writing in 1981 of the distinction between
"patriarchal values" and the "female aesthetic." Schowalter's rhetoric
reflected the influence of the new theories, as she wrote of the need for
"gynocritics" to attack the "androcentric critical tradition."[14]

In practice, that translated into an attack on the Western humanistic
tradition itself. Feminist critic Susan Gubar writes that she and her
colleagues had once believed that "women and men participated equally
in a noble republic of the spirit and that both sexes are equal inheritors of
'a thousand years of Western culture.' " But having followed the logic of
their ideological progression, Gubar wrote, they had now come to

realize that this heritage—the "treasures of Western culture" —were, in reality, "the patrimony of male writers" and thus, by implication, enemies to the cause of feminist liberation.[15]

Critic Carol Iannone points out the fundamental contradiction between Woolf's "aesthetic of transcendence" and the new feminism's political aesthetic of "sexual grievance," which has led feminists to reject the humanist tradition. "Given this incompatibility," Iannone concluded, "feminist criticism *must* eliminate the reliance on literary standards lest literary standards eliminate it."[16]

The discovery that the new theoretics of post-structuralism made it possible for feminist critics to eliminate such standards of judgment— now labeled phallocentric, patriarchical, Eurocentric, and sexist— cleared the way for feminist literary interpretation to present a radical new worldview. Now even second-rate literature could become part of the feminist canon, because literary standards had been abolished. Now books—or "texts" as they were inevitably called—could be judged by a new feminist aesthetic, feminist dogma, and even a specifically feminist writing style and epistemology suffused with "values that examine the extent to which a work reflects or services the interest of women."

Under the new dispensation, any attempt to apply standards or even reasonable judgments based on aesthetic norms could be regarded not only as politically regressive, but as an act of oppression, intellectual sexism, and imperialism. "Our language system," wrote feminist critic Leslie Rabine, "works as a system of phallic oppression enmeshed within the overall system of social oppressions: and it also mediates them all."[17] * Writes Peter Shaw:

> What starts out as sexual politics in feminist literary criticism, then—placing a concern to elevate women's condition before literary considerations—yields to radical politics, in which women's condition is glossed on a vaguely Marxist model of oppression and exploitation. At each radicalizing step, surprisingly enough, radical politics puts at least as much emphasis on gender as sexual politics did, advancing with equal if not greater insistence the ideas of a

---

* Like other radical feminists, Rabine sees phallocentrism in a variety of places, including monotheism—"One God (a phallic one)"—the family, "which recognizes One Master (the father who holds the phallus)," and language itself, which is dominated by what she calls "the phallic symbolic order."

separate women's sensibility, a separate women's writing style, and a separate women's literary criticism. Moreover, where sexual politics had demanded ever more Draconian denials of specific literary values, radical politics demands the abandonment of literary value altogether.[18]

Liberal feminism, notes Shaw, has been notably silent in confronting the extreme versions of lesbian feminism, French biologism, and Marxist feminism because it has, in effect, allowed itself to "be taken intellectually hostage."

"By subordinating literary critical values to considerations of political solidarity, and a desire not to insult political radicals," writes Shaw, "it has made itself complicit in radical feminism's most damaging tendencies."[19]

The same politicized logic informs the feminist attack on empiricism and science. Here the embrace of scholarship by ideology is most evident. "The impetus for such an analysis [the rejection of 'male' science]," Margarita Levin writes, "arises from the need for completeness—'gender' must be shown to be a social artifact suffusing *all* 'belief systems'—and, of course, from the need to explain away particular scientific studies that confirm innate sexual differences that feminists deny are 'natural.' *But the real threat to feminist ideology, it turns out, is the scientific method itself*, with its promise of objectivity no matter who the scientist is."[20] [Emphasis added.]

Ultimately, Levin notes, the feminist critique falls flat because of its failure to answer the unavoidable fact that "so-called masculinist science *works*."[21] The fact is embarrassing, perhaps, but appears to have no influence on the continuing popularity of feminist books attacking science in the curriculums of elite universities.*

Inevitably, such inversions of academic value are reflected in the classroom. When Harvard adopted a women's studies program in 1986, the sole dissenter was Harvey Mansfield, who denounced the program as "a foolish and almost pitiful surrender to feminism. This is Harvard,

---

* Levin predicts that one of the next major attacks on the curriculum will be in the form of demands for "subjective" science courses and new guidelines for scientific journals to weed out masculinist bias; new grading systems that take account of women's approach to science; and a movement for more funding of non-sexist science. She is almost certainly correct.

not the platform of a political party." The courses, Mansfield gibed, would be merely "elaborations of the opinion one already has and the confirmation of their prejudices."[22]

That seems to be confirmed by Professor Karen Howe, who taught a course called "The Psychology of Women" at Trenton State College. Howe concluded that "there is a self-selection process operating so that students choosing to take women's studies courses already think in liberal terms regarding women, compared to the general student body." She tested her students at the beginning of the semester and consistently found that most of the students were already committed feminists. In fact, she noted, "my students were already scoring so high on the scale that there wasn't any room for them to obtain higher scores as a possible result of taking the course."

The aim of the course was not to challenge the preconceptions of the students, but to reinforce them. "We begin the course with discussions of the male bias in society and psychology," Howe said. "In the course of discussing this material, the students experience a shift from the male interpretation of females that makes up a good deal of psychology to a more female-centered focus . . . they have become more aware of the presence of sexism in their socialization and society."[23]

If Socratic dialogue is the paradigm of a liberal education, the paradigm of feminist study is the consciousness-raising group, described by feminist academic Kate Lindemann:

> First, the experience is more than communal, it is collective. In the context of collective reflection women found the power to name oppressive experiences and to disassociate themselves from both external and internalized models of oppression. . . . Second, the group is dialogic, and it is without a formula, or an appointed leader. Honest, mutual sharing without regard to status has been freeing and has generated keen insights for such groups. . . . Third, the group emphasizes non-judgmental behavior. . . . Fourth, in the consideration of someone's experience, members respond with supportive, collaborative experience. . . .[24]

Unfortunately, such an environment is not also conducive to the challenging of feminist ideas, assumptions, and claims. "If you didn't buy the feminist line," one Ivy League junior says, "you knew you were going to be put down. You got the idea that you were out of it. After a while, I just stopped raising my hand."[25] The pressures to conform are not, apparently, limited to speech alone.

Elizabeth Lilla, a former editor at *Geo* and *Daedalus* was told by one teacher at Kenyon College that a female student was "asked to defend her decision to dress in a noticeably feminine manner." Other students complained they were penalized with lower grades if they did not use the ideologically approved pronoun "he/she." And in some classes, "students reported being put very much on the defensive if they disagreed with their teacher's feminist interpretation of a work."[26]

The pressures are also felt by faculty members themselves. Professors who seek to challenge feminist ideology, or even provide their students with unbiased critiques of its major premises are blackballed from women's studies programs. At Pomona College, for example, a professor of philosophy, Frederick Sontag, developed a course titled "The Feminist Critique: The Ad Feminam Argument," which he described as a philosophical appraisal of feminist theories. It was promptly rejected by the women's studies program. "I believe that if I were a woman, my course would have been approved," Sontag told *The Chronicle of Higher Education*. But the key factor in the course's rejection seems to have been its failure to meet the feminists' ideological litmus test. Sontag says the women's studies program reviewed his personal beliefs, which were deemed unacceptably skeptical of feminist dogma. The program's director all but admitted as much when she wrote that "all courses in the department proceed from the initial premise that there is something unique in women's experience," and that Sontag did not have an understanding of "the fundamental issues" in women's studies.[27]

Even so, there is an extraordinary amount of naivete about feminist pedagogy, even among academics. In his book, *Killing the Spirit*, a critical analysis of academia, historian Page Smith wrote that he suspected the atmosphere of women's studies programs was "not dissimilar to that of women's colleges in the late nineteenth century, places like Mount Holyoke, Smith, Wellesley, Bryn Mawr."[28] Smith's innocence and his sanitized fantasy, however, would not survive even a brief exposure to the realities of the feminist classroom.

At Ohio State University, for example, a woman instructor on feminism was shouted down during a class by militant lesbians. When Kenyon College's Thomas Short heard of the incident he remarked that the offending students should have been removed so that the class could continue. Recalls Short, "[I] was solemnly informed by another of my male radical feminist colleagues that that would be contrary to 'feminist pedagogy.' Feminist pedagogy, I learned, rules out any exercise of authority, since that would be male."

Short pointed out the obvious: "Ruling out anything akin to adversarial procedure will, of course, effectively protect assumptions from being challenged—and all the more so when some people are allowed to do all the talking."[29]

IV

THE OFFICIAL IDEOLOGY II:
RACE

After two decades of affirmative action, special minority studies pro-grams, ethnic student centers, minority administrators hired to deal with minority concerns, all-black dorms, and a culture in which "diversity" has become an all-purpose mantra, academia has made little meaningful progress toward increasing black success in higher education.

By the late 1980s, while the percentage of black students who grad-uated from high school rose, the proportion of black high school grad-uates attending college dropped sharply. And those who attend college often lead isolated lives. Students at the University of California at Berkeley have become accustomed to racial separation through a vol-untary resegregation in housing and social life. "On the whole," one Berkeley senior told *The New York Times*, "blacks and whites don't have relations with each other on this campus." At the University of Illinois not only are fraternities and sororities racially segregated, but black students hold a separate all-black commencement ceremony each year, with their own speakers.[1] There are other signs of failure as well.

Universities have shown a greater talent for recruiting minorities than actually graduating them.* While 60 percent of white undergraduates earned degrees from the University of Texas after five years, more than two-thirds of black students failed to graduate.[2]† At the University of California at Berkeley, the university enrolled many black students even though they had, at best, marginal academic credentials. At the same time, Berkeley quietly limited the number of academically qualified Asian-Americans it would accept. One study found that to have a 50 percent chance to win admission to Berkeley, an Asian student needed a score of 7,000 on the so-called Academic Index, while a score of 4,800 was sufficient for black applicants.[3] The result was that while Asians (and some white students) were excluded, many of the academically under-prepared black students were, in effect, set up to fail, which they did, with more than two out of three dropping out of school.[4] ‡

The message here seems clear: while large minority student counts enhanced an institution's image and sense of political and moral virtue, this *frisson* of self-congratulation was increasingly coming at the expense of the minority students themselves, who were tantalized by degrees that proved unattainable. In 1983, fewer than 600 black students nationally had composite scores of 1200 or more on the SAT—even though that was the median student score for many of the schools that were aggressively recruiting them.[5] Since then, black test scores have risen modestly, but not enough to eliminate the magnitude of the disparity. One study, for example, found that while black students admitted

---

* A 1990 study found that only 24 percent of black students had earned a degree even six years after entering college. Between 1976 and 1987, the number of bachelor's degrees awarded to blacks actually fell by 4.3 percent; with an even greater drop—12.2 percent—for black males. Blacks earned only 5.7 percent of the total bachelor degrees awarded in 1987, down from 6.4 percent in 1976.

† At the University of Texas, the average SAT score of black entrants in 1988 was more than 100 points below the average for white students. (*The Texas Review*, March 1989.) According to the Texas Educational Opportunity Plan for Higher Education, the average grade point average for first-year black students was 1.97 (compared with 2.45 for white first-year students).

‡ Black and Hispanic students made up 21.3 percent of Berkeley's freshman class in the fall of 1989. White students made up 33.1 percent of the freshman class, down from 57.9 percent in the fall of 1981. During the same period, Asian-American applications rose 7.9 percent, but admissions increased by only 2.4 percent. A bill before the California State Legislature would require the state's public universities to try to achieve a student mix that "reflects California racial and ethnic diversity by the year 2000, when whites are expected to be a minority." (*The New York Times*, February 16, 1990)

to Cornell scored in the 75th percentile, they were expected to compete
with white students who were at the 99th percentile. The average black
student at the Massachusetts Institute of Technology scored in the upper
ten percent nationally. But when measured against fellow MIT students,
the scores of the black students were in the bottom ten percent of the
class. Nearly a quarter of the black students who matriculated at MIT
failed to graduate.[6] Economist Thomas Sowell observes that "Minority
students with every prospect of success were artificially turned into
failures by being mismatched with an institution preoccupied with its
minority body count."[7]

Sowell, who is black, goes so far as to suggest that the "body-count"
mentality of the universities has fed a new racism by creating a new
stereotype of the black student. "The only large group of white students
who have a long history of being admitted to leading colleges and
universities without meeting the normal admissions standards are big-
time varsity athletes," he writes. "They too have a long history of taking
Mickey Mouse courses, receiving grades that they haven't earned—and
of failing to graduate nevertheless. Why should anyone be surprised
when such patterns have also emerged under preferential admissions for
minority students? Why should anyone be surprised that the 'dumb
jock' stereotype that has followed college athletes for decades under
these conditions should now have a racial counterpart, after similar
conditions have been created for minority students?"

Having been grossly mismatched with institutions of higher learning,
Sowell suggests, minority students have only two basic alternatives:
either obtain poor grades and "lose their self-respect" or attack and
undermine the standards against which they are measured and which
they are often unable to meet. "Given the alternatives," he noted, "it is
hardly surprising that so many choose the second."[8] *

Given the climate in higher education, administrators have been
reluctant to address the obvious dilemmas posed by the demographics of
race. Instead, they have turned to rhetoric and symbolic politics. While

---

* Sowell's analysis seems born out by the frequency with which proposals for tightening
academic standards are condemned by black students as being inherently racist and
elitist. A black doctoral student who wrote in *The Nation* that "When we hear talk
about increasing the number of 'qualified' minority students and being careful not to
'lower our standards,' we must recognize these as catch phrases for the politics of
exclusion. . . ." was merely articulating what has become the almost reflexive response to attempts to address questions of academic qualifications.

THE OFFICIAL IDEOLOGY II: RACE

denying that there was any tension between excellence and "diversity," many schools have imposed mandatory ethnic studies requirements, often with a strong victim-studies flavor. Such curricular "reforms" were closely aligned with the continuing pressure to recruit and retain minority faculty members, a process that has become so heated that even the normally bland *Chronicle of Higher Education*, was moved to describe it as a "minority faculty recruiting frenzy."[9]

These recruitment efforts have also been complicated by academic demographics. Despite twenty years of aggressive affirmative action, the number of doctorates awarded to blacks in 1988 was down 22 percent from a decade earlier. Blacks were awarded only 3.5 percent of the doctorates handed out in 1988; but even this overstates their representation on university faculties. Many black professors are concentrated in predominately black institutions; by the end of the 1980s, blacks represented only 2.3 percent of the faculty at predominately white institutions.[10]

Even those numbers do not fully reflect the scope of academia's dilemma. In 1986, more than half of the doctorates earned by black scholars were in a single field—education. In 1986, there was not a single doctorate awarded to a black candidate in architecture, astronomy, classics, European history, geology, law, German, Italian, Russian, or Spanish. Moreover, fewer than half (272 out of 547) of the black Ph.D.s chose to pursue a career in higher education, thus drastically reducing the pool of potential candidates for universities.[11]

The paucity of qualified minority candidates for academic positions has not, however, discouraged elite universities from redoubling their affirmative action efforts, thus creating a lucrative, booming, and divisive market for minority scholars. In 1988, for example, Cornell hired 24 minority professors in a single year.[12] Duke has put in place a policy of hiring a minority professor in each of its fifty academic departments by 1993. The University of Wisconsin has upped all bids with its ambitious plan to recruit 70 minority professors, including 25 senior (tenured) faculty members, in just three and a half years.

Other than eviscerating normal academic standards, the only way to achieve such a goal is to raid other institutions. Wisconsin is not alone in creating minority raids.* It has, in fact, been raided in turn. In a

---

* In the fashionable jargon of affirmative action, the goal is no longer necessarily to hire a "qualified" minority, but to find candidates who are "qualifiable," a euphemism for the abandonment of normal academic standards.

recent year five black professors departed for more lucrative offers. "We're lucky to break even," one Purdue university administrator admitted. "We're just bidding against one another. It's becoming an academic musical chairs."[13] One result has been a shift in the locus of political activity to the search committee, where the hiring and promotion of faculty has become the continuation of revolution by other means.

Filling the growing number of positions held open for members of disadvantaged groups is not as simple as merely finding qualified applicants of the appropriate ethnic or sexual identity. It is not enough to be a woman or black: only those specializing in "oppression studies" need apply. At Kenyon College, according to Elizabeth Lilla, the goal "is not simply to hire more women but to hire the right sort of women, which is to say feminists." Lilla reports that at least one non-feminist woman was denied reappointment in her department because of her "refusal to incorporate feminist materials into her courses."[14] Similar standards often apply for other minority candidates.

While black professors who decline to join the chorus of attacks on the white, racist, patriarchal West, often find little interest in their services,[15] the State University of New York at Binghamton offered an endowed chair in the humanities at a salary of more than $105,000-a-year and lavish perks to a professor notorious as an apologist for Muammar Quadaffi.[16]

University of Texas Professor Alan Gribben describes the process of ideological selection:

> In English Departments, women as well as minority academics who practice close reading, formal analysis, genre study, literary historiography, biography, textual studies or editing find increasingly that the new hiring guidelines actually impede rather than advance their hiring and promotion. A woman professor must apparently write about the scarring effects of violence-prone patriarchy to benefit from the attitudes of this "New Orthodoxy"; an African-American, Mexican-American, Asian-American, or other ethnic scholar can receive the truly lucrative academic positions only if he or she is prepared to devote a lifetime to describing the hegemonic brutality of white Euro-Americans. Simply *belonging* to one of the favored hiring classifications is no longer sufficient in the latter 1980s: one must subscribe to the sacred if dogmatic trinity of Race, Class, and Gender.[17]

One egregious example of academic racial politicking took place in 1989 at the University of Wisconsin, when UW offered a black activist/ poet named June Jordan a salary approaching $80,000-a-year if she would join UW's English Department. "We wanted to recruit stars," explained UW Chancellor Donna Shalala, "and June Jordan was precisely that kind of person."[18]

The attempt to hire Jordan was not questioned by members of the UW faculty, the board of regents, or even members of the state legislature. It thus fell to a student, Richard Abowitz, an English major at the university, to point out the unmentionable: Jordan's views on race were "extreme, dogmatic, and irreconcilable" and often tinged with anti-Semitism.[19]

"Her attitudes toward poetry and literature, toward the English language and toward America—white America, in particular—are on record for all to see and read," Abowitz wrote in *The New Criterion*. "What is amazing is that any reputable English Department anywhere would consider her a senior person of distinction, worthy of a prestigious position and a whopping salary."

Abowitz, who went to the trouble of reading Jordan's collected works, found her poetry to be "formless, colloquial, [and] banal" while her politics were "dour, shrill, and predictable." During a visit to Dartmouth College in 1987, Jordan had denounced the writing of black poetry "for art's sake," insisting that "our poetry is political or we fail ourselves as poets."[20]

For Jordan, the United States represents "the greatest evil to people seeking just rights of self-determination." She singled out Vietnam, Cuba, and Iran for accolades. In contrast, Israel was, for Jordan, a "tool of the United States in [its] deadly insistence on global domination."[21]

Her views on academic freedom were drawn from predictable models. She has argued that controversial scholars like William Shockley should be denied the right to speak on campus, claiming the imminent danger of racial genocide. In one essay, she warned that "Right now, in America, we, Black People, Third World peoples, poor people in general are being sterilized: homogenized into nonexistence, sterilized. . . . Now, and right here, the poor and the Black and the Third World peoples here, at Yale, must testify to repeated and growing prospects of private and state-supported policies to destroy and extirpate 'us' from this diseased body politic of the United States."[22]

Her attitude was reflected in her approach to language itself. In fact, it is the intersection of Jordan's racial and political views with her "scholarship" on language that is perhaps the most revealing aspect of all.

For Jordan, Standard English is "the language of the killers," or as she described it during her Dartmouth speech, "the language of people who hate me."[23]

That attitude translated directly into the way she approached language in her classroom. At one point she had her students at Stony Brook write letters protesting the alleged murder of a young black man by a white policeman. Under Professor Jordan's tutelage, it read: "Us appall, fed up, because that another senseless death that occur in our community. . . ." Not even *The Village Voice* would dignify the illiterate screed by printing it. But Jordan defends her students' use of "black english" by arguing: "Should we use the language of the killers—Standard English—in order to make our ideas acceptable to those controlling the killers?"[24]

Again, it was left to Abowitz to remark upon the obvious:

> It is very odd to think of an English teacher expressing such sentiments at a time when students are graduating from college with an increasingly feeble command of the English language. To encourage students to ignore spelling and violate grammatical rules—this apparently, is part of June Jordan's mission as a teacher of English.

Professor Eric Rothstein, the chairman of the UW English Department praised Jordan as "perhaps the most outstanding female, black poet of her generation."[25] Abowitz came to a different conclusion: "the attempt to hire June Jordan has everything to do with radical politics and nothing whatever to do with scholarship, critical intelligence, acceptable standards of prose writing, or even minimal levels of artistic achievement."[26]

Ultimately, Jordan chose to accept an offer from Berkeley, bypassing Wisconsin's "competitive offer," and Shalala's fervid recruitment effort. It was clear, however that Abowitz's critique had little influence on either the school's administration or the UW English Department. Chairman Rothstein praised Abowitz as a bright young man, but warned darkly that he "is going to have a great deal of difficulty in finding schools where people are going to be sympathetic to his arguments."[27] That is likely true.

The attempt to hire June Jordan was itself merely part of a larger offensive at the University of Wisconsin—launched after a handful of relatively minor, though troubling, incidents on campus, including one in which students wearing "black face" staged a "slave auction" during a fraternity party. UW officials used the slave auction and a handful of other incidents as the pretext for decreeing a mandatory "ethnic studies" requirement and for unveiling "the Madison Plan." The Plan calls for spending nearly $5 million over three years, largely to hire minority faculty. Funding for June Jordan was to have come from the Madison Plan kitty.

By exploiting the fraternity stunts in apocalyptic terms, the administration was able to play upon its own self-created sense of crisis and thus provide itself with the ammunition to do what it wanted to do anyway. It was a classic example of the leveraging of maximum moral indignation from the most isolated infractions. UW also announced its "Design for Diversity," a euphemism for a program that included tight restrictions on any speech that "is intended to demean the individual(s) on the basis of race, sex, religion, color, creed, disability, sexual orientation, national ancestry or age," or that creates "a hostile environment for education, university related work or other university-authorized activity." As originally drafted, the speech *dictat* was so broad and vague that officials were forced to clarify it by exempting actual classroom discussions.

The ban on racist speech, is not, however, absolute. Louis Farrakhan, the leader of the Nation of Islam, was invited to speak at UW. His invitation came at the urging of some of the very groups that had most actively argued for the racial gag rule. A notorious anti-Semite, who has praised Hitler and called Judaism a "gutter religion," Farrakhan's appearance even struck Shalala, the architect of the speech ban, as ironic. "Black students denounced some people for hiding behind the First Amendment," she told *The New York Times*, "and then they hid behind the First Amendment when Farrakhan came."[28]*

---

* UW's "Design for Diversity" could also be called "Diversity or Death" in the case of the ROTC program. In late 1989, the faculty voted 386 to 248 to throw ROTC off campus by 1993 to protest discrimination against gays and lesbians. The shutdown would affect 440 ROTC students at the Madison campus. Of the faculty vote, Shalala said: "I could not be prouder of them." (*Milwaukee Sentinel*, December 5, 1989.) Under political pressure, however, Shalala later reversed herself and ROTC was given a reprieve.

Inevitably, the shrill tone of ideological conformism has made itself felt throughout the university. At the University of Buffalo, the law school faculty voted *unanimously* to adopt a "Statement Regarding Intellectual Freedom, Tolerance and Political Harassment" that says that free speech must be limited by "the responsibility to promote equality and justice." As Paul Hollander, a professor of sociology at the University of Massachusetts, noted: "It would be interesting to know who will be authorized to define what constitutes equality and justice and just how they are to be promoted. In any event, no totalitarian could have put it better."[29]

In scenes that academics would have found unimaginable only a few decades earlier, professors have openly called for "self-censorship" in both research and classroom presentations. One Harvard professor called for faculty members to avoid using any material in classes that "might hurt a group," while a colleague told a forum in Cambridge that while artists and writers might have complete freedom of inquiry and expression, such freedom was inappropriate for the universities where the faculties were "supposed to be creating a better world."[30] Recounting the incident, *The Economist* of London noted wryly that this doctrine of academic unfreedom was delivered "to much applause" from its academic audience.[31]

In the 1960s, New Left *philosophe* Herbert Marcuse had argued explicitly that certain kinds of speech could legitimately be suppressed, even by "apparently undemocratic means" in the service of social betterment.

> They would include [Marcuse wrote] the withdrawal of toleration
> of speech and assembly from groups and movements which pro-
> mote aggressive policies, armaments, chauvinism, discrimination
> on grounds of race and religion, or which oppose the extension of
> public services, social security or medical care, etc. . . .
>   Moreover, the restoration of freedom of thought may necessitate
> new and rigid restrictions on teaching. . . .[32]

But even at the height of the student revolution, Marcuse's call for restrictions on free speech was taken seriously only by the far left. Now, having undergone a process of rebirth and academization, Marcuse's theories have been institutionalized.

Under the ironic and indeed Orwellian rubric of "diversity," schools as diverse as Brown, Emory, Penn State, Tufts, Michigan,* and Wisconsin imposed new gag laws, aimed at speech deemed offensive to the official ideology. At the University of Connecticut, students faced expulsion from classes not merely for the use of "derogatory names, inappropriately directed laughter [and] inconsiderate jokes," but also for what the school termed, "conspicuous exclusion [of another student] from conversation."[33] At the University of Michigan, a university publication gave as an example of prohibited discriminatory harassment a male student's remark that women are inferior to men in a given field. Another possible violation of the rule, students were told, would be if students gave a party at a residence hall but failed to invite someone because they thought she was a lesbian.[34] †

Even where such policies have not been formalized, the hunt for ideological impurity is often rigorously pursued. When dining-hall workers at Harvard, for example, planned a "Back to the Fifties" nostalgia party, they were accused of racial insensitivity by the dean for minority affairs. The dean, ever vigilant for whiffs of racism, detected inappropriately backward attitudes in the celebration of the pre-civil rights era (even though most of the dining hall employees were minorities themselves).[35]

Schools ranging from Vassar to Brown, Berkeley, UCLA, Dartmouth, and California State University at Northridge have attempted to censor, suppress, or discipline student journalists. At UCLA, a student editor was suspended after publishing a cartoon that featured a rooster who was enrolled as an undergraduate at UCLA. When asked how he got into the school, the rooster replies, "Affirma-

---

* After a student challenged the University of Michigan's policy, because it would restrict his right to discuss his research ideas in classes, it was thrown out by a federal judge. Tufts also later suspended its policy. A proposal to impose a mandatory "ethnic studies" requirement at Michigan failed by a narrow margin in a faculty vote, but it had administration support and was expected to be raised again.

† In contrast, some schools have been notably reticent in dealing with outbursts of anti-Semitism (Jews do not happen to be "in" this season.) After one anti-Semitic incident at Vassar in 1988, recounts Thomas Sowell, "the prime concern was not to punish the student responsible but to suppress that news from being published." When the student paper published the story anyway, it "had its money cut off." (New York Daily News, July 21, 1989)

tive Action." When the editor of the paper at Northridge reprinted the offending cartoon to protest censorship at UCLA, he too was suspended.[36] *

As the cloud of ideological conformity has spread, it has inevitably entered the classroom itself. Even the doctrine of academic freedom no longer provides immunity from harassment from the ideologically advanced. At Tufts, a professor was denounced for "racism and callousness" by one minority student, who aired the charges in the student press. The professor's crimes included recommending "Tally's Corner," a widely used study of urban anthropology; raising questions about affirmative action; and appearing to support Senator Daniel P. Moynihan's warnings about the status of the black family.[37]

Even though they are often utterly without merit, charges of "racism" can take a terrible toll, especially when the environment is so hostile to even the hint of deviancy. At Harvard, Professor Stephan Thernstrom was pilloried by campus activists for "reading aloud from white plantation owners' journals without also giving the slaves' point of view."[38] At the University of Michigan, a distinguished sociology professor was denounced for political errors and racial insensitivity because he assigned several readings deemed unacceptable to some minority members of his class on "Race and Cultural Contact." Reynolds Farley had taught the course on race relations for nine years and asked his students to read a nineteenth century defense of slavery. As a result of the controversy and harassment, Farley said he will no longer teach such courses. "Given the climate at Michigan," he said, "I could be hassled for anything I do or don't say in that class. I decided to drop the course. It certainly isn't worth it."[39]

If his reaction seems excessive, consider the case of the lecturer at the University of Pennsylvania, who was ordered into the academic gulag of "sensitivity training seminars" after he expressed surprise that many of the black students in his class seemed unaware of the thirteenth amendment abolishing slavery.[40] As the lecturer should have known, Penn's "diversity" policies leave little room for deviationism.

University of Pennsylvania Professor Alan Kors recounts the story of an undergraduate member of Penn's "diversity education" committee, who wrote a memo naively expressing her "deep regard for the individ-

---

* The protest over censoring student journalists brought together an unlikely coalition, including both the ACLU and former attorney general Ed Meese.

ual and my desire to protect the freedoms of all members of society." In response, a university administrator fired back her own memo, with the phrase circled and the word "individual" underlined.

"This," declared the Penn official, "is a 'RED FLAG' phrase today, which is considered by many to be RACIST. Arguments that champion the individual over the group ultimately privilege the 'individuals' belonging to the largest or dominant group."[41]

At Stanford, certain issues can simply no longer be discussed freely within the classroom. "It is very difficult today to get open discussion going on such issues as anti-pornography and affirmative action because people are sensitive about the feelings of minority members," Gerald Gunther, a professor of constitutional law, told *The Chronicle of Higher Education*. "It isn't a good teaching situation if you are inhibited because you feel somebody's feelings might be hurt."[42] "Things have gotten to the point," one Michigan student told *The New York Times*, "where students can't say anything about racism on campus without being called a racist."[43]

At Wesleyan University, where radicals paid tribute to their intellectual and spiritual forebears by ritually burning copies of the conservative *Wesleyan Review*, one recent graduate says, "People are very reluctant to say what they feel if it doesn't mesh with the prevailing ideology. There is a form of self-censorship in which people can't say what they really think because of fear of being labelled insensitive or, even worse, racist or sexist."[44]

In the 1980s, as the campaign for "diversity" became a form of official ideology, schools quickly embraced "sensitivity" programs aimed at excising illicit attitudes. The approach is elastic; the definition of what is racist, sexist, or "homophobic" can be adjusted almost endlessly. Academic leaders like Professor William Damon, the chairman of Brown University's education department, argue that schools should require "mandatory racial-education courses." Such courses, Damon insists, "should cover and *provide clear justification for, any racially or ethnically sensitive admissions or hiring criteria that students may see on campus*."[45] [Emphasis added.] In other words, affirmative action is dogma.

Damon's call for required courses justifying affirmative action drew a stinging response from Harvard's Stephan Thernstrom. "How about a mandatory course providing 'a clear justification' for American foreign policy since 1945?" he asked. "Or one justifying the Reagan Administration's domestic policies?" The violation of academic ethics and academic freedom would be obvious in such cases.

But Damon's proposed therapeutic course, Thernstrom wrote, "would clearly not dispassionately examine the pros and cons of affirmative action, despite the powerful criticisms of it that have been advanced by scholars black (Thomas Sowell, Glenn Loury) and white (Nathan Glazer, Allan Sindler)." This, he wrote, was not education in any normal sense of the term, but rather "an exercise in indoctrination."[46]

Harvard has hosted therapeutic workshops collectively grouped under the title AWARE—"Actively Working Against Racism and Ethnocentrism"—that have featured movies like "Racism 101" and harangues by sensitivity professional Gregory Ricks, who described both Dartmouth and Harvard as "genocidal" institutions. At one session, Ricks declared: "Throwing tampons at the male, sexist dogs at Dartmouth was educational!"[47] Ricks is a former Dartmouth *dean*—both a symbol and product of the changes in American higher education.

Brown University has put its own twist on the therapeutic ethos by creating programs specifically designed for minorities. All non-white freshmen are invited to campus three days early to attend what the university calls its "Third World Transition Program," a heavily political indoctrination session that serves to reinforce the new students' identity as members of oppressed minorities. By the time Brown's white freshmen arrive for the school year, the racial divisions have already been drawn.*

At the University of Massachusetts, the forcible six-day occupation of a university building by black activists resulted in the university agreeing to a laundry list of concessions, including an expanded cafeteria menu of "ethnic foods." In a scene reminiscent of the 1960s, U-Mass Chancellor Joseph Duffey not only brought food baskets to the students involved in the seizure of the university building, but afterward thanked the invaders "for reminding us of obligations we share as members of a community of learning."

---

* Journalist Pete Hamill wrote of Brown's Third World Transition Program: "It is race-driven; it assumes that nonwhites are indeed different from other Americans, mere bundles of pathologies, permanent residents in the society of victims, and therefore require special help. 'They're made to feel separate from the first day they arrive,' one alumnus said. 'And they stay separate for the next four years.' " (*Esquire*, April 1990)

Even so, Duffey's self-abasement did not usher in an era of campus peace. Instead, there were more racial conflicts, prompting the university to sponsor a two-day moratorium devoted to racial "re-education," complete with workshops, "support groups," and the rest of the paraphernalia of the modern therapeutic culture. As one observer noted:

> The tacit presumption underlying the workshop and the support groups is that regulating behavior and achieving civility are not enough. One must go into people's minds and "reeducate them"— a favorite word—in order to root out racism that is there *by definition*. Everyone, in this scheme of things is guilty and no one gets to be proven innocent. . . .[48]

The message to students, wrote Professor Jean Bethke Elshtain, was that "you may not know it but you are by definition racist, sexist and homophobic. The white males, of course are the most guilty of all, but nobody escapes the dragnet." Elshtain found the mind-cleansing program "unsettling," but she was also skeptical that it would have the desired effect. "My hunch," she wrote, "is that, over the long-haul, the upshot of such endeavors will not be a purified, racist-free, collective student consciousness but a simmering backlog of resentment at being labeled as a racist, even if one has never committed a racist act nor uttered a racist slur."[49]

CHAPTER

THE ATTACK ON THE WEST

All attempts to make education subordinate to politics begin with the burning of books. In the 1980s, the purge of reading lists—like the imposition of gag rules on speech—was carried out in the name of "diversity."

By mid-decade, the debate that dominated much of the academic agenda centered around the "canon," the works of great literature upon which the liberal arts curriculum had been built. At one time, humanistic education could be defined as the study of such books—the best of what has been thought and written.

"These books," St. Johns College's Leo Raditsa reminds us, "have to be read because without them you would not know the love of life or its depth or its dangers; you would not know what is worth living and dying for. . . . They give the past its words, and only the past can enable us to see the present without too many illusions and in all its richness and danger, and to recognize the likely catastrophes that only courage and intelligence can avoid."

Such intellectual experiences also required teachers, described by Raditsa as "voyagers, carrying home the treasures they discovered on their own backs."[1]

It is one of the tragedies of higher education that such vivid intellectual experiences have become increasingly rare for students. The modern university has pushed the Great Books to the margins of the curriculum, substituting instead the desiccated, narrow, and specialized scholarship of academic "research." The modern university professor is trained, promoted, and rewarded for research, not for teaching, with the result that undergraduates have limited course offerings taught by uninspired lecturers (often graduate assistants) on pedantic or "populist" subjects (such as courses on the history of rock music).

In the early 1980s, however, the humanistic ideal seemed to be making a remarkable come-back, with Stanford University taking the lead. As the 1960s atmosphere of intellectual chaos and intimidation started to dissipate, Stanford in 1980 created a new program in Western civilization, a cluster of courses centered on fifteen Great Books, including the Bible and works by Homer, Sophocles, Plato, St. Augustine, Dante, Thomas More, Machiavelli, Martin Luther, Galileo, Voltaire, Karl Marx, Charles Darwin, and Sigmund Freud. It was an extraordinary act of intellectual and institutional reaffirmation. For many undergraduates "Western Civ" was the highlight of their Stanford education.*

By any measure, it was a success. Only a few years earlier, a British journalist who had visited the campus had gibed that for most Stanford undergraduates, "the period between the second Ice Age and the inauguration of John F. Kennedy seems largely undifferentiated."[2] But by 1982, Western Civ had so changed the intellectual environment that one professor could declare: "A miracle has happened among Stanford undergraduates. They do talk about Plato at dinner and about Shakespeare on the grass."[3]

But by the late 1980s, the paradigm for the new academic revolution was the evisceration of that program under pressure from the Black Student Union—whose slogan "We don't want to read any more dead white guys" was chanted in antiphony with "Hey, hey, ho, ho, Western Culture's Gotta Go!"†

---

* The course consistently was rated favorably by 65 to 80 percent of Stanford students.

† Stanford is not alone. Its Western Civ program had been modelled on Columbia University's own famous humanities program. But that course is itself under fire, because it has an insufficient number of titles by non-white, non-male, and non-Western authors. One of Columbia's best known faculty members is left-wing literary critic and Israel-hater Edward Said, who says of Columbia's Great Books course, "They [younger faculty members] all loathe the course. They loathe it with a passion beyond description." (*New York Times Magazine*, May 15, 1988)

It was decisive for the intellectual integrity of the debate at Stanford that for the most part the content of the Great Books was ignored, while the focus of the attack was turned on their authors—now dismissed as dead, white, Western males. It was a startling triumph for unreason; especially ominous because this savaging of the humanities ultimately came not at the hands of the militants, but the university itself.

Again, the cry was "diversity," but the agenda sounded suspiciously ideological. The Great Books curriculum, one history professor charged, "has become a symbol of nineteenth century Western imperialism, a remnant of the time Europe ruled the world."[4]

"The faculty who pushed hardest to overturn [Western Civ] are 1960s leftovers," said history professor Paul Robinson, the director of the doomed course. "As undergraduates, they assumed they'd be called upon to reform the world. Twenty years later, they see themselves besieged by an America that's turned away from radical politics. They want to make the campus a haven, and attacking the course was their way of digging a line of defensive trenches."[5]

Perhaps the most effective tactic in the battle of the books was what one recent graduate called the radicals' "censorship-by-accusation."[6] When, for example, the student newspaper, *The Stanford Daily* editorialized against attempts to junk Western Civ and ran several columns defending the program, the head of the Black Student Union publicly compared the student writers to the Ku Klux Klan and the whites who chased a black man to his death at Howard Beach.[7] In the end, the threat of being tarred as a racist intimidated the vast majority of Stanford students and professors who favored the course into silence.

Bowing to the pressure, Stanford's faculty replaced Western Civ with a course called "Cultural Ideas, Values," that pointedly excluded reference to the West, and demanded that professors "give substantial attention to the issues of race, gender and class," and assign books by "women, minorities and persons of color."

The faculty's action brought a swift denunciation from then-Education Secretary William Bennett: "For a moment, a great university was brought low by the very forces which modern universities came into being to oppose: ignorance, irrationality and intimidation. The loudest voices have won, not through force of argument but through bullying, threatening and name-calling."[8]

The campaign highlighted the paradox of the canon debate. During one rally, black students agitating for the dismantling of Western Civ displayed a banner reading: "Get Your Stanford Education in Diversity" with the word "diversity" crossed out and replaced with "Racism" and "Western Culture."[9] By juxtaposing "diversity" in opposition to "Western Culture," the students were engaging—unconsciously perhaps—in the wildest of paradoxes.

Pluralism, or "diversity," is, of course, a Western ideal. It did not spring from the cultures of Africa and Asia, but from the cultures of Western Europe and the United States. This tradition, however, is being attacked by militants who believe that only black writers can speak to blacks, only women to women, only hispanics to hispanics. In the culture of "diversity," race and sex—not literary or intellectual quality, or even historical fact—are the standards for inclusion.

To make room for the new agenda, Homer, Sophocles, Dante, More, Luther, Galileo, Darwin, and Freud were tossed into the curricular ash can. Only six of the original fifteen books remain. The discarded classics have been replaced in part by Rastafarian poetry, the U.N. Declaration of Human Rights, and the writings of Frantz Fanon, the apostle of black revolutionary terrorism.

The latter's presence is the most illuminating aspect of the agenda of the new curriculum. Revealing far more than he knew, Assistant Dean Charles Junkerman wrote to *The Wall Street Journal* that fifty years ago

> John Locke seemed indispensable in answering a question like "What is social justice?" In 1989, with a more interdependent world order, a more heterogenous domestic population, and mass media and communications systems that complicate our definitions of "society" and "individual," it may be that someone like Frantz Fanon, a black Algerian psychoanalyst, will get us closer to the answer we need.[10]

The crudity of Junkerman's analysis rests not merely on its suggestion that Locke's ideas may somehow have been rendered obsolete by "mass media," but the implicit assurance that there can be no enduring human questions or standards that can be referred to in making a judgment of value. Junkerman's replacement of John Locke with Frantz Fanon also implies a sort of moral and intellectual equivalency between Locke's *Essay Concerning Civil Government*, which shaped the ideas of the Founding Fathers, his *Letters Concerning Toleration*, an historic plea for religious and intellectual freedom, and Frantz Fanon's *Wretched of the*

Earth, with its echo of Joseph Goebbels: *"when a native hears a speech about Western culture he pulls out his knife—or at least makes sure it is within reach."* 11*

Fanon's writings—now enshrined in the curriculums of schools like Stanford—flatly reject calls for negotiation, democracy, and non-violence as "quaint humanitarianism" and he derides "the Mediterranean values—the triumph of the human individual, of clarity, and of beauty" as mere "lifeless, colorless knickknacks."12 The persistent theme of Fanon's work is the necessity of violence and the defense of terrorism in the fight against colonialism. Because colonialism is for Fanon "violence in its natural state," it can be overcome only "when confronted with greater violence."13

> For example, the gangster who holds up the police set on to track him down . . . or who dies in single combat after having killed four or five policemen, or who commits suicide in order not to give away his accomplices—these types light the way for the people, form the blueprint for action and become heroes.14

At least for Stanford, this is to replace the writings of a man whose work is indispensible in understanding the roots of the American republic and modern democracy. Allan Bloom was roused to say of Junkerman's comments that Fanon "is a *demonstrably* inferior and derivative thinker to whom no one would pay any attention if he were not the ideologue of currently popular movements, and did not, as a black Algerian, fit Stanford's job description."15

None of this was to argue against the inclusion of non-Western thought or literature. The *addition* of the classics of the Orient and Islam unquestionably enriches liberal education. Stanford offered outstanding courses in non-Western cultures, again reflecting the historic development of the liberal arts. Columbia University, which originated the modern Western civilization programs, offered a course in Oriental Civilization, which could be used to fulfill the second year requirement

---

* Junkerman's doctrine of obsolescence presumably also applies to such works as Milton's *Areopagitica* and John Stuart Mill's *On Liberty*. It is not, then, surprising that there have been moves to restrict free speech on campus. In a *New York Times* op ed article a Stanford English major argued: "Stanford must realize that unlimited free speech does not necessarily increase educational opportunities," and called for a ban on "racially derogatory *ideas* on this campus. . . ." [Emphasis added.]

in its famous Contemporary Civilization program. The bulwark of the Great Books movement, the University of Chicago, required students to take a sequence in either Russian, Indian, or Islamic Civilization to satisfy undergraduate requirements in the social sciences.[16] Boston University's new humanities core also integrates classic works of non-Western civilizations into its program, without diluting its Western content or politicizing its courses.

But adding non-Western works and building upon the existing canon with due respect for the intellectual integrity of the enterprise is very different from using such texts *in place* of Western classics, as was done at Stanford. Displacing the Western texts and traditions is to sentence students to study world cultures without having any prior understanding of the West's, as if it were possible to understand the nuances of a foreign culture without having any real sense of one's own. But, ultimately, the appreciation of non-Western cultures is not what the canon debate has been about at all. Although the left invoked the concept of "diversity," with its patina of respectability and democratic legitimacy, it had a far more thorough-going critique in mind.

Implicit in the Stanford revolution was the abolition of the very idea of intellectual and literary standards—the idea that one book may actually be better than another and thus worthy of greater attention. Stanford professors like Herbert Lindenberger argued that canons that focus on great literature are intellectual tyrants; that history itself is only an arbitrary construct that can be reshaped into conformity with ideology.[17] This philosophy is embodied in the cultural relativism of the curriculum, under which all cultures—preliterate, Homeric, Italian Renaissance—are regarded as essentially equal, with none having any pre-eminent claim on our interest or allegiance.

Ultimately, the result is a system, remarks one journalistic critic, in which, "the saint and Hitler, Sophocles and a peasant's songs, all fade together against the gray background of a nihilism where good and evil, truth and falsity, are no longer considered the kinds of issues that teachers and students ought to grapple with."[18]

The irony is unmistakable.

At the end of the 1980s, the world—both East and West— from Beijing's Tiananmen Square to Bucharest to the Brandenburg Gate turned once again to the Western tradition for guidance and inspiration, recognizing in the West the fount of man's aspiration for freedom. East Germans meeting in Christian churches read the words of Martin

Luther King, Jr., who in turn had drawn his own inspiration from the philosophical tradition he traced from Plato and Aristotle to Rousseau, John Stuart Mill, and Locke, as well as the eloquent poetry of the Old Testament.

But as the world embraced the traditions and inspirations of the West, American academics were repudiating them. And their attack on the West was trickling down to the public schools.

In 1989, a report titled "A Curriculum of Inclusion," was prepared for the New York State public schools, under the direction of the state's top educator.[19]

The report indicts the current curriculum of the schools for what it calls "deep-seated pathologies of racial hatred" and urges "sweeping changes" in the curriculum. Adopting the typically shrill tone of academic victimology, the report opens by declaring that minorities have been the "victims of an intellectual and educational oppression that has characterized the culture and institutions of the United States and the European World for centuries." New York's schools, according to the report, have perpetrated "miseducation" and inflicted psychic damage on the young through "a systematic bias toward European culture and its derivatives."

The report declares that "there is something vulgar and revolting in glorifying a process that heaped undeserved rewards on a segment of the population while oppressing the majority." The "process" the report refers to is the American and Western European political tradition.

Among the racist aspects of the curriculum singled out for condemnation is the treatment of the U.S. Constitution and Bill of Rights. According to the report, teaching that the Constitution embodies "the belief in human dignity, liberty, justice and equality," reflects "White Nationalism," and ignores the reality of a political system that was designed "for articulating and aggregating the interests of the rich and powerful, who were the true benefactors of the New Anglo-Saxon Model."

More properly, the educators argued, the Constitution should be taught in the New York public schools as a "seriously flawed" document that was, in reality, "the embodiment of the White Male with Property Model." To make the curriculum more diverse and "pluralistic," the report insists, students must be taught that: "Deeply rooted in the development of the United States of America is the policy of sacrificing higher ideals on the alter [sic] of materialism and profit making, particularly when African American interests are involved."

The author not only recommends an elaborate new bureaucratic watchdog to monitor such ideological lapses, but calls for "the most stringent measures" to "root out this *illness*." [Emphasis added.]

"It is too little too late to believe that the inclusion of multicultural perspectives on the pluralism of American society can reverse long established and entrenched policies and practices. *Much more severe corrective action is needed to create the dynamics of positive change*." [Emphasis added.]

The battle for the soul of American education is just beginning.

THE HOLLOW MEN

Probably only a few students are effectively indoctrinated by politicized classes. It is quite easy, in fact, to graduate with degrees in business administration, or engineering, or medicine, unaffected by the academic orthodoxies and perhaps even unaware of their presence on campus.

But that measure is misleading. The impact of the new academic culture is not merely its success in corrupting the American mind, but in stultifying it.

American academics boast that the American university system is without peer in the world. And despite perennial pleas of poverty, American higher education enjoys virtually unprecedented riches and has encountered little resistance to piling up even more. For a decade, leading universities have raised their tuition at more than twice the rate of inflation.

But it has become increasingly difficult to ignore the void at the heart of the enterprise—a moral and intellectual vacuum in which one searches in vain for a remotely coherent sense of the meaning of a college degree in 1990.

"The one intolerable thing in education," Mark Van Doren once remarked, "is the absence of intellectual design." But it is possible to graduate from 78 percent of the nation's colleges without ever taking a course in Western civilization; from 38 percent without taking a single course in history; and from 45 percent without taking courses in American or English literature. It is possible to graduate from one-third of the nation's colleges and universities without studying the natural or physical sciences.[1]

Columbia's Jacques Barzun describes the ideal humanities curriculum by noting that it must, first of all, actually be a curriculum, "a sequence, not a batch of courses for picking over. . . . Bits and pieces will lead nowhere—certainly not to a confident familiarity and a mode of thought. Nobody should expect a 'humanized' graduate to come forth after a shallow bit of 'world lit' here and whiff of art history there."

The study of the humanities, he wrote, requires both a "common training" and a "common body of knowledge."[2]

Barzun's prescription is based upon the recognition that humanistic study is a continuing dialogue between science, history, literature, and philosophy, because the end of the liberal education is not the various specialized fields themselves, but the human being the student is becoming. In traditional liberal education, artists, poets, scientists, historians, and philosophers speak to one another, providing mutual illumination. That is the ideal; it is no longer the reality.

It is possible, for example, to fulfill the humanities requirement at Dartmouth—one of the nation's leading liberal arts colleges—with a grab-bag of courses that might consist of "Creative Video," "Costume Production," "American Popular Design," and "Women and Literature." One would also be deemed to have satisfied the liberal arts requirement for the humanities by taking a bundle of such unrelated courses as "Basic Drawing," "Introduction to Modern Brazilian Culture," "Gnosticism and Urban Christianity," and a "Seminar in the Music of John Coltrane."[3] Even with its so-called core curriculum, it is possible to graduate from Harvard without reading Shakespeare, Aristotle, or Plato. Students can pass through higher education at the nation's most elite educational institutions in abysmal ignorance of their place in history, the civilization which they inhabit, and the great philosophical debates on what it means to be human.

With its refusal to exercise intellectual judgment or to challenge what Kenyon College's Thomas Short calls the tendency of the curriculum to "the political, the obfuscatory, and the silly,"[4] the modern university has engendered its own form of post-modern academic ignorance, an agglomeration of prejudice, dogma, misinformation, and sophistry. Paradoxically, the modern student is schooled in the culture of universal skepticism, but he is unarmed in any true confrontation of ideas. This is perhaps inevitable when we have students who take courses in the economic imperialism and oppression of the West, but have no background in economics; or who are indoctrinated in the multiform evils of American society, without ever studying its history or institutions; or who explore the philosophical nihilism of deconstructionism without ever having acquired the basics of critical thinking.

What such students are left with is less an intellectual point of view than a posture of defiance; a skepticism too feeble and untrained for anything more than the clichés of fashionable prejudice. Because their ideas are seldom genuinely tested, theirs is a style without substance and ultimately without commitment, even to the doctrines of the culture itself. The situation is not without its own irony. Instead of the beliefs it has sought to inculcate, the academic culture has produced not merely unbelief, but the rejection of the very concept of belief. The graduates of the culture are drilled in the rituals of dismantling their culture, but are understandably at a loss when asked to build anything in its place.

They are hollow men stuffed with the straw of academic confusion.

How could this have happened? How could higher education so lose sight of its values, mission, and ends? How could its standards become so inverted that a scholar whose work is an attack on "coherent beliefs of any kind" can be transformed into a pillar of the humanities? How could professors who argue that language is phallus-like because it is linear be not merely tolerated, but celebrated, fêted, and tenured?

In *After Virtue*, Alasdair MacIntyre asks us to imagine that a catastrophe has occurred that is so great that our knowledge of the natural sciences is all but completely lost: physicists are killed, books destroyed, laboratories sacked. All that is left are fragments, bits and pieces of theories, experimental equipment "whose use has been forgotten; half-chapters from books, single pages from articles, not always fully legible because torn and charred." Some of the scientific terminology survives, but its meaning is largely lost, unconnected with any theoretical context or understanding of the basic principles of the now-lost science. Children are taught the partially recreated disciplines under titles like Physics, Chemistry, and Biology; heated debates develop over scientific concepts that are only dimly understood. All the while, the new practitioners of "science" would be unaware of the fact that a catastrophe had occurred at all.

MacIntyre's radical thesis was that this mythical catastrophe is in fact a description of what has happened to our understanding of the language of morality. "We possess indeed simulacra of morality, we continue to use many of the key expressions. But we have—very largely, if not entirely—lost our comprehension, both theoretical and practical, of morality." It is a catastrophe, MacIntyre writes, so thorough that it would be unrecognized by the academic curriculum, and indeed "the forms of the academic curriculum would turn out to be among the symptoms of the disaster. . . ."[5]

It is not my purpose here to pursue MacIntyre's argument. But he provides a provocative clue to the nature of academia's own crisis, which features debates—centered on terms like "the liberal arts," "diversity," "academic freedom," "the Great Books," "the university"—that presuppose a shared understanding and history that no longer exist.

But if we are seeing the results of such a catastrophe as MacIntyre envisioned, when did it occur? And how?

As fateful as they were, the events of the 1960s cannot completely account for it. We need to go back further to the time when the consensus over the ends of higher education dissolved and both teaching and the liberal arts—their fates inextricably intertwined—were demoted to marginal status within the academy. In place of the consensus about the means and the ends of education that once existed, there was now a vacuum.

When academics withdrew into their specialties, a process that accelerated after the Second World War (it being considered more "professional" to be a "scholar" rather than a "teacher"), they withdrew also their willingness to exercise judgment over the curriculum. The academic culture's fragmentation was justified by the professors on the grounds that each specialty should grow in its own direction, its allegiance to the discipline rather than to the institution; to the profession rather than to the student or to the curriculum. The focus was no longer on teaching, or the shared ends of the institution, but research within the increasingly narrow academic villages.

The traditional college, in contrast, had been founded on a metaphysic that placed man within a moral and rational universe. The purpose of the academy was to help students to apprehend this fact through a discussion of great works on the nature of man and his place in society and in creation. The disappearance of that metaphysic— unnoticed and unremarked in much of the vast literature of academic self-congratulation—undermined the foundations of the academic enterprise, especially in the liberal arts. Long before the onslaught of the student revolution of the 1960s, higher education's immune system had been destroyed. It had lost the rational standards by which it had previously judged itself, or at least the will to apply them.

Add the collapse of moral courage, the disintegration of liberalism, and the replacement of reason by intimidation, to a system already breaking apart under its own centrifugal forces, and the result is disaster.

"We are the hollow men/ We are the stuffed men," T.S. Eliot wrote, "Leaning together/ Headpiece filled with straw. Alas!/ Our dried voices, when/ We whisper together/ Are quiet and meaningless/ As wind in dry grass/ Or rats' feet over broken glass/ In our dry cellar."

In the "Hollow Men," Eliot drew upon one of literature's most haunting images—that of moral weightlessness. In the *Inferno*, Dante finds in the vestibule of hell the numberless souls of those who had been neither good nor evil—who had failed to commit themselves one way or another—and were thus condemned to chase through the underworld an empty banner which was blown aimlessly "as the wind behaves." It is a strikingly apt metaphor for the state of the modern academy.

Understanding the pathology of this decline is critical for any meaningful appreciation of the current crisis. And to help us understand the crisis, perhaps it is best to focus on one school.

The crisis of Dartmouth College, like that of academia as a whole, did not spring full-blown from the upheaval of the 1960s. The history of Dartmouth and its decline is largely the history of American higher education itself. At one time, Dartmouth played a leading role in reaffirming the value of a liberal arts education. It later turned away from that role, but was still, for a time, a potent counter-model for hundreds of institutions struggling with their sense of identity and institutional purpose and lost in curricular confusion. The seeds of our present academic dissolution lie in Dartmouth's history; but so perhaps does the key to renascence.

PART II

THE
DECONSTRUCTION
OF DARTMOUTH

VII

THE HOPKINS ERA

The inauguration of a president of Dartmouth College is an occasion of august tradition, with ceremonies stretching back to the founding of the small missionary college on Hanover plain in 1769 by Eleazer Wheelock. The new president is entrusted with the College's charter by a representative of the trustees. From his predecessor, he receives a silver punch bowl, a gift to Wheelock in 1771 and now a symbol of both the presidency and the "Wheelock Succession," emphasizing the unbroken line of both leadership and tradition.[1]

The charter of Dartmouth College was issued on December 13, 1769, but it was not until the next year that Eleazer Wheelock, travelling through the wilderness along the length of 70 miles of the Connecticut River, finally fixed upon a location for his College. The site he chose was both breathtakingly beautiful and practical, "containing about 3,300 acres on which there is, by estimation, near 200 acres of choise meadow, annually overflowed by said river, and a large brook which runs into it."

Wrote Wheelock: "This tract is pritty well watered, and well proportioned for all kinds of tillage, and for fuel. It joyns upon the falls, called White River falls . . . where is the only place for a bridge across Connecticut River, it being but eight rods wide. . . ."

Indian tribes—who had been driven off in recent Indian wars—had long used the area for hunting grounds. As Wheelock surveyed the site he determined that the College itself would stand within a mile of the river, surrounded by fields whose cultivation would provide "the principal or only diversion and way for students health &c. . . ."[2]

By the time of the American Revolution, Dartmouth College was one of only nine such institutions of higher learning in the colonies.

Dartmouth's choice for its eleventh president, in 1916, was an extraordinary one. At 38, Ernest Martin Hopkins was neither a clergyman (until 1909 all but one of Dartmouth's presidents had been men of the cloth), nor a scholar (as was his immediate predecessor).[3] But his choice reflected the changing nature of higher education and the gravity of the challenge facing the liberal arts college. The traditional college of the nineteenth century was described by historian Frederick Rudolph as "a place where nothing happened and where the president by a kind of indifference or remoteness or even superiority to mundane matters performed an effortless role in seeing to it that nothing did happen."[4] That was clearly no longer the case.

Leading figures in the American academy were already proclaiming the death of the undergraduate college. "As time goes on," predicted the president of Stanford, "the college will disappear, in fact if not in name."[5] Only a few years previously, no less a figure than Nicholas Murray Butler of Columbia had suggested the withering away of the undergraduate colleges. Heavily influenced by the German universities, with their emphasis on research and specialization, Butler and his ally Professor John W. Burgess made little effort to conceal their contempt for the undergraduate colleges or for the men who taught in them. Burgess—a dominant figure at Columbia since his arrival in 1876— regarded colleges as little more than schools "for teaching Latin, Greek, and mathematics and a little metaphysics and a very little natural science." He dismissed the traditional college teacher as little more than a "schoolmaster of superior sort," in contrast to the German professors, who lectured only on topics of their own choice, often the fruits of their personal, rigorous research. Adopting the German nomenclature, Butler and Burgess thought that colleges should fulfill the function of the German "gymnasium" where students were given the tools of specialized learning by means of drills and textbooks to prepare them for their real work, in the universities.[6]

It was this challenge that Hopkins faced as he was inaugurated in October 1916. In place of the verities that had governed higher education, there was now turmoil, confusion, and doubt. Hopkins acknowledged as much in his inaugural speech, when he said, "We are summoned into a wilderness of thought."[7]

Although he was not an academic, Hopkins was no stranger to academia. A successful business executive for companies such as AT&T, Hopkins had begun his career as an aide to Dartmouth President William Jewett Tucker, had founded and served as president of the Alumni Council, and for a time edited Dartmouth's alumni magazine. Even as his business career prospered, his ties to the College remained strong and suffused his family life. (The woman he married had been private secretary to his two predecessors as president.)

Even so, Hopkins accepted the presidency of Dartmouth only reluctantly, after he learned that he was the last Dartmouth graduate in the running. As he later recounted, he believed that what was at stake was the "unique and indispensable function" that schools like Dartmouth could fulfill.[8] At the center of Dartmouth's tradition was a passionate loyalty to the ideals of the independent liberal arts college, handed down from Eleazer Wheelock, but most dramatically personified in the person of Dartmouth graduate Daniel Webster.

The pivotal event in Dartmouth's history was the controversy that led to the Dartmouth Case argued before the U.S. Supreme Court. Fired by internal disputes and populist sentiment, the New Hampshire legislature attempted to take control of Dartmouth from its private trustees and declare it a public "university." At issue was the future not only of Dartmouth College, but of the very existence of private colleges. On October 10, 1818, Daniel Webster, representing the College, argued the case before the U.S. Supreme Court. The famous story recounts how Webster held the justices of the Supreme Court transfixed. One account described Chief Justice Marshall, "with his tall and gaunt figure bent over as if to catch the slightest whisper, the deep furrows of his cheek expanded with emotion and eyes suffused with tears."

Webster closed his case by proclaiming:

> Sir, you may destroy this little institution; it is weak; it is in your hands! I know it is one of the lesser lights in the literary horizon of

our country. You may put it out. But if you do so, you must carry through your work! You must extinguish, one after another, all those great lights of science which, for more than a century, have thrown their radiance over our land!

Finally, his voice choked with emotion, Webster uttered words every Dartmouth man for two centuries would know by heart:

It is, Sir, as I have said, a small college. And yet, *there are those who love it.*

Recounted the event's chronicler, "There was not one among the strong-minded men of that assembly who could think it unmanly to weep, when he saw standing before him the man who had made such an argument, melted into the tenderness of a child."[19]*

For Hopkins, the idea of a Dartmouth president not immersed in that tradition was unthinkable. He took the job.

Today, the academic administrator is part academic, part cheerleader, part bureaucrat, but mostly a glad-handing fund-raiser. Even as he took office, Hopkins was something of an anachronism. He did not see himself as a spokesman for the faculty, nor an advocate for the academic establishment; with both he maintained a civil, often cordial relationship, but also distance. He was a highly public figure, an active, voluble, occasionally pugnacious advocate, who took up his causes in the popular press through articles, speeches, and interviews; moreover, he was willing to challenge the *Zeitgeist*, even at great cost to himself.

Hopkins was an imposing figure who, though five feet eleven inches tall, seemed much taller, an effect enhanced by his high bald forehead,

---

* Eleven months later, the Court ruled for the trustees, declaring that while Dartmouth may benefit the public, it was neither a public nor a civil institution and that the charter was a valid and inviolate contract. The case was a critical development in the understanding of the corporation and "a bulwark of private property" because it protected private property from public encroachments.

The case transformed the face of higher education. It endorsed the principle of academic organization in which ultimate authority rested not with the faculty, but with a board of trustees. And because it now ensured that private colleges could survive, it led directly to a boom in the foundation of colleges across the country. So profound was the impact of the case in shifting the focus of higher education from the public to the private sector that one historian speculates that it "probably helped to check the development of state universities for half a century." (Rudolph, Frederick, *The American College and University*, p. 211)

his dark, heavy eyebrows and his erect and powerful bearing.[10] "The immediate impression," recalled a former colleague, "was one of dignity and reserve—dignity without stuffiness."[11] Throughout his tenure, he was accessible to both faculty and students. He was a familiar figure on campus as he moved across the green with his distinctive sloping walk. Over his three decades as president, he defined the personality and the mission of Dartmouth.

Although now little known outside of Dartmouth circles, Hopkins may well have been the best known college president of his age—which included such luminaries as Nicholas Murray Butler of Columbia, Robert Maynard Hutchins of Chicago, and Abbott Lawrence Lowell of Harvard. During his long career, he would be offered a place in FDR's cabinet, the presidency of the University of Chicago, and would be prominently mentioned as a candidate for the leadership not only of Harvard, but of Johns Hopkins and the universities of Minnesota and California.[12] But his significance rests in the role he assumed at a critical moment in history. In his three decades at Dartmouth's helm, Hopkins would come to embody the determination of the liberal arts college to resist the encroachments of the new universities; and he would emerge as a pivotal figure in a movement to reaffirm liberal education and academic freedom. The era between the wars was perhaps the last time that a concerted effort was made to arrest the drift away from the liberal arts traditions and the eclipse of the humanities. Although the drama would not be fully played out for several decades, the lineaments of modern American higher education were already being hardened into shape. The reform battles at Dartmouth, Columbia, and Chicago were the crucible in which the values of the academy were to be tested.

THE RISE OF THE UNIVERSITY

Although the forces that shaped higher education in the second half of the nineteenth century are complex and often overlap, they can for simplicity's sake be roughly divided into three phenomena: (1) the social and economic changes in society following the Civil War, including the rise of new professions, (2) the rise and growth of science, and (3) the appeal of the research university formed on the German Model.

The War Between the States not only redefined the newly reunited states, but the nature of American society. Inevitably, higher education was caught in the rush of the newly invigorated nation toward industrialization, economic growth, and expansion. In 1867, Ralph Waldo Emerson cast his eye on the American academy and declared that "a cleavage is occurring in the hitherto granite of the past" and "a new era is nearly arrived."[13]

As the war ended, the curriculum of higher education was still governed largely by the consensus generated by the Yale Report of 1828, which had anchored higher education to the study of classical languages. That consensus had rested on the belief that the disciplined pursuit of knowledge had a unity to it, and was best achieved by a study of the classics of Greek and Roman civilization. But in a society in which limitations were being swept away in the onrush of the bustling new Republic, the old colleges seemed hopelessly out of touch. Their relevance to the new professions and needs of commerce was not readily apparent; and they seemed uninterested in dealing constructively with the exciting growth of science and its numerous applications in both industry and agriculture.

The traditional college's model of classical education was explicitly repudiated in the Land Grant College Act of 1862. The author of the bill, Congressman Justin Smith Morrill had called on colleges to "lop off a portion of the studies established centuries ago as the mark of European scholarship and replace the vacancy—if it is a vacancy—by those of less antique and more practical value."[14] The bill, which turned over more than 17 million acres of public land to the states for the development of new institutions of higher education, called for the creation of at least one college in every state "where the leading object shall be, without excluding other scientific or classical studies, to teach such branches of learning as are related to agriculture and the mechanic arts." Within a century, 69 schools were being supported by the legislation.[15]

It was a measure of the intensity of the repudiation of the Yale Report in the latter half of the nineteenth century that American colleges now began offering courses in everything from agricultural chemistry, "the Feet of the Horse and Ox and their Diseases," to bookkeeping, penmanship, and orthography.[16]

There was also a powerful new model to inspire the new schools. It is difficult to overstate the influence or the impact the founding of Johns Hopkins University (opened in 1876) had on higher education. For the first time, a great graduate university on the German model had been founded in the New World. It brought with it the bracing new spirit of a university devoted to the expansion rather than the mere repetition of knowledge. The German universities were renowned for their scientific brilliance, which they had built from their focus on scholarship and the freedom of both the professors and students to pursue interests as they chose. The universities were founded on the twin concepts of *Lernfreihet* and *Lehrfreihet*, the freedom of the student to study and travel as he pleased and the freedom of the professor to pursue his scholarship unfettered. Students at German universities were free to design their own courses as they chose and study and attend classes only when they wished. Because the universities were little concerned with student issues, the German universities had few, if any, facilities outside of classrooms—no dormitories, cafeterias, or student unions. The structure of the universities was also attractive to American faculties. German universities were run by the professors themselves, not administrators. A class of mandarins with quasi-noble social standing, the German professors' domination of higher education was unquestioned and absolute.

Like the German universities, Johns Hopkins focused upon "the acquisition, refinement and distribution of knowledge," rather than upon teaching.

The result, as Frederick Rudolph noted, was a "faculty-centered institution." So central was research to Johns Hopkins that students were selected for admission on the basis of their ability to provide stimulation to the professors. "Nothing could have been more remote from the spirit of the old-time college," wrote Rudolph, "where the teachers were theoretically busily engaged in stimulating the students."[17]

The new universities also marked a decisive shift in the metaphysics of higher education. The traditional colleges had by and large been affiliated with organized religion. Now, as historian Rudolph noted, "for the acceptance of revealed religious truth the new university in Baltimore substituted a search for scientific truth."[18]

This Germanic spirit electrified a nation in search of a new model for higher education. Within a decade, Johns Hopkins had become the nation's premier Ph.D. mill, turning out scholars who would dominate— as the image of Johns Hopkins itself dominated—the faculties of institutions across the nation. The old-time college teacher was rapidly becoming obsolete. In the nineteenth century, it was theoretically possible for a professor to teach courses in rhetoric and sociology, and write articles on political economy and literature.[19] As one admirer later recalled, the college teacher "was a man who had, above all else, intellectual enthusiasm and intellectual sympathy; his learning, touched many fields, and all with a sympathetic and friendly spirit; and his work consisted largely of bringing into the lives, and into the intellectual appreciation of his students, his own sense of learning of civilization and of social relations. For this work there was needed not primarily a man of research, but a man of larger comprehension, of wide interests, of keen sympathies, and of discriminating touch. . . ."[20] Increasingly such professors seemed quaint, if not outright embarrassments in the new universities where departmentalization and specialization had become the marks of the new scientific academy. The gadarene rush to academic respectability often made no distinction between good and bad teaching. Viewing the transformation of higher education's priorities, Henry S. Pritchett of the Carnegie Foundation declared: "Research is a name to conjure with, *but in the last two decades more sins have been committed in its name against good teaching than we are likely to atone for in the next generation.*"[21] [Emphasis added.] It was 1908.

The primary model for the old American college had been the English university, whose traditions stood in stark contrast to those of the German universities. As described by John Henry Cardinal Newman, the university in the English mode was "a place for *teaching* universal *knowledge.*" This implied that it's goal was "the diffusion and extension of knowledge rather than advancement." In direct counterpoint to the German idea, Newman wrote, "If its object were scientific and philosophical discovery, I do not see why a University should have students." Nor was the product of the English university a technical expert; he was a gentleman, and the role of higher education was to inculcate him with "the force, the steadiness, the comprehensiveness and the versatility of the intellect, the command over our own powers, the instinctive just estimate of things as they pass before us . . . the real cultivation of mind."[22]

With its emphasis on the unity of knowledge, the English tradition had been reflected in the 1828 Yale report, and had been the dominant factor in the development of curricula for most of the century. But it was a tradition that had grown stale with time; its inspiration had flagged. Too seldom did the reality accord with Newman's ideal. Then, as now, the greatest weakness of liberal education was its failure to embody its own values in tangible ways. To the critics of the nineteenth century college, the focus on the classics was a mummification of education, a stiff, dull, soulless, rote scratching through the dust of dead texts, and dead ideas. At too many schools, learning consisted largely of recitation and a slavish adherence to textbooks, and there was at least a hint of truth in the gibes of those who regarded the entire institution as an anachronism. It was an old problem for the humanities. As early as 1644, John Milton was complaining of "the old error of the universities, not yet recovered from the grossness of barbarous ages," and the tendency to emphasize grammar and lexicons rather than "the solid things in them."[23] As a model of liberal learning it was unedifying and uninspiring.

Faced with such a feeble foil, the German university's appeal was all the more powerful. It was thus to the German, not the English, tradition that Harvard turned as it made itself over in the 1870s.

Charles William Eliot would hold the presidency for forty years, beginning in 1869. More than any other academic leader, he would usher in the university era in higher education. He forcibly transformed Harvard from a college into a university by instituting the elective curriculum.[24] Beginning in 1872, he introduced a radical new program of electives to replace the prescribed classical course of study. Eliot began by dropping required courses for seniors. By 1884, all requirements for sophomores and juniors had also been abolished. The next year many of the requirements for freshman were dropped, and by 1897 the only required course in the entire Harvard curriculum was freshman rhetoric.[25]*

At various times, Eliot defended the elective system by expressing his boundless faith in the sagacity and judgment of the young. He argued that a young man of nineteen or twenty "ought to know what he likes best and is fit for. . . ."[26] But his enthusiasm for youthful wisdom was not the point. He was not interested in developing a youth cult at Harvard. His goal was to make Harvard—like Johns Hopkins—a faculty-centered institution. Historian Frederick Rudolph makes the observation that in all of the voluminous correspondence between Eliot of Harvard and Hopkins' president, Daniel Gilman, neither ever made a reference to the educational or personal guidance of students. "These were irrelevant to the new orientation, to the university spirit, to the Germanism which was erecting german-style beer parlors on the edge

---

* Eliot's influence was felt at Dartmouth, where in 1882 the trustees replaced the traditional prescribed classical curriculum with one that gave more leeway in electives.

of campus," Rudolph writes.[27] Johns Hopkins had enrolled undergraduates only reluctantly, more as a public relations gesture than anything else; Harvard had always had undergraduates and was stuck with them. But in practice, their presence was regarded as only a minor inconvenience; they were by no means the preoccupation of the institution.

Its new preoccupation with research, however, was quite successful on another level. During Eliot's tenure, Harvard's faculty grew from sixty to six hundred and its endowment grew from $2 million to $20 million.[28]

In dismantling the curriculum, Eliot and Harvard flatly rejected the idea that there were certain books, courses, and intellectual experiences that all educated men should share. Both faculty and students were now free to make their own way, however eccentric, through the university. Inevitably, by shattering the concept of the unity of knowledge, the elective system fragmented the faculty, laying the foundations for the growth of departments and the development of specialties and subspecialties. Following the German model, the barriers were broken down between general and specialized studies, but more importantly, the lines were blurred between undergraduate and graduate education. Eliot had opened up what seemed to be limitless vistas of learning. The most dramatic of which was the freedom to pursue research.

"The largest effect of the elective system is that it makes scholarship possible, not only among undergraduates, but among graduate students and college teachers," Eliot said in 1908.[29]

In later years Harvard was to turn back somewhat by restoring some order to its curriculum and discipline to its system (inspired in part by an angry parent who discovered his son in Havana when Harvard believed he was attending classes). But over the forty years of Eliot's tenure, Harvard's influence had spread rapidly even to small, independent liberal arts colleges, which, Rudolph quipped, "introduced an elective curriculum and waited to become universities."[30]

Only a handful of schools could even plausibly hope to become real universities; but schools of every sort adopted the trappings and the sprawl associated with the new institutions. Their growth was fueled by the lack of any sort of agreed upon limits. New professions bred new courses; which in turn bred departments and faculties, multiplying courses, splintering schools, and fragmenting specialties.

Abraham Flexner, writing several decades later, described the American university as an "expression of the age," and as he surveyed the academic *Zeitgeist*, what he found was confusion confounded with confusion.[31]

> They have thoughtlessly and excessively catered to fleeting, tran-
> sient, and immediate demands; they have mistaken the relative
> importance to civilization of things and ideas . . . they have simul-
> taneously cheapened, vulgarized, and mechanized themselves.[32]

All of this was embodied in the curriculum. At Columbia courses were offered in "practical poultry raising," "wrestling, judo and self-defense," and "advertising research," while teachers were trained in a curriculum that included courses in "cookery," "fundamental problems in clothing," "food etiquette and hospitality," and "principles of home laundering."[33] Vassar had even established a new Institute of Euthenics, which was defined as the "science of efficient living," which Flexner found was "artificially pieced together of bits of mental hygiene, child guidance, nutrition, speech development and correction, family problems, wealth consumption, food preparation, household technology, and horticulture."

Desperate to fit the new institute into the liberal arts curriculum, Vassar published *The Meaning of Euthenics* that exulted that the new courses would deal with such questions as "What is the connection of Shakespeare with having a baby?"[34]

As early as 1884, Columbia's Burgess, one of the new mandarins of the academic order, had surveyed the scene of higher education and declared the obsolescence of liberal arts colleges.

"It will be largely a waste of capital to maintain them," he declared, "and largely a waste of time to attend them."[35] Burgess's admiration for the German university was unlimited; he had on several occasions been invited to lecture abroad and he brought back with him the absolute conviction that the Teutonic academy represented the irresistible path to the future of learning. Eager to bring his vision to fruition, he established Columbia's first graduate school and emerged as the dominant voice in the university. He had powerful allies. Columbia's president Frederick Barnard shared Burgess's enthusiasm for things German, and was disposed to abolish the undergraduate college altogether.

He was opposed by the dean of the College, John Howard Van Amringe, who valiantly defended the liberal arts ideals against the growing encroachments of Burgess and his allies. In 1905, he warned that the College was in danger of being "degraded into a mere vestibule of a professional school."[36] Which was, of course, exactly Burgess's plan. Butler's 1905 plan to compress the undergraduate program into two years with students feeding directly into professional schools was a logical extension of the various trends in higher education.

But far from presaging the eclipse of the traditional college, the attempt to strangle the liberal arts at Columbia was to generate a remarkable counterrevolution, focused on the revivification of the liberal arts.

In 1916, John Erskine inaugurated his famous Great Books course; three years later, in 1919, building on the wartime "War Issues" course, Columbia inaugurated its course in Contemporary Civilization. Eventually, Columbia would expand Contemporary Civilization into a two-year course and add general two-year courses in the Humanities and Science. As Kenneth Lynn would later write, they represented "a fundamental act of institutional reassertion" by decisively placing humanistic studies at the heart of the curriculum.[37] Years later, Columbia would reaffirm the principles that led to the development of the new curriculum by saying:

> It is no lip service to tradition to declare once more that the liberal arts program should be the heart of our interests and aims as a college. In the meaning of the liberal arts we include all studies that contribute to the art of living, as distinct from the channeled preparation for making a living.[38]

At a crucial moment in its history, higher education had found the living embodiment of an ideal when it had seemed all but dead.

THE HISTORIC COLLEGE

Against the German university with its blending of graduate and undergraduate, its specialization and preprofessionalism, Ernest Martin Hopkins counterpoised what he called "the faith of the historic college."[39]

As he was later to say at a speech at Harvard, the independent, privately endowed undergraduate college of liberal arts was "the mother of all other institutions of higher learning which have evolved from the needs of our people. . . ."

There was, he argued, a fundamental incompatibility between the goals of the university and the college. The focus of the Germanophile university was on students as potential specialists. The college, however, was concerned with man *qua* man. "Its first concern," declared Hopkins, "is not with what a man shall *do* but with what a man shall *be*."[40]

Though Hopkins and Columbia's Van Amringe were cast in the roles of "conservatives," it was they who led the great reform movement. Lionel Trilling later remarked that "it was not the progressives but the conservative party that was in the end to be proved right. The conservative fell back on the Renaissance ideal of the whole man, and on the idea of the gentleman, of the honorable and responsible citizen of enlightened and gracious mind."[41]

Hopkins intended Dartmouth graduates to be living refutations of the Germanophiles whose sterile, narrow, and desiccated scholarship was without ethical focus and devoid of humane values. Even the most brilliant and accomplished scholarship was incomplete, Hopkins insisted, if not "established on the foundation of character."[42]* Hopkins insisted that the mission of the college "is not primarily to develop intellectualism, but intelligent men." The new priorities and curriculums of the Germanophiles were inherently incompatible with such a vision. Beginning with his inauguration, he made it clear he opposed the continuing fragmentation of the curriculum "until its attitude takes on unfortunate semblance to a sprawl." And while other schools were adding new departments, new fields of study, and new courses, Hopkins declared that, if anything, he envisioned some contraction, "reverting to a curriculum of fewer subjects better taught."[43]

But the heart of his mission was the effort to breathe life into the

---

* "If the only options available to this college," Hopkins said, "were to graduate men of the highest brilliance intellectually, without interest in the welfare of mankind at large, or to graduate men of less mental competence, possessed of aspirations which we call spiritual and motives which we call good, I would choose for Dartmouth College the latter alternative. And in doing so, I should be confident that this college would create the greater values, and render the more essential service to the civilization whose handmaid it is." ("Today's Responsibility of the College," Address, September 22, 1927)

humanistic tradition. He admired William James, who had been waging his own rear-guard fight against the new *kultur* for several decades—and frequently quoted him. James shared with Hopkins a distrust of specialism and a powerful sense of the ends of humanistic education. "All our arts and sciences and institutions," wrote James, "are but so many quests of perfection . . . and when we see how diverse the types of excellence may be, how various the tests, how flexible the adaptations, we gain a richer sense of what the terms 'better' and 'worse' may signify. . . . Our critical sensibilities grow both more acute and less fanatical. . . . The feeling for a good human job anywhere, the admiration of the really admirable, the disesteem of what is cheap and trashy and impermanent,—that is what we call the critical sense, the sense for ideal values. It is the better part of what men know as wisdom."[44]

Throughout his tenure, Hopkins' relations with the faculty were cordial and based on mutual respect. On the occasion of Dartmouth's sesquicentennial, in 1919, Hopkins had declared that, "I hold it true beyond the possibility of cavil that the criterion of the strength of a college is essentially the strength of its faculty. If the faculty is strong, the college is strong; if the faculty is weak, the college is weak." But there remained an underlying tension between the president's vision and the prerogatives of the faculty.

Hopkins was profoundly skeptical of the faculty's totemistic claim of pre-eminent wisdom in educational matters. He was firm in placing limits on the powers of the faculty, opposing its attempts to control admissions. It was self-evident to Hopkins that the responsibility of saying "what kind of a college it is going to be," rested not with the faculty, but with the board of trustees.[45]

Hopkins wasted no time in asserting his leadership on the campus. Shortly after taking office, he executed what amounted to a mild coup d'etat when he appointed James P. Richardson professor of law and political science, without having consulted the faculty on the matter first. Moreover, he had decided to name him chairman of the department. Richardson would become one of Dartmouth's finest professors and most revered scholars, but the faculty were incensed.

Hopkins met with the distressed professors and told them that he intended to maintain Dartmouth's emphasis on teaching and fight the emerging trend in which faculty transferred their loyalty from the College to their departments (a mark of the emerging academic culture).

And finally, he stressed, his administration would be governed by the belief that "great truths need to be transmitted though teachers whose personalities make these truths vital."[46]

Hopkins was acutely sensitive to what he called the academic "caste system" that rewarded researchers while holding professors who taught undergraduates in disdain. It brought him directly to the issue of the "qualification and attributes" of faculty members. The American college, he said,

> has suffered injury untold by accepting standards from the graduate schools which they, in turn, accepted from abroad. . . . I know of nothing more unreasonable nor of anything more deleterious to the self-respect of the American college than that so many men of ample training and of broad learning, with real enthusiasm for contributing to undergraduates not only of their knowledge but of their zest for life should, on the one hand, lack the complete respect of their associates or, on the other, be deprived of the satisfaction of reputation because of the great delusion which has pervaded the college world, to its loss, that a record of research only, if of sufficient profundity, more than compensates for incomplete manhood or for incapacity or indisposition to recognize the real purpose of the American college.
>
> I believe the time has come when we should free ourselves from the cant and sophistries that still pervade college circles on such points as these. . . . Research is important, yes; production is important, yes; teaching ability is important, most emphatically yes. But, if it be conceded that all three are not indispensable in the individual, let us be honest enough to acknowledge that teaching ability is not the first to be sacrificed. . . .[47]

He was deeply troubled not only by the growing contempt for teaching, but the new values that were being imposed on the faculty by the graduate schools. Ortega y Gassett commented on the "peculiar brutality and aggressive stupidity with which a man comports himself when he knows a great deal about one thing and is totally ignorant of the rest." Hopkins not only shared that view, but saw it embodied in what he termed the "fetishism towards the Ph.D.," which had now become "the open-sesame to a position as a college teacher."

Hopkins believed that a Ph.D. often "tends to unfit a man for teaching," and he made it a practice to hire faculty members who had not yet finished graduate school "before [they have] become wholly permeated by its ideals and subject to influences antagonistic to the college purpose."[48]

Hopkins believed that liberal arts colleges were committing suicide by accepting the Ph.D. as the only measure of scholarly fitness. He saw it as a crucial, and perhaps fatal, surrender to the university values of specialism and research. The result of his suspicion of the new breed of academic was the creation of a Hopkins-era faculty as idiosyncratic as it was brilliant.

A portrait hanging in the College's Sanborn House evokes some of the spirit of the age. It depicts a bearded dapper figure in a pince-nez, beret, white suit, and an opera cloak flung over his shoulders. This specimen of the academic gentlemen of the *ancien régime* is David Lambuth, identified on the name plate, not as "professor," but as *"Teacher of English at Dartmouth*: 1913–1948." Dartmouth graduate Budd Schulberg described Lambuth as "a freshman's dream of what a college English teacher should look like," but Lambuth was a fierce grammarian and stylist, what Schulberg called a "big verb man," who taught several generations of Dartmouth graduates the intricacies of English prose.[49]

Another of the distinctive Hopkins-era faculty members was Lewis Dayton Stilwell, a dynamic lecturer whose penchant for costumes— when discussing World War I, he would come to class dressed as a dough-boy—and vivid rhetorical imagery forever fixed both the form and the content of his lectures on his students' minds. Gifted with the voice of a Shakespearean actor, Stilwell joined the history department in 1916, the year of Hopkins' elevation to the presidency, and became one of the moving forces behind the College's course in the "History of Citizenship," turning the required freshman course into one of Dartmouth's most memorable intellectual activities. For four decades, Stilwell was at the center of campus intellectual life; an embodiment of the Socratic method. "Standing in the midst of a cluster of students in a fraternity bar, dressed in old chinos, sweat socks, worn cordovans, and his favorite tweed jacket, a cigarette pinched between his fingers, a glass of beer in his hand, he would adopt some unorthodox position and hold forth," Dartmouth alumnus Richard Barber wrote. "Then as the heated counter-argument started, eyes sparkling, he would cut through the surface and expose our fraudulent logic and rationalizations. An awkward silence would be shattered by his booming laugh, and a quick *bon mot* would relax the tension and we would be back on the path of analysis."

When a former student once urged Stilwell to try to publish his lectures, Stilwell expressed little interest. Maybe he would someday, he said, "after I have retired for a while. Right now I am working on a new lecture I think the guys will enjoy."[50]

CHAPTER
VIII

THE LIBERAL COLLEGE

Hopkins' era was not a tolerant one, nor one inclined to give colleges much leeway in defying conventional wisdom. Although academic freedom was often invoked, it was often honored more in the breach; at many schools faculty were routinely dismissed for controversial viewpoints. Dartmouth felt the full force of those pressures and no small part of Hopkins' stature and influence came as the result of his refusal to yield.

"The goal of education," he said in 1923, "is the cultivation and development of powers to the end that we may know truth and conform to it."[1] Exposure to conflicting ideas, Hopkins felt certain, was the best way not only to develop such critical faculties, but also ultimately to know truth.

Hopkins stunned many alumni in 1924 by saying that he would welcome Lenin or Trotsky as speakers to the campus, if they were available. William Z. Foster, a leading American Communist had actually already spoken on campus, and Hopkins found himself under fire. His position was unambiguous: "If a man starts a new movement," he explained, "if a man raises some question in regard to the validity of some belief which we have regarded as sure, men will flock to that theory. There is no place where fallacies in thinking will be so quickly punctured as in the college group."[2] Four years later he expanded on his view:

> Truth has nothing to fear from error if truth be untrammeled at all times and if error be denied the sanctity conferred upon it by persecution or concealment. The method of the educational institution in its search for truth calls for diversity in points of view and emphasis upon all capable of stimulating students' thought. The great obligation of the College is to inspire men to think rather than tell them what to think. . . .[3]

Free speech, he insisted, in a famous address at Amherst College, "even for pernicious doctrine, is not antagonistic to the college purpose so long as access is not denied the student to other points of view, and so long as stimulation is given to his mind to weigh conflicting data for himself." He also grounded his position in pragmatism, observing that "as a matter of practice, entirely aside from the theory which I have enunciated, repression and censorship never work within an intellectually alert group of boys such as constitute the college."[4]

His statements were consistent with his past public positions. In 1919, at the height of the Red Scare, he had denounced the so-called Palmer Raids against American leftists.[5] His concern for civil liberties was also broadly humanistic. In 1925, he joined with other prominent academics in condemning Congress for passing anti-Japanese immigration legislation and in calling on both political parties to condemn the Ku Klux Klan, which was at the time enjoying an alarming and increasingly violent revival.

Although by modern standards Hopkins was a man of deeply conservative moral and ethical values, the attempt to categorize Hopkins by the standards of our own time serves only to emphasize the degree and depth of the transformation of the landscape in the decades since Hopkins' time. Our own age of shrill absolutism makes a poor vantage point from which to evaluate what inevitably seems to modern eyes to be a series of paradoxes. In his politics, Hopkins was a liberal Republican, who backed Franklin Roosevelt in 1932 (though he later grew disillusioned with the New Deal); he was a profoundly religious man who was hostile to fundamentalism and presided over the abolition of compulsory chapel at Dartmouth; and, though socially conservative, he was a vigorous advocate of academic freedom.

For Hopkins, reviving the liberal arts did not entail transforming colleges into catechistical institutions. A liberal education, for Hopkins, required not merely the free exchange of ideas, but the open clash of ideologies. Hopkins resisted any suggestion that the College should align itself ideologically. Throughout his tenure, Hopkins prided himself on the open-mindedness of the College, by which he defined its principled tolerance of diverse and even obnoxious ideas. The point of such tolerance was not the assumption that there was no truth or that it was unknowable; but that the search for truth should brook no arbitrary limits.

Hopkins' defense of the free exchange of views inspired a kind of passion for free speech among the students. When the Communist leader Foster visited the campus at the invitation of the Liberal Club, students and faculty feared he might be harassed. The night before, when he had tried to speak at the University of Worcester in Massachusetts the university cut off the lights, sparking a near riot. To avoid a recurrence and to assure Foster got a chance to be heard, students and faculty members met him at the train station and formed a "guard of honor" to prevent interference with the speech. Foster's speech made few, if any, converts among the conservative student body, but the incident solidified Dartmouth's reputation as a citadel of tolerance.[6] In the decade of the 1920s, Yale was known for its conservatism; Columbia for its radicalism; but Dartmouth had distinguished itself for its open-mindedness.[7]

A token of that open-mindedness arrived in Hanover in 1920. John Moffatt Mecklin came to Dartmouth after disastrous tenures at Lafayette College and the University of Pittsburgh. Mecklin had left Pittsburgh as a result of his sympathetic attitude toward the great steel strike of 1919. Despite the controversy that surrounded him, Hopkins had recruited Mecklin because he knew the brilliant sociology professor would stimulate the students. Even so, Mecklin was unsure that he could frankly discuss the strike of 1919 with his classes. Years later, in his memoir, *My Quest for Freedom*, Mecklin recalled:

> I was assured, however, that I could talk frankly. . . . That was the
> Dartmouth way. This experience was to me more or less of an acid
> test of Dartmouth liberalism. . . . I now had convincing proof that
> for the first time in my teaching career I had complete academic
> freedom. . . .[8]

Over the next two decades, Mecklin's courses would become among
the most popular on campus and as one alumnus later recalled, Mecklin
became "one of the college's most vivid and beloved characters."9

THE OROZCO MURAL

Hopkins' defense of tolerance received its sharpest test, however, not
over Communist speakers or "radical" professors in the classroom, but
from a work of art. The bitter controversy over a mural by Jose Clemente
Orozco is of interest, not only for the light it casts on Hopkins, but also
as a striking contrast to the handling of a similar skirmish over murals
that convulsed Dartmouth five decades later.

Orozco, a well-known Mexican artist, made no secret of his passion-
ately held leftist allegiances, which were also evident in the vast mural
he painted in the reading room of the Baker library. Epic in proportion
and subject matter, Orozco's spectacular mural—spread over 3,000
square feet of wall—was an astonishing and violent celebration of
liberation. It depicted the story of Aztec migration, the pre-Columbian
golden age, and the prophecy of Quetzalcoatl. Had he stopped there, the
matter might never have come to a head. As it was, these historical
panels were counterpoised with Orozco's interpretation of their modern
counterparts. His graphic, sensational, and often gruesome portrayal of
capitalism, militarism, and the evils of American education (skeletons
are depicted in academic robes), and his armed Mexican peasants rising
up against imperialism, aroused a furious reaction even before it was
completed in 1934. For Hopkins, it was to be one of his bitterest disputes
and one in which he was well aware that he was at odds with the vast
majority of the alumni.

The mural was denounced for its political content, for its jarring
modernist style and, by some critics, because it had been painted by a
non-American. The Daughters of the American Revolution and the
National Commission to Advance American Art joined in a chorus of
denunciation.10 Hopkins response was typically direct. "I had not supposed," he said, "that art was restricted by race or time, and I do not
think that it is."11

Hopkins did not waver in his support of the mural and the muralist.
For Hopkins, the issue was whether Dartmouth would continue to be "a
live institution" that not only preserved the values of the past, but was

open to new, even troubling, ideas. Nor was he penitent about the Orozco furor. Writing to a friend, he said that "I would bring in anybody to espouse any project which would be as intellectually stimulating to the undergraduate body as these murals have proved to be."[12] The very fact that opinion was so sharply divided, and that debate over the merits of the murals was raging throughout the campus, Hopkins said, showed that the controversial murals were "potent beyond anything else that we could have done" to stimulate thinking about art.

When Orozco offered to modify the mural to avoid embarrassing the College, Hopkins rejected the offer. Writing to a colleague, he said, "I should like to have Mr. Orozco feel that he has the enthusiastic support of the College in the principles for which he stands and the ideas which he wishes to represent. I have been perfectly willing to uphold my official end of this controversy and to defend the privilege and right of Mr. Orozco in the whole matter."[13]

In part to mollify disaffected traditionalists, the college commissioned another mural three years after the Orozco mural was completed. Altogether more conventional in conception, subject, and execution, the mural in the Hovey Grill, the college's dining hall, by Walter Beach Humphrey depicted events from the life of Dartmouth's founder, Eleazer Wheelock. The only controversy at the time centered around the presence of bare-breasted Indian women in the painting. One offended alumnus demanded of Hopkins how *he* would like to be depicted "surrounded by a lot of naked Indian women." All things considered, Hopkins said, he wouldn't mind at all. In fact, he would be quite pleased.[14] Privately, he advised others not to have anything to do with murals, a piece of advice his successors would—to their discomfiture—ignore.

THE STUDENT PRESS

Although his tolerance was frequently sorely tested, it also extended to the oftentimes contentious student press on campus. As an undergraduate, Hopkins had been editor of both the College yearbook and *The Daily Dartmouth*. Perhaps because of that experience, he was left with few illusions about the taste and judgment of undergraduate journalism. As president, he would let the student editors know of his disagreements with them, but notes one historian, "he would not countenance censorship," and even though it occasionally required "heroic self-restraint," he consistently defended the freedom of the student press.[15] One incident recounted by his biographer is illustrative.

In the mid-1930s, *The Daily Dartmouth*, under the editorship of Budd Schulberg, took a militant and often strident position on a strike at a local granite quarry. Because of the College's hitherto close relationship with the owners of the quarry, the paper's coverage was both embarrassing and potentially costly in lost gifts to the College. One morning, with *The Daily Dartmouth* in full cry on the strike, Hopkins picked up the paper and remarked to Professor Stearns Morse that he would have to say good-bye to a major gift he had been hoping for from the family that owned the quarry. Nor, he told Morse, was this the first time the paper had undermined the College's fund-raising efforts. "But we've lived with it," Hopkins concluded, "and shall keep on living with it."

Remarked his biographer, "Interference with the editorial freedom of the paper was out of the question."[16] His attitude was, again, a mixture of principle and pragmatism.

"I am irritated beyond measure at the whole Schulberg campaign," Hopkins wrote to a correspondent in December 1935, "but I do not see anything to do about it. . . . All in all, there is less detriment to the College in letting its publications entirely alone and allowing them to go their individual ways than there is in any attempted censorship. This is not a matter of theory, but it is plain practice. . . . In other words, trying to stimulate thought in the undergraduate mind and to express the attitude of the liberal arts college that all matters of life ought to be subject to thinking, we cannot tell the undergraduate to hang his clothes on a hickory limb but not go near the water."[17]

Once again, Hopkins' advice would have spared his successors a good deal of grief had they only heeded it.

THE APOLITICAL COLLEGE

As vigorously as he defended the free exchange of ideas, Hopkins also opposed any attempt to politicize the curriculum itself. Speakers of the left and right were welcome, but within a context of universal tolerance that exposed their ideas to searching scrutiny and contrary points of view. This was very different from the notion that the College itself, or individual faculty members, would use their status to advocate an ideological position. For Hopkins, this was propaganda and was inherently incompatible with liberal education. Hopkins said he could imagine colleges set up specifically for the defense of capitalism or to justify benevolent despotisms. But, he insisted, "they would be mere training schools, not a liberal arts institution."[18]

Hopkins' opposition to politicizing the College was also hardened by watching the experience of the German universities during the 1930s. Long the exemplar of higher education, the German universities eagerly embraced national socialism, even when it meant politicized changes in the curriculum, the introduction of violence into the university, and the effective destruction of academic freedom through intimidation. Goaded by the Nazified professoriate, German university students formed an enthusiastic pool of shock-troops for the extremists. The Nazis won control of student organizations two years before they came to power.

Throughout the 1920s, the German universities were centers of right-wing opposition to the republican government. "The anti-republican hysteria of professors and students continually led to incidents," writes historian Fritz Ringer. "Whenever a lecturer expressed anything resembling pacifist or Marxist views, there was a student riot against him, particularly if he was Jewish. Liberal governments occasionally tried to protect the victims of these campaigns; *but the university faculties generally favored the side of the students.*"[19] [Emphasis added.] In speeches and articles professors repeatedly exhorted the young to take the lead in restoring German greatness. Martin Heidegger declared in his rectoral address in 1933: "The time for decision is past. The decision has already been made by the youngest part of the German nation."[20]

As early as 1925, the faculty at Heidelberg voted virtually unanimously (there was one dissent) to condemn a colleague who had observed that German soldiers had died "in a dreadful way," during the First War. "As these attitudes spread," wrote historian Ringer, " 'freedom of learning' became an ever more one-sided concept."[21]

At the heart of the new politicization of the German universities was the assumption that all scholarship was at bottom political; or would be made so. "To write about government, economics, or society was necessarily to enter into the heated debate concerning contemporary political alternatives," Ringer observed. "The prevailing sense of crisis was so profound that even methods of analysis in the social sciences, not just the research results, acquired an immediate political relevance."

New academic disciplines arose, while others were changed into the image of the new order. German universities developed chairs in "Germanic physics" and "Nordic research." "The substantive quality of German learning," remarked Ringer, "did not benefit from these conditions."[22]

Although the German professoriate could be fierce in its defense of its prerogatives, its defense of academic freedom was notably ambiguous. "University faculties too often defended this freedom only to protect their oligarchical control by an entrenched orthodoxy," according to historian Michael Stephen Steinberg. In doing so, "they robbed academic freedom of its essential liberal content and limited its application to freedom from outside pressure and defense of internal faculty self-government. But freedom also required an internal dialogue too often lacking. By not providing this dialogue or emphasizing a critical approach, the university failed the students and the Republic."[23]

Faced with threats of student violence, German university officials reacted with timidity and attempts at appeasement. As early as 1922, officials of the University of Berlin cancelled plans to hold a memorial service for Walter Rathenau in the face of threats. University officials turned a blind eye to brownshirted students on campus, while they discouraged opposition. Officials in Munich, for example, permitted SA boss Ernst Rohm to address a student meeting at the university, but denied permission to the former mayor of Nuremberg on the grounds that he was "a politically controversial personality."

"This policy of appeasement toward student violence," wrote Paul Johnson, "became the pattern of the 1920s, the rectors and faculties always capitulating to the most outrageous demands of student leaders rather than risk troubles."[24]

Significantly, the tragedy of the German universities had no discernible long-term effect on their devotees in American higher education, who continued to regard them as the paragons of higher learning. But it deepened Hopkins' mistrust of the value system of the Germanophile academy. Writing in 1949, after the collapse of Nazi Germany, but amid the dramatic growth of the new federally-funded universities, Hopkins clearly had the experience of the German universities in the 1920s and

1930s in mind when he wrote: "Intellectualism by itself alone and in its impatience with anything except perfectionism is almost inevitably inclined towards totalitarianism of either the fascist or the communistic form."[25]*

REBUILDING THE COLLEGE

It was given to Hopkins not only to restate the faith of the historic College, but to rebuild the College itself. In the 1920s, Hopkins increased the budget for instruction from $250,000 to $900,000, and launched a building boom that changed the face of the campus.

He was also determined to give a thorough review to the curriculum, which he did in 1918, in only his second year in office. Hopkins introduced a prescribed curriculum for freshmen and forbade students from pursuing majors or minors until they were upperclassmen.[26] Beginning in the fall of 1920, a one-semester class was offered in "Citizenship." Like Columbia's "Contemporary Civilization," the new course was a joint venture among several departments, utilizing professors from the departments of history, political science, sociology, and economics. Also required was a course called "Evolution," offered jointly by the school's science departments.

Hopkins also initiated an organizational change that was crucial if he was to have success in opening the way for further reforms. The system of department chairmen serving for life was dropped in favor of a system of two-year terms, with the chairmen appointed by the president.

In 1923, Hopkins asked the faculty's Committee on Educational Policy to prepare a report that candidly listed Dartmouth's shortcomings. The report was searing: standards in some courses were flabby; teaching often uninspired and superficial; and there was too much "loafing through college."[27] With the support of the trustees, Hopkins assigned Chemistry Professor Leon Burr Richardson to undertake a thorough review not only of the curriculum, but of educational methods from institutions around the world in an ambitious effort to help redefine the College's purpose. Richardson visited 19 institutions in the United

---

* In contrast, he said, "All of the complex factors which affect man as a human being are a part of the responsibility of the college rather than treatment of man as a disembodied mind, which under its German heritage remains still to a considerable degree the attitude of the graduate school."

States and 14 in England, Scotland, and Canada. He did not visit Germany. In the summer of 1924, Hopkins himself visited both Oxford and Cambridge, the high seats of English scholarship.[28]

The curriculum that emerged from Richardson's report owed much to both the English universities and the Columbia renaissance. Like Columbia, Dartmouth dropped the B.S. degree. Distribution requirements were created to ensure both breadth and depth in the educational experience; breadth by ensuring that freshmen and sophomores were exposed to a wide variety of fields before they declared majors, and depth by making the majors more structured and coherent. A comprehensive examination in the major for seniors was introduced with the emphasis on "independent thought rather than mere memorization of facts."[29]*

But central to the changes, from Hopkins' point of view was the initiation of honors programs for outstanding students, which gave selected students free rein to study as they chose and, like Oxford and Cambridge, emphasized the tutorial method of individual instruction. Nothing could have been more remote from the universities' increasing reliance on the mass lecture; and Hopkins was acutely aware of the implicit criticism of the system in his own proposals. Only the cost deterred Hopkins from instituting British-type tutorials throughout the College. As it was, he was able to raise an endowment of $3 million for the honors tutorial program—$1.5 million from the General Education Board and $1.5 million from John D. Rockefeller, Jr.[30]

Hopkins' successes won national attention. His speeches were routinely covered in *The New York Times* and often turned up in editorial ruminations on education. Remarked the *Times*: "President Hopkins's strong and salient qualities have impressed themselves on the country as well as on the numerous and hardy and capable sons of Dartmouth."[31] In 1926, *The Chicago Journal* declared that Hopkins "has become the recognized spokesman for those who believe in the liberal evolution of the modern college and the sympathetic recognition of the inquisitive student."[32] William Allan Neilson, president of Smith College, paid an

---

* Richardson did not favor a return to a highly structured curriculum and his argument has since been used to bolster arguments against proposals for a core curriculum. In March 1990, for example, James Wright, the dean of Dartmouth's faculty, published a long article in the *Alumni Magazine*, citing Richardson as an opponent of attempts to prescribe a curriculum that would provide a common intellectual experience. Wright, however, ignored the historical context of Richardson's proposals, which were a refutation of the university-style specialism of the era.

even higher compliment, by saying that Dartmouth had provided more stimulus to educational thinking in the country than any other institution. From Columbia, Professor Roswell Magill wrote: "From all we hear here, Dartmouth is the most interesting college in the country."[33] Such was his celebrity that Hopkins was mentioned virtually every time the presidency of a major institution opened up, including Harvard. ("With all of my admiration for Harvard and my friendship for Harvard men," Hopkins wrote to a friend, "it irritates me that they feel it to be a compliment to discuss me in this connection." Said Hopkins, "I wouldn't touch the Harvard presidency with a ten-foot pole." He was nevertheless deeply honored when he received an honorary doctorate from Harvard.)[34] In the early 1920s, he was actually offered the presidency of the University of Chicago by its board of trustees, and was strongly urged to accept by John D. Rockefeller, Jr. Hopkins did, in fact, seriously consider it before declining.[35]*

Such accolades immeasurably added to Hopkins' growing legend and to his prestige in tiny Hanover. Throughout the 1930s, he continued to use his stature to focus on the curriculum. A year of language study at the College level was made mandatory and a requirement that students take two full years of science was added.

After a trip to Europe that left Hopkins alarmed about the rise of fascism and the fate of the democracies, he called for further revision of the curriculum, specifically to increase the focus on the social sciences, with a requirement that undergraduates "learn the fundamental principles of government, economics, and social relations, with the historical data illustrative of these."[36]

In 1936, Dartmouth initiated Social Science 1-2, to replace the old "Citizenship" and "Evolution" courses. The new curriculum, said Hopkins, made it "impossible for any Dartmouth man to graduate from College in complete ignorance in regard to the theory and practice of

---

* Years later, according to Hopkins' biographer, the Hopkinses were vacationing with Robert Maynard Hutchins and his wife. In the course of the conversation, Mrs. Hutchins was surprised to learn that Hopkins had once been offered Chicago's presidency. Why, she asked Mrs. Hopkins, had she never mentioned that her husband had been offered the presidency? Mrs. Hopkins, the biographer recounts, considered the question for a moment before answering, "I guess I didn't think it was important." Said Mrs. Hopkins, years later, "It didn't make our relations with the Hutchinses any warmer."

government and the sources from which this had sprung."[37]* In the fall of 1939, Social Science 1-2 was taken by all but 40 of the year's 643 freshman, thus ensuring a common intellectual experience at that level.[38]†

The course reflected the influence of Columbia on Dartmouth and it placed the College solidly within the General Education movement in higher education. The term General Education, however, was a dreary euphemism for what was essentially, the restoration of liberal education. By the 1930s, Dartmouth had joined both Columbia and Chicago as centers of what became a renaissance in liberal learning.

---

* Hopkins was deeply disappointed by the failure of the faculty to approve a fully integrated two-year program. He attributed the faculty's decision to self-interest. He was later to complain that their lack of enthusiasm weakened the program. "The instruction staff is much longer on haywire philosophy," he gibed, "than it is on practical knowledge." (Widmayer, Charles, p. 203-204)

† This point later became a subject of dispute. In 1990, James Wright, the dean of Dartmouth's faculty, wrote that the exemption of 40 students from the course—slightly more than six percent of the class—was evidence that Social Science 1-2 did *not* provide a common intellectual experience. In fact, the 94 percent rate indicates exactly the opposite. (Wright, James, "Dartmouth's Steady Course," *Alumni Magazine*, March 1990)

CHAPTER

RENAISSANCE

Columbia's move in 1919 to reinstate the liberal arts as the center of its educational program was a conscious reaction against the suggestions that Columbia's undergraduate program be allowed to wither away. But the institution's dramatic recommitment to liberal education was also driven by other changes in the college, including the new diversity of its student body.

That diversity was seen not as an excuse for the further splintering or deconstruction of the curriculum, but was an impetus for creating a shared intellectual environment through a series of courses that ensured that whatever their backgrounds, students would now have a common humanistic education.

In 1916, the faculty at Columbia had abolished the Latin entrance requirement (Greek had been dropped in 1897). The change had two fateful consequences: it represented a turning away from the traditional rigid hegemony of the Greek and Latin classics over the curriculum; and it dramatically changed the nature of the student body, as more students from public high schools became qualified to enroll.[1]

Columbia's Contemporary Civilization Course was the progeny of Columbia's "War Issues" course given during the First World War and

104

John Erskine's extraordinary Great Books course, which he introduced in 1916. As the Great War ended, attention shifted inevitably to a "Peace Issues" offering. The result was Contemporary Civilization. Erskine's canon of great literature was to serve as the foundation for both the Contemporary Civilization course and the later Humanities sequence. As much as anyone, Erskine had defined the canon that formed the heritage of the West and his list is still impressive. It is given here in full:

Homer, *The Iliad; The Odyssey*
Herodotus, *History*
Thucydides, *History of the Peloponnesian War*
Aeschylus, *Prometheus; The House of Atreus*
Sophocles, *Oedipus Tyrannus; Oedipus Colonus; Antigone; Electra*
Euripides, *Alcestis; Medea; Electra; Hippolytus*
Aristophanes, *The Frogs; The Clouds*
Percy Gardner, *Principles of Greek Art*
Plato, *The Symposium; The Republic; The Dialogues of Plato*
Aristotle, *The Ethics; The Poetics*
Lucretius, *De Rerum Natura*
Vergil, *Eclogues and Georgics; Aeneid*
Horace, *Odes; Epodes; Satires; Epistles*
Plutarch, *Lives*
Marcus Aurelius Antoninus, *To Himself*
St. Augustine, *The Confessions; The City of God*
The Song of Roland
The Nibelungenlied
St. Thomas Aquinas, *Of God and His Creatures*
Dante, *La Vita Nuova; La Divina Commedia*
Galileo, *Nuncius Siderius; On the Authority of Scripture in Philo-
        sophical Controversies; Four Dialogues on the Two Great Sys-
        tems of the World; Two New Sciences; Third Day*
J. J. Fahie, *Galileo, His Life and Work*
Grotius, *The Rights of War and Peace*
Montaigne, *Essays*
Shakespeare, *Hamlet; Much Ado About Nothing*
Cervantes, *Don Quixote*
Francis Bacon, *The Advancement of Learning; The New Atlantis*
Descartes, *Discourse on Method*
Hobbes, *Leviathan*

Milton, *Paradise Lost*
Moliere, *Les Precieuses Ridicules; Le Bourgeois Gentilhomme; Le Misanthrope; Tartuffe; L'Avare*
Meredith, *On Comedy and the Comic Spirit*
Locke, *Essay Concerning Human Understanding*
Montesquieu, *The Spirit of the Laws*
Voltaire, *Candide, Toleration and Other Essays,*
S. G. Tallentyre, *Voltaire in His Letters*
Rousseau, *Discourses on Inequality; Confessions*
Gibbon, *History of the Decline and Fall of the Roman Empire*
Adam Smith, *The Wealth of Nations*
Kant, *The Critique of Pure Reason*
Goethe, *Faust*
American State Papers: The Declaration of Independence; The Constitution; The Federalist
Victor Hugo, *Les Miserables*
Hegel, *The Philosophy of History*
Sir Charles Lyell, *The Principles of Geology*
Balzac, *Old Goriot*
Thomas Malthus, *Essay on the Principle of Population*
Jeremy Bentham, *An Introduction to the Principles of Morals and Legislation*
John Stuart Mill, *Autobiography; On Liberty*
Charles Darwin, *The Origin of Species; Autobiography*
Louis Pasteur, either Rene Vallery-Radot, *The Life of Pasteur*, or Emile Duclaux, *Pasteur, the History of a Mind*
Karl Marx, *The Communist Manifesto; Capital*
Tolstoy, *Anna Karenina*
Dostoevsky, *Crime and Punishment*
Nietzsche, *Thus Spake Zarathustra; Beyond Good and Evil; The Dawn of the Day* (Preface)
William James, *Psychology**

---

* The Columbia canon inevitably illustrates some of the difficulties of canon-making in general. The modern critic might be surprised to see Grotius and Hugo on such a list, while Jane Austen, for example, is neglected. And why *Much Ado About Nothing*, but not, say, *King Lear*? Why Jeremy Bentham, and not Pascal, or David Hume? Why Malthus, but not Spinoza or Machiavelli? But these are essentially questions of literary value, not of sex or politics.

"Contemporary Civilization" met five times a week in small classes and represented a joint effort of the Economics, Government, History, and Philosophy faculty. In 1929, the course became a two-year sequence. In 1937, it was joined by a required Humanities course, which was also extended to two years in 1947. Creating a parallel sequence for the sciences proved more difficult. Although Columbia developed a two-year science sequence it remained optional and students were required only to take two years of science from any of a half dozen fields.[2]

The first year of Contemporary Civilization focused on what the faculty felt were the central aspects of the Western tradition: "the Judaic-Christian quests for justice and love, and the Greco-Roman quests for natural law and order," as well as "the growing dignity of the individual under the influence of the Renaissance and the Reformation; the revival of experimental science with its great effects on the manipulation of man's natural environment; the Enlightenment and its search for natural law in social relations; the births of democracy, liberal capitalism, and the idea of internationalism." Readings included works by Aristotle, Cicero, and Aquinas, as well as other relevant documents.

Columbia's second year focused on what the school called "the insistent problems of the present," including welfare, the nature of capital, the prospects of full employment, the role of labor unions, the place of the United States in the world order, the constitutional basis of American Government, economic power, and political pressure groups.

Although Contemporary Civilization was established as an examination of the development of democratic institutions, the course was not turned into uncritical propaganda. Studying liberal capitalism, for example, students read Smith, Malthus, Ricardo, Bentham, Tocqueville, and Bright. But they were also exposed to a wide spectrum of critics: Marx, Lenin, Sorel, Carlyle, Comte, Dewey, Leo XIII, and Pius XI.[3]

The Columbia humanities program was even more formidable. It was not unusual for Columbia freshmen to be asked to read 100 pages of Herodotus or Rousseau overnight. But the courses embodied Columbia's belief that in order for educated men to "possess an inner life with sufficient riches to withstand the slings and arrows of fortune, they must have learned to feed their souls upon good books, pictures and music."*

The point of the course was to make the students realize that the Great Books spoke to them not as would-be specialists in history, or literature, or philosophy, but as individuals. Columbia wanted to introduce freshmen to books and to put them at ease in the presence of the great. "They learn that Rabelais and Montaigne and Machiavelli are readable," a faculty report said, "that they have something to say even to a scientific and sophisticated creature like these 20th Century freshmen."

"No less striking to freshmen," the faculty later wrote, "is the discovery that formed across time and space is a kind of ideal fraternity

---

* Columbia Humanities.
First Semester:
Homer, *Iliad*
Aeschylus, *Agamemnon*; *Choephori*; *Eumendies*; *Prometheus Bound*
Sophocles, *Oedipus the King*; *Antigone*; *Oedipus at Colonus*; *Electra*
Herodotus, Book I; Books VI, VII, VIII (in part); Thucydides, Books I, II, V (in part); Books VI, VII
Aristotle, *Poetics*; Euripides, *Electra*; *Trojan Women*; *Hippolytus*; *Medea*
Aristophanes, *The Frogs*; *The Birds*; *The Clouds*
Plato, *Apology*; *Symposium*; *Republic*
Aristotle, *Ethics*, Books I, II, III, X
Lucretius, *On the Nature of Things*
Vergil, *Aeneid*
Bible, *The Book of Job*
Tacitus, *Annals* (in part); *Germany* (in part)

Second Semester
Augustine, *Confessions*
Dante, *Inferno*
Machiavelli, *The Prince*
Rabelais, Books I and II
Montaigne, *Essays*
Shakespeare, *Macbeth*; *Hamlet*; *King Lear*; *Henry IV* (Parts I and II); *The Tempest*
Cervantes, *Don Quixote* (Part I)
Milton, *Paradise Lost*
Spinoza, *Ethics*, Parts I, IV, V
Moliere, *Schools for Wives*; *Tartuffe*; *Misanthrope*; *Physician in Spite of Himself*
Swift, *Gulliver's Travels*
Fielding, *Tom Jones*
Rousseau, *Confessions*, Books 1, 2, 5, 6, 8, 10
Voltaire, *Candide* (Part I)
Goethe, *Faust*, (Part I)

where in conversation and dispute, love and hate, veneration and contempt, still possess an intensity that our limited individual experience seldom affords."[4]

The students were treated as generalists and, indeed, the faculty members were forced to become generalists themselves. Columbia did not expect every freshman to become an expert on Plato. "All that can safely be said of even a great scholar is that he got enough on a first reading to impel him to go back a second time."[5]

Columbia's program was personified in the figure of Mark Van Doren, who combined brilliant scholarship with inspired teaching. "His lectures were conversations," a student would later recall, "launched casually with some observations, and then he would draw a student in the class into the conversation. He had a way of creating intelligence in the student through these exchanges."[6] Van Doren's effectiveness as a teacher grew out of the relationships he established with his students. Decades later, Van Doren would call students "the crucial persons with whom I spent my time."

> From the beginning, I think I assumed experience even in freshmen. Perhaps the chief novelty consisted in my assumption that nothing was too difficult for the students. Freshmen have had more experience than they are given credit for. They have been born, had parents, had brothers and sisters and friends, been in love, been jealous, been angry, been ambitious, been tired, been hungry, been happy and unhappy, been aware of justice and injustice.
>
> Well, the great writers handled just such things; and they did so in the basic human language men use whenever they feel and think. The result, if no teacher prevented its happening, was that the freshmen learned about themselves. And so did the teachers, at least if they read and talked like men of the world, simply and humbly, without assumptions of academic superiority.[7]

THE GREAT CHICAGO FIGHT

The other great force in the renascence of the liberal arts in the decades between the wars was the University of Chicago under the leadership of Robert Maynard Hutchins. The state of the liberal arts college had no sharper critic than Hutchins. It was, he complained, "partly university, partly general, partly special. Frequently it looks like a teacher-training institution. Frequently it looks like nothing at all." But unlike the Germanophiles, Hutchins' solution was not to abandon the college, but to revive it.

The University of Chicago had been founded in the nineteenth century with the explicit intention of becoming one of the nation's premiere research universities. Bankrolled by John D. Rockefeller, Jr., it had a more than reasonable prospect of achieving its goal, especially under the leadership of its first president, William Rainey Harper. The priorities of the new university were never in doubt. Promotion of faculty, Harper declared, depended "more on the results of their work as investigators than upon the efficiency of their teaching. In other words it is proposed in this institution to make the work of investigation primary, the work of giving instruction secondary."[8]

Even so, Harper was mindful of the need to maintain a balance between the research goals of the university and the larger mission of the college. It was Harper—not Hutchins—who developed the idea of merging the last two years of high school with the first two years of the university to create a new undergraduate program centered on general education. For Harper, it was a fundamental principle that "an essential element in the education of every man, and especially that of the scientist, is a study of the great heritage we have received from the past."[9]

Harper's attempt to balance the two missions of the institution did not survive his presidency. His successor, a political scientist named Harry Pratt Judson, moved quickly to put in place a curriculum of electives modeled on Eliot's Harvard reforms. Over the next two decades the undergraduate college was virtually submerged under the research mission of the university. As a later dean wrote:

> Undergraduate work was grossly neglected; even worse, the College came to be regarded by some members of the family as an unwanted, ill-begotten brat that should be disinherited. Nearly all finally agreed that we had reached a situation that necessitated a decision either to abandon the College or to develop it.[10]

That choice still confronted Hutchins when he was named Chicago's president at the outrageously young age of 30. The young president was urged by some faculty to complete the work of dismantling the college. Instead, he launched the most ambitious attempt to transform a major university in the history of American higher education.

Unlike the new sort of administrators already emerging in higher education, Hutchins did not regard himself as a conciliator or a mediator above the fray of academic politics. He saw his role as defining the educational mission of the university and did not flinch from the extraordinarily bitter controversy that would inevitably result from his proposals and that would be known as the "Great Chicago Fight."*

Hutchins developed a four-year program devoted entirely to liberal education. The plan, never completely implemented, was completely prescribed; the curriculum made allowances for no electives and no specialization. Students were subject to comprehensive examinations at the end of each course, administered by outside experts. Moreover, Hutchins defied the prevailing wisdom—and the growing departmentalization of knowledge—by creating Chicago's own academic structure, organizing knowledge not on a department basis but in comprehensive fields, through basic organizing principles.[11]

The central tenet of Hutchins' curriculum was that undergraduate education was an end in itself, not merely a preparation for graduate study.

From the beginning, Hutchins recognized that he could not entrust his radical new curriculum to a traditional faculty, hired in traditional ways.† A crucial element in the success of the college was the development of an autonomous faculty, who would be able and willing to teach the broad courses and who could be hired without wrangling and protracted negotiations with individual departments. The result was a critical mass of brilliant, dynamic, gifted teachers. "The courses," wrote Daniel Bell, "were extraordinary intellectual adventures for the teaching staff." Many of their lectures, Bell quipped were "given more to impress each other in the barnyard competition," but that reflected the extraordinary culture created at Chicago.[12] The professors were

---

* "The minimum qualifications of an administrator . . . are four," Hutchins later said. "They are courage, fortitude, justice, and prudence or practical wisdom. I do not include patience, which we are told President Eliot [of Harvard] came to look upon as the chief requirement of an administrator. . . .I regard patience as a delusion and a snare and think that administrators have far too much of it than too little. . . ."

† Indeed, the "Great Chicago Fight" pit Hutchins against the massed faculty opposition. For the entrenched academic establishment, Hutchins' resurrection of undergraduate education was an attack on the essence of the academic enterprise as they saw it. His successor, Lawrence A. Kimpton later declared, "He almost ruined the University of Chicago, and would have had he remained a few more years."

willing to teach the sections and to dedicate themselves so absolutely to teaching, Kenneth Lynn later noted, "because they knew that in doing so they defined the basic meaning of the institution they worked for."[13]

The Chicago revolution owed much to Columbia. Hutchins' youthful and irascible colleague, Mortimer Adler, was a product of Columbia, where he had studied under John Erskine and had taught the Great Books course himself.* For a time, Adler and Hutchins together offered a seminar in the great works at Chicago, where students were drilled in first principles and right ends. Their approach was a decisive rejection of the growing fashion that regarded education as value-free. It was Hutchins' aim to restore the primacy of metaphysics; for him, the notion of education without an understanding of first principles was meaningless and potentially dangerous. In 1935, he published the outlines of his theories in *The Higher Learning in America*, still one of the most remarkable documents of its kind. Hutchins' definition of the role of the university won immediate praise from Columbia's Mark Van Doren, who wrote of Hutchins' conception of liberal education:

> It can study first principles, it can concern itself with the permanent truths about "man as man"; it can cultivate the intellectual virtues; it can provide an understanding both of the past and the present in the light of which things absolutely new may be examined, it can tell us whether any given thing is absolutely new, and if it is not can remind us how it has been dealt with before; it can relate the departments of our knowledge to one another, and by discovering the common intellectual basis of all the professions can relate them. . . .[14]

But in a precursor of the academic debates of later years, Hutchins' ideas came under heavy fire from acolytes of the new educational establishment. He was accused of "absolutism" by one faculty critic, and John Dewey hinted broadly that Hutchins' attempt to inject values into education was fascistic. The rhetoric matched the increasing passion of the fights at Chicago, where Adler described the atmosphere as "overheated and . . . filled with inflammable gases."[15]

---

* In one of the more remarkable chapters in the history of American education, Adler had been one of the discussion leaders in the adult Great Books groups formed in New York's five boroughs—a group that included such scholars as Mark Van Doren, Jacques Barzun, and Clifton Fadiman.

As a result of the opposition, Hutchins never succeeded in creating a curriculum exclusively centered around the Great Books. That was left to Scott Buchanan and Stringfellow Barr who left Chicago for St. John's College in Annapolis.

The changes at Dartmouth were not as dramatic as those at Columbia and Chicago. But Hopkins did not need to go as far as either institution: Dartmouth always had been a liberal arts college; both Columbia and Chicago were full-fledged universities with long traditions of leadership by men in the German model. But the goals and the styles were strikingly similar.

The reforms at Chicago and Columbia should not be seen merely as reactions to the trends in higher education, but as attempts to modify and restrain the fragmenting whirl overcoming the universities. In the 1930s and 1940s, such a compromise still seemed possible—a Grand Synthesis that would preserve shared liberal values within institutions dedicated to specialism.

Daniel Bell summarized what he called the "working principles and commitments" of the reform movement under four headings: "Ideological," for the stress placed on society's need for a unifying principle and consensus; "Tradition," instructing the student in the history of Western civilization "in order to broaden his vistas, to make him aware of the recurrent moral and political problems of man in society, and to chart the travails of the idea of freedom. . . ."; "Contra-specialism," the rejection of the "religion of research," in favor of a return to *humanitas*; and "Integration," an emphasis on courses that paid attention to "the broad relationships of knowledge," rather than focusing on a single discipline or a specialized area of a single discipline.[16]

To those four principles he might well have added a spirit of intellectual tolerance, without which the enterprise would have been still-born.

The decisive element, however, was more basic: each institution had committed itself to what an Aristotelian would call a *telos*, a clearly defined, well articulated end that constituted the good toward which all its actions tended. That end was the educated man, imbued with the spirit of the liberal arts, familiar with the great works of civilization, and trained in the rigorous use of his rational and analytical capabilities.

By any measure, it was an extraordinary moment in history. At each school, that *telos* was mirrored in the curriculum and embodied in the vivid intellectual experiences in the classroom. In our age of token

educational reform, the thorough-going nature of the liberal arts reforms of the 1920s and 1930s is striking.

At Columbia, the Contemporary Civilization classes were seldom
larger than 30 students, requiring no fewer than 20 separate sections,
each taught by separate faculty members. At Chicago, all of the major
courses were run as staff courses. Courses met four hours a week—two
lecture hours, two for discussion.[17] The professors met weekly to discuss the courses, review materials, and explore issues raised in class
meetings. Moreover, the experience at Columbia and Chicago provided
what should have been the definitive refutation of the claim that a
teaching-centered institution was inherently hostile to scholarly research. At both Columbia and Chicago professors prepared original
articles for inclusion within the curriculum.*

Crucial to the reforms at Columbia, Chicago, and Dartmouth was the
hiring of the proper faculty. Each school recognized that its distinctive
curriculum required a distinctive, even customized faculty. At Columbia, the tradition was nourished by each generation of instructors seeking to emulate and surpass its predecessors. At Chicago, faculty
members were hired specifically to teach courses in the Great Books
curriculum, bypassing the academic departments. And, at Dartmouth,
Hopkins ensured at least some independence for the liberal arts faculty
from the dominant academic culture by short-circuiting the graduate
school initiation process, hiring faculty before they had completed their
doctorates.

The years since World War II have seen numerous reform movements
rise up, only to dwindle into half-heartedness and failure. This is because meaningful reform rests upon a thorough-going institutional commitment. The curriculum must represent a consensus over the *telos* of
the institution. There must be powerful and dynamic leadership from
either the president or key elements of the faculty. The educational
mission of the institution must be supported by the faculty. And the
classroom must be the center of the institution's intellectual life. These
were the building-blocks of the renaissance at Dartmouth, Columbia,
and Chicago. Had any been lacking—as subsequent developments

---

* By 1945, Columbia's Contemporary Civilization course was using original articles
written by faculty members on Aristotle, St. Thomas Aquinas, mercantilism, the
scientific revolution, the Puritans, the Enlightenment, labor movements of the nineteenth century, and a cyclical analysis of the English Industrial Revolution.

would illustrate—the reforms would have either been abortive (as they were at Harvard) or would fizzle out in time (as they have in countless other institutions both large and small).

THE FINAL YEARS

Despite his successes, Hopkins noted that the pressures on an under-graduate college to become a university "are subtle, constant and sometimes strong."[18] None was stronger than the lure of cash held out to schools willing to expand their graduate programs or divert their resources from undergraduate teaching to research. Hopkins repeatedly had to turn down such largess, because it was often tied to requirements for graduate work "beyond what was permitted by the limits we imposed upon ourselves." As he suspected, that was not a choice that was made by all academic executives. It was in the face of such influences that Hopkins came to the conviction that Dartmouth could maintain its identity and liberal arts tradition by maintaining its independence and not "diverting its funds or dissipating its energies in a more diversified program."[19] Hopkins saw the endless multiplication of course offerings as inherently detracting from the College's core liberal arts mission.

Hopkins was unable to resist some of the changing currents of the academic culture. He pushed hard for a two-year core social studies course, but it was vetoed by the faculty, which, Hopkins gibed, seemed to feel that students were best served "by the maintenance of conditions most comfortable to faculty convenience and desires."[20] Hopkins was also troubled to see "potentially great teachers" refuse Dartmouth appointments because they had been warned by their graduate school mentors "not to become known as teachers lest this handicap them in securing recognition as scholars."[21]

But most of all, Hopkins was troubled by the political/cultural mood of American academics—a mood of skepticism, defeatism, appeasement, and isolationism. It was inconceivable to him that any intelligent man would exchange his freedom for the "intellectual and spiritual stultification" of the totalitarian state. But in 1936, a poll by Dartmouth College's "Peace Committee" found student sentiment running more than seven to one against American support for European victims of aggression. Student sentiment was also overwhelmingly in favor of abolishing ROTC. The peace movement among students and professors remained strong even after Hitler invaded Poland. Hopkins' concern turned to outrage when in May 1940 one of Dartmouth's faculty delivered a lecture in which he said the effect of a Nazi victory on the United States would be negligible and that, far from being insane, Hitler was shrewd and insightful. The speech, Hopkins' biographer wrote, was "wildly applauded by an overflow student audience."[22]*

To Hopkins this was "not only a degradation of liberal dogma but is suicide." Hopkins, who had prided himself on Dartmouth's open-mindedness, now saw it degenerating into a refusal to make basic moral and ethical judgments. He was appalled by what he saw as the decay of the critical function, but more fundamentally by what he recognized as the failure of moral courage that was to be so distinctive of our time. When the Peace Committee asked to use a college building to stage another "peace" rally, on Memorial Day, 1940, Hopkins refused permission. For the first time in his life, he confided to a friend, "I hate my job."[23]

Hopkins sensed a shift in the tides of history. As his tenure ran down, he could hear the long, withdrawing roar of the traditions to which he had given his life.

In the autumn of 1945, the Wheelock succession was passed on to a new president, John Sloan Dickey. Dartmouth and American higher education were about to enter upon an era of frenzied, unplanned, and unprecedented growth, change, and dislocation.

---

* A final irony was that the speech was given by one of the quintessential Hopkins-era professors, Lew Stilwell.

CHAPTER

THE CENTER CANNOT HOLD

In retrospect, it is clear that 1945 is the Great Divide in the history of higher education. Even after the war, there remained a lingering fascination with the Germanophile university, which could now be harnessed for service in what was to become a massively funded government-university-research complex. But the volatile admixture of cash, prestige, and power fashioned a new sort of university.

Imbued with a post-war confidence bordering on arrogance, the modern university had developed the taste for sheer mass and weight that typified post-war America, and that would shape the nation's military, corporate, and cultural thinking. Often the lines between the various enterprises would blur as universities became research extensions of the federal government and began to think of themselves as "knowledge factories," in Clark Kerr's unfortunate, if memorable, phrase. The newly flush universities quickly adopted the rhetoric of entrepreneurship, but inherited the grammar of bureaucracy. During the student rebellion of the 1960s, the universities would be bitterly attacked for their impersonality and interlocking relationships with government and business. Many of the criticisms struck home because the universities had become so closely tied to the infrastructure of the modern world, assuming a shape that would have been virtually unrecognizable to a pre-war academic. These were higher education's go-go years in which colleges redoubled their efforts to become universities, while universities mutated into vast, impersonal, research-dominated multi-versities. Teaching loads dwindled, class sizes skyrocketed, and curric-ulums were increasingly tailored to accommodate the new priorities.

The heady confidence of academics was understandable in the years after the war. The universities had played critical roles in the greatest scientific breakthrough of the age, the building of the atomic bomb. Enrico Fermi had overseen the first atomic chain reaction at the University of Chicago; Los Alamos was technically under the aegis of the University of California; staffing for the project had been drawn from MIT, Wisconsin, Illinois, and virtually every major school in the country. One of the central figures in the development of the bomb was James Bryant Conant, the young president of Harvard, who was to play a decisive role in the integration of academic science with the waging of war.

The mushroom cloud over Hiroshima demonstrated not merely the value of the universities for national security, but opened breath-taking new vistas for the scientists themselves. Neither the government nor the academics were slow in capitalizing on the possibilities. Henceforth, the Manhattan Project would serve as a shadowy paradigm for the new university. Science, particularly federally funded science, became the dominant factor in university priorities, and the values of the laboratory quickly came to dominate the overall values of the university itself. If "scholarship" had been the focus of the German university, now the focus was funded research. Even if funds were not available, the shift to the research culture—the heart of the scientific enterprise—gradually made itself felt through the other disciplines. Richard Rhodes, the chronicler of the creation of the A-bomb was to note that it was Conant who "created the modern Harvard of eminent scholarship and publish-or-perish, up-or-out." [1]

But not all disciplines could share in the same heady growth. If the post-war era saw the coming of age of the sciences, the humanities often found themselves left behind. With the new emphasis on scientific values and research, the humanist was often odd man out, a situation exacerbated by the growing gap between the rewards lavished on the academic scientists and the scraps left for the liberal arts. That was hardly foreseen by contemporaries. At the time, 1945 seemed to mark a new high-water line for the general education movement. Harvard's publication that year of *General Education in a Free Society*—which became known simply as the Redbook—appeared to mark a radical change in the philosophy of the nation's most influential university. The report called for the creation of general, required courses in "Western Thought and Institutions," "Great Texts in Literature," and in the sciences.[2] The Redbook's ambition was sweeping. With typical Harvard confidence, it sought to develop what amounted to a comprehensive philosophy of education. But the courses and the rationale for the program were strikingly derivative of the programs at Columbia and Chicago. Like Columbia three decades earlier, the authors of the Redbook saw diversity not as a reason to fragment the curriculum, but as a reason to seek unifying principles. It found these in the study of the heritage of the West and in the Great Books.

"The root of argument for using . . . great works in literature courses is briefly this: ours is at present a centrifugal culture in extreme need of unifying forces. . . . Therefore the books . . . which have been the great meeting points and have most influenced the men who in turn have influenced others are those that we can least afford to neglect." The course in "Western Thought and Institutions" was intended to concentrate on history, "to set forth the main tendencies in the development of modern civilization." In the sciences, the Redbook envisioned "a rigorous and highly integrated introduction to the sciences as a whole."[3]

The Redbook's program influenced schools throughout the country. By implicitly placing Harvard's prestigious imprimatur on general education, it represented an unprecedented opportunity for the liberal arts on the eve of the great surge of hyper-specialization. Instead, the failure of general education at Harvard served to illustrate how dramatically the culture of higher education was changing.

The roots of the failure were deep: unlike Chicago and Columbia, Harvard never made any sort of an institutional commitment to general education, and the faculty never accepted the idea. In 1949, the faculty overwhelmingly rejected the Redbook's proposed prescribed curriculum, substituting its own plan which provided a variety of course options in each of three major fields of knowledge. "While this decision utterly destroyed the rationale of a shared intellectual experience," wrote Kenneth Lynn, "it made sense to a faculty that saw no compelling reason not to let professors stage their own shows as usual."[4] By the end of the 1960s, the so-called Gen Ed program included more than one hundred courses, and was larded with such exotic offerings as "The Role of Women in Irish Society," and the "Classical Music of India, Pakistan and Bangladesh" —a far cry from the original Redbook vision of a shared intellectual experience.

Harvard's failure tinctured academia as a whole, as college curriculums became the product of intra-faculty bargaining, reflecting the influence, clout, and power of the respective departments, rather than a coherent educational philosophy. Perhaps inevitably, academia turned to the nomenclature of liberal democracy to justify this revolution. The rush of new students into higher education—many of them financed by the GI Bill—provided a receptive audience for the argument that the transformation of the academy was the necessary result of democratization.

No single characterization captured the new mood or proved more effective than "diversity," a word resonant with the traditions of pluralism and democracy. As traditionally understood, diversity was the very essence of a liberal education, inasmuch as it reflected the clash of ideas and the suspicion of dogma that informed humanistic study. Now, however, it was contorted to serve what was essentially a political agenda. In 1947, a presidential commission began the process of codifying "diversity" as the official ideology of the American university when it declared: "We shall be denying educational opportunity to many young people as long as we maintain the present orientation of higher education toward verbal skills and intellectual interests." Many young people, the report noted, have different, nonintellectual abilities, and cannot receive a proper education if universities continued to insist on recognizing "only one kind" of intelligence. Among the diverse sorts of overlooked skills the report specified were "social sensitivity and versatility, artistic ability, motor skill and dexterity, and mechanical aptitude and ingenuity. . . ."[5]

Even at the elite levels of the academy, "diversity" proved an extraordinarily effective codeword for what would otherwise have seemed mere chaos. Chicago's Hutchins was one of the few voices raised in dissent. "Since American institutions of higher education are already so diversified that neither the faculty nor the students can talk with one another except about the weather, politics, and last Saturday's game," Hutchins wrote, "the commission's advice is a little like telling a drowning man that he can improve his position by drinking a great deal of water."[6]

SEEKING THE BALANCE

Dartmouth was far from the center of the great changes overtaking higher education. But it was not immune. The period 1945 to 1970 was to be an era of impressive growth for the College, years of transformation. Programs were added and expanded in all fields of study and the faculty was expanded and transformed. The changes were driven in part by demographics.

By the time President John Sloan Dickey took office in 1945, the enthusiasm and commitment of the early Hopkins years had faded as the faculty had aged. There were still outstanding faculty, of course— Eugene Rosenstock Huessey, the Christian existentialist philosopher; Thomas Vance and John Finch in English—but in the inevitable cycle of institutional reform the inspiration had sagged with the passage of time. There was little fresh blood, in large part because the departments were tenured-in and top-heavy.*

Many of the aging faculty members were clearly marking time; and the College came to resemble more of an amiable and articulate country club than an institution of higher learning.The faculty Hopkins had recruited in the post-1918 boom had remained, tenured and in place through the 1940s. Dickey did not make a single tenure appointment during his first eight years in office; then the floodgates opened. Between 1954 and 1966, nearly half of the faculty would retire, to be replaced by a faculty with a very different view of Dartmouth.

One of the first senior appointments was a bright young mathematician named John Kemeny, who was recruited from Princeton at age 27 and made full professor and chairman of the department of mathematics.† It fell to the young scholar to build the department nearly from scratch. He would later recall that when he arrived on campus in the early 1950s, some department offices were empty after noon; in some

---

* In 1950, 12 of the 17 faculty members in the Economics Department were full professors; in History, 12 of 13 faculty were full professors; in Government, 9 of 12; in Sociology, 6 of 8; in Psychology, 7 of 10.

† Kemeny recently remarked that the College had been under the impression that he was 31 years old at the time he was recruited. "If they had known my true age," he remarked, "the whole history of Dartmouth might be different."

departments it had become the norm for faculty to give the same lectures to the same classes year in and year out.

Under Dickey, Dartmouth struggled to find a balance between the Hopkins-era emphasis on teaching and undergraduate education and the need to have a faculty that was more research-oriented, in line with the new academic culture. But many of the changes in the years ahead amounted to a conscious reaction against many of the values of the Hopkins era. The old-time teacher-scholars of the 1920s and 1930s were now regarded with scarcely concealed disdain bordering on contempt; anachronisms and embarrassments that Dartmouth desperately wanted to do without.

By 1966, the *Alumni Magazine* would carry an article on the school's curriculum that declared—italics and all—that *"Dartmouth now proclaims itself in effect a small university."*[7] A gross exaggeration of the realities at Dartmouth, the article nevertheless reflected the zeal with which the small College had acclimated itself to the new academic *kultur*. Making note of the various pressures on schools like Dartmouth—the increased demands of graduate schools, the push for professional rather than general education, the emphasis on specialization, and the availability of research grants—another article in the same issue of the *Alumni Magazine* announced: "As a college determined to stay in the forefront of American higher education, Dartmouth *has been responsive to all these pressures of the modern world. . . ."*[8] [Emphasis added.]

No official announcement was ever made. The rhetoric remained familiar and reassuring. President Dickey continued to pay homage to Dartmouth's commitment to the liberal arts, which he referred to repeatedly as "the liberating arts." But to paraphrase Robert Maynard Hutchins' own comment, Dickey did not have the courage of Ernest Martin Hopkins' convictions.

THE DEFEAT OF GENERAL EDUCATION

The first changes in Dartmouth's curriculum came almost immediately on Hopkins' retirement. One of his major accomplishments had been the creation of the one-year, required course in social science,

"The Development of Modern, Social, Economic and Political Institutions." In 1946, the faculty dropped the course as a requirement. In its place, students could now choose from any two of eight introductory courses in economics, government, history, psychology, and sociology. The same year, under Dickey's leadership, the College introduced its "Great Issues" course, which over the next two decades would bring dozens of prominent Americans to campus to lecture on current political and social issues. (One of the first speakers was Congressman Richard M. Nixon, who spoke on "Testing Political Loyalties.")*

But as the College entered the 1950s, the dominant issue remained general education. Despite the highly structured focus of the first two years of the undergraduate curriculum, Dartmouth could no longer claim that it provided a shared intellectual experience. Nor was its program tailored to emphasize the inter-relationship between the various fields; and it lacked a structure outside of the academic major for incremental, progressive learning.

Beginning in 1948, interdivisional committees of the faculty began what was intended as an exhaustive review of the curriculum. The committee assigned to deal with the social sciences developed the most ambitious proposal, resurrecting Hopkins' vision of a comprehensive, required two-year course. The committee flatly rejected the current curricular requirements, "the election of a number of largely unrelated departmental courses," as "inadequate." Any sense of the inter-relatedness of the courses, the committee said, "is reached, if at all, largely by chance." Nor had the "Great Issues" course solved the problem. Many of the students taking the course as seniors, the committee reported, arrived woefully naive of current issues and markedly deficient in critical skills.

In presenting its alternative, the committee hoisted the banner of full-blooded liberal education, declaring that the entire College would benefit "by a common intellectual experience in the first two years" and stating as a self-evident fact that "the high degree of specialization which has taken place in American higher education over the last few

---

* The "Great Issues" course should not be mistaken for a Great Books course. It essentially dealt with current events and government policy. Its underlying goal seemed to be the creation of the well-rounded federal official—consistent with Dickey's own professional background.

decades . . . of course is contrary to the concept of a liberal arts college."9*

On February 15, 1951, the faculty rejected the proposal.10

President Dickey was not inclined to resist the new pressures. A lawyer and diplomat by trade, Dickey had served with distinction as director of the Office of Public Affairs at the State Department before being named president of Dartmouth. Now he was faced with the need to recruit an essentially entirely new faculty, while keeping the College financially secure.

In 1955, a report by faculty members, under the auspices of the American Association of University Professors, issued what *The Dartmouth* called "a scorching indictment" of the intellectual atmosphere on campus.

> There prevails among many undergraduates on this campus an intellectual apathy, a negative attitude hardly to be dignified by the term anti-intellectualism. Deep-seated indifference, casual unpreparedness, and habitual absenteeism are among the symptoms. Few of our students ever do any academic work beyond the prescribed minimum.11

The Undergraduate Council followed this jeremiad with its own report, calling for more essay exams to replace the increasingly ubiquitous multiple choice exams—the prevalence of which reflected a degree of indolence among the faculty at least equal to that charged to the students. (The multiple choice exams took far less time for the professors to grade.)12

Dickey inaugurated a review of the curriculum that culminated in 1958, with one of the more sweeping changes in the College's history. Once again, the faculty factions were called together to debate the shape

---

* The first year of the proposed social science course would be "an introduction to the present," beginning with a discussion of "the nature of man and his geographical and social environment." The second semester would be devoted to "the nature of history and the emergence of modern Western Civilization."

The second year's course would focus on the twentieth century, with topics to include "The impact of the Industrial Revolution," "the free enterprise system," "political democracy," "problems facing democratic society," "totalitarian revolts against free enterprise and political democracy," "international politics and the search for an enduring international order," and finally, "the challenge to democracy." Throughout both years, an attempt would be made to integrate the various individual disciplines.

of the curriculum and the institution's primary mission. The result was a combination of high idealism, pragmatic compromise, and outright sophistry.

Once again, the faculty rejected a required two-year Western Civilization and introductory Social Science course. In addition they adopted a ten-week trimester system that meant cutting the number of required courses from 40 to 36 (plus Great Issues); cut the number of weekly class hours for students from 15 to 12; reduced faculty teaching loads*; and raised the student-teacher ratio from 13 to 1 to 17 to 1.

What was most striking about the changes was that, in general, the reforms were focused less on either students or the curriculum itself than on the needs of the faculty. Despite its heavy use of academic euphemism, an explanation of the program in the April 1957 *Alumni Magazine* made it clear to what degree the entire proposal was faculty-centered. It argued that the quality of the faculty at the College would depend "significantly on the economic status of college teachers in general and Dartmouth teachers in particular," and insisted that increasing the student-teacher-ratio "could lead to substantial economic gains for the college teacher."[13] The faculty argued that classes of 20 to 75 were "awkward" and envisioned a much wider use of the large lectures that were beginning to dominate higher education. The agenda behind the change was dominated by concern over Dartmouth's ability to compete for faculty members with other universities. To do so, the faculty insisted, Dartmouth not only had to raise salaries, but had to "attract them by offering them closer, less-schedule bound association with students." (In other words, lower teaching loads.)

"Certainly," the faculty argued, "a close relationship between student and teacher is a valuable element in liberal education *but a low student-teacher ratio indiscriminately throughout the curriculum is a serious barrier to economic improvement of the teaching profession.*"[14]† [Emphasis added.]

All of this obviously posed a difficult public relations problem for the

---

* Instead of teaching three or four courses a semester, faculty were expected to teach only two or three. In addition, they would be given the option of concentrating their work in two of the terms, so that the third could be devoted to "independent research."

† The change in student-teacher ratio assumed "a judicious cut" in the 638 courses then offered by Dartmouth. The cut never occurred. By the mid-1960s, there were more than 700 courses; there are now more than 1,300.

College: How to justify such an abrupt shift in the priorities of the College, especially when it involves such an obvious cut in teaching, class hours, and overall requirements? *How could less possibly be portrayed as more*? The solution was ingenious.

"Suppose," Provost Donald Morrison suggested, "the focus is shifted from teaching to learning, and colleges begin to think of their task as one of *enabling students to learn without being taught*." (Italics in original.) *Learning without being taught*! How better to explain a reduction in the educational program for undergraduates than to portray it as an *improvement*; better yet as a profound shift in educational philosophy that ultimately benefits the undergraduates?

As Morrison went on to explain, "we are seeking to improve greatly the students' educational experience in ways that will require less of the teacher's time and energy."

"This," Morrison exulted, "is an exciting prospect. . . ."[15]

The key to this was to be "an independent reading program." Students would select books from a list of great works (such as Homer's *Iliad*, Plato's *Dialogues,* Chaucer's *Canterbury Tales*, and Thucydides' *History of the Peloponnesian War*) and use their free time to peruse them with a minimum of faculty involvement. While ostensibly introducing a Great Books component, the proposal was also cutting it free from the curriculum—creating a sort of academic limbo where the books might be read, but not discussed. The proposal made the free-floating nature of the reading proposal explicit when it said: "The selection of books for the list from which the student would make his own choice would be made *with an awareness that the books would often be read without access to faculty advice or library facilities.* . . ."[16] [Emphasis added.]

Vague in conception and unwieldy in administration, the independent reading program survived for less than a decade. But in its brief life it served as a powerful sales tool for the new curriculum. It evoked elements of the Great Books movement and capitalized on the long and rich tradition of self-education. No one ever becomes educated solely by what he learns in class. But at Dartmouth, that truism was reduced to a fig-leaf for a radical shift in academic priorities. Moreover, the notion of transferring responsibility to students was somewhat undermined by the administration's knowledge that student motivation was one of the chief problems at Dartmouth. Without a blush, administrators now had to extol the sagacity of the very students they had derided not only as anti-intellectual, but as apathetic, unprepared, and often absent.

Even so, Dickey was an enthusiastic evangelist for what *The New York Times* called "a fundamental shift in higher education—from teaching to learning."[17]

"By shifting the emphasis from the student's dependence upon teaching to his independence upon learning," Dickey told *The Times*, "we hope to bring the intellectual self-reliance and capacity to higher levels than is now possible."[18]

The program won national attention. The "reform" of Dartmouth's curriculum, editorialized *The Providence Bulletin*, "articulates the beginnings of a revolution in college level learning, a revolution which finds echoes in academic circles everywhere, including Harvard University."[19]

The significance of the reforms was three-fold: it marked the final defeat of formal general education at Dartmouth; it reflected Dartmouth's accommodation to the new academic culture in which the curriculum was subordinated to faculty concerns; and it acclimated the College to the practice of sleight-of-hand—doing one thing while saying another—an extraordinarily seductive habit increasingly deleterious to the College's intellectual integrity over the years.

Throughout the 1950s and early 1960s, Dartmouth continued to expand and diversify its programs. Fields like International Relations began to flourish in the 1950s, with a staff recruited from the Government, Economics, History, and later, Geography Departments. The era also saw the growth of special programs in Chinese and Russian language study, Latin American study, Oriental Cultures, City Planning, and a new center for Public Affairs.

The expansion clearly strengthened the College and made it a far more professional place than it had been in the late 1940s. But it also had other consequences, some of them unintended. The impact of the changes on the culture of the College could be seen clearly in the development of the Department of Sociology and Anthropology. In 1945, the Department of Sociology offered only 20 courses, with ten professors. By 1965, it had been merged with Anthropology; the new combined department had a staff of 17 and offered 49 courses. More importantly, however, as one observer noted, the new department "is representative of a Dartmouth faculty working under the pressures of a liberal arts college being propelled towards university status."[21]

The department's chairman, Professor H. Wentworth Eldredge, was quoted as saying that "A member of the Sociology Department teaching full time at Dartmouth *is not a successful sociologist.*" Being a teacher might have been adequate in the era of Hopkins when Dartmouth's focus was on liberal education and the teaching of undergraduates. In the new thrust toward university status, that was no longer enough. By 1965, Eldredge was declaring that a professor of sociology "is expected to supplement his Dartmouth assignments by obtaining government or foundation money to work on special projects." He would thus teach only "part-time." This reduction in teaching, Eldredge argued, was in the College's best interests because it "lightens the financial burdens of the College, increases its prestige with publications, and by forcing the College to hire more men offers a wider range of courses and personalities to undergraduates." Professor John Hurd, a professor of English Emeritus, remarked that Eldredge's attitude "is not shared by all of Dartmouth's faculty, but it does reflect the new emphases."[22]

In fact, Eldredge's comments grossly overstated the extent to which priorities at Dartmouth had changed; in contrast to many of its Ivy League siblings, it remained primarily focused on teaching. But the consensus was eroding and deep divisions had begun to appear in the faculty's understanding of Dartmouth's identity.

The same tendencies drove the continuing proliferation of courses. Professor William Smith watched the process as chairman of the Committee on Instruction. "I saw one thing that I fought and fought with little success," he recalled. "New people would come in and rather than hiring them basically to handle existing courses, they would create new courses, tailored for that person. So you began to see the proliferation of idiosyncratic, individual courses. Young Ph.D.s with no teaching experience were being isolated from teaching basic courses. Instead, they were teaching very, very specialized, esoteric, irrelevant courses. Over the last 20 years, the curriculum has been faculty, not conceptually, driven. That phenomenon was the beginning of the dilution and destruction of any coherent curriculum."[23]*

---

* Columbia's Provost, Jacques Barzun, spoke at Hofstra University in December 1963 and warned that "the best colleges today are being invaded, not to say dispossessed, by the advance agents of the professions, by men who want to seize upon the young recruit as soon as may be and train him in a 'tangible skill.' He describes the process of transformation: eminent scholars begin to teach students as if they were future fellow-scholars and specialists like himself. Emulating his approach, the young students select a major as quickly as possible to prepare themselves for this professional future.

Nothing, however, reflected the new emphases more dramatically than Dartmouth's aggressive move into graduate education. Doctorates were established in Physiology (1960), Molecular Biology (1960), Mathematics (1962), Physics and Astronomy (1964), Pharmacology (1964), Engineering (1965), Biology (1966), Chemistry (1966), Earth Science (1966), and Psychology (1967). Again the focus was on the benefits for the faculty of such expansion. An article in the April 1966 *Alumni Magazine* explained that one of the main reasons for expanding the graduate program was that "it would help in recruiting and holding a first-rate faculty of university caliber."

> This new breed of faculty . . . has had its own special influence on Dartmouth's changing program of undergraduate education. *The modern professor, more oriented to his discipline than to general education, prevails at Dartmouth as elsewhere.*[24]* [Emphasis added.]

President Dickey embraced the new trends. In his foreword to *The College on the Hill*, Dickey essentially reversed 50 years or more of institutional policy when he declared that the modern Dartmouth student "must also be specifically prepared for going on as a student to the specialized work of graduate education."

In 1954, Columbia, in a step back from general education and toward specialization, introduced majors. In 1959, under pressure from the

---

"An even stronger influence is that of the young teachers who need to establish themselves. This they can do only in one way: by showing productivity in research. . . .Accordingly, these junior professors decline to teach anything not related to their own specialties. As one of them said to me, they 'do not want to teach secondhand subjects' [e.g. general survey courses]. Firsthand subjects are necessarily narrow, and what is worse, they are treated as if everyone in the class were to become a teacher, a duplicate of his own teacher."

* This new *kultur* was eagerly welcomed by the College, the author gushed, because it "happily dovetails with the quality of the new breed of students." In the ten years from 1955 to 1965, the average College Board verbal scores for Dartmouth students had risen from 548 to 654, while math scores rose from 585 to 705. Moreover, nearly three-quarters of Dartmouth graduates were going on for advanced degrees; in the sciences, the proportion was even higher, with an estimated 83 percent of Dartmouth science majors moving directly to graduate or professional schools. As a result, the individual departments introduced increasingly specialized offerings in their departments, often redesigning the entire major, a later report said, "along the lines of pre-professional training."

departments, Columbia dropped the second required year of Contemporary Civilization. In the 1950s, the University of Chicago also found it increasingly difficult to attract young scholars to teach its general courses and was beginning its own incremental chipping away at the Hutchins curriculum.[25] And all academia watched the decomposition of Harvard's curriculum with the sort of fascination usually reserved for witnessing an unusually gruesome train wreck. The developments did not make for optimism.

By 1963, Jacques Barzun saw the trend toward specialization and fragmentation as so inexorable that opposing it "would be like trying to sweep back the ocean."[26]

Lionel Trilling lamented "as a sad and significant event in the culture of our time," the rank indifference with which his own colleagues at Columbia greeted Daniel Bell's study of liberal education, *The Reforming of General Education.* "From my long experience at the College," he later wrote, "I can recall no meetings on an educational topic that were so poorly attended and so lacking in vivacity as those in which the report was considered. If I remember correctly, those meetings led to no action whatever, not even to the resolve to look further into the matter."

"Through some persuasion of the *Zeitgeist*," Trilling concluded, "the majority of the faculty were no longer concerned with general education in the large and honorific meaning of the phrase."[27]

TRASHING THE CURRICULUM

The Dartmouth curriculum that had survived the 1950s still insisted on prescribing a general education for students in their freshman and sophomore years.* But this remnant of the traditional College was about to be assaulted.

The first blow fell in November 1964, when the faculty's Committee on Educational Policy voted to recommend sweeping changes in the

---

* The courses that constituted the freshman and sophomore curriculum were mostly broad survey courses designed for non-majors and non-specialists. In the humanities, the choices included "The Classical Foundations of Modern Society (Greek and Roman)," a general survey course on the field of art and architecture, a freshman seminar in English, "Classics of European Literature and Thought," surveys of the history of music, "The Problems of Philosophy," "The Judeo-Christian Tradition," and "Living Asian Religions."

curriculum. The committee explicitly took note of the increased emphasis on research and publication among the faculty and said that a "serious part of this Committee's deliberations concerned the health of the intellectual climate *for the professionally oriented faculty member*."[28] [Emphasis added.]

The committee rejected the notion that the curriculum should aim at a shared intellectual experience and juggled the distribution requirements so that students were no longer obliged to take sets of broad, general courses. Henceforth students could satisfy the so-called breadth requirement by taking *any* four courses in the humanities, social sciences, and sciences. Students could meet the new requirements by taking highly specialized courses and could, if they chose, take *all* of those courses *in a single department*. Students were also permitted to spread their required courses over the entire four years of their college career and encouraged to declare their majors early.[29]

"This is an upheaval," the committee's chairman, Professor Roy Forster, declared. "In a sense we are doing away with the first two years of college and scrambling up the entire curriculum by allowing students to major in the first two years and finish their distribution requirements in the last two."[30]

The faculty recommended dropping the independent reading program ("in light of the fact that the original objectives of the General Reading Program . . . are being met in other ways" which were unspecified) and—despite some opposition from the English Department—eliminating the second half of the English composition requirement.[31] In its place, the faculty created a new freshman seminar program on subjects of highly specialized academic research such as "Greek Mathematical Sciences," "The Ulysses Theme," "Latin Love Poetry," "Rogues and Pilgrims," "The Japanese Theater in Relation to Western

---

Similarly in the social sciences, the choices were centered around courses such as "Political Ideals," which focused on the intellectual roots of democratic and totalitarian governments, "Introduction to Economics," "Introductory Human and Economic Geography," "American and Foreign Governments," "The History of Europe in Medieval and Early Modern Times," "The History of Europe Since 1715," "History of the United States," "An Introduction to Human Society," and "Introduction to Psychology."

Students could take no more than two courses in any department in any of the three divisions and in the sciences and social sciences had to take courses in each of the three main disciplinary areas.

Theater," and "Comic Characterization in Shakespeare and Dickens."[32]
The seminars, which dramatically accelerated specialization, were an
interesting attempt to bridge the gap between the faculty's professional
research activities and the needs of undergraduates. The expedient was
simple. Rather than adjust the faculty's focus into areas more congenial
to the undergraduate population, they chose to treat the undergraduates
as if they were graduate students.

Professor Henry Terrie, a former chairman of the English Department
saw the curricular revolution as an inevitable byproduct of the other
changes in the College's priorities and values.

> When you try to formulate principles for distribution requirements
> you step on people's toes. This was a byproduct of the effort to
> upgrade the quality of the faculty. The byproduct was that we got
> more people with specialties. The result was that we could never
> eliminate *any* course from the distribution requirements. Instead of
> broad gauge courses in Western Civilization and Humanities I and
> II, we ended up with someone's remote specialties—everyone's
> remote specialty.[33]

The changes in Dartmouth's curriculum fell far short of the demolition of the curriculum occurring on some other campuses. For the next
20 years, Dartmouth would point to Brown University's elimination of
all of its distribution requirements as a vivid contrast to its own actions.
Indeed, Dartmouth had not gone nearly so far as Brown; but the insistence on using Brown as a benchmark really serves only to indicate just
how far academic standards had fallen in the 1960s.*

The dismantling of the curriculum and the radical shift in focus may
have led Dickey to entertain second thoughts. At the 1966 convocation,
he lamented the "growing (if largely unintended) tendency, in our fast-
paced academic communities, to downgrade the amateur as a classroom

---

* Dartmouth's grading policies were also changed in the 1960s, with the introduction of
the "non-recording option," and the remarkable provision that allowed students to
count courses toward their graduation requirements even if they failed them as long as
the failure was not the result of "flagrant neglect." Between 1960 and 1970, grade
point averages skyrocketed, from an average of 3.19 in 1960-61 to 3.8 in 1970. The
faculty changed the grading system in 1973, but the upward trend continued, if not
quite as rapidly. By 1980, more than half of the senior class graduated with some type
of honors from their major department.

customer of the liberal arts." He urged his listeners to "be alert to the possibility that some of our arts and science offerings, at all levels, have become unnecessarily professional in content and spirit, both to the disadvantage of the course itself and the very purpose of the institution."

Even so, his benediction of the new curriculum was one of resignation. The time had come, he said, "to say straight out that the future of liberal learning in the American college will increasingly rest more with the individual teacher and student that with the committee on curriculum. . . ."[34]

DISILLUSIONMENT

Even before the upheavals of the mid-1960s, there were scattered signs of discontent. By 1963, Clark Kerr, the apostle of the university as "knowledge factory," sensed that "the undergraduates are restless." The new multiversity had transformed academia and opened new vistas of professional and financial advancement for the faculty, but had done the students themselves "little good."[35]

Thousands of students flocked to the newly-great multiversities, many of them the first members of their family to attend college. Lured by boasts of Nobel laureates and academic stars on the faculty, many arrived on campus naively believing they might actually be taught by some of these eminences, only to find that the only time they saw them was as a blur in the parking lot. In any other business, it would have been called "bait and switch." In the new university, it passed for higher education.

Perhaps the most eloquent critic of the new academy was classicist William Arrowsmith, who delivered a passionate defense of what he called "the ancient, crucial, high art of teaching."

> Behind the disregard for the teacher, lies the transparent sickness of the humanities in the university and in American life in general. . . . At present the universities are as uncongenial to teaching as the Mojave desert to a clutch of Druid priests.
>
> The scholar has disowned the student—that is, the student who is not a potential scholar—and the student has reasonably retaliated by abandoning the scholar. . . .

> The irony of the situation is enough to make strong men weep. Here, unmistakably we have students concerned to ask the crucial questions —identity, meaning, right and wrong, the good life— and they get in response not bread but a stone. . . .But what fills one with rage is the callousness of the scholars, the incredible lack of human concern among humanists, the monumental indifference of the learned. . . .Why, you ask, is teaching held in contempt? Because it has become contemptible by indifference. Teaching has been fatally trivialized by scholarship which has become trivial.[36]

The manifesto of the student revolt was Paul Goodman's 1962 book, *Community of Scholars*, a seething indictment of the pretenses and frauds of the modern academy. Goodman was appalled by the slavish conformity of so many institutions to the norms of the culture and the absence of even ten schools "that strongly stand for anything peculiar to themselves." Goodman depicted senior scholars indifferent to both students and their colleagues and a society that was being satisfied with "fat syllabi, hundreds of thousands of diplomas, bales of published research," but little true education. Administrators, Goodman charged, "engage in tooth-and-nail competition" to advance their institutions, but often ended up treating the university like a department store, "increasing efficiency by standardizing the merchandise and the sales force."

Goodman's proposals were both radical and reactionary. While he envisioned a return to a more traditional relationship between student and teacher, he called for the abolition of the bureaucracy and administrative infrastructure of the university, along with the "other excrescences that have swamped our community of scholars."

Even though it was at the height of its success, the American university was ill-prepared to face the challenge posed by the student revolt. Almost casually the academic establishment had eaten away the foundations of its own institutions; but until the 1960s it was possible not to notice.

CHAPTER
XI

REVOLUTION

The 1960s were not years of reform, but of revolution—an upheaval whose symbolic Bastille was the University of California at Berkeley. In October 1964, thousands of students demonstrated outside of occupied Sproul Hall protesting the University's ban on the distribution of political literature on campus. A pitifully small contingent of police was sent to evict them, and failed.

The protests quickly turned ugly. Shouting and jeering, students threw themselves in front of a squad car, climbing onto its hood and roof to deliver speeches. One of the mob's leaders, Mario Savio, was accused of biting a police officer in the leg. Demonstrators barred the doors of Sproul Hall, making it impossible for administrators to either enter or leave the building, although some fled through windows and across a roof.

"There is a time," Savio declared as the revolt gathered momentum, "when the operation of the machine becomes so odious, makes you so sick at heart that you can't take part; you can't even tacitly take part, and you've got to put your bodies upon the levers, upon all the apparatus and you've got to make it stop. . . ."[1]

No institution embodied the new shape of American academia in a purer form than Berkeley in the mid-1960s. It was the prototypical multiversity, a term coined by Clark Kerr, the president of the University of California and the architect of Berkeley's greatness. In 1964, Berkeley's administrators could look back on triumph after triumph; their institution was the match of any in the world in the quality of its research. If the undergraduate program had been neglected, it was a small price to pay for the glories of scholarship produced by the multiversity knowledge factory.* They never saw it coming.

Nor, as the events of the next two months would illustrate, did they have any idea how to deal with it. The vacillation of the administration, the increasingly shrill and radicalized students, and the wavering of the faculty would, however, set the pattern for the 1960s student revolt. For the next two months, the university and the students would engage in a numbing round of negotiations, challenges, threats, and feints, culminating in the mass arrest of more than 800 students in early December, and a bitter student strike. Classes across the campus were cancelled. Professors who tried to continue to teach were subjected to intimidation and harassment. Teaching assistants who joined them were labelled "scabs."

In the end, the capitulation of the university, in what philosopher Sidney Hook described as "the strangest faculty meeting in the history of American education," was total.[2] With hundreds of students gathered outside roaring their approval or disdain for the various speakers, nearly a thousand faculty enacted the primal tableau of the 1960s. By an overwhelming margin, they rejected a compromise proposal supported by the administration and the university's department chairmen. Amendments that deplored the "lawlessness," of recent days were crushed.

By a vote of 824 to 115, the faculty handed the Free Speech Movement a complete and unalloyed victory over the administration.

---

* Two professors at Berkeley, Sheldin Wolin and John Schaar, described the climate of the multiversity: "By any reasonable standard, the multiversity has not taken its students seriously. At Berkeley, the educational environment of the undergraduate is bleak. He is confronted throughout his entire first two years with indifferent advising, endless bureaucratic routines, gigantic lecture courses, and a deadening succession of textbook assignments, and bluebook examinations testing his grasp of bits and pieces of knowledge. . . .It is possible to take a B.A. at Berkeley and never talk to a professor." (Quoted by Irving Howe in *Revolution at Berkeley*, New York, Dell, 1965, p. xvii)

In the aftermath of the crisis, Nathan Glazer wrote that he and other moderates "are filled with foreboding."[3]

"What student leaders learned from the academic senate meeting of December 8," he wrote, "was that extreme tactics could be used without censure from the faculty."[4]

Sidney Hook prophetically saw the implications for other institutions:

> It was a victory, with the help of the overwhelming majority of the faculty, which smashed the traditions of orderly educational process and opened the gates to the politicization of the American university system. Although the leaders of the FSM [Free Speech Movement] may not press their luck further, their actions will probably inspire others. . . .
>
> It is the *approval* of student lawlessness on the part of the faculty, no matter what its alleged causes—ignorance of the facts, resentment against the administration, weariness with the whole business, conformism, desire to curry favor with students—which constitutes the most shocking aspect of the role of the faculty in the Berkeley episode. . . .Its vote can only serve to encourage further lawlessness.[6]

Hook was one of the few academics to criticize professors who suspended their classes to deliver political speeches. He also pointed out the obvious irony: that in the name of "free speech," academic freedom had been badly bruised. Academic freedom, Hook argued, "cannot exist if the teaching, research, discussion or dialogue is disrupted by pressures, demonstrations, and strikes."

But dissidents like Hook and Glazer were ignored. Hook would later characterize the years of revolt as "a failure of nerve and an eclipse of intelligence," during which "the commonplace truths about the weight of evidence, responsible assertion, striving for objectivity, and fairness in controversy" all came to sound "like wild paradoxes."[7]

THE TRIUMPH OF UNREASON

Having conceived of itself as an adversary culture, liberalism now found itself outflanked from a direction that left it morally and intellectually vulnerable. James Q. Wilson later described the relationship between the traditional liberalism of the academy and the new revolutionary faith as the tension between justice and benevolence. He could as easily have said reason and emotion—even reason and unreason—for the relationship was largely the same. Caught up in the idealism and the manichean moral dualities of the civil rights movement of the 1960s, the campus radicals had developed a politics of compassion, sincerity, and social commitment for the oppressed and downtrodden. The academic establishment's abstract, bloodless, utilitarian liberalism of "justice— the rule of law, equality of opportunity, democratic voting," Wilson wrote, could not "easily or for long withstand an aroused sense of benevolence."[8]

Increasingly impatient with rules, procedures, even free speech itself if it was seen as hampering the realization of social virtue, the left turned to the rhetoric of hectoring dogmatism. Sidney Hook would describe the phenomenon as the "barbarism of virtue." The hard-won principle of academic neutrality upon which academic freedom was based was now being challenged, Hook noted, "by those who are imbued with a sense of virtue, who under the banners of humanity want the temple of learning to become a fort from which they can sally forth to transform society with impunity."[9]

Ultimately, Wilson noted, the politics of commitment were incompatible with the principles of liberal education. The critical faculties developed by the liberal arts led to what Wilson called "universal skepticism," but the politics of benevolence tended to "suppress the exercise of criticism." He detected in this the seeds of what was to become a rigid and often violent intolerance for unpopular ideas.

Wilson also noted the paradox at the heart of the politics of benevolence. When frustrated, he wrote, benevolence "often turns to rage and those who celebrated the critics of compassion may come to indulge sentiments of hatred."

The transition from the liberal faith in justice to the barbarism of virtue was captured in the transmogrification of the Students for a Democratic Society, destined to play such a fateful role in the decade. In 1962, SDS's Port Huron Statement had declared:

> We regard *men* as infinitely precious and possessed of unfulfilled capacities for reason, freedom and love. . . . Men have unrealized potential for self-cultivation, self-direction, self-understanding, and creativity. . . . The goals of men and society should be human independence: a concern with . . . finding a meaning of life that is

personally authentic . . . one which has full spontaneous access to present and past experiences. *Human relationships* should involve fraternity and honesty.

Citing that passage, Wilson would later write: "Within a few years, this organization, including many of those who signed this statement at Port Huron, were attacking universities, harassing those who disagreed with them, demanding political obedience, and engaging in deliberate terrorism. Nothing could have been more liberal than the 1962 statement of the SDS; nothing could have been less liberal than its subsequent history."[10]

THE POSSESSED

By 1968, the movement that had begun as a campaign for free speech, was increasingly characterized by a hard-edged and shrilly ideological leadership. On racial issues, for instance, power was passing from integrationists and advocates of non-violence to more militant, often separatist black nationalists with little patience for the evolutionist, reasoned, non-violent approach of leaders like Martin Luther King, Jr.

The movement had also become opportunistic, looking for issues or incidents around which to manufacture disturbances and provoke a reaction that would in turn help radicalize students. One of the earliest and ugliest of the uprisings occurred at Columbia, where SDS leaders used the university's plans to build a gymnasium as a pretext to occupy several buildings and shut the campus down. One dean was held hostage by the students for more than 24 hours. As the radicals had hoped, police intervention helped radicalize the student body and faculty and destroy the normal standards of discourse on campus.

When a naive Harvard radical complained to Columbia SDS leader Mark Rudd that nothing was happening at Harvard to justify a full-scale uprising, Rudd responded:

Let me tell you. We manufactured the issues. The Institute of Defense Analysis is nothing at Columbia. Just three professors. And the gym issue is bull. It doesn't mean a thing to anybody. I had never been to the gym site before the demonstration began. I didn't know how to get there.[11]

The pattern of intimidation and appeasement was set early at Columbia. A law student charged with assault and battery and physically hindering students from seeing a faculty member was arraigned before Columbia's disciplinary committee. At the first hearing of the tribunal, SDS members mounted the podium shouting "Bullshit! Bullshit!" One disrupter leaped onto the tribunal's table and scattered the faculty members' papers across the room. The panel broke up in confusion, only to return with what amounted to a slap on the wrist for the accused student. Even though the university's rules called for suspension or expulsion, the panel—thoroughly intimidated by the disruptions—voted only "disciplinary probation." Formally, the student was warned not to repeat his actions; but the message from the faculty was clear. The student answered the faculty's action with an article in the campus paper that concluded:

> To these petty little men, and the more guilty ones that control
> them, I conclude with the message of the valiant math-commune:
> "Up against the wall, motherfucker. This is a stickup!"[12]

The threat of violence was always implicit in the language of the radicals, whose shouted obscenities became a trademark of the university uprisings of the next two years. At Columbia, student radicals labelled the dean of Columbia College a "motherfucker" before an assembly of students; but by then it had become almost common parlance on campus, a symbol of contempt for authority and civilized standards of discourse.[13] At Yale, for example, Black Panther "chief of staff" David Hilliard would later deliver a rambling diatribe in which he shouted "Fuck the judicial system!" and then declared that "there ain't nothing wrong with taking the life of a motherfucking pig." There were scattered boos, but when Hilliard began shouting "POWER TO THE PEOPLE!", the crowd—students and faculty sympathizers alike—took up the chant. It was an extraordinary moment in the history of the collective suspension of reason.[14]

This should not be mistaken for systematic ideology; it was impulse, a blind will to destruction that owes more to Dostoevsky's *The Possessed* than to any other chapter of American history. The new revolutionaries saw themselves "not as Bolsheviks or as Maoists on the Long March," Peter Collier and David Horowitz later observed, "but as Vandals and Visigoths battering the gates of America from within."[15]

Author John Hersey later sought to capture the flavor of events at his alma mater Yale, in what he called "this weird state of crowd psychological transcendence. . . ."[16]

> It is, the ruinous head fever that has ravaged campus after campus in many countries of the world. . . .
> All around one fly rumors, false alarms, *real* alarms, blurring of fateful truths at the very moment of their revelation, character assassination, binges of the ego, terrors like those of nightmares in broad daylight, gestures of love out from the cover of which peel the bloodshot eyes of unconscious rage. Everyone has to choose. . . .[17]

THE RISE OF BLACK STUDIES

Few schools in the 1960s could match San Francisco State's laissez-faire attitude toward educational issues. "People are inclined to say, 'Let everyone do his own thing,' " Professor Stuart Miller, recently recalled. If that meant approving courses in "Capitalism and Body Functions," then so be it. During the 1960s, the faculty approved a minor called "Critical Social Thought" with the explicit stipulation that only courses taught by Marxist professors be counted toward the program. When Miller asked colleagues why they had supported it, they replied, "Well, if that's what they wanted to do they can do it. Let the marketplace decide."

Even so, prior to the strike, says Miller, the tolerant attitude made San Francisco State "a very exciting place to teach."

> Academic standards were going up during the Sixties and the students were getting better and better. In fact, I sort of felt that San Francisco State was going to become a CCNY West, complete with the radicalism, but also with the very high academic standards. The strike really destroyed that.[18]

San Francisco State had had a black studies program since 1966.* But

---

* As of the spring of 1968, courses included: Anthropology: "Historical Development of Afro-American Studies"; Dramatic Arts: "Improvisations in Blackness"; Education: "Miseducation of the Negro"; English: "Modern African Thought and Literature"; History: "Ancient Black History"; Psychology: "Workshop in the Psychology of, by, and for Black People"; Sociology: "Sociology of Black Oppression."

under growing pressure from black militants on campus, President John Summerskill unilaterally named a new "special curriculum supervisor" to design a new black studies program. The man he selected (without any consultation from the faculty) was Dr. Nathan Hare, a self-described "black revolutionist" who had previously been fired by Howard University for inciting students to violence.[19] Hare made no secret of his racial attitudes. Speaking at Stanford he declared: "I don't believe in absolutes, so I do not categorically reject all white men, only 99 and $44/100$ths of them." He told the audience that he would never fight in the Army, "and if I did I would shoot as much as possible at the whites around me."

Lest his message be misunderstood, Hare continued:

> They say we are too few to fight. We should vote. But I can kill 20 [white] men. I can cut one's throat, shoot another, drop a hand grenade in the middle of a whole bunch. I get only a single vote, and that's between the lesser of two evils.[20]

Hare rejected the idea that whites could teach any black courses and suggested that white students be barred from taking black studies courses. The key to education, he insisted, was not the development of critical thinking or the development of individual talents. Hare proposed replacing that "white" philosophy with one centered on "the key component of community involvement and collective stimulation."[21]

His proposed curriculum pushed his politicized agenda even further, calling not only for courses in black poetry and black history, but also in black mathematics, black statistics, and black science.[22]

It is unlikely that Hare's pseudo-racialist curriculum would have fared well under even the most cursory scrutiny by fellow scholars. But the atmosphere on campus made sober consideration impossible. Claiming that "racists" were attempting to "exterminate" all black studies programs, the Black Student Union continually escalated tensions. Radical Stokely Carmichael visited the campus to urge students to assume a more overtly revolutionary stance.

In this environment, only a few voices were raised to question the enormity of Hare's proposals. The most cogent was John Bunzel, a respected member of the San Francisco State faculty, who published an article raising a number of basic questions about the proposals. Of course some black students responded well to black instructors, Bunzel wrote. But what of other considerations, including academic standards?

He also questioned the political agenda behind Hare's insistence on "collective stimulation." Did Hare envision an academic program or a political program for community action? And how would the courses be taught? "Will those who teach in the Department of Black Studies be of the same political and ideological persuasion or will efforts be made to recruit a black staff that purposely reflects different and opposing points of view? . . . Will the Department of Black Studies mirror the views of the Black Student's Union, thereby reinforcing the Union's political goals and purposes on campus?"[23]

And finally, did Hare envision indoctrination or genuine scholarship on black history? Would Hare, Bunzel asked, "substitute propaganda for omission, or, as some have said, new myths for old lies?"[24]

Bunzel published his article in mid-1968. When he returned to the campus that fall, an administrator called him into his office to tell him that because of the article he was now "a target" of militant blacks on campus.[25] A Kennedy delegate to the 1968 Democratic National Convention, Bunzel was labelled a racist and "lackey" of the CIA by campus radicals. The campus newspaper claimed that Bunzel's critical article had cost the black studies program a half million dollars in grants. The tires of his car were slashed, the words "Fascist Scab" were painted on the family automobile, and he was the target of an attempted bombing.[26] Meanwhile, a manual of revolutionary violence was circulated, with instructions on how to use "rocks and bottles," "red pepper, darts, water guns, etc.," "zippo cigarette lighters," "ice picks, leather punches and can openers," "pipe bombs," "cherry bomb with armament," and "molotov cocktails" for use against police and non-striking students.[27]

At one point, the manual read: "Many progressive thinkers of revolutionary theory believe assassination of pig leaders is one of the necessary variables for winning our struggle. . . ."[28]

Bunzel might have expected support from the administration or his colleagues, but neither was prepared to stand up to the reign of terror. In late October 1968, the committees on Undergraduate Curriculum and Instructional Policies met jointly to consider Hare's "conceptual proposals." Members of the Black Student Union were permitted into the room and stood three deep around the table. Asking only a smattering of questions, the committee approved the program in less than an hour and a half and recommended that the faculty senate adopt it immediately.[29]

One of the few faculty members to oppose the proposal was Professor Stuart Miller. When one of his black colleagues who privately regarded the black studies proposal as paternalistic abstained, Miller asked him why he had not voted against it. "Are you crazy," Miller recalls him answering. "Do you think I want to get beaten up?"[30]

John Bunzel later wrote:

> No discussion was ever focused on the critical premise that being black is not in itself an absolute qualification for being an expert, any more than being white is in itself a qualification for being an expert. . . . A black statistician cannot by definition be a more expert statistician *qua* statistician than a yellow or white statistician. *Either the college or university is a single community with standards of scholarship that make Black Statistics as repugnant as Lysenkoist Biology or it begins a piecemeal transformation into a cockpit of ideologues and fanatics who have abandoned the search for knowledge. . . .*[31] [Emphasis added.]

The faculty's craven surrender of intellectual integrity was not sufficient to appease the militants, who immediately issued five demands that in the parlance of the era were non-negotiable.* When the university did not immediately acquiesce, they called a strike that lasted for months and tore the university apart.

Years later, Arthur Chandler, a professor of Humanities at San Francisco State, explained the lack of resistance to the demands of the militants. Much of it, he said, "though not all, can be explained by sheer exhaustion. By the time the strike was over, many people were physically and emotionally exhausted. They didn't want any more conflicts. They didn't want another confrontation. They didn't want another fist in the face."[32]

---

* (1) That all black studies courses taught in other departments immediately become part of the new department; (2) that Nathan Hare receive a full professorship with a full professor's salary (he held the rank of instructor); (3) that the university recognize a bachelor's degree in Black Studies, and that the department be given absolute autonomy in hiring and curriculum; (4) that 20 full-time teaching positions be allocated to the new department (the faculty had approved 11.3); and (5) that *all* black students who applied should be admitted to San Francisco State University, beginning in the fall of 1969.

BEHIND IVY WALLS

But it was the Ivy League that was ultimately to set the pace in the retreat of reason.

Sidney Hook was later to say that if Harvard's capitulation was to be the Munich of higher education, Cornell was its Pearl Harbor.[33] Nearly 20 years after the events, Cornell's handling of the student revolution was recalled by Allan Bloom as "a truly disgraceful event, a microcosm of the cowardly acquiescence to the establishment of tyranny. . . ."[34]

In one of the decade's many ironies, Cornell's administration, led by President James Perkins, was notable for its supreme confidence in its ability to handle any disturbances on campus. Cornell's administrators were self-acknowledged masters of the techniques much in vogue in the 1960s, such as co-opting the radicals, defusing issues, insulating top administrators from confrontations, and "continuous demonstration management."[35]

Ultimately, however, James Perkins came to personify the servility of university administrators in the face of the increasingly ominous attacks on the integrity of the university and on academic freedom. Perkins seemed to thrive on humiliation. In 1968, as he spoke at a symposium on South Africa, a black student grabbed him by the collar and dragged him forcibly from the podium. Perkins, who was described as "badly shaken," quickly fled the room.[36]

Even so, Perkins rationalized that some of the infringements on academic freedom could be justified in the cause of advancing "social justice." Perkins made it clear that faculty members who came under attack for comments either in or out of class could expect no support from him. He told faculty "they could not use the cloak of academic freedom to cover up statements which might anger black students." With a standard that accommodated the militants rather than defend scholarship and free speech, Perkins helped make what followed inevitable.

The pattern of Cornell's response to pressure was set when several black militants attempted to take over an economics class after a professor named Michael McPhelin used Western standards to criticize the failures of African economies. McPhelin's other crimes included pointing out that human resources, like natural resources, varied from country to country; that economics was a science developed by Western man;

and that individuals needed to develop traits, including cunning, appropriate to their environment. To the radicals in the class, who found this view insufficiently deferential to Third World sensibilities, McPhelin was a racist. When they sought to seize the class, McPhelin dismissed it. In less than an hour, black students had begun a sit-in in the office of the department chairman. The chairman and a secretary were, in effect, held hostage for 13 hours.

It is difficult to imagine a more clear cut case of academic freedom; but the denouement was ominous. McPhelin, a visiting professor, left campus. The chairman praised the young radicals and signed a statement pledging to bring a practitioner of more enlightened economics to Cornell—to be selected by the students.[37]

Eager to co-opt the radicals on campus, Cornell also moved quickly in 1968 to establish an Afro-American Studies Institute. Despite Perkins' best efforts, it fell short of what campus militants wanted: they demanded a fully autonomous all-black college, run by black students. To press their point, they began a series of disruptions that included removing books from library shelves to show their "irrelevance" to black students; dancing on tables in the cafeteria to underline the need for a campus "soul room"; and running through campus buildings with toy guns while knocking over vending machines. The protests became increasingly threatening. A photographer for the campus paper was beaten up by black students when he refused to surrender his film after one incident; six members of the Afro-American Society forced three whites to vacate their offices.[38]

Cornell's administration responded by granting concessions to the black students, including making the new Black Studies Program degree-granting. But in April 1969, six black students at Cornell were cited for disorderly conduct for their role in the disruptions. The charges were investigated by a student-faculty commission on discipline which voted to merely "censure" three of the six students found guilty. The punishment was the mildest form possible and the students, moreover, had the right to appeal to the faculty.[39]

Instead, early on the morning of April 19, members of the Afro-American Society, some of them armed with rifles, occupied Willard Straight Hall, the student center.* Service personnel were forced to leave immediately, while the black students expelled visiting parents staying

---

* Later estimates put the number of guns at 13 rifles and two shotguns.

in the building's guest rooms. When white fraternity boys later tried to enter Straight Hall, fights ensued and several students were injured before the whites were driven off.[40]

The image of armed black students, brandishing their weapons with impunity, shocked the nation; but more shocking were the events that followed.

The militants demanded that all charges be completely dropped against the black students. The administration, under Perkins, quickly agreed but referred the final decision to the faculty, which met on April 21. The faculty refused to accept the administration's repudiation of the student-faculty Commission on Discipline, but in a gesture of good will, invited the black students to state their case at a meeting scheduled for April 23. The militants responded by unleashing a wave of threats.

The spokesman for the Afro-American Society darkly warned that Cornell had "only three hours to live." The presence of rifle-toting militants on campus chillingly underlined the potential that threats could easily escalate into actual violence. Professors who had opposed the capitulation were denounced as racists who "will be dealt with." The militants added to the sense of menace with chanted slogans such as "Death to Pigs!" and "Death to racists!"[41]

Security officials warned faculty moderates to leave campus; some went into hiding. All the while, the administration doggedly pursued its policy of increasingly surreal appeasement.

When SDS, anxious to get a piece of the revolutionary action, seized Barton Hall the act was blessed by President Perkins as "one of the most constructive forces which have been set in motion in the history of Cornell."[42] Wrote Sidney Hook: "Worse than the student lout, white or black, who roughs up those to whom he can make no rational response, is the teacher or the administrator who kisses the hand that strikes him down."[43]

Finally, the faculty too gave in. Fearful, intimidated, anxious to atone for white guilt, the faculty voted to drop all charges against the black students—without seriously weighing the findings of its own commission; without hearing any evidence. No effort was ever made to discipline the students who seized Straight Hall or Barton Hall.

Two visiting professors on campus that Spring, Matthew Hodgart from the University of Sussex, England, and Harold Bloom of Yale, suspended their classes, declaring that "the conditions of free speech

and personal safety that have normally obtained in the academic communities of the civilized world" no longer existed at Cornell.[44]

Again, Hook delivered the harshest verdict:

> Whatever physical damage might have been inflicted on Cornell
> would have been less costly morally than the loss of self-respect
> involved in the capitulation . . . every principle of academic due
> process was jettisoned, the academic freedom both of teachers and
> students betrayed, and the hysteria of blue funk concealed by
> empty rhetoric about building a new form of "racial harmony on
> campus."[45]

Cornell was only the beginning. At Harvard, the arrest of militant,
law-breaking students resulted in the faculty's dramatic repudiation of its
own administration. A proposal from moderates declaring that "the
overriding moral issue is the initial violent seizure" of Harvard's administration building was defeated by a faculty vote of 248 to 149.[46]

The politicization of Harvard had proceeded apace from 1966 on, as
radical groups like SDS established effective beachheads in both the
student body and the faculty, where sympathizers could increasingly be
counted on to present the radicals' demands at College meetings.

With the backing of its faculty allies, SDS scored a major victory in
1968 when it gained approval for a course called "Social Relations
148-149." Taught by two young professors, the course made no pretense
of scholarly objectivity. Its SDS sponsors openly proclaimed that the
purpose of the course was to link "a politically radical interpretation of
the world" with "a commitment to action in the Movement."

Its radical agenda was apparent in the titles of its seminars, which
ranged from "Imperialism and the University," to "Women and Sex-
Role Oppression," to "Leninism." The sections were sometimes taught
by radical undergraduate members of SDS and even occasionally by
radicals with no formal affiliation to the College at all. In the spring, the
course, which was offered for university credit, had an enrollment of
900 students, and played a significant role in the radicalization of the
student body.[47]

The success of the radicals in politicizing the faculty was obvious
from its reaction to the takeover of University Hall. But the crucial test
of Harvard's commitment to academic integrity was to come on the
issue of black studies. A faculty committee headed by future Dean
Henry Rosovsky had spent 18 months developing a program of Afro-

American Studies, which would permit students to take courses in conjunction with a concentration in another discipline. The plan not only had strong faculty support, but had been endorsed by the leadership of the Afro-American student organization.

Now, suddenly, in the midst of the strike, the leadership of the Afro-American group was changed; the new, more radical leaders rejected the previously agreed-upon plan. In its place, the radicals demanded a full-fledged department that would be controlled not by the faculty or the administration, but by a joint committee of faculty and students. Moreover, it would be autonomous, hiring its own faculty, writing its own curriculum, and establishing its own standards. The proposal represented a rejection of Harvard's academic standards and principles of governance. But, the black students warned that if the faculty failed to approve it as written there would be another takeover and perhaps worse.

At the faculty meeting called to discuss the issue, members of the Afro-American group were allowed to attend and actually participate in the debate. Some faculty were disturbed by the proposal's explicit call for "radical and relevant courses," but with the consent of the student radicals, the phrase was amended to "innovative," a euphemism that provided a necessary, if thin, patina of intellectual seriousness for the faculty. In the end, the faculty voted 251 to 148 to reject the faculty's own proposal and to adopt the radical plan. The radical plan had been opposed by both leading moderates and liberals in the faculty; but it was overwhelmingly supported by younger faculty and, significantly, by faculty from the natural sciences.[48]

Perhaps no other single incident illustrated the consequences of the fragmentation of the curriculum more graphically than the apostasy of the scientists, who voted heavily in favor of the proposal. To them, the revision of the curriculum was more or less irrelevant since it affected only the *social* sciences, and would thus not affect either their departments or their students. As for the impact on the overall intellectual integrity of the institution, that seemed not to be an issue at all.

In later years, there may have been a tendency by some to romanticize the "idealism" and "commitment" of the 1960s, and to cover the sins of the decade with the gloss of nostalgia. But by 1969, Yale's Robert Brustein saw the uprisings less as an exercise in idealism "than a grownup version of the bully game called 'get the guy with the glasses.' "[49]

"The politicization of the community had liberated a lot of energy," he noted, "but it had not been particularly protective of the privileges of dissent."[50]

On campus after campus, speakers who challenged the left were routinely shouted down: the secretary of defense at Harvard, the chairman of the joint chiefs of staff at Brown, the secretary of agriculture at the University of Wisconsin. At Stanford, Vice President Hubert Humphrey was pelted with urine and excrement.[51]

UCLA cancelled a course in Anthropology because militants objected to the teacher. James Buchanan, later a Nobel laureate, resigned from UCLA, citing "an atmosphere of violence, intimidation and fear." At New York University, a speech by the South Vietnamese ambassador was disrupted when SDS-led radicals dumped a pitcher of water on his head. Militants broke down the door of a lecture hall at NYU in which *New York Times* columnist James Reston was lecturing—thus expressing their displeasure with the editorial policy of his newspaper. The chancellor of NYU, whose role it was to safeguard the intellectual environment of his institution, was impotent because, Sidney Hook noted, he "lived in fear of faculty rebuke for causing a confrontation."[52]

Hook, who had been a keen and skeptical observer of the movements and developments of most of the twentieth century, was still unprepared for the extent of the collapse of the university. In his autobiography, *Out of Step*, he called the events of the next year at NYU, his own school, "perhaps the most shocking series of experiences in my life."[53]

For most of his life, he wrote, he had thought intelligence was the supreme virtue and had "taken for granted the operation of moral courage."[54] His faith did not survive the revolution.

CHAPTER

XII

1969

From the relative security and apparent immunity of remote Hanover, Dartmouth watched the spreading anarchy on the nation's campuses with ambivalence and growing uneasiness. Some administrators apparently hoped it would pass them by completely. In late 1967, A. Alexander Fanelli, assistant to President Dickey, vetoed a proposed story by the College News Service on growing student activism at Dartmouth, saying that such a report would "create confusion" and "would be doing a disservice" to the College.[1] As late as December 1968, there was little sign of student activism in Hanover. Conservative students controlled the student paper, student government, and the student-run radio station. More than a third of Dartmouth's undergraduates had supported the election of Richard Nixon in 1968, a student writer noted in the *Alumni Magazine*, "undoubtedly far above the Ivy League average."

"If student opinion is radicalizing, there is little indication of it."[2]

Two years earlier, a small chapter of Students for a Democratic Society had been formed on campus. Although it never established more than a modest beachhead at Dartmouth, and was often at a loss for issues

151

to exploit, it provided what little political theater there was at the College. In 1967, it tried with limited success to mobilize support for a protest against College investments in Eastman Kodak after that company refused demands by community activist Saul Alinsky to retrain 600 unemployed persons in Rochester, New York.[3]

More typical of the left at Dartmouth was a young student activist named Robert Reich. The *Alumni Magazine* would later characterize Reich as "a different type of student-power activist," who emphasized negotiation rather than confrontation. "Reich is a politician by nature and a student-power activist by accident and an excess of energy."[4] Reich described himself in 1968 as "an extremely conservative establishment hippie."[5]

His election as student government president marked a sharp shift to the left. Reich's major accomplishment was the creation in 1967 of the Dartmouth Experimental College, "a flexible and non-authoritarian area" in which a student could "experiment and discover for himself."

Such counter-culture experimental colleges had sprung up throughout the country as alternative curriculums to the traditional universities and colleges themselves. Using the euphoric prose of the decade, Reich characterized the new colleges:

> Everywhere the emphasis upon community, upon involvement, upon close relationships, upon building an open and unthreatening environment. . . .
>
> The particular technique varies, but the goal is always the same—a total and personal learning experience. At Penn's Experimental College, one student instructor found himself faced with a huge lecture hall of people interested in his course on LSD; so he turned out the lights and passed out candles and incense. According to him, this brought people closer together, forced them to listen to each other. What more delightful indirect way of criticizing college education than making a success out of a competing college that claims to be more relevant, more innovative, more alive to human needs and desires?[6]

Reich's alternative college began with 20 courses and advertised itself as "an exciting and free-wheeling educational experiment." Courses ranged from American Negro history to "LSD and Frontiers of the Mind." On any given night students could discuss "Guerilla Warfare" or J.R.R. Tolkien. By later standards, many of the courses were mild indeed, including offerings in "Bridge for the Beginner" and "A Brief Look at German and Italian Opera." But it also included courses in "A Radical View of American Economic Development," "Nationalism in the Third World," and "Do You Feel a Draft?" a course described as "helping others with their draft problems."[7] Reich later boasted that the Experimental College had become so popular that it was the fourth largest college in the state.[8] (In the late 1980s, Reich, by then a professor at Harvard and guru to Democratic presidential candidates Walter Mondale and Michael Dukakis, was named to Dartmouth College's Board of Trustees.)

The most jarring evidence that the cup would not pass from Dartmouth, however, came in May 1967, when former Alabama Governor George Wallace visited the campus for a scheduled speech. Radical and black students greeted his attempts to speak with jeers and catcalls and the event quickly escalated toward violence. Wallace was forced to cancel his speech and leave campus while students rocked and pounded on his car. To the deep chagrin of the administration, the incident won national attention as an example of the growing intolerance on university campuses. CBS News commentator Eric Sevareid used the episode to denounce the "self-conscious morality" of student radicals and to warn of the dangers of the politics of intimidation.

> At Dartmouth College, several hundred students have discovered a higher meaning to the constitutional guarantees of free speech. It means the freedom to howl down anybody with a different view and to threaten him with bodily harm, as they did to ex-Governor George Wallace. These students are quite certain their morality is higher than Wallace's, a proposition now open to doubt. Their basic, unspoken conviction is that the young and left-wing are naturally pure; the middle-aged and right-wing naturally impure.
>
> It all leaves bewildered citizens groping helplessly to find the difference between the students who smashed Wallace's car and that Dallas woman who spat on the late Adlai Stevenson; the difference between today's left-wing intimidation and yesterday's right-wing intimidation by McCarthyism. . . .[9]

Mindful of its free speech traditions, Dartmouth was determined to respond forcefully to the challenge posed by the shout-down. An ad hoc committee was formed by the faculty to develop guidelines for dealing with dissent and activism. The resulting policy on freedom of expression and dissent clearly distinguished between the right of dissent, which was unlimited, and acts or threats of force which had no place within the College. It was a thoughtful and powerful restatement of the values of a liberal college, certainly one of the clearest such declarations by any major institution of higher learning in the country:

> Dartmouth College prizes and defends the right of free speech and the freedom of the individual to make his own decisions, while at the same time recognizing that such freedom exists in the context of law and of responsibility for one's actions. The exercise of these rights must not deny the same rights to any other individual. The College therefore both fosters and protects the rights of individuals to express dissent. Protests or demonstrations shall not be discouraged so long as neither force nor the threat of force is used, and so long as the orderly processes of the College are not deliberately obstructed.*

ROTC WARS

As it did elsewhere, SDS targeted Dartmouth's ROTC program, both as a means of capitalizing on growing anti-war sentiment and resuscitating itself. In May 1968, a total of 407 Dartmouth students were enrolled in ROTC, including 113 students on ROTC scholarships.[10] SDS demanded that Dartmouth immediately "deinstitutionalize" the program. It seized on the College's annual ROTC Awards Ceremony, traditionally held on the College Green, as the first opportunity to show its strength.

Calling for "direct action" if its demands were not met, Dartmouth's tiny SDS chapter threatened to disrupt the ceremony. The upheaval at

---

* The policy had the strong support of the Executive Committee of the Undergraduate Council, which endorsed a statement by a Student-Faculty Committee on Dissent that read in part: "the College should not forbid the appearance of individuals or groups holding controversial opinions. Neither should it permit expressions of dissent which employ means, such as the threat or use of physical force, which hamper the rights of expression of others. To the extent that the College cannot maintain an orderly exchange of ideas, it forfeits its mandate in the community to protect freedom of inquiry, and so gives up its right to self-discipline." The committee explicitly extended its guarantee of free speech to military recruiters. While protests against military recruiters would be permissible, the student-faculty committee said, "the blocking of access to a building or the threat or use of force against a recruiter would not." (Statement prepared by the Student-Faculty Committee on Dissent, November 6, 1967)

Columbia, where SDS had succeeded in shutting down a great university, gave extra force to the threat. While the College insisted that it had not capitulated or bowed in any way to the pressure from SDS, it took several steps designed to avoid confrontation. Most significantly, it moved the entire ceremony from the Green—the center of the campus—onto a more obscure part of the campus, Chase Field, which was surrounded by a temporary wire fence that excluded all but invited guests. Critics noted that the administration's action gave the military an apparently lower status than anti-war demonstrators who freely used the Green for their activities. President Dickey, who was less and less a factor on campus in his declining years, made it known that a "long-standing commitment" made it impossible for him to attend the ceremonies. The highest ranking College official to attend was an associate dean.

Administrators assiduously tried to avoid any police presence at the event, asking students and faculty members to assist in keeping order. That brought an ominous warning from SDS that "anti-war demonstrators will be fully justified in viewing any faculty member who polices the May 15 demonstration as an active and unforgivable participant in the U.S. military assault on the Vietnamese."[11] The actual event passed without serious incident. Two hundred protestors waved flags, sang songs, and chanted slogans, from behind the wire fences.

But SDS had scored a major victory. "The College has again bowed to pressure and nebulous threats of violence by peace demonstrators," senior Jonathan Hull complained.[12] Moreover, the Executive Committee of the Faculty ordered a study of the "compatibility" of ROTC with the College's educational goals. In October 1968, the special study committee came back with a recommendation to phase out the ROTC program and eliminate it entirely within three years.

SDS's success was remarkable, especially given its isolation on campus. Part of that had to do with Dartmouth itself. Radicals had never made significant inroads into the student body. Several years later, Laurence Radway, then chairman of the Government Department, would argue that three factors contributed to the fact that the radical coalition at Dartmouth did not amount to a "hill of beans": the type of student who attends Dartmouth College; the absence of graduate students who provided leadership for the uprisings on other campuses; and the physical isolation of the College, which tended to insulate Dartmouth from the kinds of outside influences that were being brought to bear on schools located in urban settings.[13]

But even given those factors, Dartmouth's SDS was a notably feeble affair. An internal SDS memo, for example, tried to rally demonstrators against Air Force recruiters in 1968. But its radicalism was undermined somewhat by its rather mundane warning that unless the group raised money quickly, "we will lose our annual budget of $200 from [the College] as well as our College credit number."[14]

In another communiqué, two SDS leaders candidly explained their sense of alienation from the College.

> As a group, we understandably exhibit contempt for most Dartmouth students and their middle class careers and values. Yet we know that we are from the same contemptible middle class. So we intuitively try to draw out of the student body the few kindred souls who share our minority sensibilities.
>
> Our contempt for the majority leads us to alienate ourselves from most students, while our desire to recruit more members demands that we somehow speak to students and faculty and attempt to persuade some of them to join us, i.e. renounce their former background. *The result of our ambiguous position is that we know neither how to relate to students nor why we even bother at all.* . . . So out of frustration, we try to blow their minds, shock them with our "liberated" language, bang them over the head with evidence of brutal U.S. imperialism, and create for them radicalizing spectacles such as police violence at a demonstration.[15]

That fall, they escalated their tactics. On November 25, 1968, twenty to thirty SDS members denouncing Dartmouth's alleged "complicity with the military" picketed Fairbanks South, where two Army officers had been provided space for recruiting interviews. The protest was peaceful throughout the morning, but its failure to gather any student support frustrated organizers eager to provoke a response by the College.

In the afternoon, when the two Army officers returned from lunch, the demonstrators locked arms in front of the entrance to Fairbanks and blocked their re-entry. When one of the officers tried to climb over the railing of the porch at the front of the building, two of the demonstrators grabbed him by the leg and pulled him down. The SDS members continued to block entry when Dartmouth Proctor John O'Connor appeared and tried to escort the officers into the building. The officers, seeing the futility of the effort, eventually left.[16]

Four students were specifically cited for violating the College's Guide-lines on Free Expression and Dissent. But they mounted a vigorous defense and were joined by four members of the faculty who had participated in the obstruction of the recruiters. In a statement, the four professors declared that "the issue for us is *not* one of freedom of expression." The recruiters did not deserve protection because they were "part of a machine whose ultimate function is the killing of massive numbers of Vietnamese."[17]

One of the signatories was Jonathan Mirsky, a leading radical figure on campus and a professor of Chinese language. Since at least late 1967, Mirsky had been agitating for restrictions on the free expression guaran-tees in the College's Guidelines. In November 1967, he circulated a memorandum by Boston University professor Howard Zinn, arguing that certain actions, including corporate and military recruitment "must be restricted for the health and safety of others."[18]

Echoing Herbert Marcuse's call for restricting socially obnoxious speech, Mirsky's logic defied the letter and the spirit of the College's policy but could be—and increasingly was— used to justify the disrup-tion of a wide range of activities that were deemed unacceptable by the left. Mirsky's position, however, still reflected minority opinion at Dartmouth College.

One faculty member urging a strenuous defense of the College's policy was Mathematics Professor John Kemeny. The future Dartmouth College president wrote an unsolicited memorandum to Dean Thaddeus Seymour two days after the incident, urging "severe penalties" for the radicals. Kemeny called the obstruction of the recruiters a "clear-cut and willful violation of the College's policy on dissent. . . ."

> Unless we of the faculty are prepared to enforce this policy to the fullest, we will have failed in our role as educators and anarchy will rule on the campus. It is very important that the question of whether the cause for dissent was worthy should *not* be taken into account. The faculty has taken a very strong position allowing a great deal of freedom for dissenters whether or not their cause is just. On the other hand, we have stated clearly that certain actions are not permissible, no matter what the cause is. One of these actions is the barring of a recruiter from a College building.[19]

Kemeny noted that he had not been involved in the Vietnam protests on either side. "However, the current issue is not Vietnam but order on the Dartmouth campus and the willingness of the faculty to enforce its own rules."

The College Committee on Standing and Conduct, however, which was charged with handling student discipline, gave the students only the mildest form of punishment "college discipline" —a form of probation.

COLOR WARS

Until 1969, racial tensions had remained in the background at Dartmouth. But in early March, Dartmouth's Afro-American Society, which had not previously been a radical force on campus, suddenly issued 18 "demands." Along with asking the College to address itself to "the solutions of the problems of socio-educational deprivations that paralyze the black community," the group demanded an admissions quota of at least 11 percent for black students, hiring of minority administrators, the admission of 10 to 15 "special students" who did not meet normal admission standards, the creation of a Black Studies program, and the suspension of normal degree requirements for the program. The administration was given until April 3—less than a month—to respond.[20]

The College launched into a crash program of negotiations that often lasted into the early morning. They were carried out, Dean Leonard Rieser later said, in a "climate of urgency in order that there be no climate of emergency."[21]

The *Alumni Magazine* later described the mood of the talks:

> Though the Afro-American Society never mentioned violence, the experience of other universities was in everyone's mind, and much of the College was prepared for a building seizure, or worse, if the AAS didn't get what it wanted. Wallace L. Ford '70, the Afro-American Society's coordinator, helped the rumors along by telling *The Dartmouth* the society had "plans" to handle any contingency. Rumors of administration preparations—not all of them entirely spurious—became the talk of the students and faculty, and the campus, left in the dark, prepared for the apocalypse.[22]

Within days, the College agreed to almost all of the Afro-American Society's demands. Psychology Professor William Smith was an early member of the College's negotiating team before he dropped out for reasons of health ("I couldn't stomach it, literally").

"It was," he recalled later, "raw intimidation. They caved in to pressure to create a program with no intellectual basis. They were frightened. They didn't know what to do; the pressure was tremendous and they took the easy way out."[23]

The proposals were rushed to the faculty for approval on April 16. Under them, the College agreed to create an Afro-American Studies program to begin in the fall; significantly increase the enrollment of black students; appoint more black faculty in the field of urban studies, who "need not necessarily possess the usual academic credentials"; name Samuel Smith, a black, as an assistant director of admissions; endorse additional funds for a "black recruitment officer"; and have at least one black student "nominated by the AAS" freed from regular academic duties to work in the admissions office and as a guidance counselor.[24]

More troublesome was the Afro-American Society's later 19th demand, which called for the creation of a separate judiciary committee to deal with disciplinary cases involving blacks. While the College did not accept the segregated plan, it pledged to "expedite reform of that system in consultation with the AAS," a move that resulted in the creation of a special black advisory committee on discipline.[25]

President Dickey capped the appeasement of the militants with a lengthy letter to the Afro-American Society in which he praised the black militants and thanked them for their suggestions. "You have helped us toward greater understanding and we will do our best to keep the relationship with you such that we can continue to be helped by you." Dickey hastened to note that "we who are white can never truly know the personal burden and urgency it imposes on today's black students," and said that "we will not expect the impossible from you."[26]

The statement by the AAS was also conciliatory but retained an implicit threat. The group said it was "confident that our relationship [with the College negotiators would] preclude even the consideration of violence and confrontation by any sector of the College Community."[27]

In early April, SDS sought to capitalize on the confusion at Dartmouth by declaring its solidarity with the Afro-American Society, and then announced its own non-negotiable demands to Dartmouth College: the immediate abolition of ROTC and the abolition of all military recruiting on campus.

In late January, the full faculty had considered the issue, voting against measures to shut down ROTC ahead of schedule. One result of the faculty action was the creation of a special ROTC Committee.[28] In early March. the committee voted to inform all incoming freshmen that no credit for ROTC would be given after June 1972.

As pressure built, the faculty began to bend. In late April, the Executive Committee of the faculty voted to re-open the ROTC issue by throwing it to the students in the form of a referendum. Despite its ostensible "democratic" orientation, SDS denounced the proposed vote as "repugnant and immoral." The next day, April 22, about 250 demonstrators entered Parkhurst Hall and conducted a sit-in for three hours. The demonstrators threatened to return on the 30th to "engage in an act of civil disobedience unless the faculty, administration and trustees accede" to their demands to shut down ROTC immediately.

Dickey again tried conciliation, meeting secretly with Pentagon officials and officials from other colleges in an attempt to find a middle ground. Dickey's painful and increasingly untenable position was exacerbated when he was summoned to the state capital by nervous state officials. At the meeting, Dickey gave what he later described as "an assurance such as has never been offered on this job to anybody, anywhere, anytime." The gravamen of his pledge was that if the state did not send state police, Dartmouth would maintain "the kind of order that is the absolute responsibility of the public authorities."[29]

His desperation is reflected in the minutes of the faculty's executive committee meeting on April 24, when he pleaded with the faculty "to speak to the issues of maintaining order. . . ."

Referring to the failure of the College to stand behind its guidelines on dissent by imposing credible penalties, Dickey described the Dartmouth disciplinary system as being "in disarray," and warned the faculty that public law enforcement officials would step in to maintain order if the College failed to do so.[30] At Dickey's urging, the Executive Committee adopted a tough resolution declaring that the faculty "will not tolerate any breach of the stated policy regarding freedom of expression and dissent inasmuch as membership in this community carries with it as a necessary condition to honor and abide by this policy."

The resolution called for tough sanctions against violators, specifically enjoining the Dean of the College "to take whatever steps are required to deal with individuals who do not abide by the existing policy on freedom of expression and dissent, *including the immediate suspen-*

sion of students found in clear violation of the policy with readmission contingent upon recommendation of the Committee on Administration after appropriate hearings."[31] [Emphasis added.]

Had that resolution been adopted by the full faculty, it would have provided the administration with the kind of solid faculty support that was lacking at so many other schools. But in lengthy and contentious meetings over the next two days, the faculty eliminated all references to specific sanctions and removed the expression stating the refusal of the faculty to tolerate any breach of the policy on dissent. As finally passed, the faculty resolution merely appealed "to all groups and every individual in the College community to reject any violent, destructive, or disruptive course of action." It also "clarified" the policy on dissent to make it clear that "unauthorized entry into, or occupation, of a private office" is a violation although it is difficult to imagine that anyone had ever been in doubt on the question.[32]

Having backed down from the definitive earlier statement, the faculty voted to cancel all classes for Monday, April 28, so that a special symposium on the ROTC issue could be held preceding the afternoon student referendum. The faculty also committed itself to meet again to consider the referendum results.[33]

From the College's point of view, the referendum results were a worst-case scenario. By an overwhelming margin (1,907 to 599) students voted to urge the faculty to reopen the ROTC issue. But it gave no clear guidance as to what direction the faculty should take. The SDS position—immediate abolition—received only 25 percent of the vote. None of the options received even a convincing plurality.*

Even though more than 88 percent of Dartmouth's undergraduates had participated in the vote, SDS flatly rejected the validity of the referendum. Emboldened by the confusion, anti-ROTC demonstrators staged a second sit-in at Parkhurst Hall the day after the vote, leaving before midnight, as one account later wryly noted "when the College surprised them by allowing them to stay on."

When the faculty finally voted on May 5 to reaffirm its phase-out of ROTC, setting a terminal date of 1973, SDS declared the decision "intolerable" and made plans for a more militant and dramatic stroke.

---

* In the balloting, 35.8 percent supported eliminating ROTC after the present contract enrollees graduated; 30 percent favored the faculty position; 25 percent backed the SDS option; while 8.8 percent favored retention of ROTC.

TAKEOVER

At approximately 3:15 on the afternoon of May 6, about 60 students entered Parkhurst Hall. Using bullhorns, SDS leaders ordered all administrators and College personnel to leave immediately. As a token of their seriousness, the protestors began nailing shut the heavy oaken front doors. SDS Leader Guy Brandenburg ordered President Dickey from his office; he quickly left.

Dean Seymour was at his desk when SDS leader James Van Hoy entered his office and told him to leave. "I indicated that he was welcome to stay with me and that I would talk with him about any subject that was on his mind," Seymour later said.[34] Hearing commotion outside of his office, Seymour looked out, to find his waiting room occupied by six or seven demonstrators. Confused and frightened, the secretaries had covered their typewriters and closed their desks. Seymour explained to the demonstrators that they were in violation of the policy on Free Expression and Dissent. Stepping out in the hallway, Seymour repeated his warning in stentorian tones that could be heard throughout the building. He was ignored. More doors were being nailed shut; furniture was being taken from offices for conversion into barricades.

Back in his office, protestors had taken over Seymour's switchboard; others entered and began demanding that the dean leave. Finally SDS leader John Spritzler ordered Seymour to leave immediately and tried to grab his arm. When Seymour told him that "he would be initiating violence if he touched me," Spritzler coolly responded that he was not using "violence," but only "force." Seymour was grabbed by several protestors who pushed him from the office. A large man, Seymour resisted as best he could, grabbing partitions, door jambs, and bannisters. The group forcing him out grew in size. At the head of the stairs to the basement, Seymour fell a few steps. He was pushed down the stairs and out a basement door.[35]

Seymour had had some brief warning of the attack, when a student had dropped off a note warning of the imminent takeover, half an hour earlier. Albert I. Dickerson, the dean of freshmen, was not so fortunate. Dickerson was one of the College's most beloved figures, a legacy of the presidency of Ernest Martin Hopkins, who had named him his assistant on his graduation in 1930, nearly four decades before. Dickerson had devoted his entire adult life to Dartmouth, as director of the news service, executive secretary of the Alumni fund, executive assistant to the president, executive officer of the College, director of admissions, and now dean of freshmen. After his death three years later, Dartmouth President John Sloan Dickey would describe Dickerson by saying, "In the most profound sense he personified the place, or at least he personified what most of us learned to love about the place."[36]

Dickerson was in his office interviewing a former student applying for readmission when the takeover was announced. Stepping into the corridor, Dickerson saw that the assault was well-planned, well-organized, and determined.[37] Dickerson ordered his staff to clean their desks, lock their files, and leave. His staff was, however, reluctant to go. Dickerson insisted. One woman forgot her handbag in the rush. But by the time she attempted to retrieve it, the protestors had overturned oak settees and blocked all entrances.

Until now, Dickerson's presence had gone unnoticed. One of the takeover leaders now announced loudly: "Dean Dickerson is still in his office. Get him out!"

The leader of the takeover and several of his followers entered Dickerson's office, where the elderly dean still sat behind his desk, refusing to leave. At the leader's order, several students picked up Dickerson's chair, with Dickerson still in it, and began carrying him out. At the door, the base of the chair fell off, causing the carriers to stumble. "I stood up as an alternative to being dumped on the floor," Dickerson later recalled.[38]

Eight or ten protestors, including one faculty member, joined in the effort to push Dickerson out of the building. When Dickerson protested, the SDS leader answered monosyllabically.

"Shit."

The College was not caught unprepared. A local judge issued an injunction—prepared more than a week earlier for just such an incident—ordering the building to be immediately vacated by 5:30 p.m. At 8 p.m., Grafton County Sheriff Herbert W. Ash read the injunction through a bullhorn and gave the occupiers one hour to leave. When the deadline expired, Ash once again read the injunction and extended the deadline to 10:45 p.m. Some of the more radical occupiers argued for violent resistance, but they were outvoted. Some students left Parkhurst via the back windows, but the ultimatum had no other effect. In all, Sheriff Ash read the injunction eight times. As a federal appeals court would later note, "The only consequence of his outdoing Joshua . . . was a closing of the windows."[39] Confrontation had become unavoidable.

At about 1 A.M., Governor Walter Peterson met with Dickey and other College officials at the home of one of Dartmouth's attorneys. The decision having been made to use state police to clear Parkhurst Hall, Governor Peterson personally addressed the troopers assembled at the Lebanon Armory, urging them to exercise restraint.

A little after 3 A.M., police cordoned off Parkhurst Hall, and New Hampshire State Police, backed by a contingent from Vermont, broke through the front door and entered the building. Demonstrators took up the chant "ROTC must go—now!" But none resisted arrest.[40]

In all, 54 persons, including 40 students were arrested and charged with contempt of court. If they expected the same sort of leniency from the court that they had become accustomed to from the College, the protestors were to be bitterly disappointed. With swift justice, Judge Martin Loughlin held hearings two days later and sentenced 45 of the protestors to 30 days in jail and fines of $100 each. Nine others were granted continuances to obtain counsel.*

Dean Seymour immediately applauded the court's action, declaring "the days of indulgence are over." The penalty, Seymour said, was stiff, "but it would be naive to expect indulgence from a court which allowed twelve hours for students to vacate the building voluntarily."[41]

The mood among administrators was self-congratulatory. Indeed, they had done what so many other schools had failed to do: they had acted swiftly to stop illegal activity and had done so without violence. Moreover, the SDS strategy of radicalizing the campus had failed miserably; a student strike called to protest the arrests fizzled, effectively destroying SDS as a factor in campus politics.

National reaction was positive. "Campus toughs don't have to be coddled," editorialized *The Philadelphia Inquirer*. "There are ways to deal with them. The response to trouble at Dartmouth College last week is an example. . . . There was no fuss, no nervous wringing of hands— just direct action and swift punishment."

A week after the takeover, A. Alexander Fanelli, Dickey's special assistant, wrote a memo to the president reporting that the College had received 100 telegrams and more than 100 letters, overwhelmingly supportive. "A recurrent theme, however, is the hope that the offending students will be expelled or at least suspended (with most voting for

---

* Five of the 45 later won new trials. All appeals for the jailed students, however, failed.

expulsion)," Fanelli told Dickey. Fanelli was troubled, however, by the impression that the fate of the students was up to Dickey; Fanelli strongly urged the president to "clarify this matter," as soon as possible by explaining that their discipline was out of his hands.[42]

But the ebullience at newly liberated Parkhurst was misplaced. The arrest and relatively harsh sentences for the participants in the May 6 takeover had divided the faculty. In the late 1960s it had become an article of faith among liberal academics that police should not be invited onto a campus, no matter how severe the provocation. Since it was the specific goal of SDS to provoke arrests, they became inevitable. The only real question was how severe the provocations had to be before the administration would react. As events elsewhere showed, SDS was prepared to escalate its tactics beyond the tolerance of all but the most pliant administrators. As impracticable as it was, however, the no-police principle provided a ready source of outrage that fueled the protestors' goal of using the inevitable arrests to radicalize campuses.

On May 20, a letter signed by 22 Dartmouth faculty members denounced the Parkhurst arrests as an example of "unprecedented harshness towards . . . students." Describing the students who had forcibly ejected administrators and staff and nailed the doors of the building shut, the faculty members wrote:

> These are sincere, dedicated and thoughtful young people who are raising issues of crucial importance—issues that ought to be raised. Some of us did not approve of their taking over Parkhurst, but we feel that it is to their honor that they fervently want to stop the killing in Vietnam. To deal with them on the level of calling police armed with guns and dogs, and then having them locked up in cages is wrong. It shames our whole community.

One of the signatories was mathematics professor John Lamperti, who circulated a separate letter in which he described the sentencing of the students as "a radicalizing experience." "The sense of menace, of repression, of helpless individuals being crushed by the power of the State was overwhelming," Lamperti wrote.[43]

Answering Lamperti's jeremiad, Victor E. McGee, an associate professor of psychology, circulated a letter in which he said that reading Lamperti's letter, it was "hard to imagine that he was talking about those same individuals who forcibly ejected our president and our deans from

Parkhurst Hall; who willfully violated the guidelines for dissent . . . who categorically dismissed the opinions of the majority on campus, who fearlessly and foolishly attempt to force their opinion on all of us under the guise of superior moral conviction. . . ."[44] His comments were, interestingly, echoed by the valedictorian of the class of 1969, Kenneth I. Paul, who said: "This type of pitifully misguided action must be punished firmly. Learning ceases when the integrity of procedure is flouted. The President of Dartmouth College shall not be manhandled by would-be martyrs, anachronistic Trotskyites."[45] Indeed, student support for the radicals had evaporated with the Parkhurst bust. Many students had actually gathered to cheer the state troopers as they arrested the occupiers.

But faculty opinion was another matter. If Lamperti represented radical opinion, it soon became apparent that even liberals and moderates were backing away from support for the administration. Some argued that because of the jail terms, it would be double-jeopardy for the students to face College disciplinary charges. Others demanded outright amnesty.

By the end of the month, History Professor Charles Wood had obtained 80 signatures on a faculty petition urging the College's disciplinary panel to acknowledge the College's tradition of leniency and the fact that the demonstrators had been motivated by high moral principle. Citing the precedent of the Wallace disturbances of 1967, in which the students had been suspended, but readmitted at their request, the 80 faculty members urged the disciplinary panel to impose only token penalties.[46]

Although there was continuing pressure for the College to take firm action, the mood among faculty had clearly changed dramatically in the aftermath of the arrests and it was reflected in the penalties handed down by the Committee on Standing and Conduct. Of the 40 students charged with violating the policy on free expression and dissent, only one—David Green—was expelled. Two were suspended for a year; four were suspended but reinstated in time to graduate in June. Beyond that, the committee handed down the mildest penalties possible: 27 students were placed on "college discipline," five were acquitted, and one withdrew from college altogether.[47] The two faculty members who were also charged fared less well. Both were suspended and since neither had tenure, the move effectively ended their careers at Dartmouth.

More important, however, than the lenient penalties was the shift of attitudes about the Parkhurst takeover. Within a year, the apparently successful handling of the incident had been transmuted into one of the administration's starkest failures. In February 1970, *The Dartmouth* described the handling of the Parkhurst Hall takeover as marking "the ultimate failure of the Dickey administration during its last years to effectively reach the undergraduate body."[48]

The lesson of the revisionist version of the takeover was very clearly in the mind of the man who was, by then, his successor.

CHAPTER
XIII

A CASE OF FREE SPEECH

Dartmouth's resolve to defend free speech was put to an early test. On October 15, 1969, many of Dartmouth's classes were suspended so that students and faculty members could attend workshops held in conjunction with the anti-war moratorium that day. In a statement issued the previous week, Carroll Brewster, the dean of the College and Leonard Rieser, the dean of the faculty, had declared that "every effort will be made to respect the feelings of individuals who for personal reasons of personal conviction decide not to attend classes or teach on" October 15. The College, they announced, "will try to accommodate this activity in a way which does not infringe on the rights of those who do not wish to participate."[1]

On the same day—while the College was showing its tolerance for anti-war activities—25 to 30 black students prevented Nobel laureate William Shockley from speaking at an academic conference on the Dartmouth campus. The incident and its aftermath dramatized the fragility of the College's policy on free expression and the tenuous nature of the racial accommodation of the spring.

The occasion of Shockley's appearance was a three-day meeting of the nation's most prestigious academic organization, the National Academy of Sciences. By longstanding tradition, any NAS member may submit papers he wishes to read at the meeting. Shockley, a professor at Stanford, submitted two abstracts. One was entitled, "Hidden Momentum Consistency for Amperian Current Sources of Magnetization." But the controversy centered around his second paper, whose title, "Offset Analysis Description for Racial Differences," belied its explosive contents. In it, Shockley discussed what he believed was evidence of inherited genetic differences between the races.*

Reflecting their contempt for Shockley's academically questionable sortie into genetics and race, officials of the NAS scheduled his paper for the last session on the final day of the conference, with the explicit hope that so many people would have left by the time Shockley spoke that the physicist would attract little attention.

But local papers, including the inflammatory *Manchester Union-Leader*, had given Shockley considerable advance publicity, apparently solicited by Shockley himself.[2] By the day of the speech it was obvious the NAS strategy would not succeed. A flier written by two Dartmouth SDS members (one of whom, Guy Brandenburg, had been arrested in the takeover of Parkhurst Hall and put on "college discipline" for a year) denounced Shockley as a racist and denied that he had the right to speak on campus.

"Free Speech" Obscures the Issue
We believe that Mr. [sic] Shockley should not be permitted to give his lecture because it would hurt rather than serve the people. We think that speech—and the freedom to use it—is good when it is employed to help people fight a common enemy and to better their conditions of life; but that speech is a bad thing when it is used to spread racist lies that divide people who need to be united.[3]

College officials recognized that the speech would be a crucial test of the Policy on Free Expression and Dissent. Dean Paul Shafer contacted Professor Jonathan Mirsky, who was then acting as faculty advisor to SDS, to ask whether he knew of any plans to disrupt the speech. Mirsky claimed he knew of none. Sometime later in the day, however, Mirsky later recounted, he met several black students who said they "regarded Shockley's attitude and *presence* as deeply insulting."[4] Administrators,

---

* Shockley's first paper was read without incident on October 13.

meanwhile, tried to calm tensions by assuring black students that faculty members would be on hand to refute Shockley's contentions.[5]

Two hundred spectators gathered for Shockley's speech on the 15th. Before his introduction, a statement by the president of the NAS effectively repudiating Shockley's views was read to the audience.*

When Shockley was introduced, 25 to 30 black students and a scattering of white students rose to their feet and began clapping. And kept clapping. Faculty members and administrators pleaded with the students to let Shockley speak. When he was unable to win quiet to make a statement, Professor John Kemeny wrote a message on a chalkboard, saying, "I am chairman of the Committee on Equal Opportunity. If you do not let me speak, you are ruining all the gains so far." When the clapping stopped, Kemeny urged the students to let Shockley speak, repeating his private comments that "I intend to show everyone that what Shockley says is junk." Kemeny was followed by a black student who also pleaded with the students to stop, and by Claire Ehrmann, a lecturer in Romance languages, who told the black students, "If we want Reverend Jackson to speak here, if we want the Black Panthers' representatives to speak here, we must let this man speak—it's as simple as that—and we must repudiate his arguments. . . . That's all there is to it. If we want to be free on a campus, let everybody speak."[6]

Jonathan Mirsky now rose, not to defend Shockley's right to speak, but to urge white students to walk out on Shockley or to stand in protest as a show of sympathy for "the pain the blacks feel."[7] The clapping resumed and after a while, officials abruptly adjourned the meeting. Just before the meeting ended, Dean Carroll Brewster spoke to the audience about what was at stake. "What has happened here is so grave," he said, "that I find it difficult to express my concern. You all know how I and most of us feel on the issue. But you don't fight an idea by trying to hide an idea. . . ."[8]

Mirsky took a different view. Having argued earlier that military

---

* "As a member of the National Academy of Sciences elected in 1951 in recognition of his research contributions in solid state physics," the statement said, "Dr. William Shockley has the privilege of addressing the Academy on matters he believes deserving of interest. . . ." But, the NAS statement said, Shockley "has offered no new research program and no new approach" to the field of psychometrics and had confused available data with "views concerning the management of welfare" and concluded by stating that "the NAS does not endorse his recommendations."

recruiters did not deserve free speech protection, he now added certain views on race to his list of unprotected speech: "Shockley should have been 'allowed to speak'—if a white person makes the judgment. For a black, no."

Mirsky charged that the NAS decision to let Shockley speak demonstrated "reckless insensitivity," and he accused white faculty of caring less about the "feelings" of black students than about their actions. Mirsky flatly denied that limiting speech would backfire on left radicals, because "their *words* are not, for their audience, part of a long history of slavery, murder, and exploitation. Shockley appears a genuine threat to blacks." By "merely" clapping, Mirsky wrote, the blacks showed "moderation," while the faculty members who pleaded for Shockley's academic freedom showed "inertia, insensitivity, and perhaps a bit of cowardice."[9]

Seventeen students, all black, were charged with violating the policy on free expression. Administrators were fully aware of the stakes. The day after the incident, the peripatetic A. Alexander Fanelli, special assistant to the president, wrote a private memo to Dean Rieser saying that "it seems to me we need a *formal statement* of some kind by a responsible officer of the College regarding the seriousness of the incident with Shockley to underline the fact that a university cannot function if only some people have the right to speak and others are arbitrarily denied that right. The absence of such a clear statement would imply the College either condones or does not take seriously this violation of free speech." Professor William Smith, who had been an original member of the College's negotiating team with the AAS in the spring, pleaded with the administration to take a hard line. "If the College authorities and faculty do not condemn in word and deed, promptly and firmly, this outrageous denial of freedom of speech this institution will have lost its right to be considered an institution dedicated to academic freedom and free and open inquiry."[10] But again, the final disposition was out of the administration's hands. Moreover, the question quickly grew beyond simply free speech.

The full implications of Dickey's concessions to the Afro-American Society in the spring now became apparent. The 19th and final demand from the Afro-American Society had been the establishment of a separate black judicial committee to hear all disciplinary matters involving black students—in effect, judicial apartheid at Dartmouth. Instead of rejecting the separatist demand out of hand, the administration compromised, creating a Judicial Advisory Committee for Black Students (JAC) and gave black students the right to request the JAC to investigate any charges and to make recommendations to the College Committee on Standards and Conduct (CCSC).

Although it was only advisory, the College had accepted the principle of judicial apartheid and had institutionalized it in College rules and procedures. That committee was now in place, heavily dominated by radicals, including Jonathan Mirsky.

In the wake of the Shockley incident, leaders of the Afro-American Society met with Dean Carroll Brewster to inform him that the JAC's advisory status was no longer acceptable. The AAS was now demanding a fully autonomous separate judicial body. Brewster made it clear he would oppose any racial division of disciplinary matters.[11]

The next week, representatives of the AAS returned, this time with a memorandum unilaterally declaring that as of October 16, the CCSC "is no longer recognized as having control or power over the Black Judiciary Council and the Afro-American Society recognizes only the BJC" as having authority over black students.

"The above is not be seen as a 'demand' by the Dartmouth Afro-American Society, but rather as a statement of fact," the memo flatly declared.[12] The Afro-American Society had simply presented the College with what it regarded as a *fait accompli*, denying the authority of the College over black students.

Each of the 17 students was invited to appear before the CCSC to defend himself against the charges relating to the Shockley incident. None appeared. Instead, the Judicial Advisory Committee for Black Students—which now styled itself the Black Judicial Council—conducted its own "inquiry," and issued a 29-page report in late November.[13]

Declaring that the black students had acted "in self-defense," the committee completely exonerated all 17 students, recommending that all College charges be dropped. The committee argued that because Shockley's address was "defamatory" to blacks, "it could not claim the constitutional protection which the First Amendment affords and 'free speech,' academic or otherwise, is not an issue." The report accepted Mirsky's argument in full. The students, it said, "saw in Mr. [sic] Shockley's speech an attack on their future security and . . . we are convinced of the reasonableness of that fear."

"It is understandable," the committee declared, "that black students felt they had to rely on their own resources to prevent a damaging attack on themselves or their race. . . ." The report said that white faculty members and administrators "immediately lined themselves up both physically and rhetorically with Mr. [sic] Shockley. . . ." Given that environment, the students had no choice but to resort to "self-help."

Independent parties who examined the incident found the committee's logic specious and its finding without merit. After a detailed investigation of its own, even the left-leaning New Hampshire Civil Liberties Union concluded that Shockley "was denied his right of free speech." Declared the NHCLU: "Academic freedom is lost for all men once the practice is established of defining areas of heresy in which any man can be silenced and prevented from exercising freedom of speech."[14]

Legal experts contacted by the College also rejected the committee's findings.*

The continuing viability of the College's policy on free expression and dissent clearly demanded a statement by the College rejecting the selective-free speech arguments of the JAC. Instead, on December 4, the CCSC in issuing its findings, claimed to have found "extenuating circumstances." The committee handed down the mildest possible sanctions, placing the 17 students on "college discipline for one term, without restrictions." No attempt was made to answer the JAC report, except to say that "the report of the JAC is a serious one and has to be taken seriously."[15]

If the intention was to appease the Afro-American Society or the JAC,

---

* A private memo by Dean Carroll Brewster describes the reaction of Yale law professor Joseph Goldstein. The Yale professor "objected seriously" to the idea that blacks can only be judged by other blacks, an argument he found inherent in the JAC report. Moreover, Goldstein said, it was incumbent on any institution of higher education to vigorously protect the rights of any visiting scholar to investigate and teach whatever he chose. "Particularly, no such action as was taken against Shockley can be permitted by an institution, action which is clearly coercive and attempts to dictate how one teaches and does his work." Goldstein suggested two standards by which the College should measure discipline: (1) the protection of the integrity of the institution; and (2) the protection of the educational future of the student. Goldstein rejected any penalties less than suspension as a "firm statement about the future." (Memo to file by Dean Brewster, December 10, 1969)

it failed. All eight members of the black judicial panel resigned in protest, accusing the College of showing "an inflexible attitude."[16]

But their outrage could not conceal the fact that the College's decision in the Shockley case was an abject surrender of principle that effectively eviscerated the policy on free expression. It would cast a very long shadow.

CHAPTER
XIV

STRIKE

John Kemeny was named Dartmouth's 13th president on January 22, 1970, after a 16-month national search by a joint trustee-faculty committee. He had been on the Dartmouth faculty since 1952, one of the College's most brilliant, dynamic, and internationally famous acquisitions. An outstanding scholar, gifted teacher, and respected faculty leader, Kemeny was also to prove to be a paradox of sorts, a mercurial figure given to unexpected and often unannounced changes of direction.[1]

The new president was in every respect remarkable. Born in Budapest in 1926, Kemeny's family fled to the United States in 1940. At 14, Kemeny spoke fluent German and Hungarian and was comfortable with Latin. Although he knew no English when he was enrolled at New York City's George Washington High School, he graduated three years later—before his 17th birthday—first in his class of nearly 1,000. The next month, the young prodigy entered Princeton. Although his work there would be interrupted by service in the Army, he would graduate summa cum laude in 1947. By then, he had already established his mark on science.

In 1945, while still in the Army, Kemeny had been assigned to serve as a mathematician in the theoretical division of the Manhattan Project, based in Los Alamos, New Mexico. As the final touches were put on the first atomic bomb, Kemeny worked on some of the earliest prototypes of computers designed to solve complex theoretical and mathematical problems—a heady experience for an undergraduate and one that would shape the career of the future author of the computer language BASIC.

In 1946, he returned to Princeton, where he was elected to Phi Beta Kappa, and earned enough credits to graduate the next year with degrees in both mathematics and philosophy. While pursuing a doctorate at Princeton, he was selected as a research assistant by Albert Einstein, who recognized the talent of the brilliant young graduate student. Einstein put Kemeny to work on the development of his Unified Field Theory; and at one point, it appeared that the young assistant had achieved a stunning breakthrough by working out an improved version of the theory Einstein was formulating. But, as Kemeny himself later observed, his concept was "beautiful in its simplicity but, unfortunately, not consistent with the facts."

Despite that setback, Kemeny's academic career was exceptional both for its accomplishments and its diversity of interests. After obtaining his doctorate from Princeton, Kemeny was named to the Princeton faculty as Fine Instructor of Mathematics, specializing in logic, but two years later he shifted to the Department of Philosophy where he was named an assistant professor.

For Dartmouth, the young Hungarian mathematician/philosopher was a timely and triumphant acquisition. In 1953, when Kemeny was given a dual appointment as Professor of Mathematics *and* Philosophy, he symbolized Dartmouth's commitment to revitalize itself with a new breed of faculty member. Almost all of the senior members of the mathematics department were in the process of retirement, so it fell to Kemeny to rebuild and reshape it. From 1954 to 1966, he chaired the department, recruiting an entirely new faculty and inaugurating a doctoral program in mathematics that was the first program of its type in the Faculty of Arts and Sciences. As a leader of the faculty, he played a central role in the various revisions of the curriculum, and as a member of the board of governors of the Mathematical Association of America and chairman of its panel on teacher training, Kemeny played a key role in the formulation and propagation of the "New Math" throughout the nation's schools. He also found time to develop BASIC and co-design the College's pioneering computer time-sharing system. By the late 1960s, as Dickey faded from the scene, few members of the College community had more influence. In the years immediately preceding his election as president, he had served as Coordinator of Educational Plans and Development, had chaired the College's Committee on Equal Opportunity, and served on the ad hoc committee studying Dartmouth's educational programs—with special attention to the question of educating women.

Despite that auspicious prologue, Kemeny's presidency was quickly plunged into the radicalism of the era. The announcement on April 30, 1970, that U.S. troops had entered Cambodia signalled the beginning of another spring of chaos for colleges and universities that were already reeling under waves of campus protests, some directed at supporting the Black Panthers. (Yale, for example, mobilized in "solidarity" with Panthers charged with the murder of a young black man, Alex Rackley.)*

President Kemeny's reaction to the Cambodian invasion and threats to go on strike was difficult to predict. He had opposed a faculty resolution denouncing the war in the fall of 1969, arguing that it was inappropriate for the College to take political positions because such action was "coercive to the minority." On any political issue, he said, "the president should separate his personal views from institutional policy."[2]

A year and a half earlier, Kemeny had urged stiff penalties against SDS protestors who had obstructed Army recruiters. As late as May 2, it appeared he would oppose any strike at Dartmouth. Speaking to the annual meeting of class officers, he described how he had met with a delegation of seven student leaders earlier in the day.

> I think you can be very proud that we have student leadership of this caliber and that this campus is willing to work to solve this very difficult issue . . . without blowing up the campus, *without going on strike as several of our sister institutions are,* and without coming to a terrible confrontation.[3] [Emphasis added.]

---

* Rackley was bound, gagged, and tortured before being shot twice, in the head and the chest. His mutilated body was found in a marsh near Middlefield. Another Panther implicated Panther leader Bobby Seale in the murder, claiming he had given the order to "off the pig." Some of the defendants later confessed to their role in the torture/ murder of Rackley, and Seale was freed as a result of a hung jury. But in the spring of 1970, the innocence of the Panthers was a matter of blind faith among campus radicals.

He was apparently misinformed. The next day, a Sunday, 300 Dartmouth students and faculty met and called for an all-college meeting to vote on whether to join the coming national student strike. As originally envisioned, the strike was to center on three major "demands": that the United States immediately and unilaterally withdraw all troops from Southeast Asia; that the U.S. end "its systematic repression of political dissidents, and release all political prisoners, such as Bobby Seale, and other members of the Black Panther Party" [presumably without trial]; and finally that universities "end their complicity with the United States war machine by an immediate end to defense research, ROTC, counterinsurgency research and all other such programs." At the meeting on Sunday night, the last two demands were dropped; but the second, relating to black repression, was restored the next day (but not before black students had withdrawn their support for the strike). In its final form, the strike call demanded the "immediate withdrawal of American troops and support" from South Vietnam and Cambodia and called for an end to "repression of the black community and of dissenters."[4]

A spokesman for the group's steering committee said that professors would be urged to suspend regular classes and devote their class time to discussion of the strike issues. The goal of the strike, a spokesman said, was "to try to close Dartmouth down, in its normal workings and open it up for a meaningful focus on the issues of the strike."

The Dartmouth, in effect, turned itself into an organ of the strike committee by publishing an editorial (also published in student papers at Brown, Cornell, Princeton, Harvard, Penn, and Columbia) endorsing the shut-down of the College, arguing that "the significance of classes and examinations pales before the greater problems outside the classroom." With more passion than logic, it insisted that a strike "recognizes that within a society so permeated with inequality, immorality, and destruction, a classroom education becomes a hollow, meaningless exercise."[5]

The strike leaders were not asking for a strike *against* Dartmouth, as much as a strike *by* Dartmouth—the politicization of the institution at the expense of its academic mission.

The vote on the strike was scheduled for 10 A.M., Tuesday, May 5. But by then the issue had been decided: the campus had been shut down, classes cancelled, and the strikers' main goals implicitly endorsed—by the President of Dartmouth, John Kemeny.

It was a stunning reversal for a man who had only a few months ago explicitly rejected the politicization of the College; and who had appeared to rule out a strike less than 48 hours earlier.

After the meeting of the strike committee on Sunday night, a delegation of five students contacted Kemeny and went to his house for a midnight meeting. Kemeny peppered the students with questions: How long would their strike last? What activities did they plan? How would they handle non-strikers? The students explained their plans to launch anti-war canvassing throughout the state and indicated that they envisioned a two or three week shutdown. An account by two strike leaders recalls:

> In the course of the one-and-one-half hour meeting Kemeny switched from being the devil's advocate to exploring the possibilities of the kind of strike that was being proposed. He thought through some of the problems out loud and suggestions as well as criticisms came from all quarters. Mrs. Kemeny was present and made a very strong argument to her husband that the community was facing a serious crisis and that there were times when even an institution such as Dartmouth had to break out of its traditional posture and respond.
>
> By the time the meeting had ended Kemeny had made it clear that he was actively considering his own role in the proposed strike, although he gave no hint as to what it might be.[6]

Throughout the next day, Kemeny met with College officials and department chairmen. He also had a second meeting with student strike leaders, who left "convinced that he would not actively oppose the plans they had outlined to him."[7]

The takeover of Parkhurst and its aftermath was a precedent very much in everyone's mind. The College's forceful reaction to what had been a provocative act by a handful of radicals trying to impose their will on the community, was now seen by the students and some faculty as "an unnecessary and harmful confrontation" that had symbolized the breakdown in communication between the administration and students.[8] Kemeny had come into office pledging to improve communication; the failure and isolation of Dickey's administration was taken as an instructive lesson. That night, Kemeny announced the strike.

"There comes a time," Kemeny declared in a radio broadcast, "when there are priorities over and beyond that which we have traditionally considered the fundamental purpose of the institution." Kemeny announced the suspension of all normal academic activities for the rest of the week. The next day, May 5, would be set aside as a "day of mourning" and "soul-searching" for the students killed at Kent State, while the rest of the week would be devoted to what Kemeny described as "education of the deepest form" during which the College would "engage in a collective exercise of formulating plans for the future."[9]

He began his address, paradoxically, by reminding his listeners of his recent declaration that "institutions as such cannot effectively take stands on controversial issues," and that as president he had to separate his own sentiments from the official position of the College. Having insisted he could not commit the College to a political stance, he then proceeded to commit the College to the strike, which he called "an attempt . . . to unite the entire community in joint effort to see whether all of us together might be more effective in changing national policy than any group could be on its own."

In a radical departure from the standards of academic comity, Kemeny did not call for a debate, but rather for "united action" and the development of "collective wisdom." It was unclear what role he envisioned for those students and faculty who might not adopt the "collective wisdom" or who chose to dissent from the united front he envisioned. There is no hint in his remarks of concern for the coerced minority that he himself had cited only months before.

In what amounted to a litany of collective guilt, Kemeny declared that "civilization in this country has reached a stage that I find totally intolerable," managing to touch on the problems of poverty and hunger ("that could be easily eliminated"); urban decline; the failure of the civil rights movement ("too slow, too little, and too late"); and the "scandalous record of this country" in the treatment of American Indians. He continued the theme discussing the tragic deaths at Kent State, declaring that "all of us are at fault."

Kemeny announced that he had joined a number of academic leaders by signing a statement that urged the president "to take immediate action to demonstrate unequivocally your determination to end the war quickly."

Kemeny urged "as large an attendance as possible" at the strike meeting set for the next morning and called a general faculty meeting for the next evening. Kemeny made it clear he did not envision that the meeting would have the form or the substance of a democratic or open debate. There would be no "parliamentary rules and motions and de-bates on small points of wording," he said, *"because the issues are too serious."* This was not, of course, strictly logical. The gravity of the issue and the passions it had aroused made the democratic guarantees embodied in the rules and motions and debate absolutely essential for a fair and free discussion; by declaring them irrelevant, Kemeny was endorsing a thoroughgoing politicization of the mechanism of College governance. He couched this amazing anti-democratic *coup d'etat* in religious terms. He envisioned the faculty meeting, he said, to be held "somewhat in the style of a Quaker meeting," where presumably the collected faculty would sit in silence and wait for God to discuss the strike issues with them.

Kemeny said that as he listened to the students and faculty radicals, the word "unity" had appeared again and again. along with "frustra-tion" over the difficulty of bringing it about. He could, of course, have pointed out that this frustration over the lack of unity on a political issue as divisive as the war was a sign of intellectual pluralism and diversity of opinion—the mark of an institution committed to liberal learning. Instead, he came to the conclusion "that indeed we are in extraordinary times, that it is indeed a time when the community should take united action, and if there is anyone who can bring such united action about it is the President of the College."*

So that the strike would be complete, Kemeny also urged all College administrators to "do whatever they can to make it possible for all employees of Dartmouth College to participate in the discussions" (outside of the faculty few Dartmouth staff were to take Kemeny up on his offer; most shunned strike activities).[10]

To appreciate the radical departure of Kemeny's action, one need look no further than the eloquent statement issued nine months earlier by the Committee Advisory to the President, which reaffirmed the apolitical character of the liberal college. The signatories, including several senior faculty members, declared that

> a university cannot adopt an official moral stand on a political or
> other issue outside the institutional framework by majority vote (or
> *a fortiori* by minority coercion), without forfeiting its place among

---

* Kemeny's emphasis on "unity" is notable because of its implications for the evolving definition of "diversity," which was to be a trademark of his administration.

the primary institutions in our society where an individual can freely assume his own moral stance.

The university, whose essential function it is to investigate and teach, is one enterprise where the individual moral beliefs of its members are *not* overlaid and possibly misrepresented by official standards. Other independent organizations exist or can be formed in order to promulgate specific moral persuasion, and one must endeavor to preserve the university as the ultimate forum for debating individual morality.[11]

Kemeny had wholeheartedly endorsed that posture in the fall, making his conversion now all the more surprising.

The morning following his speech more than 2,500 students and faculty voted to participate in what was now in effect a presidential-strike. Normal campus activities were replaced with strike "workshops" that were scheduled throughout the day. Classes on the history of nation states, the rise and fall of civilizations, on Montaigne, Mill, Montesquieu, and Shakespeare were suspended. Meanwhile, in Spaulding Auditorium, strike-related films were shown continuously, including "Interview with Bobby Seale" and "Off the Pig," (both on the Black Panthers); "People's War" and "Vietnam, Land of Fire" (both filmed in North Vietnam); and, somewhat incongruously, "Isle of Youth," a Cuban-made film glorifying Castro's Caribbean paradise. Workshops ranged from "The Justification of Power," given by three faculty members, to more practical sessions, such as "Establishment of an Underground Railroad to Canada for Draft Resisters" and "Resisting the Military."* A fast was held to raise money for the Black Panther Party.[12]

Professor Jonathan Mirsky, who had argued against the right of either military recruiters or Dr. Shockley to speak on campus, now had an audience of more than 1,000 at his own seminar on Cambodia in which he expounded on the strike's main goal, "the liberation of the oppressed."[13] Despite Mirsky's record as an outspoken opponent of political tolerance, the June issue of the *Alumni Magazine* called Mirsky "the embodiment of moral conviction."

An almost giddy emotionalism seemed to have gripped the faculty. In

---

* Other workshops included: "Methods of Tax Protest," "White Racism and Oppression in America," "Psychological Factors in Racism," "What Can Be Done to End Racism," "Political Repression in the United States," "Impeachment Technique," "Has Democracy Failed?," and "Dartmouth Complicity."

a letter later sent to the parents of Dartmouth students, a faculty member was quoted as saying of the strike, "This has been the most exciting day of my life at Dartmouth."[14] The mood of the week was reflected in a diary kept by Sociology Professor James A. Davis, one of the strike's most enthusiastic supporters.

> SUNDAY NIGHT, MAY 3, "Telephone calls . . . meeting . . . do something! . . . End up at a strike committee meeting in Bartlett Hall. Fantastic organization the strike committee. . . . Never saw a more democratic and efficient committee. . . .
>
> MONDAY. Meetings, meetings, meetings. Cancelled a class for political reasons for the first time in my life. . . . Long, long meeting of strike committee Monday night, Tuesday morning rather. Astounding. Left, center, right, all working in harmony (*actually there isn't any right among Dartmouth students*, but they would have been welcome). . . .
>
> TUESDAY. . . . Several lost days here. (Maryssa Gerassi later said, "It was the longest and shortest week I can remember.") . . . I remember a few meetings last spring during the Parkhurst events . . . a million years ago. Not the same College.[15]

Throughout the strike, Kemeny tried to put the best face on events, insisting on the strike's educational value, while downplaying its political dimensions. Those pretensions were undermined somewhat when *The Dartmouth* editorialized that: "our purpose was not to learn something but to *change* something—the destructive policies of the Nixon administration which cause war abroad and repression at home."[16]

Privately, at least, Kemeny realized that. Despite his non-political public stance, he personally drafted a plan to modify the academic calendar in the fall for the specific purpose of giving students "a mid-fall vacation just before election day," so they could campaign for anti-war candidates.[17]* His plan was apparently inspired by Princeton's ambi-

---

* Kemeny's proposals for campaign holidays may have been one the factors that drew an urgent warning that the shift toward overt College involvement in politics could imperil the College's tax-exempt status. On June 4, Comptroller James W. Stevens wrote to all faculty, officers, and students: "A number of students and faculty, either individually or in organized groups, are engaged in political activities which might be interpreted as being for the purpose of influencing legislation or as participating in political campaigns on behalf of candidates for public office. It is vitally important that Dartmouth College as an institution, as distinguished from its students, faculty and staff, not be involved in any of these activities."

tious political program. Princeton's faculty not only voted to actively support political campaigns to elect doves and defeat hawks, but voted to turn over its research facilities, including the computers at the University's Woodrow Wilson School of Public and International Affairs, to student campaigners.[18]*

During the week of the strike Kemeny was clearly exulting in his role as campus hero. On Friday night the president of Dartmouth College showed up at a fund-raising concert by the rock band The Youngbloods, told the students how proud he was of them, and threw a lemon to the audience—a derisive reference to a conservative newspaper's comment that Kemeny was "a lemon." Reported the *Alumni Magazine*:

> A thunderous standing ovation ensued and the normally undemonstrative Kemeny was seen to give two short waves as he made his way across the dirt floor to the exit. Only when he and his wife Jean had completely left the field house did the applause finally die down.[19]

It is a measure of the excitement of the week that Religion Professor Hans Penner afterward discussed naming the lemon tree as the College's new symbol.†

On Friday morning students voted to continue the strike. The continuation of the strike beyond Kemeny's original one week of soul-searching resulted in another hasty adjustment by Kemeny and the faculty. At a faculty meeting on May 8, the faculty voted "by a near-unanimous voice vote," to award full credit for course work as of May 4; students could complete the course work for a grade, but they were given until September to do so. Students who wished to pursue political action rather than complete their studies were free to do so without penalty. The strike newsletter exulted that the "immediate 'strike enemy'— academic responsibility—has been removed by faculty resolution."[20]

Describing the attitude of the faculty, Professor Davis wrote "You

---

* In a memo to Professor Robin Robinson, Kemeny said he had "been playing around with the 1970-71 calendar to see what modifications might be feasible. I have come up with one scheme and you may be able to come up with a much better one." Kemeny's original idea was to have a mid-fall recess from October 23 to November 4, and cancel Thanksgiving vacation. If fall term classes began on September 21 and ended on December 12, Kemeny wrote, "we would break almost exactly even."

† Faculty members later presented Kemeny with a lemon tree as a token of their admiration.

don't just give orders to 3,200 young men who showed the idealism, initiative, and good sense Dartmouth students did this week. You don't issue orders to your partner."[21]

The strike quickly fizzled out, but looking back over the week, the strike newsletter noted with satisfaction, "Last week this entire community became politicized."[22]

Faculty members like Hans Penner agreed, but carried the lesson even further. "Let us admit that the notions of a neutral community," he later wrote, "of the intellect exercising itself for itself alone, of a discipline relative only to itself, are false when they are taken as characterizing the academic community."[23]

The effort of more sober analysis was left to Jeffrey Hart. The English professor had continued teaching throughout the strike, announcing that all of his classes would meet as usual. Hart insisted that *from an academic point of view*, the works of Samuel Johnson were more important than Cambodia or Kent State. Hart recalled that at least 80 percent of the students in his class continued to attend despite the strike.

Afterward, amid the lingering euphoria, Hart was virtually alone in noting that Dartmouth had "crossed an invisible line" and by doing so had opened for the first time the question of whether Dartmouth was going to remain a serious educational institution. The message of the occupiers of Parkhurst Hall the year before had been that the political demands of the protestors were more important than the academic activity of the College. But, Hart noted, that had been the action of a small minority of students and faculty. He contrasted that with the 1970 strike.

Given the inflamed emotions—"absurdly inflamed in my view"—it may well have been prudent to suspend classes, Hart said.

> But what was the *meaning* of that suspension? The suspension could only signify that the primacy of politics was being asserted *inside* the college as an institution. Thus, in various gatherings, Cambodia could be discussed and discussed at great length; but the normal classes in Samuel Johnson had to cease. For some mysterious reason the political matter could not be discussed outside of class hours, in the afternoon or in the evening. It had to replace classes. The meaning of this could scarcely be clearer. *Politics had moved into primacy, temporarily at least, within an educational institution.* [Emphasis added.] The genuinely disturbing thing— the line that was crossed—was the acquiescence of the academic community, an acquiescence almost total, in that meaning.[24]

CHAPTER

HANGOVER IN HANOVER

John Kemeny's first years in office could not have posed a sharper contrast with the final years of John Sloan Dickey's administration. Not since Hopkins had there been a leader with a clearer academic agenda or—at the beginning of his tenure—more ambitious to place his mark on the curriculum. Kemeny was a creature of the new academic culture but he was intellectually acute enough to be troubled by it.

As he took office, Kemeny seemed to aim at nothing less than an institutional renewal; he proposed innovations that might have reversed or at least stemmed the trends that were eroding the liberal arts traditions at Dartmouth. But ultimately he failed; and his failure marked the degree to which both the culture and politics of the College had changed.

Since at least the late 1960s, the weaknesses in Dartmouth's curriculum had been evident. Professor Raymond Barratt, who lead an abortive reform movement, had noted the new atmosphere on campus and the growing academization of the faculty. "The needs of the student are overlooked as compared to the strong emphasis on professionalism," he had charged.

By the early 1970s, the need for a revival of the liberal arts at Dartmouth was acute. Kemeny tried to rise to the occasion. In a speech entitled, "The Future of Liberal Arts Education at Dartmouth," Kemeny warned against the seemingly endless proliferation of courses and the fragmentation of the curriculum. His central premise, "We cannot teach everything," echoed Hopkins' own inaugural address that warned against curricular "sprawl."[1] What followed was an unusually sharp critique both of Dartmouth's curriculum and its yearning for the status of a full-fledged university:

> Why then do we have a tremendous urge for completeness in departmental offerings? Why is it that no self-respecting history department would be without an expert in the history of Afghanistan? Why is it absolutely necessary to have an expert on every single musical instrument or an expert in every branch of mathematics that has ever been invented? These pressures lead to a proliferation of courses and a fragmentation of the curriculum. As a result, the catalog contains a tremendous number of specialized courses. This may possibly enhance the reputation of our departments but it is a major disservice to the student and, after all, it is the students that the curriculum is designed to serve.[2]

The drive for completeness and comprehensiveness, Kemeny recognized, would eventually extinguish the common mission of the College. If the faculty is built on the premise that it must have experts in each sub-area of every specialty, he said, "you get to the point where members of a department cannot talk to each other about their interests." And because the experts now speak only their own language, no other professors are competent to "pinch-hit" in courses outside of their immediate expertise. "Eventually," Kemeny noted, "one reached the regrettable situation in which individual courses are owned by individual faculty members."[3]

One of the most popular arguments for this endless duplication of course offerings was that without a comprehensive curriculum, Dartmouth would be unable to attract good students. "My response," Kemeny said, "is that most good students go elsewhere."

The challenge for Dartmouth was to provide an "overview of the breadth of human knowledge and activity." He was direct in his critique of Dartmouth's current curriculum, which merely required students to take four courses each in the humanities, sciences, and social sciences.

Kemeny bluntly labelled the scheme, "basically a *smorgasbord* approach. . . . The student samples a little of this and a little of that, and one hopes that it all adds up to a great meal."[4]

The flaw was fundamental. Why, he asked, were the distribution requirements built around the arbitrary division of knowledge into three categories? The division of the faculty into humanities, sciences, and social sciences was for strictly "administrative purposes," Kemeny said, "and at least to my mind they do not in a natural way correspond to divisions of human knowledge."

"Perhaps," he quipped, "it would make equally good sense to require each student to take four courses from the most senior members of the faculty, four courses from middle-age faculty members, and four courses from junior faculty members."

Kemeny insisted that he had no magic plan and that there was no foolproof design for the curriculum. But he set out his own vision broadly, in terms that sounded suspiciously like general education. He wanted to see "course sequences for non-specialists" in the major areas of human knowledge.

> And by an area I mean something more meaningful and more homogenous than a division. I see nothing magic in three. I don't know whether there should be seven, eight, or nine major areas into which one partitions human knowledge. I would like to see all of the faculty within an area cooperate in the development of first-rate course sequences, specifically for the non-specialists, and I would like to see each student explore several such areas in some depth.[5]

The major barrier to such reform, Kemeny said, were the graduate and professional schools, whom he called "the villains of the piece." They were the main impetus, he said, for placing strong requirements of pre-professional training on students that had eroded undergraduate interest in general education.

Kemeny brought to his critique of specialization the powerful example of his own career. When faculty members or students insisted that the primary role of higher education was to prepare them for today's world, Kemeny could point out that although he was a world-renowned computer expert, he had never had a class in computers or computer science. "The reason is very simple," Kemeny later said, "when I went to college and graduate school, there weren't any computers."[6]

What he *had* gotten, he insisted was an education whose breadth enabled him to adapt his skills to changing technological circumstances. "There was something about the way we learned to think, something about the way we learned to attack new problems and the fact that we were able to come up with some completely original new ideas that allowed us to make these breakthroughs." No amount of vocational or highly specialized professional training can do that, Kemeny insisted.

His point was direct: if the College prepared students only for the present, their knowledge "would be useless 25 years from now." In fact, he said, "we have too many specialists who are specialists and nothing else. . . . And there is enormous danger that we keep training our specialists in more and more narrowly specialized areas." As his own career testified, "problems have an annoying habit of cutting across a spectrum of different disciplines. . . ."[7] But even though that meant an ever-growing need for individuals capable of somehow drawing together and synthesizing this knowledge, it was instead being fragmented and compartmentalized.

The only counterweight to this tendency was the liberal arts education, which Kemeny saw as "the best possible training for decision makers."[8] If Kemeny's defense of the liberal arts from a scientist's point of view was provocative, he was also not hesitant to raise the issue of the relationship of morality and higher education at a time when the connection was regarded by his colleagues with embarrassed silence.

Citing the spread of public immorality in the mid-1970s, Kemeny said that "it is clear that specialized vocational education is not the answer to returning to a more moral path." Again, only a liberal education held out that prospect:

> A liberal education that places stress on the historical values, on questioning of the present system, no matter what that system may be, and on examining our own values, still seems to be the best hope of returning our civilization to fundamental principles of morality.[9]

At times, he even could sound like a proto-Allan Bloom, as when he derided the "complete permissiveness" of an educational system that encourages student to "question everything—which perhaps is good— but to believe nothing, which I certainly do not consider good."[10] He again cited personal experience to make his point.

> My daughter who is about to enter college, said to me not long ago
> that she knows it is wrong but the way she was taught in school it is
> just terribly difficult for her to have faith in anything at all, and she
> desperately wishes she could have faith in something.[11]

Kemeny's ambitions for the curriculum were evident in his inaugural address, delivered on March 1, 1970, in which he declared that the "faculty is too fragmented; there are too many walls," and announced the formation of a presidential commission to develop "constructive plans for the reorganization of the faculty."[12] It was also a clear indication of Kemeny's own conception of the role of the president: he was not content to be either a caretaker or fund-raiser. He was positioning himself in the tradition of presidents like Harvard's Eliot, Chicago's Hutchins, and Dartmouth's Hopkins who were the intellectual leaders of their institutions and architects of fundamental restructuring.

Riding the crest of popularity from the strike, Kemeny had reason to be confident as he presented his Grand Strategy to the faculty. But confronting the College's academic departments was a far more complicated matter than taking on the president of the United States.

The style of leadership that seemed so dynamic when addressed to the issue of the strike suddenly seemed autocratic when the faculty's own interests were at issue. The scope of the changes Kemeny envisioned can hardly be overstated: he was challenging the intellectual and organizational basis of the culture that had grown up at Dartmouth over the last two decades. The kinds of sequential courses he envisioned had been rejected repeatedly by the faculty.

And they rejected them again.

Because Kemeny had tied his prestige so closely to the plan, its ignominious burial was especially bitter—and all the more painful for coming in his first year. In May 1970, he had been the "Golden Boy," a year later *The Dartmouth* quoted faculty critics who charged Kemeny was "becoming a one-man show," that his dealings with the faculty were "heavy handed" and often "cursory."[13]

Other efforts to reform Dartmouth's curriculum also fared poorly. Perhaps the most ambitious was a proposal for a two-year liberal arts program drawn up by two faculty members, Michael Platt of the English Department and Edson Chick of the German Department. The two professors designed their proposal to address "the current absence of purpose that afflicts the liberal arts college in America." They were concerned with the increasingly technical approach to education and expressed the hope that a new liberal arts course would "instill habits of reflection on those issues which are of fundamental significance for human life."

Based on the St. John's College Great Books program, their proposed course of study would take students in their first year from *Genesis* and Homer through Plato, Aristotle, Lucretius, Plutarch, Augustine, Aquinas, and Dante, including such non-traditional readings as *Njal's Saga* and Ibn Kaldun's *The Muqaddimah*. In the second year, students would study Montaigne, Machiavelli, Shakespeare, Bacon, Descartes, Hobbes, Pascal, Vico, Swift, Locke, Montesquieu, Hume, Adam Smith, Rousseau, Burke, and Tocqueville. Despite the broad sweep of the program, it also would have required intensive study of certain thinkers; four weeks were set aside for the *Iliad*; while 28 class days—almost 19 weeks—were devoted to Plato and Aristotle.

Under their plan, students would have spent two-thirds of their freshman and sophomore years on the liberal arts sequence. "Regular, intensive and continuous" writing assignments were an essential element of the program.[14]

Kemeny was initially sympathetic, providing money for Platt to teach a pilot course. But in 1972, the liberal arts proposal was flatly rejected by the faculty's Committee on Instruction. The committee gave three ostensible reasons for rejecting the course: (1) it was irrelevant; (2) there were no competent faculty members at Dartmouth who could teach it; and (3) it was superficial.

The first objection seemed a hangover from the 1960s, while the third objection of superficiality seemed to ignore the syllabus the two professors had drawn up. What was most striking was the claim that Dartmouth College simply had no faculty who could teach a basic course in the liberal arts.

"If indeed no teacher at Dartmouth College is competent to conduct a course in the greatest works of Western civilization," Dartmouth senior Algis Valiunas wrote in *The Dartmouth*, "then our teachers' education must be sadly lacking." Moreover, he noted, the faculty's reservations about its own competence "presumes—unwittingly, I suppose—that what now passes for a liberal education must in fact be merely a sham."[15]

Kemeny would serve as president until 1981, but his tenure saw no major revision in the distribution requirements or the organization of the faculty.

The fact that a president, popular with the faculty and students, with the backing of the trustees, with world-class scholarly credentials, and with a powerful vision, failed to make even a modest impact on the curriculum is powerful testimony to the inertia of the academic culture.

His pretensions to academic statesmanship and curricular leadership derailed, Kemeny became a bureaucrat—and a very effective one.

He might have had no alternative in any case. Along with virtually every other college and university president in the country he was faced with a new crisis: finances. Kemeny was to call the 1970s "the most prolonged financial crisis in the history of American higher education."[16] The era of retrenchment radically changed the agenda of academic administrators. The time when schools could experience rapid growth in faculty, staff, and academic programs had passed; and academia woke up after the Arab Oil embargo to a massive fiscal hangover. "While fortunately we never ran out of money," Kemeny later wrote, "neither did we have the luxury of forgetting financial problems even for a single year."[17]

For Kemeny, the financial constraints meant that the best Dartmouth could now hope for was to maintain what he called "a steady state," with the emphasis on maintaining the status quo, rather than embarking on new initiatives. "It has not been a period in which one could think of great new projects to launch," he wrote at the end of the decade.[18]

Colleges and universities in the mid-1970s seemed to fall back exhausted and depressed from the binges of the 1960s. Higher education was now obsessed with its financial well-being, as it had once been with politics.

For Kemeny and Dartmouth there was also the question of co-education. Or more precisely, the finances of co-education. Since the admission of women had the overwhelming support of students, faculty, and alumni alike, the central issue was how to admit women without drastically expanding the College. How, in other words, could Dartmouth add 1,000 women to 3,000 men without bankrupting the school?

The solution, known as the Dartmouth Plan (or D-Plan), was the masterpiece of Kemeny's administration, reflecting both his style and the priorities of the College. Kemeny resurrected old plans to run the College year round—creating a four-quarter school year that included the summer as a co-equal session. Under the plan, the student body would increase by 25 percent to 33 percent, while the faculty would increase by less than 15 percent from 1970-71 levels. The great selling point to students was the system's flexibility, permitting students to fashion their own schedules, and engage in off-campus activities. Graduation requirements were also further cut from 35 to 33.*

No other change during his administration, Kemeny would later write, was "comparable in magnitude to coeducation and year-round operation."[19]

The D-Plan was a singularly successful political stroke, but complaints about the new system came early and continued to grow in intensity. In 1976, one visiting committee concluded: "We are unanimous and strong in our conviction that quite regardless of the factors of economics and student population logistics, the quarter system as it exists in the Dartmouth Plan *impedes and probably makes impossible the coherent education of students in the Humanities*." [Emphasis added.] In 1978, an Evaluation Team of the New England Association of Schools and Colleges issued a devastating critique of the new plan. Virtually every area of "stress" on campus, it said, related to the D-Plan, "which imposes a relentless academic pace, disrupts the development of social relationships, and makes it difficult for Dartmouth's newly diverse student body to realize its identity." Other complaints were even harsher. The College's own committee on year-round education, the so-called Wright Committee, bluntly declared that the "pedagogical and educational disadvantages of the year-round system outweigh its advantages." And Professor Charles Wood, in a report to the faculty concluded after an eight-month study that it was "the greatest stumbling block to the realization of an enhanced intellectual and extracurricular life for students." In 1980, Duke University considered adopting a plan similar to Dartmouth's but after a closer look dropped the idea.[20]

Another byproduct of the D-Plan was the further fragmentation of the faculty itself. Because the faculty's teaching loads were divided among the various terms, the full faculty would never again be able to meet as a whole—too many were gone at any given time. "The Dartmouth Plan," quipped one faculty member, "was for you to be out of town."[21]

---

* The requirements were later restored to 35, which is the current requirement.

Despite the growing chorus of dissent, however, Kemeny dismissed his critics. "We made a large commitment to a significant increase in the student body and in new faculty," he said in 1980, "without building a huge number of new buildings. It is still true today that we cannot possibly accommodate anything like our present student body without our present plan in nine months of the year."[22]

He acknowledged faculty complaints that the year-round calendar had made research more difficult—they no longer had a summer term without students in which to pursue their scholarly activities. Some faculty members pushed for more generous sabbaticals. Kemeny had a different idea.

In his 10th annual report, Kemeny suggested that the problem could be solved if faculty members would simply be more zealous in protecting their leave time from interruptions. For example, he said, they should simply drop their committee activities. But more to the point, he urged faculty to be aggressive in avoiding students. Faculty, wrote the president, "should either not make themselves available to students in a term when they have no teaching obligations or limit such appointments to no more than two afternoons a week" —a remarkable statement from the academic leader of a liberal arts college where as Kemeny himself said in his inaugural address, "undergraduates will forever remain first-class citizens."[23]

CHAPTER

A QUESTION OF RACE

A significant number of black students matriculated at Dartmouth for the first time in 1968; Native Americans were actively recruited beginning in 1970; and starting with the class of 1976, women were admitted. Integrating the three groups into the Dartmouth family was not without its difficulties. It was hardest for black students. Isolated and overwhelmingly white, Hanover was not a popular location for many black students seeking an Ivy League education. Until 1968, Dartmouth had graduated a total of only 130 black students dating back to 1828. But Dartmouth did try to encourage minority attendance in the 1960s. In 1963, Dartmouth and a group of about 20 private preparatory schools had formed a consortium known as "A Better Chance" (ABC), for the express purpose of preparing promising minorities for college. In 1968, 18 ABC students applied at Dartmouth; 12 were admitted, nine actually matriculated. But by the late 1960s such efforts were no longer deemed sufficiently aggressive.

In the wake of the assassination of Martin Luther King, the College named a special Committee on Equal Opportunity, whose report (known as the McLane report) urged that Dartmouth move quickly to "substantially" increase the number of black students.[1] It also called for more active recruitment of black faculty and administrators. In 1968, Dartmouth had no black administrators and only a single black faculty member. The number of black students, however, quickly rose as the College moved aggressively into affirmative action. The class matriculating in 1968 included 29 blacks; in 1969, the number was 82. By 1976, Dartmouth had 306 black undergraduates.[2]

Throughout his administration, President Kemeny was to prove an enthusiastic and aggressive advocate of affirmative action at the College.* For Kemeny, the one glaring failure of the 1970 strike had been the lack of involvement by black students. If anything, the strike had only further alienated blacks who regarded the whole affair (with some justice) as an exercise in self-indulgence by their pampered white counterparts who were more concerned with avoiding the draft than with the problems of minorities.

The alienation of campus blacks was underlined when Cleveland Webber, the president of the Afro-American Society, failed to show up at the strike rally, even though he had been expected to speak. A former Chicago gang member before being admitted to Dartmouth at age 24, as a "special student," Webber summed up the black reaction to Kemeny's strike by writing:

> It didn't mean too much to us, the strike that is; it only meant that white students were allowed to participate earlier in their annual spring protest that was quite successful; successful in that it did lead to an earlier summer vacation and their day on the cover of

---

* His enthusiasm for quotas came in spite of the role of quotas in his own life. In 1920, the Hungarian regime of Admiral Horthy had passed racial laws restricting college admission, requiring "that the comparative numbers of entrants correspond as nearly as possible to the relative population of the various races and nationalities." The law was, of course, aimed at Jews, who would be limited to no more than five percent of the available places in the universities. It was thus one of the first steps that led to the mass emigration of Hungarian intellectuals, many of whom, like Kemeny, were to work on the Manhattan Project.

Dartmouth itself had a somewhat mixed record with quotas. Near the end of his presidency, Hopkins had acknowledged what many other Ivy presidents would have preferred to have kept quiet: the fact that the College had informally restricted the number of Jewish students admitted. Although Hopkins was more candid about the practice, he and Dartmouth were subjected to widespread criticism.

Time (fellow brothers of the world; thank you for letting me be
myself, uninhibited expression). . . . In the meantime Black people
(benignly neglected) are being genocided [sic]. . . .[3]

The repudiation of the strike by black students seemed to merely add
another layer of white guilt onto the already heavy burden the administration had assumed. Like many of their counterparts, Dartmouth's
leaders went out of their way to provide forums where they could be
reminded of their racial iniquities. One such forum was Dartmouth's
1970 Commencement, where, at the administration's behest, Wallace
Ford, a black senior delivered a "special address."

After 200 years of "oppression, 300 years of blood, 300 years of
brutal and inhuman treatment," Ford said, blacks should no longer be
surprised "by whatever America tries to do to us. . . . What goes around
comes around, *and it's time for the other folks to be surprised.*"[4]
[Emphasis added.] Parents attending the ceremony probably were.

A "PERCEPTION OF INSTITUTIONAL RACISM"

The McLane report, issued by Dartmouth's Committee on Equal Opportunity, had insisted that "It would be wrong to say that standards are
lowered or eased" for minorities "since most of the selection criteria used
for normal applicants are not applicable." A nice bit of sleight of hand.
The report went on to urge the College to "adjust to the individual needs"
of promising minority candidates and not force them to conform to the
traditional curriculum and expectations of the College, which the report
called "a traditional but arbitrary system. . . ." The "classical pattern is
not sacrosanct," the report said. "The educationally impoverished student from the ghetto, the Indian reservation or from the culturally deprived areas of rural New Hampshire and Vermont may require
something different from the classical pattern of collegiate education."

The bald statement that the traditional liberal arts education was not
necessarily suitable for minorities and other disadvantaged students
was, of course, remarkable. It was not at all self-evident, for example,
that a student from rural Vermont who may have been educationally or
culturally deprived should, in essence, remain so and would not benefit
from the College's liberal arts education.

The report's breezy dismissal of the traditional liberal arts curriculum as an "arbitrary system" was a direct attack on humanistic scholarship itself. The authors implied that academic standards were either capricious, erratic, and whimsical (the first definition of the term "arbitrary"), or autocratic, despotic, and tyrannical (the second generally accepted definition of the word). In either case, the report represented a decisive turning point for the College because it seemed to repudiate not merely the traditions, but the legitimacy of Dartmouth's educational program.

The McLane report provided official justification for the implicit lowering of academic standards in the name of racial diversity, and it sanctioned the argument that traditional education in the humanities had been arbitrarily created to served the class interests of white, Western males and was thus oppressive, racist, and patriarchal.

While the McLane report glossed over its subversion of the curriculum and the serious academic deficiencies of minority students, by 1976, the College could no longer ignore the substantial number of black dropouts and those with low grade point averages. The report noted that "the academic stanines of the black students are, on the average, substantially lower than those of the other students in the class. . . ." Almost a quarter of the black students were failing to graduate.[5]

A committee, headed by Stanley Smoyer, was formed to re-examine the issue. Its final report expressed concern "over indications that many blacks are not as well prepared, academically, as their white counterparts."

> This disparity puts them in an unfavorable, and perhaps unfair, position, not only academically, but in other phases of campus life. *The tensions created in a student by academic difficulties are likely to be reflected in his or her other campus activities and thus lead to general discontent.*[6] [Emphasis added.]

Brushing aside such concerns, the Smoyer committee called for an even more aggressive quota system to create a student body that would "more nearly reflect the racial composition of the nation." It also called on the faculty to begin discussing the imposition of a new requirement, under which all Dartmouth students would have to take a course "relating in some way to the Third World."

The tortured logic of both the McLane and Smoyer reports was shaped and prodded by the goal of having a student body that mirrored the racial makeup of the country as a whole—a position that represented the triumph of ideological optimism over demographics. The problem can perhaps be best illustrated using data from the late 1980s.

Not only was the proportion of black high school graduates significantly lower than for the population as a whole, but by 1985, only a little over a quarter of black high school graduates was enrolled in college. In raw numbers, there weren't enough academically prepared minority students to make proportional representation possible.

But the problem for an elite institution like Dartmouth was even more acute. Nationally in 1987, the average combined SAT score of white students was 926; the average score for blacks was 728.[7]

But at Dartmouth, 85 percent of the entering students finished in the top 10 percent of their high school classes, and the entering class had median SAT scores of 1330—*six hundred points above the national average for black students who took the test*. The goal of proportional representation—endorsed in both the McLane and Smoyer reports— simply ignored the magnitude of the disparity. There were, of course, high achieving minority students, but they were being eagerly recruited by other institutions as well.

The idea that a highly selective institution like Dartmouth could somehow abolish or rectify the massive disparities in the educational preparation of disadvantaged groups required a policy of placing political correctness ahead of intellectual integrity.

In 1976, it was left to a minority report of the Smoyer committee to point out that this quota could only be met by "the admission of substantially greater numbers of academic risk students," which "would be counterproductive to achievement of increased overall academic strength of black undergraduates."[8]

At the heart of the Smoyer report was the committee's contention that there existed at Dartmouth a "perception of institutional racism."[9] The basis of that charge was a report—known as the Redding report—by three undergraduates. As evidence of the charge of racism, however, the student report cited only four or five incidents over seven years and ignored statements from senior black faculty members who said they had not encountered instances of discrimination.[10]

The Smoyer report's acceptance of the "perception" of discrimination was described by the minority report as "unfounded . . . misleading and inappropriate."[11]

The lack of evidence was, however, beside the point. For the issue was now one of symbolic politics, which was entering into the curriculum itself.

BLACK STUDIES I: SAN FRANCISCO STATE

San Francisco State University's black studies program set the pattern for the new discipline. Some of the early faculty members hired for San Francisco's program had, at best, unorthodox qualifications. One woman who lacked a bachelor's degree was named an associate professor. Another had had his teaching credential revoked by the California public schools after it was found that he called his white students "honky," while addressing black students as "brother" and "sister." "But most incredible of all," recalled an observer asked to evaluate his teaching by the California State Department of Education, "he had his 'baby panthers' in uniform threaten white students right there in the classroom, particularly when they demonstrated that they knew more history than he did. They smacked a billy club into their open hands inches from the 'offender's' head at this teacher's signal." The teacher was, nevertheless, hired for San Francisco State University's black studies program and eventually became its chairman.[12]

San Francisco State's experience with black studies led to the proliferation of ethnic studies courses, and eventually to the creation of a School of Ethnic Studies. In 1981, San Francisco State created a new program of "general education." Its fate reflected the degree to which the concept of "general education" had been radically transformed in the years since 1945. One of the program's main purposes was to bail out the ethnic studies programs. Under the new program, students could meet requirements in the arts and humanities with courses such as "La Raza Cinema," "American Indian Literature," "The Sports Experience," and "Modern Rhythmic Gymnastics." Professor Stuart Miller, who chaired the General Education Council that approved the scheme, cast the sole dissenting vote. "In their eagerness to bail out black studies," he later said, "my colleagues opened the door to those courses, and then did not feel they could discriminate against everyone else getting into the act to capture the pieces of this bonanza. So courses in physical education, recreation, industrial arts, and home economics, of course, became magically transformed into humanities and social science." When the academic senate tried to correct some of the worst abuses several years later, Miller recalled, students from ethnic studies programs "mostly black and Hispanic, packed the room and behaved very much like Hitler's black shirts in the Weimar Republic, muttering thinly veiled threats of physical violence against senators. . . . Rest assured, if white students had behaved in that fascist manner, it would have received wide coverage in the press and expulsions would have justifiably followed."[13]

Miller was hardly a reactionary. In the 1960s he had worked with Paul Goodman to help set up an experimental college. He had also worked with the Black Student Union in the 1960s; was sympathetic to their demands that more black poets, playwrights, and novelists be included in course reading lists; and believed that American history courses should give more emphasis to the black experience. "There was," he said, "some legitimacy to that claim, and at first they wanted high academic standards. It was not Langston Hughes instead of William Shakespeare, but in addition to Shakespeare."[14]

He also played an early role in a special education program modeled after the City University of New York's much ballyhooed SEEK program which attempted to recruit young blacks—many of them high school dropouts. The program was, however, quickly seized by radicals in the Black Student Union, who demanded control over the selection process. "All a black applicant had to do," Miller recalled, "was mouth a few Marxist clichés or revolutionary rhetoric and he was selected. As a result, the thugs took over, and the black students I was working with, who were intellectually oriented, got beaten up and pushed aside. This was when I had nothing more to do with the program."[15]

BLACK STUDIES II: DARTMOUTH

Dartmouth's program officially began in the fall of 1969, with its own director and with 52 students enrolled in its first year. The number of students rose to 223 in 1970-71; but fell to 158 in 1971-72. Despite the decline in student interest, the program continued to follow the laws of academic fission and the number of courses rose from five to 18.[16] Problems became apparent almost immediately. Significantly, the man chosen to run the program was not a full faculty member. In fact, he had not yet completed his doctorate and his administrative experience was limited to a stint in the Peace Corps. Moreover, the faculty had ceded much of the control of the program to student members of the Afro-American Society.

One of the recommendations of the College's Committee on Equal Opportunity (headed by then-Professor John Kemeny) had been the creation of a special center for black students. In early 1970, after Kemeny had been named president, the College announced that it was designating Cutter Hall as the "focus of a multi-purpose experiment in the Afro-American area." It is unclear what form the administration envisioned that experiment to take, but once the building was turned over to the Afro-American Society the College quickly lost control. The Afro-American Society announced that Cutter Hall, which was to serve as the center for the society and for the new Black Studies Program, would be renamed "El Hajj Malik El Shabazz Temple." Black Muslim leader Malcolm X had visited the hall the year before his assassination. In his last year, the students explained, he had adopted the name El Hajj Malik El Shabazz.

The new Black Center was also closed to whites. Reported *The Dartmouth*:

> No white persons will be allowed in The Temple except on official business, AAS Chairman Cleveland Webber announced yesterday.
> He said that this will be done to provide a space on campus where black students can be free from dealing with whites.[17*]

Because the black studies program was not only housed in the "temple," but affiliated with the Afro-American Society, it inevitably took on a separatist flavor. A later faculty study of the program concluded that "non-blacks had been, if not actively discouraged from participating in some Black Studies courses, made to feel *persona non grata*. . . ."[18]

---

* As an indication of the mood of the time, *The Dartmouth* editorially applauded the separatist trend. The paper noted the objections to the center's "formalized separation of the races," but declared that "it is clear that mere physical integration of races is not and has not been a solution to racial division . . . it is naive to think that the time is still here when we can sit down at a lunch counter and talk out our differences. White society lost that chance quite a few years ago." (April 3, 1970)

An analysis by the Dean's Office was more pointed: "Black imposed constraints of separation and White acquiescence guaranteed that the program would not be taken very seriously or given the same kind of consideration that other new programs would be given."[19] The marginal status of the new program was compounded by the rapid turnover in the young, inexperienced administrators. In the first three years of the program, it went through four different directors. Not until 1972 did the program get its first doctorate-bearing faculty members. "Perhaps," as one analysis said, "the appointments were made in haste or without adequate research."[20]

"Mismanagement, isolation, discontinuity, and distrust are the logical results of this kind of beginning," the report from the dean's office concluded.[21] A faculty report came to the same conclusion, saying that "successful operation of the program was virtually impossible during these years. The faculty recruited for the Program was by and large relatively inexperienced and without sufficient academic background and training. Demands were made upon this faculty which would have sorely tried even 'older hands' who felt completely secure in the institutional environment . . . there was internal confusion concerning its educational philosophy. The Program was too isolated from the rest of the academic community. There was, apparently, little insistence that the Program observe normal practices of academic and budgetary accountability."[22]

An attempt was made to salvage the program in 1973. The faculty's Committee on Instruction called for several changes, including a new emphasis on academic scholarship instead of "socio-cultural" activities. But the key recommendation was the proposal that all regular faculty members in the department be made as half-time appointments with other departments. Moreover, it called for a moratorium on any new appointments until a later, more comprehensive review of the program. Joint appointments were crucial to the academic respectability of the program because they would tie it to existing departments whose standards would be reflected in any new hires. Such a system would, however, inevitably reduce the autonomy of the black studies program.[23] In the end, unwilling to challenge the independence of the department in the name of academic quality, the faculty voted in 1973 to reject the proposal[24]—thus dooming the program to several more years of chaos. Eventually, joint appointments were mandated, but the program continued to drift. Between 1973 and 1977, three faculty members were hired. Two of them left before they completed their doctorates.[25]

One of the program's core courses, "Introduction to Black Studies," which was offered in the fall of 1974 reflected the ambivalent standards and focus of black studies at Dartmouth.[26] Although the course included a number of readings, its structure was more on the order of an encounter group than an academic exercise. The professor set the tone for the course on the first page of the syllabus by noting that "the dehumanizing aspect" of the course was that "the educational 'system' demands that I give you some sort of a grade."

The requirements of the course included what the professor called "ramblings," which he defined as follows:

> Customarily, a rambling is a piece of paper (or more) with words written on it dealing with any topic, making any point, saying anything, complaining about anything, explaining anything, including yourself. It can also be a cartoon, a painting, photographs, a protest document, a lyric poem, a drawing, sculpture, and so forth; but please do not bring food items or live animals. A rambling is not a theme! A rambling is not a term paper. *Your spelling, punctuation, and grammar will not be corrected.* Your footnotes will be ignored. The only specifications I make are please write (preferably type) so that some other human can read it and relate it to Black Americans. [Emphasis added.]

The professor said that he would try to put together "an underground journal printing of those ramblings that seem to be worth sharing with others. . . ."[27]

Another requirement of the course was something called a "dyad interview," which translated into pairing the students off and assigning them to talk to one another. Students were instructed to "try to find out" such information as their partner's "schooling," "past activities," "previous hangups," "former pleasures," "involvements," and "hostilities," as well as current attitudes on "anything important relating to race." The professor detailed possible subjects:

> religion, politics, social relations, sex, the arts, the drug scene, homosexuality, Gay Liberation, Women's Lib, campus protest, Black Panthers, neo-colonialism, the Vietnam war, any other way [sic], the draft, Black Muslims, freedom, communism, education,

the flag, the future of the country, Watergate, SCLC, the way the campus ought to be, stereotypes, NAACP, Pan-Africanism, Black Nationalism, the Black Mistique [sic], soul, Black Power, Black Liberation and so forth.[28]

The product of this would be a paper that would include a profile of "your dyad mate," a narrative history of "your relationship," "inferences you draw about your dyad mate relative to race relations," and "your frank evaluation of your dyad mate as you see him/her."

In the late 1970s, the black studies program severed its ties with the Afro-American Society, moved out of the temple—now known simply as "Am"—and scaled back its community action projects. But the program's official brochure made it clear how hard it was for the program to shed its political background and its often confused focus. The brochure described the purpose of the program—now called the African and Afro-American Studies Program—as "an invitation to all students to help open up that portion of American history *which has remained hidden in a mist of untruth and evasion.*" (Emphasis added.) Among the thinkers whose works were to be studied, the brochure listed Eldridge Cleaver and Angela Davis.

Ultimately, however, the black studies programs were dead-ends. Their marginal status and lack of consistent intellectual content limited their influence. To have any substantive influence on the curriculum as a whole, they would have to strike an alliance with other powerful special interest groups. None would prove so potent as women's studies.

CHAPTER
XVII

A CHAMPION OF THE LEFT

During the 1970 strike at Dartmouth, History Professor Marysa Gerassi had exulted that the shutdown was "the longest and the shortest week I can remember."[1] A native of Pamplona Spain, Gerassi had a master's degree and doctorate in history from Columbia University and had taught at Dartmouth since 1968. Almost from the moment she arrived in Hanover, she emerged as a powerful and active champion for the left on campus.

As early as 1971, Gerassi (who would revert to her maiden name of Navarro after her divorce) declared, "There is no doubt of discrimination at Dartmouth. It is stronger in some areas than in others, but it exists at the level of the student body, the adminstration and the teaching staff." She served as an adviser to Third World students on campus, was organizer of the Women's Caucus in 1970, and chaired the Ad Hoc Committee on the Status of Women in 1971 and 1972.[2] That year she not only won tenure for herself, but played a central role in the faculty decision to adopt the ambitious goal of appointing women to one-third of all faculty positions over the next decade.

Navarro's stunningly successful career at Dartmouth—her transition from radical activist to administrative powerhouse—is instructive of the changes in academia as a whole, exemplifying the rise of what Stephen Balch and Herbert London described as "a network of journals and professional organizations, university departments and academic programs" that marked the institutionalization of 1960s radicalism in higher education.[3] Navarro served on the Committee on Admissions; the Committee on Graduate Studies; the Committee on Organization and Policy; and the President's Commission on the Reorganization of the Faculty. She also served on the Ad Hoc Committee on Native American Studies; the Council on Native American Studies; the Committee on Instruction; the Council on Academic Freedom and Responsibility; the Affirmative Action Review Committee; and was named Vice-Chairman of the History Department. Navarro was a member of Concerned Women Faculty; an alternate member of the Committee Advisory to the President; was on the Governing Board of the Student Center; and a member of the Fraternity Board of Overseers.

In the 1980s she was named associate dean with responsibility for overseeing Dartmouth's entire social sciences faculty.

From the mid-1970s on, Navarro played a leading role in the creation of the first formal women's studies program in the Ivy League. The core of the movement was a group of about 20 women who met regularly to discuss women's issues on campus and to coordinate efforts to introduce women-related courses into the curriculum. Her views would be influential in shaping the program's orientation.

Navarro brought to Dartmouth's program a national reputation backed by considerable influence in the new discipline of feminist studies. She was listed on the masthead of *Ms.* magazine and served on the editorial board of the feminist academic journal *Signs*, one of the leading journals that sprang up around the women's studies movement. Such journals played a crucial role because they provided feminist scholars a forum for their work and an instrument of cross-validation so critical in the academic environment. *Signs* represented the radical as opposed to liberal wing of feminism and it placed heavy emphasis on lesbian feminism, French structuralism, socialist feminism, and Third World feminism, with articles like "Displacing the Phallic Subject: Wittig's Lesbian Writing," in which the writer critiques "phallogentricism"—described as the central role of the phallus in Western society. The phallus, the writer argues, provides "the organizing principles for all standard systems including that of law" and all "standard forms of communication."[4]

In the summer of 1984, *Signs* devoted its entire issue to a discussion of lesbian concerns. Articles included: "The Mythic Mannish Lesbian: Radclyffe Hall and the New Woman," "Distance and Desire: English Boarding School Friendships," "Sexuality, Class and Conflict in a Lesbian Workplace," "Ourselves Behind Ourself: A Theory for Lesbian Readers," "Homosexuality, Homophobia, and Revolution: Notes toward an Understanding of the Cuban Lesbian and Gay Male Experience, Part I," "The Politics of Transliteration: Lesbian Personal Narratives," "Lesbian Sexuality in Renaissance Italy," "and "The Military and Lesbians during the McCarthy Years."[5]

Articles from the journal would be frequently assigned as required reading in the Dartmouth women's studies program and Dartmouth faculty members were frequently published in its pages.

In an article titled, "Multiple Jeopardy, Multiple Consciousness: the Content of a Black Feminist Ideology," for example, Dartmouth sociology professor Deborah King wrote that "a black feminist ideology fundamentally challenges the interstructure of the oppressions of racism, sexism, and classism both in the dominant society and within movements for liberation," and declared that "black women must develop a political ideology capable of interpreting and resisting that multiple jeopardy."[6]

Dartmouth's Marianne Hirsch appeared in the pages of *Signs* arguing that the concept of a "lesbian continuum" can liberate women from masculine theory and language outside of "patriarchal concepts."

"She asks," an editor's note reads, "whether all our theories about women's sexuality and mothering are not still so enmeshed in the language of male thinkers that our very experiences as we describe them become a shadowing forth of some man's theory."[7] Hirsch cited feminist critic Adrienne Rich's vision of "compulsory heterosexuality as an institution enforced by physical violence and false consciousness," that "calls many of our assumptions into question. . . ." Rich, she wrote, "demonstrates rather convincingly" that such male-centered perspectives were so dominant, that even feminist scholarship was part of the "institution" of compulsory heterosexuality. (For some time, Hirsch posted a sign on the door of her Dartmouth office reading: "SISTERHOOD MEANS REVOLUTION," which she explained reminded her of "the familial metaphors which have organized the thinking and the rhetoric of the feminist movement.")[8]

The lack of scholarly distance from one's subject is explicit in academic feminism. In 1977, Navarro had chaired a session of the *Primer Simposio Mexicano Centroamericano de investigacion sobre la mujer* held in Mexico. The group's final report, cited approvingly by Navarro in a 1979 article, had declared:

> On the one hand [Latin American women] must take part in social change through an alliance with the working class which fights for socialism, because it is generally admitted that capitalism is structurally able to make only partial reforms. On the other, and simultaneously, women must struggle for their specific demands, not only at the economic level but also for a cultural revolution that will modify the ideology that lingers on after the socio-economic system has changed.[9]

The same article made it clear how far Navarro was prepared to take her politics.

> Because such feminist scholarship has its roots in the women's liberation movement, its examination of social institutions, artistic paradigms, and academic assumptions has a strong militant quality. *In general, for feminist scholars, empirical knowledge is not an end in itself but a means of denouncing sexual inequalities in order to redress them.* [Emphasis added.]

Thus, in startlingly blunt terms, Navarro had cast off the notion that scholarship —the study of ideas, the search for facts, the assembling of data—was an end unto itself. Instead, for Navarro, it was to be put in the service of specific political goals. Empirical knowledge that did not serve feminism's political agenda was to be ignored or suppressed. As it turned out, she was very much in tune with the times.

CHAPTER
XVIII

A QUESTION OF GENDER

By 1977, Dartmouth was offering seven courses in women's studies in a variety of departments. They included "Women and History," "The Politics and Literature of Marriage," "Women and Literature: A Feminist Perspective," "Women, Politics and the Law," and "Women, Identity and Vocation in American History." The mid-1970s was a period of growing activism and prominence for feminists at Dartmouth.[1] In 1976, Marysa Navarro had been a convener of the Wellesley Conference on Women and Development, while three other faculty members— Elizabeth Baer, Marilyn Baldwin, and Blanche Gelfant—attended the charter meeting of the National Women's Studies Association. Baer also attended the International Women's Year Conference in Houston a year later. Both groups, Baer later wrote, focused on the same theme, which she described as the "new integration of race, class and sex."[2]*

---

* At the San Francisco meeting, Baer reported, "Third World, Lesbian, Student, and Staff Caucuses made impressive contributions and the National Women's Studies Association convention ended with a renewed recognition of these major groups of women." She concluded her report: "The enormous joy that was perhaps the most keenly felt especially by lesbian women and minority women will provide significant energy for the future."

In 1977 and early 1978, eight women faculty members drafted a proposal for a formal women's studies program at Dartmouth. Their proposal argued that a "structured Women's Studies Program would diminish duplication of effort, encourage students to pursue the study of women, provide validation and visibility for the new scholarship and improve scholarly interaction."[3]

"The Women's Studies program at Dartmouth," they explained, "arose in response to a legacy of devaluation of women, a devaluation exemplified by the failure of traditional academic disciplines to analyze or incorporate into their theory and practice the specific experiences and role of women in culture." It was axiomatic for the new program that "the history of 'mankind' is characterized by the fundamentally divergent experiences and expectations of the two sexes" and that "new methods and new theoretical frameworks" were necessary to correct "the legacy of women's devaluation."

In the spring of 1978, acting with impressive speed, the faculty approved the new program.

The Dartmouth women's studies program made no secret of its ambitions. A later report declared that the faculty's endorsement was not merely a recognition of the growth of feminist scholarship "but also a commitment to make feminist scholarship an integral part of our curriculum." Feminist scholarship "has set out its dissatisfaction with the received androcentric tradition," it said, but was now ready to move on, "both substantively and methodologically" by delineating "the basis of its own authority."[4]

It endorsed the definition of the purpose of women's studies articulated by Catharine Stimpson, who set out three "intellectual objectives," "the *deconstruction* of false axioms, logic, and conclusions; the *reconstruction* of reality, the addition to the record of the facts of women's lives; and the *construction* of general ideas and theories."[5]

In a proposal to the National Endowment for the Humanities, Navarro expanded on that definition.

> In its deconstructive aspect, Women's Studies has directed attention
> to the documentation of sexual inequality in society and of andro-
> centrism in the established literature of the various disciplines. The
> reconstructive project has uncovered positive but neglected images
> of women. . . . The work of both these projects has been conducted
> largely within the traditional disciplines. . . .

Now, however, Navarro continued, the Dartmouth program was interested in the third, the "constructive" phase of activity. "This involves a concerted effort not only to challenge the traditional paradigms through which, for example, historical research has been interpreted, but also construct a more adequate conceptual framework for investigating women's role in society and culture. . . . Factors such as class, ethnicity, geographical locale and historical context will be taken into account."[6]

Having established a beachhead in the curriculum, the program quickly assumed a high profile in campus life. In its first year-and-a-half of existence the new program co-sponsored 25 guest speakers on campus, representing much of the pantheon of current feminist politics and scholarship.[*]

The new program also proved successful in attracting both foundation and federal support; no small factor in ensuring its continued existence and growth. In 1978, a Lilly foundation grant supported the first of the program's new courses: Women's Studies I, which commenced in spring 1979.[7]

The syllabus of the course clearly reflected its political intentions. "Women's Studies," it declared, "is not only *about* women in society, it is *itself* a force in the evolution of women's roles." As if to emphasize the centrality of this political agenda, the identical wording appears on the syllabus of Liberal Studies 105—"Women's Studies: Deconstruction & Reconstruction," offered the next year.

Women's Studies I (and Liberal Studies 105) also promised to make full use of the various new theories and methodologies that were emerging. "We will be very attentive," the syllabus said, "to theory as well as innovative methodologies in our exploration of the issues central to Women's Studies."[8] Navarro's own contribution was equally revealing. With Colette Gaudin, she taught "History and Theory of Feminism," which explored the question: "What is the primary source of the subordination of women—men or the economic and social structure?"[9]

---

* Speakers included radical activist turned academic Annette Kolodny, who spoke on "Women as Text"; lesbian feminist Mary Daly, who spoke on "The Meta-Ethics of Radical Feminism"; Catharine Stimpson, who spoke on "The New Scholarship About Women"; and Adrienne Rich, who read her poetry. Other topics included, "Love, Friendship and Eroticism," "Women's Power, Women's Secret: Why Are Men Worried," "The Unlovely Domain: Work, Home and the Subordination of Women," "Critical Approaches to Writing by Afro-American Women," and "The Doctor's Dilemma: Sin, Salvation and the Menstrual Cycle in Medieval Thought."

Readings focused on radical, Marxist, and Freudian interpretations of feminism. Required reading included *Beyond God the Father* by radical-lesbian-feminist Mary Daly, who in the late 1970s, had closed her classes at Boston College to men; and *Capitalist Patriarchy and the Case for Socialist Feminism*, edited by Zillah Eisenstein. In her introduction, Eisenstein writes that the ongoing discussion of socialist feminism, "reflects the new understanding of how the system of male supremacy is reproduced through the sexual ordering of society, both consciously and unconsciously."[11] Chapters in the book include: "Mothering, Male Dominance and Capitalism," "Emerging from Underdevelopment: Women and Work in Cuba," "When Patriarchy Kowtows: The Significance of the Chinese Family Revolution for Feminist Theory," "The Combahee River Collective: A Black Feminist Statement," "A Report on Marxist-Feminist Groups 1-5," and "The Berkeley-Oakland Women's Union Statement," which reads in part:

> We recognize that our liberation and that of other oppressed groups cannot be achieved within the existing system. Therefore, our struggle against sexism necessarily involves us in the struggle against capitalism, racism, imperialism, and all other forms of oppression, and must be waged simultaneously with these struggles if we are to achieve our vision of socialism. . . . We too are oppressed by [imperialism] that wages war against revolutionary struggles for liberation and destroys the cultures and resources of Third World countries. . . .[12]

A chapter on "Feminist Theory and the Development of Revolutionary Strategy," stresses the primacy of politics, arguing that "feminism recognizes that political philosophy and political action do not take place in separate realms."[13]

A third course, titled "Deconstruction and Reconstruction," made the theoretical bent of the program even more explicit. Taught by Elizabeth Baer and Martha Rich, the course purported to examine gender with "special attention to images of women in popular culture." The reading list was again ideologically uniform.[14]

Students in the class were required to turn in a three to five page term paper that could take one of three forms. Here the line between academic work and activism blurred almost to invisibility. The syllabus reads: "For those of you eager to apply feminist theory learned thus far, you

may review a book, a film, a speaker *from a feminist perspective. . . .*"
No provision is made for students to write reviews from alternative or
critical perspectives.

A second option for students "with an interest in activism" was to
write an "advocacy" letter. "This will involve choosing an issue about
which you have (or would like to develop) an opinion—child-care,
abortion, human rights for gays, the ERA—and doing enough research
to assure an informed opinion. Then identify a target person—someone
in Congress, someone who has spoken out against your stand, director
of an appropriate organization—and write a letter to that person, stating
your opinion and calling for action. *Actually send the letter*; hand in a
copy of the letter to us, accompanied by a 2-3 page position paper,
summarizing your research and the rationale for your opinion."[15]

Discussing the final project for the class, the two professors listed
what they regarded as some of the more "exciting" projects done by
previous classes, including, "a proposal for a rape crisis center in
Hanover" and "a history of women in the comics."

DECONSTRUCTING THE CURRICULUM

The influence of the new philosophies was not confined to the small
number of classes formally designated as ethnic or women's studies at
Dartmouth.* Florence Howe, co-founder and director of the Feminist
Press is not alone when she argues that the goal of academic feminists in
the nation's 530 women's studies programs is the wholesale reconstruction of the curriculum—affecting every discipline. "One cannot as a
rule simply add new perspectives without changing traditional ways of
thinking."

The formulation of this view is captured in Dartmouth's Marianne
Hirsch's comment that "It doesn't really work to just add one woman and
stir." As Hirsch said in 1984, the goal of the program was not merely to
"revalue" all academic disciplines in the light of feminism, the goal was
the "reconstruction of reality."[16] In 1988, the Women's Support Task
Force added its endorsement to proposals to make gender studies
courses mandatory at Dartmouth—a requirement modelled on the Col-

---

* In the 1987-88 year, 500 students, nearly 14 percent of undergraduates in residence
took core or associated courses in women's studies at Dartmouth.

lege's current Third World requirement. Hirsch has acknowledged that if feminists can transform the curriculum as a whole, the need for a separate program will disappear.

Dartmouth English Professor Brenda Silver makes the agenda of the attack on the canon explicit:

> The attitude is, "What do I have to take out to teach a book by a woman or minority?" And that's the wrong question. What we're really dealing with here is a major epistemological question. We're dealing with men who have created the world from their point of view and [assume] from there springs the truth. And women's perceptions are really very different—even about basic things such as what constitutes knowledge, what constitutes truth, how it is disseminated.[17]

In the years since its beginnings, the feminist "reconstruction" effort at Dartmouth has focused heavily on revising the canon of literature taught in the classrooms. But women's studies is interested less with restoring the place of neglected authors than with how they fit into the ideological schema.

In "Women and Writing" offered during Dartmouth's 1989 summer term, Emily Dickinson, Edith Wharton, Marianne Moore, Gertrude Stein, Elizabeth Bishop, and Edna Millay were all ignored in favor of black lesbianfeminist [sic] Audre Lorde's *Sister Outsider*; lesbian-feminist Adrienne Rich's *On Lies, Secrets and Silence*; and a collection of writings by Third World feminists titled *This Bridge Called My Back*.[18]*

The degree to which feminist ideology has permeated the Dartmouth curriculum is hinted at in an article in the *Alumni Magazine* by recent graduate Karen Avenoso. Her exposure to feminist ideology did not come in one of the basic women's studies courses, but in two literature survey courses, including one on "Medieval Literature." Both classes, she says, were taught by feminists "who had included women authors and feminist literary criticism in their syllabi."[19]

Her introduction to the women writers and to the feminist critique of

---

* Other required texts include *I Love Myself When I'm Laughing, And Then Again When I'm Looking Mean*, by Zora Neale Hurston; *Reena*, by Paule Marshall; *Silences*, by Tille Olsen; *Women and Writing*, by Virginia Woolf; and *Writing and Sexual Difference*, edited by Elizabeth Abel.

the literary canon, led her, she wrote, to "question the notion of 'major' and 'minor' fiction, *even examine the very definition of literature.*"

Avenoso also provided a revealing glimpse of the feminist classroom at Dartmouth. As part of their "critique of traditional male teaching styles," she wrote, feminist faculty members like Carla Freccero, a professor of French and Italian, encourage the students to "question the nature of professorial authority. . . ."[20] Ideological authority is another matter.

Freccero has taught Women's Studies 10, "Sex, Gender, and Society." The course's required reading included *Women, Race and Class*, by Communist Party activist Angela Davis, which Freccero describes as "an exemplary pedagogical text" that provides "a much more thorough and varied history of U.S. 'feminism' than any I have seen. . . ." It is an indication of her own educational philosophy that Freccero regards Davis's neo-Stalinist orthodoxy as a virtue. (Davis is a winner of the Lenin Prize.) "Thus," she writes, "students are given the opportunity, too rarely provided, to experience how fruitfully and intelligently the thinking of Karl Marx can be applied when it is not being parodied or reductively imitated."[21] Or, Freccero might have added, when it is not challenged or critiqued, or subjected to historical analysis or alternative points of view. In fact, the entire course seems structured to avoid such questions.

In the classrooms like Freccero's, Avenoso wrote, "Women's Studies discussions are often organized in a 'rotating chair' fashion in which students call on each other. Such approaches lend an unusual sense of community to the field." When students share their papers with one another, it is in an "amicably critical" atmosphere, before a "supportive audience."

Now a disciple of post-structuralist feminist theory, Avenoso proudly boasts: "I can do a deconstructionist reading of the name of John Milton's Eve." She also accepted the feminist claim that "all intellectual perspectives can be said to have a political origin," and declares that its political focus was "one of the program's greatest strengths."

"Like some (but not all) students in the program," Avenoso wrote, "I have found that an increasing political activism has paralleled my involvement in Women's Studies."[22]

That overtly political focus was to become increasingly obvious as women's studies grew in stature and influence with the Dartmouth community. In the spring of 1990, Dartmouth was scheduled to host a

"Humanities Research Institute," funded by the Andrew W. Mellon Foundation and the National Endowment for the Humanities. The focus of the humanities institute was to be "Gender and War," specifically, "how war confirms and reproduces the cultural construction of masculinity and femininity, and how gender roles and representatives serve to perpetuate war." A brochure advertising the program promised to pay particular attention to "the politics of Nazism and its roots in masculine identity."[23]

As always, Navarro remained at the forefront of the movement.

NAVARRO ON REVOLUTION

Don't you know
They're talkin' about revolution. . . .

The lyrics of rock singer Tracy Chapman appear on the first page of the syllabus of "Women and Social Change in the Third World," which in the spring of 1989 was offered by Professors Marysa Navarro and Leo Spitzer.[24] The course focused on women in Cuba, Mozambique, Algeria, and the Palestinian uprising. It naturally satisfied Dartmouth's non-Western graduation requirement.

The reading list did not include any general overview of the history or sociology of revolution or social unrest; the basic texts in the field were neglected, while the books that were required were essentially advocacy texts. They included *For Their Triumphs and For Their Tears*, by Hilda Bernstein; *Call Me Woman*, by Ellen Kuzwayo; and *God's Bits of Wood*, by Sembene Ousmane. Readings were also assigned from *Capitalist Patriarchy and the Case For Socialist Feminism*—a staple text of the Dartmouth women's studies program.

The basic book for the course was Sheila Rowbotham's *Women, Resistance & Revolution: A History of Women and Revolution in the Modern World*. In her introduction, Rowbotham describes the book "as part of a continuing effort to connect feminism to socialist revolution," by correcting the "masculine bias" in mainline Marxism.[25]

She ridicules liberal, democratic feminism by calling the individual "emancipated" woman "an amusing incongruity, a titillating commodity, easily consumed." Rowbotham's ideological goal is far more dramatic than equal pay for equal work.

It is only when women start to organize in large numbers that we become a political force, and begin to move towards the possibility of a truly democratic society in which every human being can be brave, responsible, thinking and diligent in the struggle to live at once freely and unselfishly. *Such a democracy would be communism. . . .*[26] [Emphasis added.]

For students in the class Rowbotham was required reading on such subjects as: "Varieties of imperialism/varieties of opposition," "Bourgeois Reformism and Revolutionary Change," "Women and the Russian Revolution," "Marx and Engels on Women's Liberation," and "Violence and Liberation."

The class's first assignment is to read Sembene's *God's Bits of Wood*, a novel about a 1947 strike in French West Africa. The book apparently is selected to link Marxism with feminism by showing women as "doubly colonized"—oppressed as both proletarians and as women.

The connection between the oppression of women and the central discovery of Marxism, the class exploitation of the worker in capitalism is still forced. But when the connection between class, colonial and sexual oppression becomes commonplace we will understand it, not as an abstract concept, but as the something coming out of the experience of particular women.

If that connection is not explicit enough, students are assigned to read a review essay on *God's Bits of Wood* by another Marxist feminist critic, Karen Sacks, who quotes Rowbotham and endorses her point of view. Sacks praises the novelist, who "lays out for us the revolutionary possibilities with respect to women, colonialism, and class struggle that are inherent in our everyday lives."[27]

The class discussion of the book's Marxist interpretations is entitled: "Terminology in context: 'oppressive situation'; 'consciousness of oppression'; 'colonialism'; 'double colonialism?' "

The syllabus indicates the direction the discussion takes:

According to Karen Sacks, Ousmane Sembene shows us that "consciousness is as much consequence as cause of action," and that in the course of the strike "women become conscious of their independent relation to capitalism as well as of their particular kin ties and interdependence with male proletarians." Do you agree with this analysis? During the strike, did women also become conscious of themselves as a group that is doubly colonized—by the French as well as by their menfolk?[28]

Leaving Africa, the class turns to a discussion of the Paris Commune and a discussion of the distinction between what the professors call "bourgeois reformism"* and "revolutionary change," and then devotes a class period to a discussion of Marxism and women's liberation. Four readings are assigned for the discussion of Marxism, all from a Marxist point of view.[†]

The subsequent discussion deals with the dilemma of feminists in the post-revolution Marxist state:

> If patriarchy (and thus women's oppression) predates capitalist society [the syllabus reads], can it be assumed that a revolution which changes the economic basis of society in a socialist direction would consequently effect a revolutionary change in women's social, economic and political power?[29]

Subsequent classes are devoted to a discussion of anarchist and socialist feminists and the Russian Revolution (Stalin was a sexist) before turning back to the Third World. One class is devoted to "Algeria, Intifada and Iran," while a second class period is devoted entirely to "Violence and Liberation." The main texts for the discussion of violence are Rowbotham and Frantz Fanon, whose work is rapidly becoming a fixture in *au courant* university curriculums. Fanon's works have considerable significance in the history of Third World violence; but the class is assigned no readings from Gandhi, Martin Luther King, Jr., or anyone else who might provide a contrary perspective. (It perhaps goes without saying that Mother Theresa does not qualify as an acceptable commentator on women in the Third World.)

At the end of the course, three full class periods are set aside to

---

* It is perhaps worthy of comment that this is the formulation used by the Chinese government in denouncing the recently suppressed democracy movement. It is a phrase now seldom found outside of the Forbidden City, Albania, and American universities.

† The assigned readings were: Part II of *The Communist Manifesto* by Karl Marx; "The Origins of the Family," by F. Engels; a reading from Rowbotham; and "Marx & Engels on Women's Liberation," by Hal Draper in *International Socialism*.

discuss Cuba, with topics including: "The Macho, the Virgin, and the Whore: women and men in pre-revolutionary Cuba," "Women, Feminism, and the Cuban Revolution," and "Women in Cuba after thirty years of revolution."[30]

The readings range from elegiac praise of Castro's paradise, ("One of the most exciting aspects of the Cuban Revolution is the way the country's economic and social progress involved a constant physical dialogue between leadership and masses"),[31] to fervid apologias for the regime, in which Cuba's shortcomings are explained as a result of its underdevelopment and its "transitional" state. There are, of course, other ways of looking at Castro's statecraft. But not here. Such balance was apparently superfluous in the new age of "diversity."

CHAPTER
XIX

OF INDIANS AND ART: THE
DIVERSITY WARS

On February 25, 1979, during a hockey match between Brown and Dartmouth, three students dressed as Indians skated onto the ice before a full house at Thompson Arena to lead the forbidden wah-hoo-wah Indian cheer. Some in the audience joined the cheers. Some booed. Some remained silent. The College chose to overreact.[1]

Campus radicals, eager to gain the maximum amount of political leverage from the incident, denounced the prank in apocalyptic terms; their tone was matched by College officials. President Kemeny, who had cast himself as the leading force in the new diversity of campus life, called the incident "horrendous" and "in the worst possible taste." The president declared a moratorium on classes so that the campus could discuss the issues of "racism and sexism" at Dartmouth.

By the middle of the 1970s, the push for diversity had evolved into a critique of the College's culture and its traditions. A later faculty report would characterize Dartmouth as an institution "devoted to the education of privileged, white, North American males" while its traditions were the products of its insularity, "its orientation to the wilderness, its isolation from urban centers and its small size."[2]

Dartmouth's bucolic setting, the report said, had promoted the "development of a student body devoted to outdoor activities as well as study." That emphasis on "physical prowess," had contributed to the image of a Dartmouth student as someone who "studies hard and plays hard," a formulation, the faculty would declare, that was "less benign than it seems at first glance." The fraternity system in particular would come in for attack as being "not terribly high-minded," because it promoted "the use of alcohol and tended to foster demeaning attitudes toward women."

> This hermetic situation—a small group of fairly uniform male students isolated in a wilderness of great beauty—did not encourage an openness to individuals and ideas that differed from the clear-cut norm.[3]

Minority students and women were said to suffer from "feelings of exclusion," a condition allegedly reinforced by the College's traditions: including the Indian symbol and freshman orientation week.

Every freshman is invited to participate in an outdoor experience in northern New Hampshire, on spectacularly beautiful property owned by the College. The trip includes mountain climbing, canoeing, hiking, and a highly personalized introduction to the College. The freshman trip, President Dickey had said, "gives the College its distinctive personality."

The trip also embodied Ernest Martin Hopkins' vision of the College, captured in his often quoted adage:

> I would insist that the man who spends four years in our north country and does not learn to hear the melody of rustling leaves or does not learn to love the wash of racing brooks over the rocky beds in spring—who has never experienced the repose to be found on lakes and rivers; who has not stood enthralled on the top of Moosilauke on a moonlit night or has not become a worshipper of color as he has seen the sun set from one of Hanover's Hills; who has not thrilled at the whiteness of the snow-clad countryside in winter or at the flaming forest colors of the fall—I would insist that this man has not reached out for some of the most worthwhile educational values accessible to him at Dartmouth.

Now this tradition too was targeted. In its later report on "diversity," the faculty would list the orientation trip as one of three major barriers to the realization of true diversity because it "tends to create the wrong impression about the values that the College regards as important and reinforces the stereotype of the Dartmouth student as the rugged outdoor type." But most important, the trip was insufficiently serious; the report seems haunted by the concern that too much fun is being had. With a puritanism that often accompanies attempts to politicize an institution, the report urged more attention be paid to "discuss serious issues, such as threats to the environment through which the students are hiking," and suggested freshmen be assigned books that would "shed light on diversity."[4]

NATIVE AMERICANS

The aggressive recruitment and admission of more Native Americans to Dartmouth was the keystone of President Kemeny's diversity campaign. In his inaugural address, Kemeny announced his intention to renew the commitment of Dartmouth's founder, Eleazer Wheelock, to educate Native Americans. Dartmouth had clearly not lived up to Wheelock's early vision. Only one Native American actually graduated from Dartmouth in the eighteenth century. The total number of Indians attending the College between 1770 and 1865 probably did not exceed 71, and only 28 Native Americans attended Dartmouth over the next hundred years. Kemeny's goal was to recruit at least 15 Native Americans per class; in the fall of 1970, there were 19 Native American students at Dartmouth.[5]

Emulating the tactics of the black students on campus, the Indians began agitating for their own department of Native American studies. In December 1971, Native American students issued a series of demands that included not only an Indian Studies Program, but also the abolition of the College's use of the Indian symbol, which it denounced as racist.

The group's manifesto included nine specific points. They were: (1) "That athletic teams shall refrain from the use of the Indian mascot." (2) "References to athletic teams as the Dartmouth 'Indians,' or any allusion thereof must cease." (3) "Dartmouth cheerleaders, band, students, and alumni must cease use of 'wah-hoo-wah' and 'Dartmouth on the warpath' cheers." (4) "The Indian caricature on the basketball court must be removed as must the 'Indian' head on athletic uniforms." (5) "Programs should not refer to the Dartmouth football schedule as the 'warpath'." (6) "Publishers of the Dartmouth Alumni Magazine should refrain from the use of any allusion to 'Indian-ness'. . . ." (7) "The Indian murals in the Hovey Grill must be removed." (8) "College stationery letterheads and College property should not depict an 'Indian' caricature." (9) "The College should discuss with local merchants the abolition of 'commercial exploitation of Indian images' on such things as Dartmouth sweatshirts and notebooks."[6]

The Native American militants had strong support from radical faculty leaders. At a symposium in January 1972, Marysa Navarro denounced Dartmouth as "a very Waspish institution despite the presence of its Indian and Black students." She called the Indian symbol "derogatory and insulting."[7]

The College reacted quickly, naming a special study group to investigate the possibility of creating a separate study program. With impressive speed, the faculty approved the new program in 1972, along with the creation of four new courses. "There is no intellectual reason why the history of Native American people should not be considered an integral part of a liberal arts education," the faculty concluded. "There is no intellectual reason why the great religious frames of reference of the Native American people should not be an important component of learning in the humanities." The faculty did not, however, address the question of why a separate program was necessary, rather than incorporating this material into the existing departments of Anthropology, Education, and History. By now the pattern of special interest curricular politics was too well established to require any justification. Once the demands were issued, approval was almost automatic.

In October 1974, the trustees followed up by scrapping the school's historic Indian symbol. Although the symbol was an integral part of the school's traditions and well-loved by the College's loyal alumni, the trustees felt they must accommodate themselves to the mood of the times. Within the wider context of academic and social change, it seemed a minor enough issue. But the exorcism of a centuries old tradition was not so simple. In committing itself to creating the new atmosphere on campus, the College chose to go to draconian lengths to snuff out even the slightest survivals of the pre-diversity Dartmouth. But despite administration warnings and threats, the Indian continually showed up on illicit t-shirts and sweat-shirts; fans at games continued to ignore the *dictat* not to wah-hoo-wah. The College might have simply looked the other way. But in an era of symbolic politics, the Indian symbol became a rallying point for the various factions vying for the soul of the College. As trivial as it was, the College's adamant stand made the Indian symbol a powerfully divisive force in campus life.

A CASE OF EMOTIONAL VIOLENCE

The Indian incident at the hockey game was merely a trigger for tensions that had been building for some time. Two days after the hockey game, 200 students assembled in front of Parkhurst Hall to air a series of grievances, many of them hopelessly unrelated to the Indian prank. They included the College's policies toward South Africa, the alleged unfair treatment of the black studies program (it was being reviewed); and the College's insufficiently vigorous affirmative action policies. Radical fervor had, in fact, been building since late January when a member of the faculty, Assistant Professor of Education Peter Kelman, called for a mass demonstration during Dartmouth's Winter Carnival to demand the admission of more women and minorities. Despite the fact that Dartmouth was well ahead of other Ivy schools in its affirmative action program, Kelman denounced the school as "racist, sexist and elitist."

In an omen of what was to come, radicals on the faculty denounced *The Dartmouth* for daring to actually publish pictures of the skaters dressed as Indians. Professor Michael Green of the Native American Studies Department wrote a letter denouncing the paper:

> That Dartmouth students chose to present themselves as racist caricatures is unfortunate; that the college newspaper chose to publicize this example of class insensitivity without critical judgment is appalling. Either *The Dartmouth* should make a public explanation for selecting this picture for the front page, or cease to pretend that it is a publication for all segments of the population.[8]

Although the students responsible for the Indian demonstration at the hockey game turned themselves in to College officials, the faculty was not in a mood for leniency. Despite the College's tolerant attitude toward such protests as the one that prevented William Shockley from speaking, the College's Committee on Standing and Conduct voted to suspend the students. In justifying the decision, a member of the disciplinary committee, Karen Blank, argued that the pranksters had "violated the rights of Native American students who had come to this college expecting to thrive and grow as individuals without having to live with stereotypical attitudes imposed on them." Then she proceeded to propound a curious new doctrine of imputed victimization.

> When they [the Indians] received their letters of acceptance from Dartmouth, they were not told that, because of their backgrounds, they would be the victims of *emotional violence*. The long deliberated decision to suspend represented an institutional stance that such *victimization is not tolerated*.[9] [Emphasis added.]

What was striking about such logic was its radical inversion of traditional understandings of free speech. There are, of course, exceptions to the absolute right of expression for so-called "fighting words" or speech that creates a real and present danger of violence—real, physical violence, not "emotional violence." That doctrine recognized a clear distinction between expression and action; it enshrined the principle that speech alone was not a crime and that mere words could never, by themselves, constitute an act of violence or assault, no matter how inflammatory or obnoxious they might be.

But Blank's new doctrine abolished all such distinctions by regarding ethnically offensive speech not merely as distasteful, but as an act of victimization and ersatz violence. No actual damage or danger need be shown; the emotional victimization of the downtrodden class was assumed and decisively overrode any other considerations.

Blank's argument was, for all practical purposes, identical to Jonathan Mirsky's justification for the shout-down of William Shockley in 1969 and the denial of free speech rights to other speakers of whom he disapproved. Ten years later, this was no longer merely a doctrine of the campus left; now, as Blank noted, it "represented an institutional stance. . . ."

Still, the suspension of the students (and perhaps Blank's logic) was too much for Kemeny, who amended the students' penalty to "college discipline with restrictions." His decision was praised by English professor James Epperson who said that the students "were thoughtless and stupid, but they didn't intend the actions to be humiliating."*

---

* In a column on this issue, William F. Buckley, Jr., quipped: "My guess is that the students who have gotten into so much trouble at Dartmouth . . . have no hostility

Student groups, however, felt they had a powerful issue and pressed their hand. Chanting, "we're fired up, won't take no more," students representing both the Native American Society and the Afro-American Society held a protest on the College Green. Afterward, the College's Winter Carnival snow sculpture was spray-painted black and red. One of the students explained that the vandalism represented "minorities' desire to be an intricate [sic] and accepted part of the Dartmouth Community."

"We are not sorry we defaced the snow sculpture," one activist shouted during a rally. "It stood for a Dartmouth tradition that black and native Americans have not been a part of. . . . All minority groups are glad to see it happen because someone finally made a statement that everyone can see." (No one was punished for the incident.)[10] At the March 9 moratorium, Kemeny pleaded with the students for understanding, telling them that "this college cares deeply about you"—though the impression he made by walking out immediately after unburdening himself of this message was not favorable. The moratorium may have conjured images of his 1970 triumph. But it just wasn't the same.

MURALS AGAIN

The politics of diversity posed an even more difficult dilemma in deciding the fate of the mural in the Hovey Grill depicting Eleazer Wheelock and a group of Indians. Because the mural by Walter Beach Humphrey, a Dartmouth graduate of the class of 1914, was painted shortly after the controversial Orozco mural, there is a certain symmetry in their stories.

As a series of large oil paintings illustrating the song "Eleazer Wheelock," Humphrey's mural was intended, at least in part, to placate some of the traditionalists at the College who had been offended by Orozco's mural. The College's founder seemed a safe subject and, indeed, the only qualms it generated centered around the notable presence of bare-breasted Indian maidens.

The controversy over Orozco's mural had marked perhaps the strong-

---

whatever of a racial kind against the American Indian, any more than—let us say—one naturally supposed Al Jolson was anti-black because he sang in black face. But they are being treated as though they had conspired the massacre of Wounded Knee. . . ."

est test of Dartmouth's commitment to tolerance and free expression. President Hopkins would later say that it was the only issue where he knew he stood in opposition to the majority of alumni.

The demand by the Indian students that the Hovey Grill murals be removed not only threatened to revive the mural wars, but challenged the College's commitment to free expression head-on. The administration's response was to be one of the most unedifying chapters in Dartmouth history.

Administrators announced that they wished to make regular use of the Hovey Grill for College events but were "thwarted by the presence of Walter Beach Humphrey's Eleazer Wheelock murals, which women and Native Americans say are objectionable. . . ." President Kemeny had met with Indian student leaders in the summer of 1979, and later said that he "made it clear that I would, under no circumstances, agree to censorship of art, and I was assured that this was not the issue." Even so, Kemeny first tried to remove the murals and have them stored in the College's art museum, but that proved to be impossible (the murals were so firmly attached to the walls that any attempt to remove them would destroy the painting). As a result, the College announced, "a decision has been made to cover the murals."

Interestingly, undergraduate leaders seemed to have a better grasp of the issues involved in this decision than did the president of the College. The Undergraduate Council voted overwhelmingly to condemn the action, arguing that "permanent covering of the Hovey Murals constitutes the suppression of freedom of expression and of free choice." Moreover, the undergraduate group argued, the sensibilities of any one group on campus ought not be considered in absolutist terms. In a reversal of normal roles, the students were cast in the role of lecturing the administration on the basic principles of mutual tolerance and free speech. "Respect for one group's views," the council said, "does not mean the exclusion of, and should not be at the expense of, another group's position."[11]

The administration had placed itself in an untenable position. By seeking to placate the Native American students and the campus left, it had offended many alumni and placed itself in a highly ambiguous moral position *vis à vis* its adherence to the principles of diversity and academic freedom. It chose what was perhaps the worst possible option.

Kemeny announced that henceforth the Grill would serve as a rotating art exhibit "with an emphasis on the history and traditions of the College," but during the spring term, when the Hovey Grill was used for "special events," the original murals would be uncovered. What this meant was that when the students were using the Grill during the fall and winter, the mural was covered with "painted wallboard," but when alumni groups visited campus, the wallboard would be removed and the mural displayed. When no alumni events were scheduled, the Grill was locked, lest students be exposed to the offending images. Once the alumni left, the mural would once again be covered and students once again readmitted to the sanitized Grill. (This policy was continued by Kemeny's successor, David McLaughlin, who displayed the mural during alumni events, only to cover them later. Eventually, they would be permanently covered.)

This dance of the veils ultimately antagonized all groups; and its hypocrisy—displaying them for alumni, then quickly covering them up when they left—badly undermined the administration's moral credibility on the issue.

The policy was denounced both by artists and art critics. Professor Matthew Wiencke chided the administration for "blatant visual and graphic demonstration of censorship." Art Professor Robert McGrath called it "short-sighted and injudicious,"[12] while *Washington Post* art critic Ben Forgey described the College's policy as "burying your head in the sand."[13]

The contrast between the handling of the Hovey and the Orozco murals highlighted the difficulties of political censorship. By any standards, the Orozco murals had the potential of offending large numbers of students and alumni: they were overtly anti-Christian, anti-capitalist, and highly critical of the educational system. Christ is depicted wielding an axe, chopping down the cross; a scene that might be considered blasphemous. The mural is, moreover, located in the library reading room, perhaps the most heavily used area in the entire College; more students are exposed to the Orozco mural than the Wheelock mural by several orders of magnitude. And yet the Orozco mural remained untouched and uncovered.

Wilcomb Washburn, director of the Office of American Studies at the Smithsonian Institution, and a 1948 graduate of Dartmouth, called the internment of the murals "naive and embarrassingly anti-

intellectual," and noted that it reflected the administration's unwilling-
ness to "come to grips with the real issue—freedom of speech." Describing the Orozco murals, Washburn pointed out that by some standards, they were "outrageous."

"They insult the Church, the military and a teacher is portrayed as a
dead corpse. It is insulting, *and yet they remain*. It is an issue of free
speech."[14]

For Kemeny, the issue was not one of principle, but of responding to
pressure and balancing the interests of powerful constituencies. If that
meant pursuing a policy that was intellectually indefensible, that was the
price the College was willing to pay.

HERETICS: THE RISE OF *THE DARTMOUTH REVIEW*

In retrospect *The Dartmouth Review* seems almost inevitable. The rapid pace of change and the decade-long *kulturkampf* inevitably created its own reaction. Dartmouth boasted one of the most fervently loyal alumni bodies in the Ivy League, and since the days of President Hopkins had relied heavily on them for financial support. But both students and alumni were considerably more conservative than the faculty. During the 1970s, as Dartmouth embraced fashionable leftism, that gap widened ominously. Those divisions, however, had seldom been a problem, because of the virtual absence of an organized and articulate opposition group on campus. The silence that had made the right seem invisible during the 1960s had made conservative sentiment easy to ignore for most of the 1970s.

At the start of the 1980s, however, uneasiness over the dismantling of many of the school's traditions had given way to outright opposition, culminating in the election of Dr. John Steel, a La Jolla, California, physician, to the board of trustees over the vigorous opposition of the administration. The election had been a referendum on the policies of

President Kemeny, and the results were a shocking repudiation, which may have contributed to Kemeny's decision to step down the following year. Both Steel's election and the creation of *The Dartmouth Review* reflected changes in the national political mood; but both were also uniquely Dartmouth developments.

Although the divisions in the community over the future of Dartmouth were growing increasingly acute, the administration insisted on regarding the issues as little more than public relations problems. When possible, the College denied the existence of conflict; when that became impossible, it sought to discredit critics; and if that was not sufficient, it moved to silence them. It was to become a familiar Dartmouth pattern.

When the young editor of *The Dartmouth*, Greg Fossedal, denounced the College's attempts first to stymie and later to discredit Steel's candidacy for election to the board of trustees, the governing board of the newspaper, which was controlled by Dartmouth administrators, forced him out as editor. If the idea was to gag Fossedal and other conservative dissidents, the move was a fateful miscalculation.

Along with some of the brightest young writers on campus, the deposed editor quickly decided to found a new newspaper, without any ties to the administration or the College. *The Dartmouth Review* was born with strong support not only from conservative alumni who provided financial backing, but also encouragement from such national conservative luminaries as William F. Buckley, Jr., Patrick Buchanan, Russell Kirk, and William Simon. Over the next decade, the *Review* would become both an irritant and an obsession on campus. As early as 1981, College spokesmen denounced the paper for "mudslinging" and charged that it "deals in hate."[1] A College spokesman called it a "baneful" influence on campus.[2] Over the years, critics have accused it of filling its columns with "sheer venom" and "unrelieved nastiness."[3] By the mid-1980s, the College's official spokesmen routinely described the paper as racist, sexist, and homophobic. (This despite the fact that several of the paper's top editors have been women or racial minorities.) Not to be outdone, two separate faculty reports would describe the paper as a barrier not only to "diversity" on the Dartmouth campus, but also as a negative influence on the College's "intellectual environment"—an extraordinarily tall order for any student newspaper.[4]

The College's squeamishness was, however, selective; it did not extend to the publications of the left. Rather the contrary: Dartmouth has in the past officially recognized and even funded papers such as *Black Praxis*, *womyn's re/view*, and *Stet*. An official College publication describes *Stet* as "a student-run publication whose purpose is to present alternative writings and images on campus. In the past, this has included articles and literature written from Marxist, feminist, and traditionally liberal perspectives, as well as humorous pieces."[5] The description is euphemistic. One recent issue, for example, praises not only the Nicaraguan and Angolan revolutions, but also the "Afghan revolution, which continues to suffer at the hands of US proxy wars." Another page features crude drawings of hammers and sickles and guerrillas firing AK-47s, surrounded by slogans that include: "Long Live Albania," "Free South Africa," "Marx Lives," "Smash the Patriarchy," "Castro," "Che," "Victory to the Intifadah," "Lenin," "Krupskaya," "Stalin," and "Mao." The paper's masthead lists Professor Carla Freccero as one of its "workers"—it eschews the title "editor" as impermissibly elitist—and Professor Leo Spitzer has served as its faculty adviser.[6]

Stet's rhetoric is impressive in the consistency of its stridency and its angry pre-perestroika Leninist orthodoxy. "The two-party system in the United States is as totalitarian as the one-party system in the USSR," it declares, and predicts that "The people will smash Yankee Imperialism as well as Russian revisionism."[7]

Stet is, however, the soul of moderation in comparison with *womyn's re/view*, which once ran a cover featuring a nude woman, bound and gagged with what appears to be a horse's bridle—to make a "political" statement about pornography.[8] The paper describes itself as "an ongoing effort to create alternative linguistic and visual modes." It rejects all "conventional spellings which refer to wymin as a subset of man" and thus variously spells "women" as wimmyn, wimyn, wombyn, womben, and womyn. The issue with the bound nude woman on its cover listed several faculty members on its masthead (as sisters), including Professors Freccero, Ivy Schweitzer, and Marianne Hirsch.*

---

* The paper formally disassociated itself from "Dartmyth College" in 1987 "rebelling against its phallocentric, racist ideologies." The issue with the bound and gagged nude woman was, however, published while it was still affiliated with the College. The issue gives "special thanks" to the Women's Issues League, the Education Department, the Gay Students Association, and *Stet*.

It included essays, art work, and poetry, including "Angry Feminist Poem," which read in part:

> Could you tell me, please
> How not to get fucked-over
> I wanted to tell you
> How not to fuck me over
> How not to fuck my sister over
> But couldn't stay angry long enough
> To be sure.[9]

Another opus in verse, called "Insatiable II" began:

> Who watched who
> drag anyone's head
> push it
> in anyone's groin
> slap anyone's face
> gag who
> Wrench anyone's breast
> hear who
> beg and stoop and moan
> with Ahhh
> YOU BITCH
> SUCK IT
> better yet
> shave anyone's lips down there
> like a someone
> of five
> wrench it out of anyone
> NO YES NO
> straddled
> over the pool table . . .

And so on for six verses.[10]

In its Spring 1988 issue, *womyn's re/view* devoted a full page to an analysis of feminist graffiti, which "speaks of our bonding, our frustration, our anger, and, ultimately, our oppression." Examples of feminist graffiti that were analyzed included "castrate the capitalist patriarchy" ("it incorporates the ideas of socialist feminism"); "Anarchy Now" ("i wrote it because it was empowering. . . . i wanted to break the system apart, to blow it up."); "Dead Men Don't Rape"; and "W.I.T.C.H. is everywhere" ("there were only five of us witches, but i had the feeling that we were everywhere, the subversive elements were permeating everywhere.")

The back page of the issue includes "Contraceptive hints from the *womyn's re/view*" ("The best contraceptive for a woman?? Another woman, of course.")

Exercising what it regarded as its linguistic playfulness, the paper also offered a lengthy list of "feminist ice-cream flavors," including "chocolate castration," "wimmim walnut," "luscious lesbian lime," "clitoral chip," "cunnilingus coconut chip," "fruity phallic frogurt," "oreo orgasm," "double dutch diaphragm," and "lovely labia licorice."[11]

I have described the content of the papers here at some length to give some idea of the atmosphere in which *The Dartmouth Review* would be judged, and the standards of taste and decorum expected from Dartmouth publications.

Over the years, the *Review* was guilty of several notable lapses in taste. One article referred to a senior professor as "This quim queen of a professor [who] just can't separate English from her neurotic obsession with the human crotch." Of another, "His knowledge of classroom etiquette lies somewhere between a moderately educated welfare queen and a bathroom attendant." The paper routinely referred to those it disdained as "moronic" and "sleazy." Criticizing the College's affirmative action policies—a favorite theme—the paper could not resist a poke at President Kemeny's physique, opining, "Dartmouth's affirmative action policy is now, like former President Kemeny, fat and out of control."[12]

But the most serious lapse in judgment came in 1982, when the paper ran a column titled, "Dis sho' ain't no jive, bro," signed by editor Keeney Jones. The column was intended as a satire, with several targets, and was inspired by a sequence in the hit movie *Airplane*. In the movie, two black passengers are conversing in unintelligible argot, which is translated by multilingual actress Barbara Billingsley, who happens to speak "jive."

The *Review*'s "jive" column, though signed by Keeney Jones, was, in fact, not written by him. It was reportedly based on notes taken by another *Review* staffer of her roommate's syntax and vocabulary, and was written into a satire by another senior staffer, and signed by Jones.[13] It read, in part:

'Firmative action be having bad [good] 'fects on us blacks. It be gettin' into Ivy schools from the inner city, even do we not be bustin's our gizzards doin' work. But where the Ivy be at? Now we be comin' to Dartmut and be up over our 'fros in studies, but we still be not graduatin' Phi Beta Kappa. . . .[14]

The intended targets of the satire were multiple: reverse discrimination and the lowering of College standards under the rubric of "diversity"; the widespread assertion that "black English" was an admirable alternative dialect; and the College's penchant for racial pandering. But the column provided College authorities with a powerful target, and they eagerly seized on the spoof as a sign of the paper's alleged "racism."

The "jive" column was later disavowed by the paper's editor and condemned by some of the paper's conservative supporters, who questioned its taste. Congressman Jack Kemp resigned from the paper's board of advisors. Even eight years later, "Dis sho' ain't no jive, bro" is routinely cited by the administration and faculty, even though its author and most of its readers have long since graduated. One recent editor refers to the legacy of the column as "an albatross around the necks of current editors who are frequently forced to explain it."[15]

From the beginning, the *Review* was rendered suspect in the eyes of the College by the strong support, both moral and financial, the paper received from national conservatives. For some critics, that outside backing meant that the paper would be seen as a "subsidized alien presence on campus." But what such criticism does not take into account is that despite its outside support, the *Review* has always been written and edited by students—with all that implies for its consistency, judgment, and temperament. Its writing is often brilliant, occasionally obnoxious, and sometimes sophomoric (much of it *is*, after all, written by sophomores). At times nasty, unfair, and irrelevant, at others powerfully on target, the *Review* employed the full armorarium of outrageousness, satire, and wit to prick at the most cherished postures and attitudes of the Dartmouth culture.

It also represented something radically new on the campus. The *Review* appeared at a moment when the revolutionary spirit of the 1960s had ossified into place as the orthodoxy of the 1980s. It was not so much that conservative values were held in disdain, they were simply ignored. Conor Cruise O'Brien has commented on the left's penchant for neglecting its adversaries and for dismissing "even their most influential writings, unread, with a sneer."[16] At Dartmouth, the *Review* helped change that.

Most disconcerting of all for the veterans of the 1960s was that the source of this reactionary upsurge was the students themselves. "It was no longer the leftist students who had the energy, the wit and the new ideas necessary to launch a successful assault on a stuffy, Philistine conservative establishment," observed one of the paper's founding editors, Benjamin Hart. "The Sixties were gone. Today it is conservative students who are writing the satire, ridiculing the pompous and comfortable members of the liberal establishment, many of whom had not heard, or had, a new idea in over a decade."[17]

At Dartmouth, the phenomenon was perhaps magnified by the College's intellectual insularity and physical isolation. *Newsweek* writer Larry Martz, himself a Dartmouth graduate, found on his return to campus in 1988 that faculty liberals at Dartmouth, "live in a world that seems almost hermetically sealed, with an astonishing lack of awareness for the values of . . . the mainstream."[18]*

"There is a kind of liberal bigotry at Dartmouth and elsewhere," Chauncey Loomis, a former chairman of the English Department, declared. "The liberal way of thinking becomes the only way, and they do their best to blind themselves to that."[19]

By the end of the 1970s, President Kemeny had been reduced to pleading with students not to write critical letters to the *Alumni Magazine*, and was given to manichean declarations that implied that one was either for immediate disarmament or a warmonger; that one either believed in College funding for lesbian groups or was a woman-hater.[20] Into this atmosphere of ideological pietism, the *Review* and its ideological warriors crashed upon the scene as an uninvited, unwelcome, and highly embarrassing guest.

The paper freely satirized the College's penchant for the jargon of "diversity" and "feelings." Dinesh D'Souza, who would later go on to a

---

* Administrators, for example, appeared genuinely surprised when they were criticized for inviting Angela Davis to be the *keynote speaker* at the College's celebration of 15 years of co-education in 1988. They declared themselves baffled that anyone would take exception to the introduction given her by then-Dean of Faculty Dwight Lahr, who called Davis "an example of how one committed black woman has chosen to make a difference," but made no reference to her Communist Party affiliation or to her allegedly violent past.

job in the Reagan White House and the American Enterprise Institute, penned devastating send-ups of the regnant ideology, including one in which he invited readers to create their own politically correct phraseology from three rows of buzz-words popular among administrators. Examples: "profound dialectical relationship," "genuine human dialogue," and "meaningful communal oneness."[21] The paper was often outrageous in its spoofs. To highlight their opposition to College funding for the Gay Students Alliance, several editors proposed College funding for the "Dartmouth Bestiality Association," arguing that the group would meet "the need to raise people's consciousness about alternative sexual orientations."[22] The administration solemnly turned them down.

The paper also had a more serious agenda. It called for a reform of the College's curriculum to put greater stress on the "great ideas" of Western civilization and it opposed the excesses in the College's affirmative action quotas. It questioned the academic merit of some of the special "studies" programs and it urged the restoration of the Indian symbol.*

The paper won early plaudits. Even such liberal journals as *The New Republic* took note of the paper, saying "it has succeeded where countless tenured professors have failed—in stirring up animated debate on campus." Former Treasury Secretary William Simon said that the *Review* "proves that the tedious old cliches which have dominated academic life for so long are now defunct." William F. Buckley, Jr., was even more enthusiastic, calling the paper "a vibrant, joyful, provocative challenge to the regnant but brittle liberalism for which American colleges are renowned."[23] A measure of its success is the number of staffers who have gone on to become authors and influential journalists, including Benjamin Hart, Gregory Fossedal (formerly with *The Wall Street Journal*), Dinesh D'Souza, and cartoonist Steve Kelley.

The College, however, was manifestly unamused. As the paper drew national attention, the shrillness of the administration's reaction inten-

---

* It's zeal for the Indian symbol was somewhat ambivalent. One early editor acknowledged that he couldn't care less about the symbol. But again, the administration's rigidity on the issue seems to have given it a special status: because it was the one form of expression banned on campus, its display—on t-shirts, bumper-stickers, or on illegal banners—became a symbol of dissent and non-conformity. It was also a virtually guaranteed way to get a rise from the College. Every time College security officials ripped down the banner at a football game and imposed fines on the students holding it, the *Review* was handed more martyrs and converts.

sified. Both administrators and faculty insisted they objected to the style of the paper rather than its content. But Economics Professor Colin Campbell was unconvinced. "The faculty critics are not honest when they say they object to the style," he said. "It's really because of its politics."

Both at its best and its worst, the *Review* tested the College's commitment to tolerance and to the diversity of *ideas*. It was a test the College failed, not merely once, but repeatedly in a series of blunders that would make the student weekly a national media phenomenon. In that sense, Dartmouth's administration created the *Review*. None of its success, national publicity, messianic zeal, or financial support would have materialized had not the College itself repeatedly and ineptly risen to the paper's provocations.

The College's refusal to observe even elementary standards of fair play provided the *Review* with a moral stature it could never have achieved on its own. The treatment of *Review* staffers led the paper's conservative supporters to overlook the paper's occasional deficiencies and lapses in judgment; while the College's insistence on dismissing the paper as racist, sexist, and homophobic meant that the legitimate issues the *Review* has raised were seldom given a fair hearing in the Dartmouth community. It is hard to avoid the feeling that the debate over the *Review* has become a convenient substitute for arguing about more fundamental issues.

In *Poisoned Ivy*, Benjamin Hart has recorded the story of the *Review*'s early days, a tragi-comic farce of Dartmouth's efforts to strangle the infant paper in its crib.*

Almost from the moment of its inception, the College threatened legal action to block the *Review*'s use of the title "Dartmouth," even though a good number of the businesses in Hanover freely appropriate the College's name without objection from the institution.[24] What really concerned the College was the *Review*'s breach of Dartmouth's monopoly on communications with alumni. Benjamin Hart quotes an attorney for Dartmouth objecting to the paper on the grounds that "we don't think it's a good idea for alumni to receive two opinions about what is happening on the campus," because that would be "very destructive and divisive."

---

* "I'm not curious enough to want to read it," Kemeny told *The Washington Post* after Hart's book was published. "And besides, if I bought a copy of it, the money would go to some cause that I absolutely hate." (*The Washington Post*, December 5, 1984)

"One opinion is better than two," the College's attorney explained, "because two opinions tend to *divide* the community. . . ."[25]

Perhaps no other comment reflected the distance the College had travelled since the era of Hopkins. But the College's campaign of petty harassment had only begun with the threat of legal action. When a widow of a wealthy alumnus wrote a check for $10,000 to the paper, the College intercepted it and refused to release the money, yielding only when the outraged donor threatened to cut the College from her will unless the money was forwarded forthwith.[26] Switchboard operators for the College denied knowledge of the paper's existence when callers sought to contact the *Review*.[27] In October 1981, a College employee was caught dumping hundreds of copies of the paper into the garbage. The College threatened to arrest *Review* staffers if they tried to distribute the paper at football games. Alumni who contributed were pressured to drop their support. The College announced as "official policy" that no interviews were to be granted to *Review* reporters. When a freshman reporter for the paper called the Council on Student Organizations for information on student groups—information freely available to all undergraduates—the secretary said that she had been instructed by the president's office not to release the information to any *Review* staffer, because "students are entitled to information about [student] groups, but not students affiliated with *The Dartmouth Review*."[28] And in what was surely one of the most bizarre incidents in the history of College-media relations, Dartmouth's administration actually charged Greg Fossedal with allegedly "misappropriating" a press release that was displayed on a hook below a sign reading "Cleared for Release." *The Washington Post* later referred to charges against the young editor as "nebulous,"[29] but Fossedal was subjected to a nine hour hearing before a disciplinary committee of faculty members, some of whom had been openly hostile to the *Review*.* The panel found the young editor guilty of "misappropriation" and put him on "college discipline" for committing a flagrant act of journalism. Afterward a dean defended Dartmouth's curious approach to due process: "The CCSC [the disciplinary panel]

---

* Michael Green, chairman of Dartmouth's Native American Studies Department, a frequent target of the *Review*, presided at the tribunal that heard the case against Fossedal. In a 1984 interview with *The Washington Post*, Green said of the *Review*: "It's almost as though folks take the ideas of children seriously. That is what I find so absolutely staggering."

does not have to prove guilt beyond a reasonable doubt. If evidence of guilt exceeds the evidence of innocence, we have to respect that."[30]

No incident in the paper's early career, however, drew as much attention as the attack on young Benjamin Hart by one of the College's black administrators, Samuel Smith, while Hart was attempting to distribute copies of the newspaper. In the altercation, Smith attempted to push Hart through a plate glass door, kicked and punched him, and when Hart tried to restrain the attacker in a headlock, bit him.*

Smith subsequently received a court-imposed fine and probation and a week-long suspension *with pay* from the College for the attack on the student journalist. The incident cost Smith three lower incisors. Hart was forced to get a tetanus shot. But what made the incident truly extraordinary (and ludicrous) was the aftermath. Meeting three days after Smith's attack on Hart, Dartmouth's faculty voted 113 to 5 to censure not the administrator who had attacked an undergraduate, but *The Dartmouth Review*.[31]

In what was to become something of a College ritual, faculty members rose one after another to denounce the student paper as racist, sexist, and elitist. Declared Professor William Cole: "It's about time these racists *were run out of town*."[32] Cole's attacks, however, were not confined to mere rhetorical expression.

In early 1983, a young reporter for the *Review*, Laura Ingraham, sat in on one of Cole's Music 2 classes. Her subsequent article reported how Cole arrived late, left class for periods of as long as ten minutes at a time, and spent at least half of his lecture on "the race question," referring to students as racist and sexist. The course was a notorious "gut" on the Dartmouth campus; its syllabus was three lines long. Requirements included a "journal" that did not have to be about music at all, while the final exam was a collective "name that tune" test.

"Nothing worries Bill Cole," wrote Ingraham. "Not students, not regulations, not teaching. Nothing."[33]

After the article ran, an angry Cole went to Ingraham's dorm room early on a Saturday morning and pounded on the door for nearly 20 minutes. "You cocksuckers fuck with everybody," Cole shouted at reporters for the *Review*. "You have fucked with the last person."[34]

---

* The incident harkened back to the legacy of 1969. Smith had been named an assistant director of admissions as a direct result of the College's hasty settlement with the Afro-American Society in April of that year.

Later he announced that he was cancelling his class until the *Review* apologized to him. The Dean of Faculty told Cole that he could be fired if he did not meet with his classes. Cole's behavior met with no other sanction, despite the fact that he repeatedly referred to students affiliated with the *Review* as "motherfuckers" during a class session.[35]

Again, the faculty provided almost unanimous support for Cole. A fellow music professor announced that if he were Cole, he would have "busted [Ingraham's] kneecaps."[36] Others helped raise money for Cole's abortive libel suit against the *Review*. (He later dropped it.) Even after Cole shouted at another co-ed walking across the campus green that "I'm going to fucking blow you up!" the administration took no action, even though the female student reported the incident and expressed concern for her physical safety.[37]

In any other circumstance, the use of physical threats and obscenities by a member of the faculty against a female undergraduate would have resulted in vigorous action by the administration. But the administrators in Parkhurst Hall remained silent. By then, Kemeny had long since retired and been replaced by a new president. The *Review* and other conservatives had welcomed the choice of David McLaughlin as Kemeny's successor in the expectation that his selection would usher in a dramatically new atmosphere on campus. They did not understand how profoundly the College had changed.

XXI

COUP D'ETAT

Years afterward, David McLaughlin would summon up a memory from the waning days of his undergraduate career at Dartmouth.

"I remember standing and watching the entire campus arrayed across the lawn of Dartmouth Hall [during Green Key weekend] and watching the fraternity hums. The whole community was stretched across that wonderful expanse of landscape. You felt that the College was embracing you and you could embrace it back in a special way."[1]

Few students in the College's history had been embraced as thoroughly by Dartmouth's traditions or had embraced them as thoroughly in return. McLaughlin served as president of the Undergraduate Council, president of his junior class, lettered in three sports, and in his senior year set three gridiron records, ranking as the fifth leading pass receiver in the nation.

Later called the "most visible and perhaps the most admired member of the class of 1954,"[2] McLaughlin was awarded the Barret Cup for leadership, scholarship, and character; and was honored as the College's best all-around athlete of 1953-54. He graduated Phi Beta Kappa.

Eschewing a career in pro-football for business, McLaughlin had been similarly successful, rising to the presidency of the Toro Company at age 39 in 1970 and to the chairmanship in 1973. His ties to Dartmouth had remained strong. He served as chairman of the Board of Overseers of Dartmouth's Amos Tuck School of Business Administration and in 1971 had been named to the Board of Trustees of the College. In 1977 he became chairman of the Dartmouth Board of Trustees.

McLaughlin's selection as successor to John Kemeny as the fourteenth president of Dartmouth came as a surprise, but was not completely without precedent. Ernest Martin Hopkins had also been a businessman and William Jewett Tucker had been a veteran member of the board of trustees.

The choice of McLaughlin signalled another of the College's attempts to achieve a sense of balance. The Kemeny years had been a period of turmoil in which change—coeducation, the various studies programs, the suppression of the Indian symbol—had come too rapidly and spawned the counterrevolutionary *Dartmouth Review*.

As a trustee and later as chairman, McLaughlin had supported or at least acquiesced in Kemeny's policies; but he was a safer alternative. If alumni ties had grown strained in Kemeny's latter years, who better to assuage concern than the quintessential Dartmouth man himself? And in an era in which financial concerns were paramount, who better to run the College than an experienced chief executive officer? Likeable and competent, McLaughlin was a man whom others instinctively came to trust and rely upon. He was also an insider whose conservative instincts were well known. In 1979, as board chairman, he had taken what appeared to be a strongly conservative stand:

> On campus, the pervasive voice of dissent over Vietnam in the late 1960s has evolved into a multitude of single interest groups, each believing that they are entitled to immediate answers. While Dartmouth has responded to accommodate the new social environment, it has never been our intent, and it is not now, that the rights of the special or single interest elements should ever override or compromise the rights of the greater College community.[3]

McLaughlin stressed the need to assimilate, and perhaps modify, the changes of the last decade "to assure that they reinforce the traditional values of the College."

For alumni whose teeth had been set on edge for most of the last decade, McLaughlin's words were reassuring; they also hinted at a return to normal life at Dartmouth.

Despite their different worldviews, the transition between Kemeny and McLaughlin was expected to be smooth and painless. From the trustees' perspective, there was no reason to believe that McLaughlin would not prove one of the College's most successful presidents.

Five years later, McLaughlin would resign virtually in disgrace; hounded by an unrelentingly hostile faculty and alienated from both the right and the left.

The events that destroyed McLaughlin's presidency were ostensibly centered around two main issues: the restoration of ROTC on campus and the shanties erected on the Dartmouth Green to protest South African apartheid. But as Winston Churchill once remarked, great quarrels "arise from small occasions, but seldom from small causes."[4] At stake was the question of who really ran Dartmouth College.

THE MAN FROM TORO

Unfortunately, David McLaughlin entered upon the presidency at a singularly inauspicious moment in his own career. In only two years, McLaughlin's company, Toro, had gone from what *Forbes* called "one of the year's hottest growth items,"[5] to a company on the very edge of disaster. Under McLaughlin's leadership, Toro had grown rapidly throughout the 1970s with revenues rising from $57 million in 1970 to $350 million by decade's end.[6] McLaughlin aggressively pushed the company into a radically expanded product line—including snow-blowers and chain saws—to take advantage of the Toro name. By the end of the decade snow-removal equipment accounted for half of Toro's $17.4 million annual profit. McLaughlin confidently projected revenues of $700 million within five years.[7]

He did not, however, take into account the weather.

The winter of 1979-80 was notable for its light snowfall; and booming Toro suddenly found itself with bloated inventories. Sales of snow-blowers dropped to $40 million from $130 million only a year earlier. The disaster was compounded by the next winter, which was also dry. Snowblower sales plummeted even further in 1982, to only $5.8 million.[8] Toro's setbacks multiplied. A garden tiller was recalled; a lawn hose-and-reel system had to be redesigned. And in what seemed a final act of divine displeasure, Mount St. Helens rained ash over one of the cities Toro had picked to market a new low-cost mower trimmer.[9] Overall, Toro's total sales dropped 38 percent, from $400 million to $247 million and the bottom line plunged into the red. The losing streak would extend for ten consecutive quarters, with cumulative losses of more than $30 million. To cut costs the company laid off 27 percent of its 4,000 employees and fired 125 managers, including the man McLaughlin had personally recruited as president.[10]

Two weeks later, McLaughlin resigned to become Dartmouth's president.

"It turned out that [McLaughlin's resignation] was a hell of a good thing," Toro board member Thomas Keating, a former chairman of Honeywell, Inc., told *Business Week* magazine. "It would have been hard for Dave to face up to the fact that [his way] wasn't working."[11]

Perhaps unfairly, but also inevitably, the timing of his selection as College president fueled suspicion that the trustees were simply bailing out a friend. McLaughlin did not arrive in Hanover trailing clouds of glory.

The precipitous fall from grace at Toro would have shaken the confidence of any man, especially someone whose career had been as uniformly successful as McLaughlin's had been. The new president kept up a brave front, throwing himself into his new duties with what the *Alumni Magazine* called "a passion for efficiency."[12] But a profile of McLaughlin five months into his tenure paints a startlingly different man than the executive *Forbes* had praised only three years earlier for his "relaxed" style and "effortless" achievements.[13]

> Tall and thin, McLaughlin is, understandably looking a little haggard these days, a little gray, though the warmth and directness of his striking blue eyes temper the fact considerably. He is a tightly controlled man, a former athlete strangely without fluidity. He moves slowly, in a sort of locked deliberateness, a suspension in tension, and speaks completely without gesture. If David McLaughlin were ever to be taken off guard, it's safe to say no muscle of his body would betray the fact.[14]

If McLaughlin would later seem diffident and insecure in his relations with the faculty, he was determined to be master of the College's administration. At Toro, McLaughlin had been known as a "hands-on" manager deeply involved in the details of running the company.[15] He transferred his style to the College, moving quickly to replace Kemeny's administrative holdovers with his own men and demanding absolute loyalty. When McLaughlin decided that the *Alumni Magazine* was excessively independent and insufficiently deferential, he forced the editor out. The associate director of foundation and corporate relations, David Dawley, later resigned, lambasting McLaughlin for creating a "stifling" atmosphere within the administration. Dawley accused McLaughlin of creating a "secretive" and "hierarchical" environment in the administration that discouraged discussion and dissent. "The feeling is, if you want to speak out, get out."[16]

His style with the faculty could not have been more different. Stung by the criticism of his appointment, and subjected to continual browbeating from the liberal faculty, McLaughlin pursued a policy of aggressive diplomacy bordering on appeasement that included a 30 percent salary increase for the faculty. If he expected the pay boost would make him more popular, or even acceptable to the faculty, he was disappointed. He was also disappointed in his attempts to appease faculty sentiment on other issues.

Privately, he assured friends and alumni of his affection for the now-banned Indian symbol. But on campus, he denounced it as inappropriate and racist. When liberal faculty members renewed attacks on the Hovey Grill Indian murals, he tried to have them removed, covered them up again, uncovered them for alumni events, then had them permanently covered. He cut the budget of the liberal Tucker Foundation, but did little to bring balance to the increasing leftward tilt of the speakers brought to campus.

His attempts to straddle the issues lost him the respect of the traditionalist alumni and won him no points with the liberal faculty. It was a pattern to be repeated again and again throughout his presidency.

Part of the explanation for his vacillation and ambivalence can be laid to his apparent intimidation by the faculty. But contributing to that was his weak grasp on many of the educational issues at the heart of the College, including the curriculum.

In his inaugural address, for example, McLaughlin struck a decisively conservative note, quoting Ernest Martin Hopkins' credo that the "goal of education is the cultivation and development of our mental powers to the end that we may know truth and conform to it." And he warned against the "tendencies toward overspecialization, excessive utilitarianism and curricular discontinuities. . . ."

But several comments also made it clear that despite his decade as a trustee, McLaughlin did not fully comprehend how Dartmouth had changed over the last twenty years. When for example, he said that "It serves us well to remember that the College has never wavered from its original purpose," he appeared to write off much of the recent history of the College.

Even more puzzling was his reference to the national movement in favor of core curricula. "Many of our sister institutions are today rediscovering the value of a disciplined undergraduate curriculum in the liberal arts, *which Dartmouth—in steadfast pursuit of Wheelock's vision —never abandoned.*"[17] [Emphasis added.] It is difficult to believe that a former chairman of the board of trustees would imagine that Dartmouth *had* a core curriculum or would believe that it had never watered down its curriculum.* As a matter of simple fact he was incorrect, as Kemeny certainly knew. But it revealed a more fundamental weakness; McLaughlin never had more than a marginal understanding of curricular reform and was thus destined to be ineffectual in implementing significant changes.[†] Even so, shifts in the curricular center continued apace.

In the waning years of the Kemeny administration, faculty committees had proposed modestly tightening the College's distribution requirements, but the proposals had not been adopted. One of the proposals, however, had a better fate. The committee proposed that

---

* In fact, McLaughlin was apparently not alone among the trustees in his limited understanding of the curriculum. In a 1983 interview, Walter Burke, then chairman of the trustees, was asked about a required course in classic Western civilization. Burke responded: "That sounds like a great idea to me, but I don't know that my opinion is all that vital on that. *But I do remind you that the distributive requirements at Dartmouth never did back off that, whereas a good many other institutions did.*" (*The Dartmouth Review*, December 5, 1983.) Although Dartmouth did not eliminate the distribution requirements, it *did* water them down. As late as 1989, members of the trustees would continue to insist that Dartmouth had a core and that it had never loosened its distribution requirements.

† The only notable change enacted under McLaughlin was the requirement that students complete 12 academic terms rather than 11 and spend their entire senior year in residence.

students be required to take one course in "a culture or cultures outside of Western Europe and North America." The proposal was not new; similar suggestions had been made as early as 1960.

In the fall of 1981, the faculty gave final approval to what was to be known as the "non-Western requirement." The new requirement did not result from student agitation. In fact, student opinion was sharply divided over the proposed new requirement. A poll taken in early January 1980, found 40 percent of the students opposed to the idea, while 39 percent favored it.[18] Faculty support was, however, overwhelming and the new requirement was passed virtually without dissent.

The term "non-Western" was somewhat misleading, because East-West considerations appeared to be irrelevant in the choice of courses.* Latin American studies were included, for example, but not courses on Brazil. Arabic and Native American Studies were considered non-Western; but not Hebrew or Russian. College spokesmen were at pains to describe the rationale of the program. "If it is something coming from Spain," Registrar Douglas Bowen explained, "then it wouldn't count, but ancient Mexican culture would. In the same way, studies about black culture stemming from Africa is allowed, but American black culture is not."[19]

Bowen was wrong. By 1989, a course such as "Black Theater, U.S.A." was counted towards the "non-Western" requirement. So too was "Early Black American Literature" and "Modern Black American Literature." Political considerations seem to have had a powerful role in shaping the new requirement. Although courses in Anthropology, Geography, and Government are included in the non-Western program, there was no course in Economics in 1988-89.[20] Some courses, such as "American Music in the Oral Tradition," appear to have been included only because they were taught by a black faculty member. The commitment of the curriculum to non-Western cultures was also problematic. While it includes oppression courses such as "Women and Change in the Third World," Dartmouth offered no course in Japanese until recently, even though the non-Western requirement has been in place since the early 1980s.[21]

A more accurate characterization of the "non-Western" requirement was offered in recent years by the College's Women's Support Task

---

* In 1990, students could select among 115 courses to satisfy the non-Western requirement.

Force, which referred to it as the "Third World" requirement, a term that seems far more candid about its political agenda.[22]

The new requirements also highlighted the gaps in Dartmouth's curriculum. Professor Jeffrey Hart did not object to the new policy, but called it frivolous. "It's only a gesture in a total cultural vacuum," he said in 1981. "When you are not required to take Plato, while you have a non-Western requirement, where does it fit?"[23]

Hart delivered a devastating critique of the liberal arts curriculum at the College. "An old professor of mine, at Dartmouth, memorably defined the 'citizen' as the person who, if necessary, could re-found this civilization," Hart wrote. "In no sense at Dartmouth are we even attempting to nurture civilization in that sense. The present curriculum has many virtues. It contains brilliant individual courses. But most Dartmouth seniors do not know much more about the civilization of which they are a part than they did as freshmen."[24]

During a 1982 symposium on the future of the College organized by McLaughlin and then-Dean Hans Penner, Hart proposed the establishment of a new comprehensive course in Western civilization, modelled on the Humanities I and II course at Columbia, where Hart had graduated in 1952 and where he did his graduate work in the mid-1950s. As a Columbia professor Hart had taught a section of the famed Humanities course and had imbibed the spirit of that remarkable period.

Hart characterized the Humanities I and II courses as "Athens and Jerusalem" and "Reason and Faith" —"the drive for universals, and the drive to crystallize the sacred. The great polarities, forced, in major texts, to the extreme." The course accomplished a number of things for students, Hart argued:

> Perhaps most important, it made intelligent conversation possible among undergraduates. They actually had interesting things to talk about with one another, an unusual situation, and, as they experienced it, a cheerful and stimulating one. Moreover, even the very least of students had the impression that he (Columbia was male) had been somehow dealing with very important matters. And he was right.
>
> But for the good students, even for the fair-to-middling students, the course was a revelation. . . .

For Hart, the Columbia courses were the paradigm of liberal education because they provided

> a necessary corrective to provincialism, which seems always on the verge of inundating us.
>
> It demonstrated that a powerful history of thought and feeling lies behind the present moment. By providing the students with a common body of knowledge, it liberated them: they had something other than trivia to talk about with one another. It did the same for the faculty, allowing them to transcend in a good way the limits of their professional specialties.

Hart also made a passionate plea for the values of the West. Although other cultures had undeniable value, he insisted that because Dartmouth students were heirs to the culture of the West, "it therefore seems reasonable to acquaint ourselves with *that* civilization before examining others." More pointedly, he attacked the relativism inherent in much of the faculty thinking.

> The non-Western world has done some interesting things in the lyric and the narrative, and in some instances it has rich traditions of religious meditation. But there does not appear to be any non-Western equivalent—aesthetically or intellectually—of, say, Dante or Beethoven. There is no African or Asian Shakespeare or Mozart. And certainly nothing comparable to the Western tradition of systematic philosophy. If a Chinese—the most impressive of non-Western cultures—wants to be a philosopher, Confucius and Lao-Tse do not take him very far. He must engage Hume, Kant, Wittgenstein. There are very good reasons why this is so, having to do with the creative tension between Athens and Jerusalem, which persists in the Western tradition.[25]

McLaughlin was sympathetic to Hart's proposal and actually endorsed it in principle. It was a promising beginning. Although Hart's proposal ran against the current of the academic culture at the College, it was based on one of higher education's most successful models. He had made a powerful and eloquent case for the new course and the national mood seemed ripe for a significant reformation of liberal education.

Nothing ever came of it. McLaughlin invited Hart to lunch and told him that he had concluded that the College could not afford the Humanities course. But by then, McLaughlin's views were more or less irrelevant in any case.

ROTC, AGAIN

Abolished at Dartmouth in 1969, ROTC had made a remarkable comeback in the Reagan era. Nothing revealed the new generation gap on campus or its paradoxical reversal of roles as clearly as the debate over restoring the program. In February 1985, the Student Assembly voted overwhelmingly to endorse the restoration of ROTC; faculty opposition was adamant.

McLaughlin's position on the issue was typically ambivalent. He was widely known to be sympathetic to ROTC. In 1983, a poll showed students favored the restoration of a Naval ROTC program by a two to one margin. But faculty opposition was strong and McLaughlin was not prepared to fight on the issue. He killed the NROTC proposal. But rumors of ROTC's resurrection continued.

In order to assure its veto power over any further attempts to bring ROTC back, the faculty declared in 1984 that "any educational program, including ROTC, introduced to the College" was subject to faculty approval. Although the faculty had long been pre-eminent in curricular issues, its power had always been technically advisory. Before the faculty's self-declared veto, the ultimate authority of the trustees had never been seriously questioned. However, neither McLaughlin nor the trustees moved decisively to reaffirm the traditional balance of power at the College, a failure that would cost the president dearly.

In 1985, the faculty voted overwhelmingly—113 to 39—to reject ROTC. The vote was a direct challenge to McLaughlin and the trustees with whom the final decision rested.

The issue now was twofold. The first was ideological, the widespread loathing of the military and American foreign policy among the faculty. The second was the issue of authority. Who had final say over the curriculum?

After years of appeasement, McLaughlin, pressed by the Trustees, chose now to take his stand. A week after the faculty's vote, McLaughlin announced that he was restoring ROTC in spite of the faculty mandate.

For both McLaughlin and the trustees, it was a heady declaration of independence from faculty dominance. But it was also a startling reversal.

Even before the decision was announced, 52 alarmed faculty members signed a letter to the administration to avert what they said would be a "leadership crisis" at the College if the president defied the faculty. Anthropology Professor Hoyt Alverson acknowledged to *The Dartmouth* that ROTC had been a low priority item for the faculty. "The issue is what happens when something is rammed down your throat," he said. "Then it becomes a high priority." The next month, a poll found three-quarters of the faculty dissatisfied with McLaughlin's leadership. Shortly afterward, the faculty voted 167 to 2 to form an ad hoc committee to examine "College governance."

In January 1986, the faculty committee's report was completed. It referred to a "sense of widespread unrest" among the faculty and declared that Dartmouth was in the midst of a "leadership crisis."

The report called McLaughlin's decision-making style "antithetical to the effective governance" of the College and rebuked him for ignoring the faculty's role in governance and his alleged insensitivity to educational concerns.[26]

The report was not the first faculty assault on McLaughlin. The previous November had seen the academic department heads vote 26 to 1 to express "no confidence" in McLaughlin's ability to make a decision on the future of the Dartmouth Hitchcock Medical Center.

It was also clear that the faculty had never completely forgiven him for his business background. "Many of us," Classics Professor Edward Bradley told *The Boston Globe*, "feel that his experience as a corporate manager is indelible. He continues to act as if we are a corporation and he is the chairman. The faculty are the employees. The alumni are the shareholders and the students are the consumers."[27]

But the ultimate goal of this latest report was never in question. The chairman of the ad hoc committee declared that its aim was to "re-establish the central role of the faculty in the decision making process. . . ." Said the report:

> The sentiment seems practically universal among the faculty that it has been frustrated in its attempt to play its traditional, proper and necessary role in the governance of the College.

Despite the claim of monolithic opposition to McLaughlin, some faculty members spoke up in McLaughlin's defense. "All his genuine achievements are put in a context where they really don't count," said English Professor Donald Pease.[28] But, significantly, McLaughlin could not count on his own administration for unqualified support. Marysa Navarro, who had been elevated to an associate deanship, described the attack on the president as "a strong report that very much reflects the sentiment of the faculty. There's a great deal of unease on the campus and we find that echoed in the report."[29]

The faculty report was accepted by the Executive Committee of the Faculty and forwarded to the full faculty, where a motion of "no confidence" would be debated. By the time the issue came up, however, the College had plunged even deeper into chaos—the result of one of the more bizarre episodes in American higher education.

THE SHANTIES

In the absence of a catalyzing issue like the Vietnam war, student activists had fixed upon the issue of South African apartheid as the focus of their discontent. Across the country, pressure was applied to university administrations and trustees to divest their holdings in companies doing business in South Africa. For the first time since the early 1970s, campuses became the scenes for sit-ins, rallies, teach-ins, and other re-enactments of 1960s activism. But the most dramatic tactic of the new movement was the shanty. By erecting primitive, ramshackle shanty-towns on college campuses, the demonstrators sought to graphically depict the plight of South African blacks.

On November 15, 1985, members of a group calling itself the Dartmouth Community for Divestment (DCD) began building a shanty-town on the Green. The group accompanied the shanties with two demands: that the College immediately divest itself of all holdings in companies that "trade with or have subsidiaries in South Africa," and that the trustees turn over all authority to invest College resources to a "committee on ethical investment" to be selected by the "Dartmouth community."

From the beginning, the administration's response to the shanties was confused, inconsistent, and often self-contradictory. Two days after their appearance, College Dean Edward Shanahan hand-delivered an order demanding that the DCD remove the structures that same day. His position seemed clear. "If you do not remove the shanties," he wrote, "it will be necessary for the College to remove the structures."

The shanties remained. The College did nothing. When the demonstrators defied his order and built *another* shanty, the College took no action and College spokesman Alex Huppe said "there is currently no plan by the College to dismantle the shantytown."[30]

Faculty support for the demonstrators was vociferous. On November 20, 50 faculty members had joined with 300 students in a march on Parkhurst Hall to express solidarity with the divestment activists. Earlier in the year the faculty had unanimously endorsed divestiture.[31]

The administration's handling of the issue was complicated by McLaughlin's absence from Hanover. Without the president on the scene, Shanahan was unwilling to take decisive action on his own. But McLaughlin's return did little to clarify matters. Still smarting from the confrontation over ROTC and painfully conscious of the looming clash with the faculty, McLaughlin backed off from Shanahan's hard line. Somewhat cryptically, McLaughlin said that the dean's order to remove the shanties was "not meant in quite the way it was interpreted."

The president then announced that the shanties would be permitted to remain on the Green "as long as they are serving an educational purpose."* McLaughlin, however, had failed to defuse the situation. On January 9, as the president was having lunch with a reporter from *The New York Times*—to discuss the "leadership crisis" at Dartmouth—student demonstrators entered his office and announced a sit-in. McLaughlin left immediately and the 30 activists proceeded to occupy Parkhurst Hall for roughly four hours. Dean Shanahan denounced the takeover as "clearly disruptive" and indicated that the students would be subject to disciplinary action. But no penalties were ever imposed.[32]

Four days later, the arts and science faculty voted unanimously to ask the College to immediately begin divesting South African holdings.

Even so, enthusiasm for the shanties was difficult to sustain. On January 21, *The Dartmouth* editorialized that "Today the spirit that surrounded the construction of the shanties has faded and support of the DCD has dwindled." The shanties had actually become self-defeating

---

* An interesting subject of speculation might be the question of how he would have reacted had the shanties instead been wigwams? And if the issue had been the Indian symbol instead of divestment?

for the pro-divestiture activists, the paper said, and urged that they be dismantled.[33] The timing of the editorial was ironic.

That night, 12 students, mostly staff members of *The Dartmouth*'s *bête noire, The Dartmouth Review*, began taking down the shanties. Calling themselves the Dartmouth Committee to Beautify the Green Before Winter Carnival, the group's purported goal was to "reduce the disgraceful huts to pieces of wood suitable for transport and donation to more worthy charitable causes in the Hanover region." Arriving at the Green at around 2:45 A.M., the students used sledgehammers to attempt to dismantle three of the shanties. Two students were sleeping in a fourth shanty and it was not touched. The "attack" lasted less than five minutes before campus police arrived. The students handed the police a letter, explaining their actions. According to the police report, the students stopped dismantling the shanties immediately and were "very cooperative."

"They didn't give the officers any trouble," College Proctor Robert McEwen said.

The students later said they had acted as a result of frustration over "administrative inaction and after about one week of a general abandonment of the 'shanties'." They noted the administration's early threat to remove the shanties. "Since then, the only action the College had taken has been the provision of police protection and spotlights which illuminate the 'shanties' at nighttime."[34]

Despite the political overtones, the incident had all the markings of a College prank. "At the time our biggest concern was whether we'd make our ten o'clock classes the next day," one of the students later said. The student did not actually join in the dismantling of the shanties, she said, "because I fell in a snow bank I was laughing so hard."

The incident reflected both the strengths and weaknesses of the *Review*; the shanty assault was provocative, brash, and decidedly outside the normal bounds of campus journalism. The staffers' lapse was compounded by the fact that they had inadvertently chosen Martin Luther King, Jr.'s, birthday for their demonstration. A recent editor of the paper notes that in retrospect many *Review* staffers regarded the shanty removal exercise as "not the wisest solution to the problem."[35]*

---

* Another former *Review* editor, Dinesh D'Souza also agreed that the shanty attack was "ill-advised." The students, D'Souza argued, should have gone ahead with their original plan to build a Soviet-style gulag on the campus Green to highlight their argument that the Green was not a proper forum for "political architecture."

But again, it was the College's reaction to the *Review*'s prank that made the incident a national media sensation.

Militants on campus held a rally the next day to denounce the "attackers" as "fascists and maniacs." Speakers used the occasion to speak out on a myriad of issues, including racism, sexism, and homophobia. The extravagant rhetoric was indicative of the tone the debate would take over the next few days. Professor Thomas Roos lashed out at the attempted shanty removal, calling it "brownshirt bullying on the order of Kristallnacht." Others compared the students with the Ku Klux Klan, "cross-burners," and "terrorists."[36]

The Dartmouth's reaction was symptomatic of the new mood on campus. The day after editorializing that the shanties should be dismantled, it declared: "The students who participated in Tuesday morning's attack on the shanty town should be expelled from the College."[37]

Demonstrators—calling themselves the "Dartmouth Alliance Against Racism and Oppression"—once again occupied Parkhurst Hall. They were joined by a number of faculty members and even administrators, including Carla Freccero, Ivy Schweitzer, Leo Spitzer, Deborah King, and Gregory Ricks, assistant dean of the College.[38] Ricks had been one of the main speakers at the anti-*Review* rally, where he called the attempt to take the shanties down a "vicious, violent act with scary overtones," and demanded the administration move quickly to punish the students. During the speech, Ricks called the *Review* "a societal ill" and "garbage."[39]

Although he was an administrator, Ricks remained in the building throughout the occupation, "and often expressed support for the protestors," *The Dartmouth* reported.

"My heart is with this," Ricks told the paper.[40]

Members of the Afro-American Society burned in effigy the figure of one of the students involved in the attempt to dismantle the shanties and then conducted a mock trial in which it found the student—who was black—guilty of racism, calling him a "nigger."[41]

McLaughlin was out of town. But he cut short his alumni speaking tour in Florida to return to Hanover and his occupied office. When demonstrators demanded to know why McLaughlin had been absent from campus on Martin Luther King, Jr.'s, birthday, McLaughlin was apologetic. "My absence," he said, "wasn't an attempt to be insensitive to your burning need."[42] Through Shanahan, McLaughlin had made it clear he was concerned about the takeover of Parkhurst Hall, but that he was more concerned "with what happened on the Green."[43]

The faculty executive committee added to the growing atmosphere of crisis by calling an emergency meeting to consider declaring a College-wide moratorium on classes. "Even if the administration doesn't call off classes," declared Philosophy Professor Walter Sinnott-Armstrong, a member of the faculty executive committee, "the faculty itself does have some power. After all, they're the ones who teach the classes." Shortly afterward, Patricia Palmieri, an assistant professor of education, told the student demonstrators that a random sampling of members of the executive committee had revealed "very strong support for the students."

Professor Carla Freccero assumed a leading role in the takeover, leaning out of the window of Parkhurst to tell other faculty members to rally support for the occupiers. Discussing the situation in McLaughlin's office where students had been standing on his desk and turning over papers, Freccero declared, "It's too late for them to go into the hall. They've been pushed around by too many administration voices." She urged other faculty to let the executive committee know that the refusal of the protestors to leave the administration building was not "an act of wanton stubbornness."[44]

McLaughlin continued to straddle the issue. "I absolutely abhor any destruction of property," he said of the attempted removal of the shan-ties, "but it would be inappropriate for me . . . to condemn the act until due process has occurred."[45]

But the matter was taken out of the president's hands. The day after the takeover of Parkhurst, the faculty's executive committee implicitly endorsed the takeover of Parkhurst by cancelling all classes for Friday, January 24. The protestors who emerged from Parkhurst after their 30 hour sit-in, *The Dartmouth* reported, emerged "with an air of victory." The victory was sweeping in scope.

They had not merely succeeded in disrupting the operations of the College, but had succeeded in turning the incident into a grand political issue.

The "teach-in" declared by the faculty vote was "for the purpose of engaging a campus-wide discussion of racism, violence, and disrespect for diversity and opinion, as most recently demonstrated by the act of demolition of the shanties on the Green."[46] The faculty action clearly seemed to prejudge the case of the 12 students who still faced possible

disciplinary action for the shanty cleanup attempt. Avoiding such preju-
dicial action had appeared to be McLaughlin's main concern. But again,
the president reversed fields.

The same day as the faculty vote, McLaughlin issued an open letter to
the Dartmouth community:

> On Friday, January 24, Dartmouth College will commit the institu-
> tion to a discussion of the issue of human dignity on this campus. It
> is a matter of such vital importance that I ask all members of this
> community to join me in using these hours of learning and reflec-
> tion to improve the quality of caring and the climate of tolerance at
> Dartmouth. In effect, the work of the College is being totally
> redirected for one day of study. . . .
>
> We stop on this day to assess just what kind of a family we are
> and want to be. . . .
>
> Friday is an important day in the life of this institution, and I
> urge that you make a personal commitment to be part of the spirit
> and work of this day-long event.

McLaughlin announced that all athletic events had been suspended
and urged all supervisors to encourage College employees to attend
teach-in activities. "It should be emphasized," he said, "that this is not
a holiday. It is a day of work—the humane work of learning and
understanding."[47]

The teach-in was a marathon consciousness-raising session focusing
on racism, sexism, classism, homophobia, and unrelenting criticism of
the 12 students involved in the shanty incident. *The Dartmouth* reported, "the consensus in the hall was that the College should severely
punish the individuals who destroyed the shanties, take stronger measures to remove the College name from the title of *The Dartmouth
Review*, and that administrative and student action be taken to make the
College a more tolerant and accommodating place."

But if the consensus was intolerant of the shanty removers' tactics, it
strongly endorsed the tactics of the anti-apartheid activists. A panel of
faculty members agreed that the takeover of Parkhurst Hall was acceptable, even laudatory. Sociology Professor Deborah King declared that it
was "a privilege to be in Parkhurst. . . . This was a democracy of
distress, a community of sufferers that was at Parkhurst."[48]

The attempt to remove the shanties assumed nearly mythic propor-
tions as the day wore on. "Every quip about the shanties, every joke

about the Gay Students Association, if carried to its logical extent, is a sledgehammer on the Dartmouth Green," proclaimed Nancy Vickers, a professor of French and Italian.[49]

McLaughlin was forced to sit more or less in silence throughout the entire day of speeches, exhortations, and demands. He felt constrained from commenting by his role as the ultimate decision-maker on discipline for the 12 students; but his silence was also a product of his political position on campus. His position could not have been weaker.

Three days after the faculty-declared strike, the faculty met to debate its motion of no confidence in McLaughlin. Professor after professor rose to denounce and ridicule the president. Biology Professor Melvin Spiegel accused McLaughlin of making Dartmouth into "the laughingstock of the nation," and declared that if he had any respect for the College he would resign. With his customary immoderation, music professor William Cole declared that "bigotry, racism and intolerance" had characterized McLaughlin's administration.[50]

In the end, the no confidence motion did not come to a vote, but the sentiment of the faculty was clear and the damage irreversible. McLaughlin's ability to lead was eviscerated.

Just as the activists on campus has used a minor prank to mobilize a sweeping attack on "racism," "sexism," and "homophobia," the faculty had been able to capitalize on the resulting furor for its own purposes. As a perceptive reporter for *The Dartmouth* later wrote: "The faculty took advantage of the previous week's events, elaborating frequently on the relevance of students' complaints to their own gripes."[51]

Battered and beleaguered, McLaughlin agreed to prosecute the 12 students involved in the shanty incident for "malicious damage to property, unlawful and disorderly conduct, harassment, abuse, coercion, and violence." His decision marked another turnaround for the administration. The day after the "attack" on the shanties, Dean Shanahan said that the students might not be disciplined at all because he knew of no College rule that barred the removal of structures that were illegal to begin with. Faced with relentless pressure, however, McLaughlin overruled the hapless Shanahan.

The politicization of the faculty at the teach-in was an ominous indication of the degree to which ideology would govern the disciplinary process. Less than two weeks after the Parkhurst takeover the Committee on Standards found 29 students guilty of violating College rules for their participation in the sit-in in the president's office, *but decided to impose no penalty whatsoever.*

The committee justified its refusal to impose any sanctions by saying that its decision had been made "in light of how [their] actions were motivated by strongly held convictions about the educational goals and responsibilities of the College," and "how the issues to which [they] are committed are vital for Dartmouth and the larger society. . . ."[52]

The same committee then turned its attention to the case of the *Review* staffers involved in the shanty incident. The difference in approach was unmistakable.

Despite the request by the students that the proceedings be open, the committee limited outside observers' access to the tribunal. The committee refused the students permission to have their attorneys cross-examine witnesses. Nor would any of the committee members step aside because of possible bias, even though one student member was a former editor of *The Dartmouth*, which had called for the students' expulsion, one was a faculty member who had publicly called the 12 students "evil," and one was an administrator who had called the defendants "heartless chicken-shit people."[53]

In the end, the committee handed down draconian sentences. Four of the students were expelled. Seven were suspended for two terms; one student was suspended for a single term.[54]

The decision was unprecedented. As former *Review* editor Dinesh D'Souza recalled, when members of the Afro-American Society had defaced the Winter Carnival snow sculpture in 1979, "they were hailed for their bold consciousness-raising, and classes were cancelled in their honor." When a College administrator had actually assaulted the *Review*'s Ben Hart, he had been suspended for *a week, with pay.*[55]

However questionable the students' conduct may have been, theirs was an act of political expression based on their own "deeply held convictions." No one had been injured. No operations of the College had been disrupted or impeded. But that didn't matter. The College appeared oblivious to the appearance of its double standard. On February 11, the same day the penalties against the conservative students were handed down, the shanties were finally removed from the College. When 18 demonstrators attempted to obstruct the removal of the shanties, they were arrested for trespassing and obstruction.[56] The College intervened to have all charges dropped, and a month later the Committee on

Standards refused to impose any penalties on the obstructors, once again citing extenuating circumstances.

But the arrest of the students blocking the shanty removal roused another furious reaction. When the College's trustees met on campus, they were confronted with 200 anti-apartheid activists. Again the harshest rhetoric was directed at McLaughlin. To loud cheering, a former Boston mayoral candidate told the students: "You've got a president here whose hands are deep in the blood of the people of South Africa."[57]

Activists presented the board with petitions declaring that it was "imperative that President McLaughlin be replaced as soon as possible." They were joined by 104 faculty members who signed petitions that said that "this failure of leadership in the College's most important affairs cannot continue."

The trustees' response was ominously vague and inconclusive. "The trustees of Dartmouth College," board chairman Walter Burke said in a prepared statement, "are spending much of this meeting studying issues raised by the recent events on campus and the faculty governance report."[58]

But the incident had already badly damaged Dartmouth's public image. Even the liberal *Boston Globe* was appalled by Dartmouth's handling of the case. In an editorial titled "Sledgehammers at Dartmouth," the paper said:

> The dangerous precedent of this case involves the college's attitude toward a free press. Apparently the amount of punishment was related to each student's position on the *Dartmouth Review*, an independent student newspaper financed by prominent conservatives.
>
> The *Review* has frequently been less than civil in its treatment of fellow students, *but that sometimes happens with a free press.* [Emphasis added.]

The damage, the *Globe* editorialized, had already been done "to the college's position as a forum for the free expression of ideas and opinions." But as if to underline the fact that the College had chosen for itself the worst of all possible worlds, it also expressed concern that the events on campus would easily result in a turn back to "an establishment institution (white, male and elite) unfriendly to women, minorities, and even white males whose interests go beyond winter carnivals and Indian mascots."[59]

Faced with such criticism, the board of trustees chose once again to treat the problem as essentially one of public relations, lashing out at the press for its coverage. One trustee complained to the *Globe* about "the media's unrealistic and one-sided portrayal of Dartmouth."[60]

Belatedly, McLaughlin bestirred himself and ordered a new hearing for the 12 conservative students. Whatever credit he may have deserved was dissipated by the fact that the students had initiated legal action which the College felt certain it would lose. McLaughlin acted only because he had little choice.[61] At the same time, McLaughlin announced that the College was again asking *The Dartmouth Review* to remove the word Dartmouth from its title. Once more he was acceding to pressure, this time from a faculty vote of 120 to 2 to demand the name change.[62] The same day McLaughlin announced the move against the paper, he also dropped all civil charges against the students who had blocked the removal of the shanties on February 11.[63]

On March 26, the new disciplinary committee rendered its verdict on the *Review* students; again it imposed unusually severe penalties. One student was suspended for three terms, three others for two terms, and the remaining six students were suspended for one term.[64] In what was becoming an embarrassing pattern, McLaughlin again temporized, asking former New Hampshire Governor Walter Peterson, who was then president of Franklin Pierce College, to independently review the case— a responsibility that was technically and morally McLaughlin's own.

McLaughlin's prolonged indecisiveness destroyed whatever standing he retained among the faculty; but it also left his own natural political base disillusioned and disgusted. New Hampshire Governor John Sununu, a trustee of Dartmouth, charged the administration with caving in to "a vocal, persistent, one-sided perspective."[65]

"The College community," Governor Sununu said in a prepared statement, "insisted on making the entire issue to appear to be one of racism and discrimination, rather than one of freedom of expression." He called the penalties imposed on the 12 students a "tragedy."

Trustee John Steel said of the disciplinary process, "that either the system we have in place does not work, or the people in charge of the system don't know how to make it function fairly." McLaughlin and the trustees themselves, Steel declared, "should have been on trial for permitting the escalation of the shanty episode."[66]

But the most devastating criticism of McLaughlin's leadership came from former Treasury Secretary William Simon, who wrote to McLaughlin as "an old acquaintance from your years in business." Simon told McLaughlin that "there is a universal feeling that the fundamental rules of fair play have been trampled upon in recent weeks at your institution." Simon delivered a somber verdict on McLaughlin's conduct:

> There are very few times in life when a man in a position of leadership is called on to make the really tough and unpopular decisions. On these occasions, a man either rises to the occasion or he fails the test. He either leads, or follows. There is never a middle ground. In this case, you were called on to make such a decision and, sadly, you did not rise to the challenge. I'm told that winters are very long up in Hanover, but they are nothing compared to the long winter of discontent that you are bound to suffer as a result of your handling of this case. Shame on you."[67]

Speaking to *The Valley News*, Simon provided McLaughlin's epitaph, "He has made nobody happy because of his cowardice."[68]*

---

* Dartmouth was not the only school whose values were tested by shanty episodes. During the spring of 1986, anti-apartheid activists at Yale erected shanties on Beinecke Plaza. Anxious to avoid confrontation, the administration allowed the shanties to remain in place for a week before removing them. The militants reacted by blocking the entrance to a university building. To its credit, the university quickly cleared them away and began disciplinary proceedings. At stake was the principle that coercive tactics should never be allowed to take precedence over reason and free discussion in an institution serious about its commitment to liberal learning and academic freedom. This was the principle at the heart of Yale's policy on Freedom of Expression drawn up painstakingly by a committee headed by one of the College's most distinguished faculty members, historian C. Vann Woodward. The occupation of Beinecke Plaza was the policy's first major test.

With astonishing speed its principles were repudiated by both the faculty and the administration. No sooner had the charges against the protestors been issued than 156 faculty members objected, deploring the "use of force" against the "peaceful demonstrations." The faculty letter drew a blistering response from Professor Donald Kagan:

> That is the low level of sophistry to which we have become accustomed in the last two decades. It is as if a family, having found that a mob had moved into its house while it was away, called the police to have them removed only to be condemned for resorting to force to get their house back. As George Orwell

In early April, McLaughlin accepted Peterson's recommendations to further soften the penalties against the *Review* staffers. In the end, six of the students had their suspensions lifted altogether and were instead given four terms of probation. Four students were given suspensions of a single term. (Two of the students had decided earlier not to appeal their penalties.)

McLaughlin's decision was met with outrage among activists; 22 protestors immediately occupied the Baker Library bell tower, forcing the library to close early and hundreds of students to leave.[69] Again, penalties for the radicals were light. All but one of the students involved in the occupation received $100 fines and varying lengths of probation or "reprimands." There were no suspensions.

McLaughlin criticized the decision saying that "the sanctions imposed do no reflect adequately the seriousness with which the community views these actions. . . ." But his comments were muted. His concern, he said, was increased substantially by "the perception on the part of many" that the College had been less than evenhanded. But he made no move to alter the decision.[70] Realistically, he no longer had any moral authority on campus and was, in any case, a lame duck.

SAFE SEX AT DARTMOUTH

The *Review* had not, however, exhausted its penchant for mischief; and again it was to challenge the College's core values. Nowhere were the differences over the content and goals of a Dartmouth education more dramatically drawn than on the sensitive issue of "safe sex." In

---

used to say, only an intellectual could believe that. No ordinary person could be such a fool. Such dishonesty and inversion of common sense have been all too usual on campuses in recent years. . . .

The Executive Committee of Yale College refused to take disciplinary action against the occupiers of Beinecke Plaza and the administration quickly retreated. Instead, it turned over control of the Plaza to a special committee chaired by a professor described as one of the most vocal supporters the anti-apartheid demonstrations. His committee quickly ruled that the illegal shanties were now legal and could now be returned to their former location, monuments to the efficacy of intimidation. For the moment, Kagan declared, "principle and freedom from disruption, intimidation and coercion are dead at Yale." (Kagan, Donald, "Basic Principles and the University," *Academic Questions*, Fall 1986)

1986, Dartmouth stepped up its "sexual awareness" efforts, including the publication of *Partners in Sex*, written by the College's director of health education and distributed to all Dartmouth students.

The campaign reflected the College's emphasis on diversity by taking great pains not to stigmatize any sexual practice, especially those popular with such "disadvantaged" groups as gays.*

Such solicitude for minority sexual practices was made explicit in another brochure, "Safe Sex," which was distributed to students at Dartmouth's 1987 Winter Term registration, along with a kit that included two condoms, a "rubber dam," (for oral/anal and oral/vaginal sex), and a tube of lubricant. Among the "safe" sex practices delineated by the brochure were "dry kissing," "masturbation on healthy skin," "oral sex with a condom," and "external water sports" —which involves urinating on one's sex partner. The brochure hastens to caution that while "urinating on skin without open cuts and sores is safe . . . urine that enters the mouth, vagina or rectum can spread viruses such as AIDS or hepatitis B."[71]

The brochure—distributed to students free of charge—also discussed such "dangerous" practices as "fisting" (forcing one's hand or fist into the rectum or vagina of one's partner) and "rimming" (oral/anal contact).

In early 1987, *The Dartmouth Review* published details of the brochure in graphic detail. But the most revealing aspect of its exposé was a transcript of a conversation between a student and a Dartmouth health administrator. (One can assume the administrator felt that her comments were meant to be in confidence, which perhaps explains their candor.)

The *Review* staffer called the health office saying that she was curious about anal sex. She had never engaged in it, she said, and thought that it sounded dangerous. Her reluctance is evident from the transcript. Part of the transcript later published in the *Review* showed the health administrator saying:

---

* An official College publication on "Gay and lesbian issues at Dartmouth" refers to "the homosexual minority [which] has been suppressed and kept largely invisible for much of Western history," and notes that they have been the victims of "severe moral condemnation and social hostility." The brochure pledges that the College, including the deans, chaplains, and the staff of the Affirmative Action Office will be "understanding and helpful to gay students."

Anal intercourse is something you could talk to more in depth with a physician, but that would be done certainly slowly and with lubrication, and with gentleness and with caring for each other it would probably not be painful. It's just whatever is mutually satisfying for both of you. . . .

The student then asks about fisting: "So I guess that's something you can try after you get used to anal sex?"

Administrator: Yes, mm-hmmm, and its an individual preference of course. Whatever's comfortable and feels natural to you. . . .[72]

The *Review*'s revelations again drew the national spotlight to Hanover. The Phil Donahue show devoted an episode to the subject and featured an editor of the *Review*, who described the Dartmouth safe sex program in considerable detail to a national television audience of millions. For an institution obsessed with public relations it was a nightmare nonpareil. What was most striking about the controversy was Dartmouth's aggressive moral agnosticism, which reduced human sexuality to an intricate series of physical and hydraulic maneuvers about which its sole concern was errant microbes and unrestrained fluids.

Professor Jeffrey Hart later commented on the dispute by recalling the Sherlock Holmes story in which the case is solved because of a dog which did not bark. "In dealing with a work of literature," he wrote, "critics sometimes call this 'the presence of the absence': What is *not* present in the Dartmouth 'safe sex' kit—and no doubt in this it resembles others—is the manners and the substance of civilization."[73]

EXIT MCLAUGHLIN

In early October 1986, David McLaughlin announced his resignation as Dartmouth's president. Two weeks after his resignation, a group of feminists calling themselves "womben to overthrow dartmyth" dumped "simulated bloodied tampons" on the grass in front of the area where McLaughlin was speaking during Dartmouth Night ceremonies. The group explained that it was attempting to "graphically illustrate the presence of womyn at dartmyth," and said it was distributing "bloodied tampons in protest of both the alma mater 'men of dartmouth' and the governing structures of dartmyth college."[74]

But afterward, McLaughlin saved his strongest reaction for students who unfurled an Indian symbol at the weekend's football game against Harvard. By now thoroughly acclimated to the *kultur* of the College, McLaughlin denounced the use of the Indian symbol as "unfortunate and unacceptable," and said it was "antithetical to everything this College believes in." Freedom of expression, McLaughlin told *The Dartmouth*, was "not the point."[75]

In contrast, McLaughlin said that the tampon incident was a "separable issue," and was "not related" to his "deep concern" over the events of the weekend. (Later he would allow that the protest by the womben to overthrow dartmyth was "immature and in poor taste.")[76]

The tampon incident was only one indication of the feminist insurgency on campus. During convocation, two members of the radical feminist Women's Issues League (WIL) tore up their programs and threw them on the stage to protest the singing of "Men of Dartmouth." After a rape on campus, WIL mobilized a campaign against sexism at the College. Because of WIL's radicalism and often shrill rhetoric, some feminists formed a discussion group "for women who were interested in joining a feminist group that was somewhat more moderate than WIL."[77] But the attempts to provide a moderate alternative were undermined by McLaughlin himself, who only days after the tampon incident appeared to endorse WIL. "WIL's concerns are felt by the majority of women on this campus," McLaughlin said. "The women's movement is more confident and the issues that women are addressing are more substantive and more to the heart of the institution than [when coeducation was instituted]. It's a much more mature and confident approach."[78]

At the top of WIL's agenda was the creation of a Women's Resource Center that would serve as "common ground" for feminist activities on campus. McLaughlin moved with considerable haste to accommodate them. In December, a task force was formed to study the proposal, heavily weighted with campus feminists.* By April, the Task Force had issued its report unconditionally endorsing the WIL proposal.[79]

The report characterized Dartmouth traditions as "often inimical to

---

* The committee was chaired by Professor Marianne Hirsch, whose office sported a sign reading "SISTERHOOD MEANS REVOLUTION." See Chapter XVII.

the inclusion of women and minorities," and blamed those traditions for causing "pain, stress and discomfort" to women at Dartmouth.[80]

The Women's Support Task Force declared that women at Dartmouth were in need of programs that would help them "confront their marginal status" and that would educate them "about their own role in the social inequities of sexism."

"They need both support as women and enlightenment as members of an environment marked by gender inequity." As evidence of Dartmouth's oppressive atmosphere, the report cited examples of fraternity newsletters featuring "articles" along the lines of "Why Beer Is Better Than Women."[81]

Creating the center, the task force said, would clearly convey the message that Dartmouth was taking an "unequivocal public stand against sexism and racism." The task force also envisioned close ties between the women's studies program and the center. The Task Force called for a "close structural and programmatic relationship" between the Center and the academic program—a relationship that would be secured by the permanent presence of two faculty members as well as the women's studies coordinator on the center's governing board.[82] But it was also clear from the report that the Center was not to be an academic institution.

The Task Force envisioned the Women's Resource Center as a "supportive context" where women could discuss "rapidly changing gender roles." The Center would also provide opportunities to "study and discuss structures of exclusion and prejudice that severely affect all members of the Dartmouth community, and women and minorities in particular," and would serve as a coordinating center for women's activities on campus. It also made it clear that the center would serve as a jumping off point for further efforts to reform the curriculum. Noting that "in many areas" in the curriculum, Dartmouth had already "come to reflect and to include the new scholarship on women and gender," the Task Force complained that some fields had retained their independence from the feminists, lamenting that "many students graduate from Dartmouth without having been exposed to the study of gender issues." Although it exceeded the Task Force's brief, it added its endorsement to proposals to make gender studies a College graduation requirement that would be modelled on "the third world requirement."[83]

The creation of the Center exemplified the new dynamics of campus curricular politics in which curricular changes (the creation of a politicized women's studies program) generated pressure for politicized campus institutions, which in turn applied more pressure to change the curriculum.

The College's verdict on David McLaughlin was not completely fair. His accomplishments, particularly in the area of College finances and new construction were considerable.

But he lacked time. Hopkins had three decades, Dickey more than two, Kemeny had 11 years. McLaughlin found himself in trouble from the start. His fall from grace, however, was not merely an individual failure, but an institutional one that raised troubling questions about who actually ran Dartmouth. Ostensibly, this question had been answered by Daniel Webster's case before the U.S. Supreme Court, which had made it clear that the ultimate authority of the College rested with the *trustees*. But in the 1980s, their authority, or more to the point, their willingness to exert their authority was subjected to its fiercest trial. McLaughlin's fall had revealed them to be, as a board, largely impotent.

"The problem is the board, it's not the president," Trustee John Steel later reflected. "It wasn't McLaughlin."[84]

"I think the board let [McLaughlin] get himself in positions he wasn't quite sure how to get out of, and the board stood there and watched."

As a result of this failure of moral courage, Steel said, "the faculty have gotten themselves in a position where they are controlling the store because the president and board don't want to fight them anymore. They don't want to go to the trouble of saying here's the way we want things and here's the way it's going to be and then deal with the objections. The board is actually coached by the president and some members of the board who sit on other boards of other institutions who say, 'Gee, let's not stir these waves, let's not force them to take ROTC. Let's just raise their salaries like they asked."

Indeed, after McLaughlin was deposed, the trustees felt sure they understood the lesson of the debacle. As they sought a successor for McLaughlin in late 1986 and early 1987, they had no stomach for more confrontation with the faculty. Said one trustee (with something of the despairing shrug that Lionel Trilling had described in the 1960s): "They [the faculty] wanted one of their own."[85]

CHAPTER

XXII

ONE OF THEIR OWN

In April 1987, they got one of their own. After an unorthodox search that included hiring a professional head-hunter, the Dartmouth Board of Trustees named James O. Freedman, the President of the University of Iowa, as the College's fifteenth president. Freedman's selection was a recognition of the changed character of the College and the new alignment of power within it. Not since 1822 had a president been named who had no previous ties to the College. At Iowa, Freedman had established and led a $100 million fund-raising campaign aimed at endowing professorships and fellowships; he had revitalized Iowa's honors program; and made Iowa a leader in the area of international studies. His politics were, moreover, muted and ambiguous. Although he cited Supreme Court Justice Thurgood Marshall (for whom he had clerked as a young lawyer) and radical journalist I. F. Stone as his personal heroes, Freedman had also testified on behalf of William Rehnquist's nomination as chief justice of the U.S. Supreme Court.[1]

Most important of all, however, was the contrast with his predecessor. Unlike the rancor that greeted the selection of David McLaughlin, Freedman assumed the presidency under auspicious circumstances. He

271

benefited from comparison. Where McLaughlin was regarded as a somewhat autocratic manager, Freedman was a consensus-builder. Where McLaughlin had been a businessman, Freedman had at least some scholarly credentials. McLaughlin could reminisce about his gridiron triumphs, but as the *Alumni Magazine* gushed, Freedman "read books." Above all, Freedman was an adept academic politician who could be counted on not to provoke unnecessary disputes with the faculty or to impinge on their authority in any way. The new president was also an eloquent orator. "McLaughlin gave orders," the *Alumni Magazine* remarked. "Freedman gives speeches."[2]*

THE NEW UNIVERSITY

Like John Kemeny nearly two decades earlier, Freedman was anxious to make his mark on the College but he intended to do so by following the lead of the faculty. In his inaugural address, Freedman declared his intention to make Dartmouth more "intellectual" by making it more attractive for "loners," and he posed as the leader of a crusade for the "life of the mind." The alternative to his leadership, he implied, was a return to the "Animal House" image that continued to embarrass both faculty and alumni.[†]

Freedman chose as his text the basic question of Dartmouth's identity: was Dartmouth still merely a College or should it become a full-fledged university?

Dartmouth's administration had already added thick new layers of university-style bureaucracy. Between 1977 and 1987, the number of

---

* Early in his administration, the *Alumni Magazine* published a picture of Freedman—tieless with his sleeves rolled up—working on one of his speeches at an electric typewriter, with the caption: "Drafting his arguments in his Webster Avenue study, James O. Freedman makes a pitch for recruiting more women, minorities and foreign students while beefing up the international curriculum." (*Dartmouth Alumni Magazine*, January/February 1988)

† Dartmouth probably deserves some of its reputation as a party school and its fraternities do seem to have a history of excess. But "Animal House" was never more than a caricature of life at the College. Even so, nothing focuses the mind so wonderfully as having one's school portrayed on the silver screen as the home of toga parties and food fights. Some faculty members seem to have been permanently scarred by the experience.

"administrative and professional employees" had shot up by nearly 25 percent, even though the number of Arts and Sciences faculty members and College service employees had actually *declined* in the same period.[3] Dartmouth now awarded doctorates and boasted a range of professional schools including its Medical School, the Tuck School of Business, and the Thayer School of Engineering. Institutions with far less reason to do so had long since declared themselves "universities." Even so, Dartmouth's presidents had always been mindful of the traditions of the College.

Unburdened by such sentiments and sympathetic to demands of the ambitious, research-oriented faculty, Freedman decided to challenge the traditions head-on. In October 1988—less than two years into his presidency—Freedman addressed the general faculty and called on the College to "emphatically" clear away "whatever ambiguity may still remain about the true character of Dartmouth's academic enterprise."[4]

Citing Dartmouth's evolving identity, Freedman declared: "Lest there be any doubt of the result of this long course of evolution, it is important for us to assert confidently and unambiguously that Dartmouth *is* a liberal arts *university*." As both the president and his audience knew, he was dealing with more than the technical nomenclature of institutional identity. Although he insisted that Dartmouth could maintain its unique traditions and that he did not foresee becoming a "traditional large-scale, highly impersonal research university," he clearly envisioned a shift in priorities toward research and graduate education. University status would mean increased research grants for Dartmouth and a larger faculty, which would spend more time on "scholarship."

His position was consistent with his own career. Educated at Harvard (B.A.) and Yale (J.D.), Freedman's experience had not been in liberal arts colleges, but in large universities. He had taught at the University of Pennsylvania for 18 years, including three years as dean of the law school. He had spent five years at the helm of Iowa, where he had pushed an aggressive research and expansion agenda.* Less than two years

---

* Freedman was not above some sleight-of hand in the academic career game. When he turned down the presidency of Indiana University, he had pledged his eternal fealty to Iowa. Said Freedman: "I have been very happy at Iowa. I worship this university, and I enjoy living in Iowa City." Less than eight weeks later, he quit. He may have gotten out just in time. Iowa was left holding the bag for an ambitious $25 million laser center that

before accepting the Dartmouth job, Freedman had been one of five finalists for the presidency of the University of Texas, a prototypical megaversity whose mission and personality could not have been more alien to Dartmouth's.[5] More recently he had been a candidate for the presidency of Indiana University, another large, research-oriented institution.[6] Perhaps because of his university focus, he referred to Dartmouth College as a "liberal arts university" in interviews with Iowa newspapers even before entering on his duties in Hanover.[7]

In his speech to the faculty, Freedman was at pains to allay concerns that becoming a university involved any retreat from Dartmouth's collegiate traditions or that the expansion of research would come at the expense of teaching. But the message was, at best, mixed. Freedman's *ex cathedra* proclamation of the new Dartmouth University was actually part of a two-part thrust. It came only days after the release of the faculty's "self-study report" prepared for the New England Association of Schools and Colleges, which was routinely reviewing Dartmouth's accreditation.[8] Freedman's "university" address was intended as an amplification of that report and was timed to coincide with its release. What Freedman was saying diplomatically, the faculty report said directly.

The faculty self-studies were uncompromising in urging Dartmouth to get on with its transformation from an undergraduate teaching-centered liberal arts college to a university in which research is a "dominant element." But most striking of all was the report's adamant

---

he had sold to the legislature as a way to boost the university's status (he also promised it would add as many as 12,000 jobs.) The legislature approved the plan largely on the basis of Freedman's assurances that three of the nation's top laser researchers would come to Iowa if the center was built. After his departure, it turned out the three scientists had no intention of coming to Iowa and denied Freedman's claims they ever had. The entire incident left a bitter taste in many Iowa legislators' mouths. Said State Representative Jack Hatch, chairman of the House Education Appropriations Committee: "I think President Freedman purposefully misled the legislature. . . . It was very fortunate for him that he left when he did." (Hatch's father was a Dartmouth student for two years in World War II.) Hatch's sentiments appear to be widely shared among both political parties. A state senator went even farther, calling Freedman and other top administrators "laser liars." Says one representative, "That whole laser fiasco has been an albatross around the university's neck." A student columnist for *The Daily Iowan* took perhaps the most cynical view, writing, "You might say [Freedman] pushed the $25 million facility through the legislature just in time to get it on his resume and get the hell out of here."

assertion that this was a change that had *already taken place and was now irreversible*. By calling Dartmouth a university, Freedman was only acknowledging a *fait accompli*, the report insisted.

> At least some administrators and trustees believe that Dartmouth is facing a choice whether to continue the traditional emphasis on the college nature of the institution or fully develop its university nature. *We have, however, already passed this particular decision point; an about-face, returning to the liberal arts college of the past is an impossibility. . . .* "9 [Emphasis added.]

The faculty report painted a disturbing picture of a divided institution that had failed to face up to the implications of its *de facto* new identity. One result was what the faculty called an "alarming" gap between what students had been led to expect from Dartmouth College and the very different goals and priorities of the faculty. Dartmouth, the report said, was "a house divided."10

Although Freedman was at pains to stress the continuity of his vision with that of his predecessors—he even cited Ernest Martin Hopkins— the radical shift in priorities was clearly evident in the faculty report. The faculty's three major criteria for judging Dartmouth's "intellectual environment" did not include undergraduate teaching.11* Moreover, the faculty considered the curriculum only as an outgrowth of the new research emphasis, which "will stimulate changes in the curriculum and in the intellectual environment." The fact that the report no longer regarded the curriculum as the central means to change the intellectual environment was the legacy of treating it as an afterthought of economic, professional, and political agendas. In more than four decades, nothing had illustrated as graphically the extent and the depth of the transformation of Dartmouth since the Hopkins era.

At the core of the report was the self-image of the Dartmouth faculty. "The faculty have established a clear sense of who they are and what they want Dartmouth to be," the faculty report declared—and the

---

* The three criteria were: (1) "The commitment to research and the depth, breadth and excitement of the resulting scholarship"; (2) "The intensity and pervasiveness of formal and informal discussion of ideas, theories, events, and artistic expressions"; and (3) "The variety, level of involvement and spontaneity or self-direction of artistic and cultural activity."

faculty did not want to be regarded as teachers in an undergraduate college. Instead,

> they see themselves as professional scholars who want to work in a university environment with a greater exposure to graduate students. . . .
>
> The faculty, in effect, have adopted the research university as the appropriate model for themselves and for their students. The students, not surprisingly, have not adopted that model. More importantly, the sense of Dartmouth as a college is reinforced by many of the actions of the administration, the language often used in official documents and by many of the structures of the institution. In short, many of the students have plenty of reason to believe that their view of themselves and the institution is the "officially" correct one. The point to be made is that the house is divided. . . .[12]*

One survey found that nearly half (48 percent) of Dartmouth faculty would leave Dartmouth if they had the chance, the vast majority opting for a research university rather than a liberal arts college.[13] Faculty in all divisions, the report declared, tended to feel they spend too much time in the classroom and evaluating student work;[14] while 70 percent of the students said they do not have enough contact with their professors.[15] Only 55 percent of students—and an even lower percentage of honors students—said the curriculum satisfies their intellectual needs.[16]

Acknowledging the growing gap between the faculty and other elements of the College, the report noted that "the Dartmouth faculty is further down this path than the administration or the students."[17] At the end of this path, the faculty foresaw significantly expanded graduate programs. Although the relative absence of teaching assistants had been one of Dartmouth's distinguishing characteristics, the faculty now envi-

---

* In the faculty report, two groups come in for particular attack: students and *The Dartmouth Review*. "The faculty are not satisfied with the students." In particular, faculty members are disappointed because students have shown little interest in engaging in specialized research, which the faculty interprets as a sign that undergraduates "do not care about the life of the mind." The *Review* was accused of not only weakening the intellectual environment, but of being one of three major barriers to "diversity." (The other two are fraternities and the freshman orientation trip.) The faculty's methodology was interesting. All of the members of the Committee on Intellectual Environment—which included Marysa Navarro—cited the *Review* as a negative influence on campus. When the faculty were asked an open-ended question about the College's intellectual weaknesses, however, some mentioned anti-intellectualism among students, but none mentioned the *Review*.

sioned the more frequent use of graduate students in the classroom. Both the faculty and Freedman also urged that undergraduates be more actively involved in the faculty's specialized research. In effect, the idea was to deal with the dilemma of specialized faculty dealing with generalist undergraduates by simply treating the undergraduates as if they were graduate students—and declaring it a reform. At research universities faced with criticism over the lack of student-faculty contact, the undergraduate-as-graduate expedient had proven popular, but for a liberal arts college such sleight of hand would mark a significant departure.

If the College adopted the changes it was recommending, the faculty report insisted, "it will be a different place, but not one mimicking other institutions. It certainly will be more intellectual 'like Harvard' but that does not mean that it need be any less personal, community oriented, service oriented, cohesive, appreciative of the outdoors, or any other of its traditional, positive values."[18] The lure it was offering was tempting: we can have all this, it said, without having to choose. We *can* be Harvard, and still be Dartmouth.

It was the archetypal academic fantasy.

Allowing for both exaggeration and the tone of special pleading in the self-study reports, there is considerable evidence to support their contention that Dartmouth had *already* changed its identity and mission. "The question is no longer *whether* Dartmouth is a college or a university," Graduate Dean P. Bruce Pipes told the *Alumni Magazine*, "but *what kind of* university Dartmouth is going to be."[19] [Emphasis added.] Funding for university-type research was growing at Dartmouth. In 1988, the College's faculty brought in $38 million in research grants in more than 400 separate projects. By the standards of major research institutions that was a mere pittance. But it represented a one year increase of 20 percent.[20]

The notion that Dartmouth was compelled to move aggressively toward increased research to attract and hold its faculty was part of academia's own version of the trickle-down theory, under which faculty research, no matter how recondite, will trickle down and benefit undergraduates.* In Dartmouth's case the argument was essential because it

---

* Recondite is surely the most appropriate term for Dartmouth's newest graduate degree. Although it has no doctoral program in English, students can now obtain a Master's Degree in "Electro-Acoustic Music." To ensure its exclusivity, the program will admit only six students at a time.

allowed the school to claim to be all things to all people; that it could
expand its research focus and its graduate programs without any loss to
undergraduate teaching, which had always been Dartmouth's strong
suit. But there were signs that the theory worked less well in reality.

Between 1972 and 1988, the number of faculty members at
Dartmouth increased by 38.4 percent. But many of those positions were
created for part-time instructors, who have come to play a larger and
larger role in classroom instruction at Dartmouth.* Many of them were
hired, in part, to allow the regular faculty more time for research, which
has become an increasingly dominant criterion for promotion and tenure
at the sacrifice of teaching and the College's traditional close, Socratic
relationship between professors and students.[21]

The tragedy, says Henry Terrie, the recently retired chairman of
Dartmouth's English Department, is that while Dartmouth had the
potential to be the best liberal arts college in the country, "Dartmouth is
never going to be a first-rate research university." Dartmouth cannot
compete with Stanford or Harvard, he observes, "unless you cannibal-
ize your own people. We will always be a second-rank graduate
school."[22]

Both Freedman and the faculty reports had given only glancing
attention to the question of such tradeoffs. But the accreditation report
written by Hanna Gray, the president of the University of Chicago,
failed to fall in behind the College's own rosy scenario.[23] Although she
praised Dartmouth, the Chicago president found no evidence that
Dartmouth had undertaken "a rigorous and realistic examination of the
choices, tradeoffs, and decisions to be made" in the shift from undergraduate college to university. The faculty reports had little to say about
how much it would cost and where the money would come from.
Genuine planning "means setting priorities," she said pointedly, "*an
issue the reports have not explicitly confronted.*" [Emphasis added.]

This was a particularly embarrassing point because the College already had received a strong warning about its financial limitations. A
consulting firm hired to prepare a fiscal profile of the school had warned
in early 1988, well before Freedman's speech, that the College faced

---

* Because so many of the new hires were part-time, the 38.4 percent increase translated
into only an 11.6 percent increase in full-time equivalent positions. So-called "visi-
tors" made up only 13 percent of the full-time equivalents in 1982-83. By 1987-88
they accounted for nearly a quarter—23 percent—of the full-time equivalents.

financial strains. Specifically, it cautioned that the College's endowment and revenue structure "are suited more to a college" and that while they might be able to support a university-type operation "they are unlikely to be able to do so comfortably."[24]*

Gray was even more critical of the faculty's report on graduate education, which argued for making the expansion of graduate programs a top priority for Dartmouth. She found the rationale for the expansion of graduate programs "incomplete in some respects, founded almost completely on internal considerations." Putting it more bluntly, the Chicago president said, "there is more emphasis on what graduate students might do for Dartmouth than on what Dartmouth might do for them."

The aftermath of Gray's report provided a revealing glimpse of Dartmouth's public relations apparatus and its approach to dealing with both the public and alumni. Ignoring the substance of the report, College spokesman Alex Huppe told a Washington, D.C., reporter that Gray's committee had "thoroughly studied" Dartmouth's curriculum—which was not true—and "had high praise for it and the strength of our faculty" —which was true up to a point, but fell well short of candor and accuracy.[25]

Huppe's approach reflected the College's basic strategy of ignoring problems and denying the existence of legitimate opposition to the College's policies.

In that spirit, Freedman came to Dartmouth as the great moderator, sympathetic to the faculty, a self-proclaimed adherent to the ideals of civility and tolerance, and someone well-attuned to the changing direction of higher education. Only the deliberately malicious could oppose him.

"If I had a pipe dream," Freedman confided to *The Boston Globe* in his first months in the presidency, "I'd like to be the Abraham Lincoln of Dartmouth—to heal the warring factions."[26]

His ambition would not survive the year.

---

* Dartmouth's endowment per student was less than one-third of Princeton's, for example.

CHAPTER

XXIII

DIVERSITY TRIUMPHANT

The incident that was to again convulse the Dartmouth campus was, in effect, a re-run. In 1983, *The Dartmouth Review* had become embroiled in a prolonged controversy over an article criticizing the teaching methods and intellectual standards of Professor William Cole's music classes. Now, five years later, the *Review* returned to Professor Cole's classroom. A student who was not connected with the *Review* tape recorded one of Cole's lectures and then gave the tape to the paper, which published the transcript on February 24, 1988. The article was part of an ongoing critique of the College's curriculum.[1] In the same issue, the *Review* exposed the unprofessional performance and lack of academic standards of a white English professor. Earlier in the month, the paper had run the results of a cultural literacy test in which Dartmouth students had performed abysmally. (Only half, for example, could name any three of the liberties guaranteed in the First Amendment.)

The transcript of Cole's class—the accuracy of which has never been seriously challenged—depicted a vintage Cole performance. Cole was captured in a lengthy and formless ramble that included the status of

Indians, his youth in Pittsburgh, nuclear waste disposal, and his thoughts on crime and poverty, salted throughout with obscenities and racial epithets. Even *The Boston Globe*, which later denounced the *Review*, was forced to admit that "from all reports, Cole's course . . . is what students call a gut course."[2]

The day after the article was published, four *Review* staffers went to Cole's classroom. Although Cole had eventually dropped his 1983 libel suit against the *Review*, the paper's attorneys now advised the editors to offer Cole a chance to respond to the new story. The reporters called Cole several times to make the offer, but each time, Cole called them racists and hung up. Even so, the decision to go to his classroom and confront Cole in person was, perhaps, questionable. Given Cole's past conduct, it should have been obvious that such a confrontation could turn ugly. As it did.

According to the students, Cole reacted angrily, shouting racial epithets and obscenities. The students demanded an apology. An official College report later said: "Throughout the altercation, Professor Cole asked the reporters repeatedly to stop taking pictures and to leave his classroom. When the picture-taking and vexatious harassment continued, he lunged at the camera and dislodged the flash attachment." The attachment was broken.[3]

The impulse to treat the incident as a racial attack was, by now, almost reflexive for the College. Despite Cole's conduct, campus indignation was directed not at the professor, but at the student reporters, who were immediately brought up on charges of harassment by College officials in an atmosphere that quickly became overheated.

Seizing on the incident, the Afro-American Society and an assortment of militant groups mobilized an all-out attack on the *Review*. At a rally attended by about 250 Dartmouth students and faculty, the Afro-American Society denounced what it called the "racist, elitist attack" on Cole and demanded the immediate suspension of the students involved. Radical faculty member Carla Freccero demanded that the College take action against the paper "in light of the persistent and malicious racist, sexist and homophobic attacks" by the *Review*. Claiming to represent a group she called "Concerned People of the Dartmouth Community," Freccero demanded that the College sue the paper to block its use of the name "Dartmouth" and (again) publicly disassociate itself from the paper.[4]

The campaign quickly escalated beyond simply the incident involving the four students and Professor Cole. Campus activists launched a boycott of all *Review* advertisers, a campaign that included picketing of businesses whose advertisements appeared in the paper.[5]* Taking on the trappings of a 1960s "happening," a candlelight vigil in support of Cole was held Wednesday night, March 2. (It later turned out that the "candlelight vigil" was organized with the active involvement of Dartmouth administrators.)[6] A rally of more than 400 students and faculty held the next day was a kaleidoscope of the Dartmouth left, featuring speakers from the Native American organization on campus, the Hispanic forum, the Women's Issues League, the Dartmouth Gay-Lesbian organization, and even the Upper Valley Committee for a Free South Africa. Each group in turn denounced the racism, sexism, and "homophobia" of the College in general and the *Review* in particular. Music Professor Jon Appleton declared: "We must find a way to put an end to Jim Crow, to jingoism, to sexism and to just plain ignorance that the *Dartmouth Review* seeks to foster on campus."[7]

The Black Caucus at Dartmouth, which claimed to represent black faculty, administrators, and staff at the College, wrote to Freedman on March 3, lamenting "the nightmare of white supremacist rhetoric" that it claimed was now "reasserting itself" at Dartmouth and referred to the *Review* staffers as "a small group of bitter adolescents, who do not hold degrees or expertise in any field."[8]

There were, of course, less strident voices. *The Dartmouth*, which seldom missed an opportunity to savage its competitor, called the confrontation with Cole "shockingly disrespectful." "But," the paper asked, "was it racist?" In the end, it concluded that "no concrete evidence indicates that this was a racist attack." The "clear issue is not racism," the paper concluded, but the "inexcusable behavior of four Dartmouth undergraduates."[9] Still serious, but hardly apocalyptic.

Another columnist in *The Dartmouth* raised a more basic question. Although recent graduate Brian Foley felt that the *Review* had descended to "mudslinging" in its coverage of Cole, he was not prepared to dismiss the other issues raised by the *Review*'s account of Cole's conduct. If the paper's account of Cole's classroom behavior was, in fact, accurate, Foley wrote, how was Dartmouth going to address such conduct?

---

* After initially resisting, the Dartmouth Bookstore agreed to join the boycott.

"Can professors do *anything* they want in a classroom, even beyond the limits of good taste?" Foley asked. "If the *Review* story is true, then embedded in Dartmouth's official response to it will be our school's answer to the question. . . . 'Whom is Dartmouth for?' It is a question worth posing again. The contention in the *Review* article is that Dartmouth exists for its students, and that students should not be subjected to the type of behavior Cole allegedly practiced that day in class. . . ."[10]

Another student, junior Doug Anderson, wrote, "If the expression of these students constitutes harassment, then so does the slightest impoliteness." But he recognized that the incident between Cole and the students was about something else. "I expect these students will not really be tried for their actions, but rather for their cause; I have already heard the cries of those who want to silence the *Review* and expel its members."[11]

But such reasoned approaches were quickly pushed aside. The campus left was adamant in insisting the issue was solely one of racism. And they received unexpected but crucial backing from the College's president. Although the four *Review* staffers faced College disciplinary hearings as a result of their "vexatious oral exchange," President Freedman addressed an anti-*Review* rally, condemning what he called acts of "disrespect, insensitivity and personal attack." While he did not directly address the *Review* case, Freedman left no one at the rally in doubt about his reference when he declared that there was no room at Dartmouth for "racism, sexism and other forms of ignorance."[12] Indeed, if the message was not clear enough, a spokeswoman for the College News Service said that Freedman's speech "implicitly, if not explicitly, expressed his support of Professor Cole as a tenured member of the faculty." Later Freedman told *The Boston Globe*, "I feel dreadful about the attack on Professor Cole."*

Freedman's comments were remarkable, all the more so given his experience as a former law school dean. When asked whether he thought his comments might prejudice the hearings on the students' conduct, Freedman said, "Not for a minute." But an attorney for the

---

* Freedman, however, denied he was making any comments at all on the Cole case. "To comment now on the specifics of those events might create an atmosphere in which the independence of the judicial processes of the College would be compromised."

students later described his remarks as a "classic example of prejudgment of the facts by a president of the university."[13]

U.S. Appeals Court Judge Laurence Silberman, a 1957 graduate of Dartmouth, later noted that the disciplinary proceedings against the students "took place against a backdrop of undisguised college hostility to the political views expressed in the *Dartmouth Review* as well as the polemical and excessive terms in which those opinions were sometimes cast." The College's claim that the hearings were not prejudiced by any official actions, Silberman noted, "seems at odds with President Freedman's speech attacking the *Review* while disciplinary proceedings were pending, as well as the continuous stream of material sent to alumni from professors and college officials" that criticized the paper.[14]

Freedman later defended his conduct, insisting that his primary consideration had been maintaining calm on campus and that he had hoped that his comments might allay some of the racial tensions that had been building. But he did so at the expense of the four students. "I couldn't believe President Freedman could attribute racial hatred on my part without even talking to me and on the eve of my disciplinary hearing," one of the students, Christopher Baldwin, later testified.[15] Indeed, only a week after Freedman's denunciation, the College's disciplinary panel found all four students guilty of harassment, invasion of privacy, and disorderly conduct. Three students were suspended (one student until the fall of 1988, two for more than a year, until the fall of 1989); a fourth student was placed on probation.*

The College's handling of Professor Cole was rather different. Although noting that Cole had "lunged" at the journalists' camera, broken the flash attachment, and used "profanity" in his confrontation with the students, the two administrators assigned to investigate the incident, Dwight Lahr, the dean of faculty, and Richard Sheldon, the humanities dean, concluded that Professor Cole's conduct, "is understandable and constituted a justifiable and moderate response." The deans praised Cole for "the restrained way in which he responded to" what they described as "clear provocation and harassment by the four reporters." Their

---

* By way of comparison, the students' attorneys later found evidence that a Dartmouth student accused of sexual assault had been given a suspension of only a single term.

report went on to praise Cole as "an unusually talented scholar whom Dartmouth is fortunate to have on its faculty."[16]*

The matter was not so easily exorcised.

A New Hampshire judge would later order the College to reinstate two of the students, after it was discovered that a member of the disciplinary panel had written letters denouncing the *Review*. The College hearings, Judge Bruce Mohl ruled, did not meet the test of fundamental fairness.

Although Mohl found no "persuasive evidence that Dartmouth College had retaliated against or otherwise pursued disciplinary action against the plaintiffs on account of their association with the *Dartmouth Review*," the hearing found damaging evidence that reflected poorly on the fairness and integrity of the College's disciplinary processes. In one letter introduced into evidence, College Dean Edward Shanahan wrote to Cole personally to tell him that he was stepping down as head of the disciplinary panel so that he could "become personally involved in the attempt to develop the case" against the student who had actually taped Cole's class. Other administrators had apparently helped organize anti-*Review* demonstrations. One administrator had written to Dartmouth fraternities, "Re: Vigil Supporting Professor Cole," emphasizing that it was "important that people show their support or concern. . . ."[17]

"IT'S TRUE TARGET . . ."

The incident seemed to have an almost mesmeric effect on the community, bringing to the surface the accumulated bitterness of the last decade. Conservative faculty members who were believed to be associated with the paper were dragged forward to answer for their

---

* In a letter to Cole, Lahr reiterated his praise for "the restrained way in which you responded to . . . clear provocation and harassment." Lahr went on to tell Cole that "the strong language you used was understandable and constituted a justifiable and measured response." (Letter from Lahr to Cole, March 24, 1988.) A memo to the four *Review* staffers the same day noted that the "alleged damage to the flash attachment in the course of the incident clearly resulted from his attempts to stop the picture-taking and only came after his repeated requests went unheeded." Thus, breaking the flash attachment was, apparently, a "justifiable and measured response."

"crimes." Professor Carla Freccero and other radical faculty tried to have Professor Jeffrey Hart formally censured for criticizing Cole and for his association with the *Review*.*

Freccero's motion, accusing Hart of "undermining collegiality and encouraging racism" was denounced as "vindictive, mean-spirited and an exercise in group-think," by Psychology Professor William M. Smith, who urged his colleagues to boycott the session. "Intellectual and reasoned discourse on this campus?" Smith wrote in a letter to *The Dartmouth*. "It is getting worse rather than better, it seems to me."[18] The faculty tentatively approved part of Freccero's censure motion after a hour-long debate on March 28, but because of a procedural maneuver, the full motion never came to a formal vote. Still, this attack on a nationally respected member of the faculty was clearly a low point in the history of academic freedom at the College.

The same day that Freccero's motion was being debated, President Freedman addressed a specially assembled meeting of the Dartmouth faculty.[19] Freedman condemned the *Review* for "dangerously affecting—indeed—poisoning" the College's intellectual environment.

Freedman would later say that he had been persuaded to make the speech by a meeting with 75 black students. Interestingly, after his frequently stated commitment to the powers of reason and the life of the mind, he now grounded his actions on *emotion*. "This was an emotional dimension that was absolutely authentic, truly heartfelt," he recalled. "It was just emotionally searing to sit there and hear students speak. It was so difficult for them to speak, the depth of their feeling was so great that I never experienced anything like it."[20]

Invoking his "moral responsibility" as Dartmouth's president, Freedman went to great lengths to reaffirm his commitment to free speech, even "speech that expresses unpopular, obnoxious, even detestable points of view." But, he insisted, "the issue that the *Review* presents has nothing whatever to do with freedom of the press." The paper was not only indecent, Freedman declared, it was "irresponsible, mean-spirited and cruel."

---

* Despite the charges against him, Hart was never an adviser to the *Review* and at the faculty meeting (the first he had attended in years) he disassociated himself from much of the paper's coverage, much of which, he said, "didn't belong in campus journalism." Hart nevertheless refused to join in a blanket condemnation of the paper. "They are provocateurs," he said. "They mean to be. They stir up a lot of questions that people don't like stirred up."

Freedman charged that the student paper "recklessly sets out to create a climate of intolerance and intimidation that destroys our mutual sense of community and inhibits the reasoned examination of the widest possible range of ideas." The College, he said, could not stand by while the paper "maliciously engages in bullying tactics that seem virtually designed to have the effect of discouraging women and members of minority groups from joining our faculty." Freedman even went so far as to imply that the *Review* did not deserve the normal protection accorded to the press, because its reporters were merely "ideological provocateurs *posing* as journalists."* Quipped *The Wall Street Journal*, "This must make Allan Bloom . . . an ideological provocateur posing as a best-selling author."[21]

If Freedman had hoped to win the allegiance of the faculty by his attack on the reviled newspaper and by embracing the rhetoric of diversity, he was not disappointed.† The faculty quickly adopted the speech as representing its own views. Marysa Navarro reportedly wept as she thanked Freedman for his support.[22] "I was attacked by them," she complained, "but nobody would defend any of us the way you have defended us today." Navarro was unstinting in her praise of the new president. "The *Dartmouth Review* stance," she told *The New York Times*, "indicates he is capable of action."[23] Cole was equally ecstatic. "I think that someone had to grab the bull by the horns," he said.

Freedman denied any intent to intimidate or censor the newspaper and insisted that by attacking the *Review*, he was merely exercising his

---

* Contrast Freedman's attitude toward the *Review* with this description of the origins of the First Amendment: "The framers, to an even greater extent, expected the widest, fiercest diversity among publications: newspapers, essayists, pamphleteers debating and vilifying not only one another but public figures with whom they disagreed. It was this diversity among contending voices, with readers free to choose, that the framers understood by 'press,' and intended, in the First Amendment, to protect. . . ." (Renata Adler, in *The New Yorker*, June 16, 1986)

The phrase "ideological provocateurs" encapsulated Freedman's fundamental lack of understanding of free press issues. Was he suggesting that journalists with a point of view were not really journalists? That ideological provocateurs were not protected by the First Amendment? What about reporters for *The New Republic*, *The Nation*, and *Rolling Stone*? Was Freedman denying them protection under the First Amendment?

† Afterward the *Alumni Magazine* gushed: "FACULTY'S FRIEND: Freedman's standing among those he likes to call his 'colleagues' is beyond dispute. The faculty liked him from the start; they loved him after his *Dartmouth Review* speech on March 28." ("Rising Sophomore," *Dartmouth Alumni Magazine*, Summer 1988)

own First Amendment rights to criticize ideas he found objectionable. In that respect, he was certainly right. But as the culmination of nearly a decade of enmity between the College and the paper and in the context of the repeated legal threats, boycotts, and suspensions of *Review* staffers, Freedman's claim was disingenuous. There was too much history. That much was clear to Navarro, if not to Freedman. "With a longer perspective," she told a local newspaper, "this is going to be the end of the *Review*. . . ."[24]

Still, there was much about Freedman's speech that was puzzling, including the distinction he was drawing between "obnoxious" and "detestable" speech which deserved protection and the "perversely provocative" ridicule that demanded the denunciation of the entire College. Was he suggesting that speech was protected only so long as no one's feelings were hurt?

Most basic of all, however, was the question of why the president of one of the nation's major institutions of higher learning would devote an entire speech to *a student newspaper*. Given the College's zeal in reprinting and distributing Freedman's speech, Freedman clearly regarded his remarks as a major policy statement, perhaps even as *the* defining speech of his young administration. But how a conservative undergraduate newspaper inhibited the free exchange of ideas—more so than, say, the occupation of campus buildings, bloodied tampons thrown at administrators, dogmatically politicized classrooms, or efforts to censure the speech of a colleague—was left unexplained.

When *Newsweek* editor Larry Martz visited the campus he was "astonished" at the openness of some Dartmouth faculty in calling for the suppression of speech with which they disagreed. Professor Freccero, for instance, had recently succeeded in having a symposium featuring the South African ambassador cancelled. And when the officially sanctioned student newspaper, *The Dartmouth*, editorialized against the creation of a Women's Resource Center, radical feminists on campus not only denounced the piece, but argued that the paper had no right to print it at all. "A lot of people around here just have a basic lack of understanding of free speech," the paper's former editor remarked.[25]

Freedman chose to address none of this and took no action on threats reportedly levelled at blacks who worked for the *Review*.

Also noteworthy was his silence on the "decency" of other publications on campus—for example *Stet*, which declared in a recent issue that

"Men Who Oppose Choice Should Fuck Themselves." Apparently, such speech does not affect the intellectual environment at Dartmouth in any negative way. Or certainly not in any way that calls for the College president's personal condemnation.

But if Freedman's rhetoric was clearly disproportionate to the incident that inspired it, it *was* proportionate to the political pressure brought against the administration from the left. The "true issue," Freedman reiterated, was not one of free speech. The "true target" of the *Review*, Freedman said, "is diversity," which Freedman described as "differences and otherness, in all their rich dimensions."

Then came his declaration:

> Dartmouth will not turn back from its steadfast commitment to diversity—it dare not if it seeks to maintain and enhance its intellectual distinction—and it will not abide having faculty members or others cruelly ridiculed and insulted on the basis of their race or gender no matter what the camouflage.

Having set out ostensibly to attack the ugliness and perversity of the paper, Freedman had gone far beyond his original brief. He was no longer talking merely about the incident between the four students and Cole. By making the defense of "diversity" the centerpiece of his assault on the *Review*, Freedman was acknowledging that the essential conflict was, in fact, not over *style*, but over *substance*. The paper's sins were *not* merely of taste and lack of civility, but of ideology—its rejection of the official doctrine of "diversity." Its crimes, finally, were *political*.

Freedman insisted that he was not attacking conservatism *per se*, allowing that Dartmouth "*needs* conservative voices—they serve to nourish our diversity"; and he endorsed the influence of Edmund Burke, John Henry Cardinal Newman, Matthew Arnold, James Madison, and Henry Adams—a list notable for the lack of contemporary, or even living, conservatives. Freedman liked his conservatives at a distance and dead. The *Review* was neither.

Obscured somewhat by the president's baroque rhetoric ("The parts should be as rich and heterogenous as we can make them, so that the whole can be as unique as we can shape it.") Freedman was propounding a radical doctrine. Freedman had drawn a line to define the limits of acceptable ideas; attacks on "diversity" were decisively excluded.

Freedman was shrewd enough to recognize that he was in tune with the academic *Zeitgeist*. In the 1980s, no academic administrator hurt his standing by calling for more research, denouncing racism, or upholding "diversity"—which was increasingly a code word for curricular fragmentation, politicized instruction, race-conscious hiring policies, and the enhanced status of radical gay and lesbian organizations on campus. As Freedman spoke, major universities across the country were in the process of imposing limits on speech that was regarded as sexist, racist, "homophobic," or otherwise hostile to the official ideology of "diversity." If the new university has a purpose—beyond the well-being of its faculty—it is to extirpate or, as an alternative, *cure* "reactionary" attitudes through programs of therapeutic education. Such a revolution—enshrined at schools as prestigious as the University of Wisconsin, the University of Michigan, Brown, and Penn State—was a logical result of the academic triumphs of the 1960s radicals who had shouted down and denied free speech to those with whom they disagreed, on the ground that opposing points of view were immoral and "dangerous."

The new doctrine was summed up by Yale student Margaret Anne Gallagher, who wrote in a critique of her own school's policies: "It is not enough to enforce a civilized code of behavior. We must pry into men's souls and wipe out incorrect thinking, undesirable emotion. The crusade against prejudice is no less than an attempt to drive evil out of men's hearts, to create a New Man." Gallagher regarded such policies as totalitarian:

> In America today, there are certain issues that cannot be discussed both honestly and safely. Race is one. On campus, a statement about race is evaluated not in terms of its truth or falsehood, but as to whether it forwards or frustrates the quest for racial equality. What is taking place is a vigorous battle to extend this special status to questions of sex and sexual orientation, to ensure that all statements on these subjects are judged not by their truth or even their sincerity, but by their political effect.[26]*

Gallagher's comments had been inspired by two cases at Yale. In one, a divinity student was punished for posting an announcement of a debate

---

* Wrote Gallagher: "The problem at Yale and elsewhere, is not just liberal bias against conservatives, or even a disregard for free speech per se. It's the abandonment of objective standards of action in favor of subjective evaluations of actions."

on the resolution, "Resolved: CIA Discrimination against Homosexuals is Justified." Another divinity student, a woman representing the Gay-Straight Lesbian Coalition, objected and filed a sexual harassment complaint against the student. The administration sided with the woman and advised the student to remove the poster. When another student, however, posted the notice to protest what he saw as a "ludicrous violation" of free speech, the harassment charges were transferred to him. Ultimately, according to Gallagher, he was kicked off campus and denied the right to participate in graduation ceremonies *for posting the notice of a debate*. Administrators warned him that unless he apologized he might never receive his degree at all.[27]

The case of Wayne Dick was almost identical to the case of the divinity student, except for the ultimate disposition. Dick, a Yale junior, was disciplined for displaying posters that satirized Gay Lesbian Awareness Days (GLAD). In a flourish reminiscent of the early days of *The Dartmouth Review*, Dick designed his own poster, advertising Bestiality Awareness Days (BAD), including advertisements for one lecture entitled "PAN: the Goat, the God, the Lover." Citing a Yale rule against "harassment, intimidation, coercion, or assault, or any other act of violence against any member of this community, including sexual, racial, or ethnic harassment," the faculty placed Dick on probation for the rest of his undergraduate career.

Outgoing Yale President A. Bartlett Giamatti maintained a studied silence about the case, despite its obvious free speech implications. But he was succeeded by Benno Schmidt, a noted First Amendment expert, who ordered a new hearing. Dick made it clear he regarded the process as a test of the limits of speech and his position was difficult to gainsay. "If my sentence is not overturned," Dick asked, "please advise me as to other views that I am also not allowed to criticize, so that I won't unknowingly violate my probation." This time, under heavy pressure from an outraged public and with the support of Yale Law School Dean Guido Calabrese and historian C. Vann Woodward, he was acquitted.

In a scene difficult to imagine taking place at Dartmouth under James Freedman, Calabrese appeared as a witness on Dick's behalf, saying at one point that while Dick's poster was "tasteless, even disgusting," that was "beside the point. *Free expression is more important than civility in a university*."[28] [Emphasis added.]

But the result was less striking than the fact that the charges were

brought in the first place at all in a modern university—that speech
would be regarded as "harassment" in an institution devoted to the free
exchange of ideas. Yale's President Schmidt seemed to acknowledge as
much in his inaugural address. "To stifle expression because it is obnoxious, erroneous, embarrassing, not instrumental to some political or
ideological end is—quite apart from the grotesque invasion of the rights
of others—a disastrous reflection on ourselves," he declared. "There is
no speech so horrendous in content that it does not in principle serve our
purposes. . . ."[29]

That had been Ernest Martin Hopkins' firm policy for three decades at
Dartmouth. But now, in 1988, it was difficult to imagine Schmidt's
words being spoken by a president of Dartmouth College. He had, in
fact, already repudiated them.

FROM BELGRADE TO HANOVER

Despite the hosannas from the Dartmouth faculty, Freedman's speech
did not play as well elsewhere as it did among the faculty. *The Wall Street
Journal* described Freedman as the "Bull Connor of academia."[30] Former treasury secretary William Simon derided Freedman for his "Orwellian doublespeak, his judicial double standard, and his selective
enforcement of the First Amendment," saying that the Dartmouth president's conduct "should embarrass any principled liberal who cares
about fairness and the free exchange of ideas."[31] A similar note was
sounded by Freedman's colleague, John Silber, president of Boston
University, who said of Dartmouth's handling of *The Dartmouth Review*
that "it is obvious that the right to dissent has been perverted into an
Orwellian right to support the politically correct."[32] *The Washington
Post* editorial board labelled the *Review* "nasty . . . smug, intolerant,
offensive and unhelpful," but noted that a College like Dartmouth was
"an institution that, above all others, is supposed to stand for the free
exchange of ideas."

Addressing itself to Freedman's emphasis on civility, the *Post* noted:

> While polite discourse and reasoned discussion are ideal compo-
> nents of a college education, so are challenges to accepted wisdom,
> tolerance for controversial political views and, above all, free
> speech. It may be provocative for students to criticize professors as

well as for journalists to confront the subjects of their stories, but both are regularly done without penalty all across the country every day. And notwithstanding campus fashions or faculty preferences, these rights belong to those on the political right as well as those on the left.[33]

Wilcomb Washburn, the director of the Office of American Studies at the Smithsonian and a 1948 graduate of Dartmouth, charged that the argument implicit in Freedman's *Review* speech—that speech should be protected so long as it does not "hurt" or "wound" anyone—was a "strikingly new understanding of free speech."

"People who are hurt by strong expressions of disagreement belong not in a university," Washburn wrote, "but in a Trappist monastery."[34]

Some of the most telling criticism of the College's judicial process and the conduct of its president came from Judge Laurence Silberman. A former ambassador to Yugoslavia, Silberman formally declined the College's Daniel Webster Award because he did not wish to appear to endorse Dartmouth's handling of free speech issues. As he did so he observed, "It does not seem inconceivable that we shall arrive at a point where there is greater toleration of dissident views in Belgrade than in Hanover."[35]

But his concerns were shrugged off by the administration. When Judge Silberman proposed that the Alumni Council form a faculty-alumni committee "devoted to encouraging toleration and diverse intellectual and philosophic views on campus," Freedman said there was no need for such an undertaking and it was rejected by a three-to-two margin. Judge Silberman resigned from the council.

What disturbed Judge Silberman was what he saw as the "pervasive hostility on the part of the faculty and college administrators to any criticism of the college's current course." Most appalling of all was the self-righteous dogmatism of the new official ideology. Silberman got the strong impression that "in the official opinion of the college, there is a morally right and wrong answer to those questions."

> Therefore, those alumni who advocated the "wrong answer" were not entitled to be represented —at least in significant numbers—on the governing organs of the college, and those students who advocated the "wrong answers" to those questions were to be discouraged from expressing their views in too assertive a fashion.[36]

Silberman detected not merely a dogmatic and moralistic rigidity on the part of the College, but the same troubling tactics once associated with McCarthyism. Where McCarthy had robbed his opponents of moral legitimacy by branding them as communists, the Dartmouth administration and faculty now used "racism" and "sexism" and "other 'isms' loosely in that same fashion to label their critics as morally inferior."

Recalling the principled stand that many conservatives took against the excesses of Joseph McCarthy, Silberman expressed disappointment that so few liberals had spoken out, particularly alumni in journalism and the law who "should understand the fundamental values at stake" in the matter.[37]

Some liberals did express misgivings about Freedman's free speech policies. Civil libertarian Nat Hentoff wrote that while he found the *Review* "often outrageous, tasteless and cruel," it was nevertheless "within the vintage American tradition of savagely satirical polemics. . . ." The real issue at stake was not the Cole incident, Hentoff concluded, but "the content and the style of *The Dartmouth Review*." A "majority of the faculty," he noted, "have been waiting for a chance to at last teach these obnoxious students a lesson."[38] But Silberman was right. Other than Hentoff and Harvard Law Professor Alan Dershowitz, the response of liberals, both inside and outside of academia was largely one of silence.

In the aftermath of the Cole affair, Dartmouth's administration adopted a tone of bland reassurance; the rhetoric of benign indirection that seems to characterize almost all of its communications with the media and alumni. A recent Dartmouth graduate, now a reporter for a Southern California newspaper, who attended an editorial luncheon with the College's new president and the editorial board of *The Los Angeles Times,* was struck by what she called "the sanitized version" of the College Freedman was selling.

"At lunch at the Times-Mirror building that day," she wrote, "I saw a learned scholar sink to the level of undiscriminating salesman, telling twisted truths to market a college that doesn't—and shouldn't exist."

"Unfortunately, as crafted by alumni and the president for media and prospective student consumption," she wrote, "the College remains little more than a bland Hollywood fantasy. . . . But perpetuating a pristine fantasy is bound to backfire."[39]

CHAPTER

THE DARTMOUTH MIND

In the fall of 1988, drawing inspiration from the presidential sanctification of diversity, the faculty, through its self-study reports, demanded that Dartmouth "offer a curriculum which will expose students to the concerns of women and minorities," intensify its affirmative action programs for both faculty and the student body, and search out and eliminate unacceptable attitudes.[1]

"The word 'diversity'," however, the report said, "is too limited a concept" to grasp the faculty's millenarian vision. Nor was mere tolerance any longer sufficient. Now diversity had to mean welcoming individuals "precisely because of their experiences and because of their race, culture, creed, gender, disability or sexual preference." It also envisioned a far more aggressive posture regarding the forces of reaction.

> Dartmouth should identify and actively confront those forces which hinder the creation of a community liberated from sexism and racism. The white male population must learn not merely to tolerate women and minorities, but to make them welcome, to rejoice in their presence and to learn with them.[2]

The alternative to such rejoicing was also spelled out: "The continuation of conditions, practices and organizations which actually foster unacceptable attitudes," the report declared, *"should not be sanctioned."*[3] [Emphasis added.]

Although the faculty report on "intellectual environment" had noted that the faculty "do not take very seriously the debate about core curriculum which is taking place nationally,"[4] the report reflected extraordinary interest in making the curriculum more "diverse." The faculty members addressing diversity noted that there had been proposals to make women's studies courses mandatory and remarked darkly that "questions" remained about more traditional courses, which they described as tending "to center on books written by and about white men." Turning for inspiration to the revolution that brought down Stanford's Western civilization program, the faculty members declared "it would help if every professor teaching a traditional course found some way to introduce the issue of diversity."[5]

By 1989, it was hard to imagine how Dartmouth's curriculum could be any more diverse than it was. Beyond the introductory English course, there is no guarantee that any two graduates of Dartmouth College will read the same books or take even a single course in common.*

Until a few years ago all students in the introductory English course were expected to read Milton's *Paradise Lost*. That requirement has, however, been modified. Some faculty members replaced Milton's epic with Joseph Conrad's *Heart of Darkness*. In one section in the fall of 1989, Conrad was teamed with a text titled, *Re-reading America: Cultural Contexts for Critical Thinking and Writing*, a collection of 76 readings on "social justice, cultural assimilation, feminism, family, education, work, television," described by the editors as "topics that raise controversial issues, meaningful to college students of all races and backgrounds."

> We propose here a coherent curriculum in which women and minority writers are central, not peripheral . . . [the editors wrote]. These writers do not shy away from issues like racism and gay parenthood. . . . The anthology's rhetorical diversity fosters flex-

---

* It is possible to get a degree from Dartmouth, with a major in English Literature, without taking a single course in Shakespeare.

ible reading and writing skills. And by putting a rock lyric or other non-canonical text next to a traditional scholarly essay, we invite students to question what the academy recognizes as "legitimate" discourse, what it does not recognize.[6]

Because Dartmouth students can fulfill all of their divisional requirements in a single department, it was possible in 1989 for a student to graduate with a humanities program consisting solely of "Stage Design," "Film Culture," "The Creative Process: Videotape," and "The History of Clothing and the Psychology of Dress." Readings for the latter course included portions of *The Official Sloane Ranger Handbook* and *The Official Preppy Handbook*. Students were required to keep a journal "consisting of three or four entries per week to record observations and attitudes (their own and others) about clothing and fashion at Dartmouth," and had to write a short term paper on the subject "How Hanover Dresses: clothes for sale in the Hanover stores." A second paper was to focus on "an aspect of the psychology of dress," while the third was directed to "a fashion designer or aspect of fashion." Class activities included historical surveys of clothing and several videos, including one titled "Not By Jeans Alone."[7]

Dartmouth does offer an outstanding course in the Great Books of the West, a course known as Humanities I and II. But such was its status on campus that it was not offered in 1988-89.[8]

The social science requirement followed a pattern similar to the humanities. Under the Dartmouth curriculum, students could satisfy their four-course social science requirement with a mixture that might have included "Adolescence," "Introduction to Computer Mapping," "Peoples of Polynesia," and "Folklore." Students could fulfill a quarter of the social sciences requirement by taking Sociology 29: "Sport and Society," which described itself thus:

> The Sociological study of sport and society can be approached in a number of ways: as a mechanism for the transmission of societal values; as a means of social participation; as a collective symbol and ritual; as an organized pattern of legitimated conflict and violence; . . . and as a social problem. From these general themes specific socio-psychological topics such as leadership, communication, conflict and cooperation can be emphasized, *along with the issues of race, sex, "sport politics," and the ubiquitous problem of social inequality*. This course examines sport as a complex socio-

cultural phenomenon possessing political and economic consequences for individuals, groups and society as a whole. [Emphasis
added.]

The requirements for the course were modest. A single term paper
was required. Neither of the two exams—mid-term and final—were
essay exams. Instead, both were fill-in-the-blank, multiple choice tests.

The course included a slim reading list, as well as several movies,
including "One on One," "North Dallas Forty," and "The Great White
Hope."[9]*

Another option for the student in search of a social science course
might have been Education 9, "Humans and Other Animals," a study of
animal oppression, which includes readings in *Bambi*, *Animal Liberation*, and *The Question of Animal Awareness*. Some suggested ideas for
research papers in the class include: "The history of animal mascots in
United States school athletics," "Animals at Dartmouth—a survey,"
"Survey of classmates as to how they think hamburgers or fried chicken
or pork chops happen."[10]

One could easily satisfy the entire social science requirement with
oppression courses, adding Sociology 19, "Black Womanhood in Culture and Society," ("We will explore the nature, extent and consequences of the multiple discriminations of race, sex and class as the
context in which these women shaped their social roles and identi-
ties . . . "); Sociology 81, "Corporate and Governmental Deviance," (a
tour of the high-spots of left-wing paranoia over the last two decades,
from Iran-Contra to the Karen Silkwood case)[11]; as well as Sociology
31, "Prejudice and Oppression." This last course is particularly notable
for appearing to develop, beneath the usual academic jargon of oppression studies, an elaborate theory of "thought crime" that removes the
humanity of the guilty parties, while making mere attitudes into acts of
violence.

"This course," writes Professor Bernard Bergen in the syllabus,
"will explore the nature and character of prejudice from a social psychological point of view." He continues:

---

* The 1986 Student Course Guide described "Sport and Society" as a course that many
students take "as a joke." The professor, the guide said, "lost control and student
interest through unorganized, random lectures. . . . Some students showed up at
discussions just to sign in. . . ." Its primary value seems to be as a fulfillment of the
social science distribution requirement.

The starting point for the course will be a view of prejudice as a particular way of knowing another person that is the commission of a violence on the other.

The prejudiced subject is like a knowledge machine that runs by itself, and the effects of that machine are a violence on the other who is the object of knowledge. The course will attempt to understand both the origin and character of prejudice as a totalized knowledge of another that is sealed off from sources of change, and the origin and character of its violent effects on the other who is the object of that knowledge.

Readings include Black Panther Eldridge Cleaver and (of course) Frantz Fanon.[12]

Another option for fulfilling the social science requirement is Sociology 27, which applies the full panoply of diversity education to "Perspectives on the American Family." The thrust of the course can be gleaned from a quiz in the course's main textbook which includes such questions as "The traditional nuclear family is the healthiest form of family. True or false." To which the answer is: FALSE.[13] In fact, the course as a whole is vigorously devoted to rooting out such anachronistic stereotypes and to exploring the strengths of "blended" families, including the "lesbian blended family."

The course's main textbook is notably unsubtle in pushing that agenda. "The traditional nuclear family is a powerful cultural symbol that fails to reflect the diversity of family forms in contemporary America," the authors write.[14] It is a gross and potentially dangerous error to regard the intact nuclear family as normal, students in the class read, because such attitudes are a "significant distortion," unfairly stigmatize other "life styles," and make it harder for such alternative units to feel "self-esteem."[15]

One article in the text examines: "What kind of family is a lesbian family? What are its advantages? Problems? What kind of kin relationships does this family have?"[16]

Gay and lesbian families might be healthier than traditional heterosexual nuclear families, the authors write. This is because gays and lesbians are freed from patriarchal gender roles, such as "husband" and "wife." "Freedom from such roles is often regarded as one of the major advantages of the gay lifestyle," the textbook declares.[17]

In the sciences at Dartmouth, any four courses will suffice to meet the

College's graduation requirement, even if they are all taken in a single department. Graduates are deemed scientifically literate even if their program consists of courses unrelated sequentially, conceptually, or in content.*

The prospects for significant reform are scant. Shortly after Freedman's denunciation of the *Review*, Professor James Wright delivered a similar attack before the Alumni Council and he rejected calls for revisions in the curriculum—dismissing "Mr. Allan Bloom . . . Mr. Bennett and this *Review* claque of curriculum reformers" and characterizing Bloom as a "classic case of someone who hasn't coped at all with the transforming world in which he lives; not at all."

"Certainly we continue to modify, to amend, to evolve our curriculum," Wright said. "But this modification and evolution and amendment generally means *adding new courses because of new fields and because of changes in knowledge.*"[18] [Emphasis added.] In 1989, Wright was named dean of the faculty.†

That fall, Dartmouth officials announced that they were reviewing the College's policy on Free Expression and Dissent. Although officials again stressed their commitment to free speech, one administrator, Alvin Richard, the College's affirmative action officer, said that the College needed to redefine the policy in such a way "that will satisfy both the gender aspect and racial aspect." Specifically, he cited the *Review*, remarking that it often defended itself "under the guise of freedom of expression." A Dartmouth senior writing in a campus newspaper put it even more directly.

"The time has come," he declared, "to hinder the expression of any forms of discrimination, racism, sexism or homophobia that make any member of the equal members of this community feel isolated, sup-

---

* One-third of Dartmouth undergraduates major in the Humanities; 45 percent major in the Social Sciences; 22 percent in the Sciences.

† Wright also emerged as a zealous defender of Dartmouth's curricular status quo. In March 1990, he published a lengthy defense in the *Alumni Magazine* arguing that Dartmouth's curriculum had *not* become "softer, less focused, and less directed." Moreover, he insisted that the modern curriculum was consistent with the goals and values of Ernest Martin Hopkins. Predictably, Wright did not mention Hopkins' numerous warnings against specialization, the university-style model, or what he had termed curricular "sprawl" that resulted from the endless proliferation of courses. (Wright, James, "Dartmouth's Steady Course," *Alumni Magazine*, March 1990)

pressed, repressed, or oppressed. . . . The time is now to get rid of the offensive *Dartmouth Review* as a voice on campus. . . ."[19]*

Professor Cole's wife, Sarah Sully, a professor of French, assigned her class an essay on the conflict between her husband and *The Dartmouth Review*. When one student defended the newspaper, she gave him a "D" arguing that because the essay was "racist" she could not give it a higher grade. When her grade was overturned, she resigned, declaring: "What's happening at Dartmouth is what happened in Nazi Germany. . . . It's what happened when the Jews were being shipped off to concentration camps and the German people looked the other way. That's what's happening at Dartmouth."[20]

Earlier in the year, Dean of Faculty Dwight Lahr had unveiled a radical (if abortive) escalation of the College's affirmative action effort—proposing what became known as the "minority first" policy. Lahr's plan would give preference to the hiring of minority faculty and only secondary emphasis to their fields or the academic needs of their department, the curriculum, or the students.

Such a radical plan was necessary, Lahr insisted, because the College still lagged behind its affirmative action goals. Again, he blamed *The Dartmouth Review* and cited it as a pretext for the new policy. "The very presence on campus of an irresponsible newspaper that can abuse freedom of the press with total impunity . . . is not likely to alleviate anybody's fears," he said. Lahr's plan for a "more dynamic and effective" diversity campaign won strong support from the faculty. One of those endorsing Lahr's plan was Professor Richard Crowell, chairman of the Mathematics Department, who said he did not foresee the proposal having much of an impact on his department.[21]†

The push for diversity also assumed unusually creative forms.

In late 1989, the Student Assembly voted to bar the Central Intelligence Agency from campus because it discriminated against homosexuals. "Denying the CIA this opportunity," the assembly declared,

---

* The charge of racism and sexism against *The Dartmouth Review* is difficult to sustain. The paper named Kevin Pritchett, a black, as its editor-in-chief in 1990. Two previous editor-in-chiefs had been Indians from the subcontinent and three had been women.

† This was, perhaps, because in 1987-88, only four blacks were awarded Ph.D.s in mathematics in the United States. ("Only 4 Black Americans Said to Have Earned Math Ph.D.'s in 1987-88," *The Chronicle of Higher Education*, August 2, 1989)

"would make a significant symbolic statement by reaffirming Dartmouth's dedication to its diverse student body."[22]

In early 1990, the International Student Association (ISA), a leading force for diversity on campus, celebrated its new-found clout by temporarily renaming the ISA Center "Fidel Castro International Center" in honor of one of the world's last remaining Stalinists.[23]*

Diversity was also the overriding theme of the 1989 Convocation, from the prayer that sought forgiveness for prejudice based on "skin color, nation, gender, sexual orientation, religion," to the heavily didactic—and mandatory—sensitivity training sessions. The Convocation speaker, Henry Louis Gates, one of the luminaries of the academic diversity movement, called upon the students to "rethink the role of a liberal education without the conceptual residue of cultural nationalism or geneticism."[24] Gates has been notably successful at parlaying his politics into academic advancement; he is member of the new class of academics who have made their "oppression" pay very well indeed.

After Gates had edited a particularly egregious issue of *Critical Inquiry* devoted to "race," writer Harold Fromm had described him as a member of "the Evangelical Guru and Guilt Industry that tells its members 'I'm okay, you're okay, the rest of the world's rotten' while their garages fill up with Rolls Royces or their vitas with grants."[25]

Dartmouth gave him an honorary doctorate.

As part of the Convocation theme, all members of the class of 1993 were required to attend a program titled "Social Issues at Dartmouth," which included a series of politically-attuned skits. These too were a legacy of the "Cole incident." In April 1988, the administration had ordered the initiation of "retreats" and orientation programs "on racial issues." It also began a series of "roadshows" that included skits and lectures in dormitories "that would explore problems of racism."[26]

Chris Smith, a freshman in the fall of 1989, reported that one of the skits, aimed at inculcating proper attitudes toward homosexuality, acted out a scene in which an out-of-the-closet lesbian invites a straight classmate to go camping, mentioning that they would be able to go skinny-dipping together. As an example of unenlightened thinking, the heterosexual is depicted as wrongly regarding this as a come-on. "But,"

---

* It is not clear why Deng Xiaoping, the Butcher of Beijing, was slighted. In any case, the decision was later rescinded.

recounted Smith, "the valiant lesbian explained that she was not attracted to the woman; the heterosexual student realized that she had been wrong, and the two skipped off together into the woods."[27]

Chris Smith wrote that he had come to Hanover "ready to spend four years learning 'the best that had been thought and said.'. . . . Granted, it was naive, but I never expected that my expectations would be so crushed by intellectual pedestrians with Ph.D.s. From convocation to sensitivity training sessions, Dartmouth seems to make an anti-heroic effort to inculcate a worship of the inane."[28]

Dartmouth also gained itself a national image of sorts through its RAID roadshow (Responsible AIDS Information at Dartmouth), which preached the gospel of condoms, rubber dams, and spermicide in a vaudeville routine that featured rock music, skits, and colorful "condom races." The shows—dramatized successors of Dartmouth's earlier safe sex programs—were chock full of valuable information and helpful notions.

"The rubber dam was originally designed for dentists," one speaker told students, "but now it is highly recommended for all anal/oral/vaginal contact. What you need to do with the rubber dam is place it over the orifice of interest, before any exchange of bodily fluids. Make sure to hold it in place while contact is being made."* According to an account by William R. Grace, an editor of *The Dartmouth Review*, the speaker continued: "We also suggest, if a rubber dam is not available, using microwavable plastic wrap. . . . Saran Wrap, it's not just for breakfast anymore." Recounted Grace:

> At this Reverend [Gwendolyn] King [Dartmouth's assistant Christian Chaplain], jiggling perilously with laughter, fell off her seat and onto her knees, repeating between gasps for breath, "not just for breakfast anymore, Saran Wrap—oh Lord!—it's not just for breakfast anymore."

Once the hilarity had died down, students in the audience were then asked to participate in a game called "Time That Condom," a race

---

* Michael Fumento, author of *The Myth of Heterosexual Aids* (New Republic Books, 1990), remarks that the heavy emphasis on the rubber dam in safe sex programs reflects attempts to "democratize" AIDS, by helping to "keep up the pretense that there is basically nothing homosexuals do that heterosexuals do not. . . ." (p. 148)

accompanied by the theme from the movie "Chariots of Fire" ("Go!—Go!—Go!—spermicide!—spermicide!—spermicide!—spread it all over the tip!—pull it down!—pull it down!—go!—go!—go!")[29]

One searches in vain for any indication that the participants in any of these adventures should be concerned with something other than technologically sound techniques for avoiding guilt, microbes, and babies; or that the fluid-exchangers and speedy condom appliers are actually human beings whose obligations to one another might occasionally transcend the proper application of rubber dams.

THE WALLS KEEP TUMBLIN' DOWN

On November 13, 1989, President Freedman addressed the faculty of Arts and Sciences and announced that Dartmouth's Board of Trustees had voted to divest all of the College's holdings in companies doing business with South Africa. The decision came only 48 hours after the chairman of the board of trustees had reaffirmed his opposition to divestment.

Over the years, Dartmouth had adopted policies that had significantly reduced its investments in South Africa. Specifically prohibited were investments directly in South African firms, financial institutions making loans to the South African government, and companies that did not follow "certain employment and other policies there." By 1989, less than two percent of the College's endowment was invested in companies doing business in South Africa. But the ardor of the anti-apartheid forces on campus had not been dampened.

On Thursday, November 9, pro-divestment demonstrators invaded the Hanover Inn, where the trustees were holding a cocktail party, to demand immediate and total divestiture. The group was led by Asir Ajmal, a well-known campus activist and writer for *Stet*. In one of the more striking ironies of the weekend's events, Ajmal would sport a hammer and sickle on his cap—at the very same time the Berlin Wall was tumbling down. In *Stet*, Ajmal had contributed to the College's intellectual atmosphere with such statements as: "Mao Tse Tung has taught us that the contradiction between landlord and peasants is one between the people and their enemies and that between peasants and workers is a contradiction among the people. While the latter can be resolved through Marxist-Leninist education the former *will require violent means for its resolution.*"[30] [Emphasis added.]

College spokesman Alex Huppe offered to arrange a meeting between a delegation from Ajmal's group and the trustees, but according to an account later published in *The Dartmouth Review*, Ajmal rejected the offer, because the demonstrators were "non-hierarchical."

The next day, 300 demonstrators congregated in front of Parkhurst Hall, demanding a meeting with the trustees. Among their specific demands was immediate divestment and the "retraction of the invitation to South African member of parliament Peter Soal" to speak on campus. Speakers at the demonstration included representatives of the Committee on Palestinian Rights, who compared Israel with the South African regime.[31] Negotiations between the protestors and the Dean of the College Edward Shanahan resulted in the trustees' agreement to meet with the radicals the next morning, a meeting attended by about 100 students. The meeting featured emotional speeches and African chants.

Even so, Trustee Chairman George Munroe made the board's position clear: it had no intention of divesting. The trustees' responsibility, he said, was to the endowment and the educational mission of the College and thus had to be concerned primarily with maximizing returns. Munroe, who had participated in a fact-finding mission to South Africa, declared: "The eventual future of South Africa will be decided by South Africans," and insisted that American investment in South Africa was doing "more good than otherwise." His position was supported by other trustees, including Robert Danziger, who argued that continued investment gave the College greater leverage over the conduct of companies doing business in South Africa.[32]

Within 24 hours, the trustees had voted to divest.

Word that an announcement would be made on Monday was apparently passed to the "Upper Valley Committee for a Free South Africa" which circulated posters around campus publicizing the expected announcement. According to *The Dartmouth*, "More than 250 student observers joined members of the faculty in cheers and cries of approval as soon as Freedman made the announcement." One radical student leader was quoted as saying he was "speechless" and "overwhelmed by the victory."[33]

The trustees' statement explaining their turn-around was an extraordinary document. While recognizing that "many firms continuing to do business in South Africa are making positive contributions to the lives of their employees and the political process in South Africa," the board said it had decided that such considerations were overridden by the "great symbolic meaning to many within and outside the College" and the board's anxiety "that disputes over such investments undermine Dartmouth's ability to achieve some of its educational goals."[34]

What the trustees seemed to be saying was that their decision was based not on principle, but solely on the imperative of symbolic politics. Because there were those inside and outside of the College who objected to the investments, it said, and because "disputes" over the issue might disrupt the College, better to yield now, whatever the merits. Future archaeologists of the academic mind will find few more striking artifacts of the culture of acquiescence. In effect, the board declared that the College was now held hostage to any group willing to use the threat of disruption.

Typically, the *Review*'s analysis was the most direct. "As one reads the communique," it editorialized, "it becomes increasingly obvious that the trustees were swayed by the recent spate of protests and sit-ins on campus and not by any sudden altruistic impulse. . . . A mob of unruly agitators effectively browbeat the Board of Trustees into divesting and dictated through their illegal and irresponsible actions the specific terms of Dartmouth's financial policy."[35]

The euphoria of President Freedman's announcement—and the spirit of diversity triumphant—carried over into the rest of the faculty's meeting. After hearing Freedman, the faculty approved yet another new special studies program in "Latin American and Caribbean Studies."

The principle architect of the new program was Maryssa Navarro, who urged her faculty colleagues not to consider the "financial burden" of the new program (that was the problem of the administration, she said), but to judge it on its curricular merits alone.

"In a world that's changing very rapidly, the walls that have been standing a long time are breaking down," she declared.[36] She was not referring to the collapse of the Berlin wall, and certainly not the walls of Fidel Castro's concentration camp on the Isle of Pines (a subject notably absent from her class discussions of Cuba). Instead, she seemed to be referring to the collapse of those final remaining barriers of intellectual integrity and academic comity that stood in the way of the advent of her own particular brand of scholastic Third Worldism and the idolatry of totalitarianism in the guise of diversity. In that respect, she was quite right.

PART III

WHAT IT MEANS

CHAPTER

THE FATE OF AN IDEA

For those who don't pay close attention to events in higher education—
and that includes the vast majority of parents, legislators, and donors—
much of what I have described at Dartmouth will sound shocking and
many will conclude that Dartmouth's problems are Dartmouth's alone.
They are not. The crisis of values in higher education is deep and
pervasive.

Unlike the upheaval of the 1960s, the universities of the 1990s are the
victims of a revolution *from above* that has robbed higher education of
much of its traditional content, while distorting its values and its basic
principles. Given the proclivities of the typical academic administrator
of the 1990s, a seizure of an administration building by militant radicals
would be simply redundant.

From surveys that chronicle mass ignorance to clownish curriculums
that have turned out college graduates unable to think critically or write
a simple letter, the evidence is compelling that the dominant academic
leftism has proven itself adept at disemboweling the liberal arts and at
propagating its own crabbed, sullen, and totalitarian dogmas—but inca-
pable of providing students with a quality education.

In the midst of this, Dartmouth is not anywhere close to being the worst case. A student at Dartmouth who is careful in his selection of classes and teachers can still obtain quite a fine education. Dartmouth cannot even be described as being in the vanguard of radicalization. In the politicization of the humanities, for example, schools such as Brown, Duke, Yale, and the University of California at Irvine are far in advance of Dartmouth. The number of radical professors at Dartmouth is dwarfed by the number of recycled militants at schools like the University of Wisconsin, Stanford, and the University of California at Berkeley. Even Dartmouth's most extreme outrages need to be placed in context: other schools—the University of Massachusetts and the University of Pennsylvania—have gone to more draconian lengths in throttling dissent and creating "sensitivity" gulags. Nor is the crisis confined to the Ivy League; among smaller schools, it is the rare college where "diversity" has not become the reigning ideology.

In 1983, Bertell Ollman—unable to believe his own good fortune—exulted that a "Marxist cultural revolution" was under way in America's universities *and that no one seemed to know it was happening.*[1] Since then, having coupled itself with academic feminism, the various mutations of post-structuralism, and professorial self-interest, the revolution has moved from victory to victory, for the most part still unrecognized, almost never opposed. If faculty members refuse to confront the subversion of their own profession, it is not surprising how little that parents, alumni, and even college trustees know about what is happening.*

---

* It is not surprising that Irving Kristol has cited the performance of university trustees as the most powerful illustration of "the impotence of non-ideological pragmatism when confronted with an aggressive ideology. . . ." Wrote Kristol:

> They loyally spend time and energy raising money to finance (among other, more sensible things) left-wing humanities and social science departments, "women's studies" programs that are candid proselytizers for lesbianism, programs in "safe sex" that promote homosexuality, "environmental studies" that are, at bottom, anti-capitalist propaganda, and other such activities of which they surely disapprove.
>
> When I point this out to them, they are likely to mumble an embarrassed, evasive reply. The sad truth is that they would prefer not to know what is going on within the institutions they supposedly govern. Such willful ignorance protects them from thinking about issues that are ideological (they don't know how to do it) or getting involved in an argument with highly ideological types on the faculty (they don't know how to do this, either).

Nor are students much savvier, at least at first. A handful, it is true, are converted to the orthodoxies of their professors. For most, however, the result is not politicization, but the inculcation of vacuity.

At stake is more than merely the triumph of the left: what we are seeing is the demolition of the very idea of liberal education. It is a collapse that is embodied in students who learn quickly that ideas are not for analysis and dispute, but ideologically dangerous minefields that are best avoided altogether. The modern university has so lost touch with its original mission that instead of imparting a sense of intellectual adventure, it teaches students to adopt the techniques of evasion and dissimulation. Deprived of their cultural patrimony and ignorant of the traditional liberal values of tolerance and free and disinterested inquiry after truth, they learn to ape the styles and rhetoric of political correctness, to cynically manipulate the system that provides them with grades and degrees. But the posture is as hollow as their education. One suspects that many of them would learn as much or more by watching *Jeopardy* than they do paying $18,000 a year for "TV: A Critical Approach" and "Rock 'n' Roll Is Here to Stay."

Any worthwhile reform of higher education will be a daunting task, but one that begins with the recovery of language. The loss of meaning and integrity of such terms as "diversity," "pluralism," "academic freedom," and the "liberal arts," has been decisive in the decline of academic values. But the recovery of higher education involves more than merely restoring academic standards, it means recognizing with Richard Weaver that ideas have consequences. That in turn demands the reclamation of the tradition that acknowledges that truth is ultimately knowable by the use of right reason. It also means the frank recognition that despite the undeniable value of non-Western cultures, the intellectual heritage of the West is indispensable in our search for meaning, dignity, and freedom. The rigor, honesty, and restlessness of the West's quest remains unique in human history and represents the closest man has come in his ongoing search for answers.

So we have the paradoxical and scandalous situation where most of the trustees of practically all the private universities are "conservative" in the sense that they vote Republican, while the institutions they preside over have, in the past two decades, been taken over by the left. These days, those trustees don't even have the nerve to propose any well-known conservative for a college presidency. (*The Wall Street Journal*, February 29, 1990)

This is a challenge that the academic mandarins are unlikely to concede without a fight. For although Marxism is dead, the academic attack on "coherent beliefs of any kind" continues unabated. Having lost its utopian model, the left has turned its considerable talents to negation. Despite the abject failure of its doctrines in practice, the left can continue to undermine the foundations of the West using its privileged positions in the academy, armed with the academic weapons of its own devising, and clad in the armor of its incoherence and incomprehensibility. Because it is embedded in an environment in which it is seldom challenged and which offers it the most prestigious possible auspices, the academic nihilists' capacity for destruction is enormously threatening, all the more so for being wrapped up in the language of benevolence and delivered through institutions of power and authority.

Is reform then possible?

Allowing for the differences in times and circumstances, Columbia, Chicago, and Dartmouth proved that it is—providing there are administrators, trustees, and faculty who share a clearly defined educational purpose, moral sensibility, and intellectual courage and discrimination.

The restoration of higher learning requires, indeed, a moral recommitment to the student as a complete human being, who is not to be condescended to, manipulated, shielded from controversial ideas, or cured of unacceptable ones. That, in turn, demands a restoration of "the ancient, crucial, high art of teaching"[2] in schools where the curriculum is no longer an after-thought to the careerism of the faculty, but an expression of a philosophical and institutional *telos*.

Faculty members have been at the forefront of the fragmentation of the curriculum and the politicization of scholarship. They must also, inevitably, play a critical role in the restoration of the intellect. The creation of the National Association of Scholars, a national, nonpartisan organization specifically designed to combat the politicization of scholarship and to help reverse the intellectual decay of the universities is a major development in the fight for academic integrity, even though it scarcely rivals such redoubts of trendy left scholarship as the Modern Language Association in influence.

One suspects that there are other voices that would be raised if the environment were not so one-sided and intimidating; too many moderates and conservatives have simply chosen to absent themselves from the ordeal of faculty meetings. That reticence may also be coming to an end. And thanks in part to *The Dartmouth Review* and its brood of journalistic disciples on campuses across the country, students now have a means to challenge the radical orthodoxy on campus.

But faculty members who take up the fight against the adulteration of the curriculum and the standards of intellectual integrity must also be able to look for support from administrators and trustees who take an informed, active, and persistent interest in defending and reasserting quality in education. Alumni should demand honest information from the institutions that are so zealous in tapping them for donations and they should demand accountability from trustees and administrators who are responsible for what goes on within their institutions.

Alumni, indeed, need to overcome their nostalgia for their *alma maters* when that *alma mater* bears slight resemblance to the college they attended in 1940, 1950, or even 1970. Wayward schools can be given a jolt if they are no longer remembered in the wills of alumni and if alumni decide to send their children to schools that still honor the liberal arts, such as St. John's College, Thomas Aquinas College, the University of Chicago, Columbia, Notre Dame, Providence, William & Mary, Boston University, Hillsdale College, the University of Dallas, St. Anselm's, the University of the South, Washington & Lee, Wabash, Whitman, Pepperdine, and Hope.

In the same respect, the great fountains of academic largess, Congress, state legislatures, and foundations alike can quickly win the attention of academe because they speak the higher learning's most eloquent language, money. Their dollars have drawn professors from the classroom and have propped up the most outrageous mutations of the academic culture. To paraphrase H. L. Mencken, in the modern university conscience is that small voice saying that your funding might be jeopardized.

The prospects for Dartmouth are, of course, uncertain. But what an electrifying message it would send if Dartmouth were to declare and enforce a commitment to tolerance, free speech, and the renewal of the liberal arts in the teeth of the academic *Zeitgeist*. Under Ernest Martin Hopkins, Dartmouth did just that and became a beacon for hundreds of schools seeking an alternative to the pressures of university conformism.

In its current condition, such a conversion is difficult to envision. But we live in an age in which orthodoxies even more rigid than Parkhurst Hall's or even the Modern Language Association's have fallen of their own weight. Nor is the struggle as uneven as it appears.

"No scheme," Jacques Barzun reminds us, "lasts forever." The source of his optimism was simple. The "bearers of culture continue to be born; the desire for culture is innate."[3]

If so, then it is the oligarchies of academe, so dominant, smug, and intolerant that they dismiss critics as mere "gnats," who are themselves the creatures of a passing moment.

NOTES

PROLOGUE: WINTER 1989

1. Syllabus, Women's Studies 22, "History and Theory of Feminism," Winter Term 1989
2. Flax, Jane, "Postmodernism and Gender Relations in Feminist Theory," *Signs*, Summer 1987
3. Ibid.
4. Jaggar, Alison, *Feminist Politics and Human Nature*, Sussex, The Harvester Press, 1983, pp. 255, 260, 261
5. Lorde, Audre, *Sister Outsider*, Freedom, California, The Crossing Press, 1984, see p. 145; "Trip to Russia" and "Grenada Revisited: An Interim Report"
6. Moraga, Cherrie and Anzaldua, Gloria, eds., *This Bridge Called My Back: Writings By Radical Women of Color*, New York, Kitchen Table: Women of Color Press, 1983, p. 213
7. Ibid., p. 241
8. Jaggar, Alison, op. cit., p. 8
9. Ibid., p. 385
10. Harding, Sandra, *The Science Question in Feminism*, Ithaca, Cornell University Press, 1986, p. 28
11. Levin, Margarita, "Caring New World: Feminism and Science," *The American Scholar*, Winter 1988
12. Ibid.
13. Harding, Sandra, op. cit., p. 9
14. Ibid., p. 250
15. Levin, Margarita, op. cit.
16. Syllabus, op. cit.

THE CRISIS

1. Lewis, C.S., *The Screwtape Letters*, New York, Bantam Books, 1982, p. 75
2. Freedman, James, "Speaking the Language of Intellectual Ambition,"

315

Address to Dartmouth College General Faculty, October 26, 1987, in *Speaking at the Outset: Four Addresses by President James O. Freedman at Dartmouth in 1987*, Hanover, Dartmouth College, 1987. In that version, Freedman's remarks appear as: "But an unqualified emphasis upon Western civilization blocks access to non-Western civilizations and legitimates an assumption of European and American cultural superiority. That assumption is as damaging to our nation as it is menacing to the world that our students will be compelled to understand and to shape." In the summer of 1988, however, the *Dartmouth Alumni Magazine* quoted a slightly different version of the same speech, this one quoting Freedman as saying, "*To the extent that* an unqualified emphasis on 'western civilization' blocks access to non-western civilizations, it legitimates an assumption of European and American cultural superiority *that will not withstand analysis*. That assumption is as damaging *to our students individually* as it is menacing to the world they will be compelled to shape." [Emphasis added.]

3. National Endowment for the Humanities, "50 Hours: A Core Curriculum for College Students," Washington, D.C., October 1989

4. Interview with author, February 15, 1990

5. Cox, Archibald, *Report of the Fact Finding Commission Appointed to Investigate the Disturbances at Columbia University in April and May 1968*

6. Hook, Sidney, *Academic Freedom and Academic Anarchy*, New York, Cowles Publications, 1970, p. ix

7. Hook, Sidney, *Out of Step*, New York, Carroll & Graf, 1988, p. 505

8. Hook, Sidney, *Academic Freedom and Academic Anarchy*, op. cit. p. 35

9. Shaw, Peter, *The War Against the Intellect: Episodes in the Decline of Discourse*, Iowa City, University of Iowa Press, 1989, p. 167

10. Ibid., p. 65

11. Bennett, William, Speech at Stanford University, April 1988, reprinted as "Why the West," *National Review*, May 27, 1988

12. Oakeshott, Michael, *The Voice of Liberal Learning: Michael Oakeshott on Education*, ed. Timothy Fuller, New Haven, Yale University Press, 1989, p. 29

THE POLITICIZATION OF ACADEMIA

1. Howe, Irving, "The Treason of the Critics," *The New Republic*, June 12, 1989

2. "Literary Critics Meet, and Find Politics Everywhere," *The New York Times*, January 1, 1990

3. " '60s protesters, '80s professors," *U.S. News & World Report*, January 16, 1989

4. Kolodny, Annette, *The Lay of the Land*, Lincoln, Nebraska, University of Nebraska Press, 1975, pp. 3-4 and 146

5. Boggs, Carl, "The Intellectuals and Social Movements: Some Reflections on Academic Marxism," *Humanities in Society*
6. Jacoby, Russell, "Radicals in Academia," *The Nation*, September 19, 1987
7. Dickstein, Morris, "Columbia Recovered," *The New York Times Magazine*, May 15, 1988
8. quoted in Collier, Peter and Horowitz, David, *Destructive Generation: Second Thoughts About the Sixties*, New York, Summit Books, 1989, p. 176
9. Balch, Stephen H. and London, Herbert, "The Tenured Left," *Commentary*, October 1986
10. "Literary Critics Meet, and Find Politics Everywhere," op. cit.
11. Trilling, Lionel, *Beyond Culture*, New York, Viking Press, 1968, p. 3
12. Howe, Irving, *A Margin of Hope*, New York, Harcourt Brace Jovanovich, 1982, p. 289
13. Trilling, Lionel, op. cit., p. 26
14. quoted in Krupnick, Mark, *Lionel Trilling and the Fate of Cultural Criticism*, Evanston, Northwestern University Press, 1986, p. 145
15. Ibid.
16. Chace, William M., *Lionel Trilling: Criticism and Politics*, Stanford, Stanford University Press, 1980, p. 125
17. quoted in Krupnick, Mark, op. cit., p. 178
18. Trilling, Lionel, "Mind in the Modern World," Thomas Jefferson Lecture in the Humanities, National Endowment for the Humanities, 1972, New York, Viking Press, 1973
19. See Chace, William, op. cit., p. 147
20. cited in Krupnick, Mark, op. cit., p. 98
21. Shaw, Peter, *The War Against the Intellect*, op. cit., p. 65
22. quoted in Krupnick, Mark, op. cit., p. 148
23. Trilling, Lionel, "Mind in the Modern World," op. cit.
24. Wellek, Rene, *The Attack on Literature and Other Essays*, Chapel Hill, The University of North Carolina Press, 1982, pp. 3-4
25. Ibid.
26. Heller, Scott, "A Constellation of Recently Hired Professors Illuminates the English Department at Duke," *The Chronicle of Higher Education*, May 27, 1987
27. Jameson, Frederic and Kavanagh, James, "The Weakest Link: Marxism in Literary Studies," in *The Left Academy II*, New York, Praeger, 1984, pp. 3-4
28. Ollman, Bertell and Vernoff, Edward, ed. *The Left Academy: Marxist Scholarship on American Campuses*, New York, McGraw-Hill, 1982, pp. 2-3
29. Ibid.
30. Shaw, Peter, "Declining Discourse," *Society*, March/April 1986

31. Ibid.
32. Campbell, Colin, "The Tyranny of the Yale Critics," *The New York Times Magazine*, February 9, 1986
33. Jameson, Frederic, op. cit., pp. 10-11
34. Hassan, Ihab, "Pluralism in Postmodern Perspective," *Critical Inquiry 12*, Spring 1986
35. Susman, Warren I., *Culture as History: The Transformation of American Society in the 20th Century*, New York, 1985
36. Himmelfarb, Gertrude, "Some Reflection on the New History," AHR Forum, 1989
37. Shaw, Peter, "Declining Discourse," op. cit.
38. Baker, Houston A., Jr., "Caliban's Triple Play," *Critical Inquiry*, Autumn 1986
39. Jameson, Frederic, op. cit., p. 3
40. Ibid., p. 4
41. Ibid., p. 10
42. Shaw, Peter, *The War Against the Intellect*, op. cit. p. 62
43. Tuttleton, James W., "Politics and art in the criticism of F.O. Matthiessen," *The New Criterion*, June 1989
44. "Undergraduate Program in English and Textual Studies," Syracuse University, 1990 (Distributed to Faculty of the College of Arts and Sciences by the Office of the Dean, February 16, 1990)
45. Ibid.
46. Letter to author, February 26, 1990
47. Haverford Catalog, 1989-90, p. 33
48. Ursinus College, Catalog, 1990-91
49. Carleton College, Academic Catalog, 1989-90
50. Williams College, Bulletin, 1989-90
51. Rudolph, Frederick, *The American College and University*, New York, Vintage Books, 1965, p. 413
52. "Academic Freedom and Tenure," *AAUP Bulletin*, Autumn, 1968
53. Cited in Shaw, Peter, *The War Against the Intellect*, op. cit., p. 75
54. Ibid., p. 75
55. Ibid., p. 76

THE OFFICIAL IDEOLOGY I: FEMINISM

1. Nuechterlein, James, "The Feminization of the American Left," *Commentary*, November 1987
2. "Scholars Seek Wider Reach for Women's Studies," *The New York Times*, May 17, 1989
3. "History Convention Reflects Change From Traditional to 'Gender' Studies," *The New York Times*, January 9, 1988
4. Ibid.

5. "Scholars Seek Wider Reach for Women's Studies," op. cit.
6. Lane, Ann J., *Women's Studies Quarterly*, Summer 1985
7. *Proceedings*, Seventh Annual Great Lakes Colleges Association Women's Studies Conference, 1978
8. cited in Shaw, Peter, *The War Against the Intellect*, op. cit., p. 74
9. Rabine, Leslie, "Searching For The Connections: Marxist-Feminists and Women's Studies," *Humanities in Society*
10. Jaggar, Alison, op. cit. p. 383
11. Ibid., p. 371, p. 382, and pp. 383-4
12. de Beauvoir, Simone, "Women and Creativity," *French Feminist Thought*, London, Basil Blackwell, 1987, p. 31
13. Moi, Toril, *French Feminist Thought*, op. cit., p. 2
14. Iannone, Carol, "Feminism vs. Literature," *Commentary*, July 1988
15. cited in Shaw, Peter, "Feminist Literary Criticism," *The American Scholar*, Autumn 1988
16. Iannone, Carol, op. cit.
17. Rabine, Leslie, op. cit.
18. Shaw, Peter, *The War Against the Intellect*, op. cit., p. 80
19. Ibid., p. 86
20. Levin, Margarita, "Caring New World: Feminism and Science," *The American Scholar*, Winter 1988
21. Ibid.
22. *The Harvard Crimson*, November 24, 1986
23. Howe, Karen G., "The Psychological Impact of a Women's Studies Course," *Women's Studies Quarterly* XIII:1 (Spring 1985)
24. cited in Jaggar, Alison, op. cit., p. 365
25. Interview with author
26. Lilla, Elizabeth, "Who's Afraid of Women's Studies?" *Commentary*, February 1986
27. "Pomona professor says course was rejected due to his sex," *The Chronicle of Higher Education*, May 23, 1990
28. Smith, Page, *Killing the Spirit: Higher Education in America*, New York, Viking, 1990, p. 289
29. Short, Thomas, "Education and Indoctrination," *Academic Questions*, March 1986

THE OFFICIAL IDEOLOGY II: RACE

1. "Black and White on Campus: Learning Tolerance, Not Love, and Separately," *The New York Times*, May 26, 1988
2. "B.A. Lite," *Texas Monthly*, January 1990
3. Williams, Walter E., "Race, Scholarship and Affirmative Action," *National Review*, May 5, 1989
4. Ibid.

5. Ibid.
6. Ibid.
7. Sowell, Thomas, "The New Racism on Campus," *Fortune*, February 13, 1989
8. Ibid.
9. "Affirmative Action Goals, Coupled with Tiny Number of Minority Ph.D.s, Set Off Faculty Recruiting Frenzy," *The Chronicle of Higher Education*, August 2, 1989
10. Ibid.
11. Bunzel, John H., "Minority Faculty Hiring: Problems and Prospects," *The American Scholar*, Winter 1990
12. "In Rift at Cornell, Racial Issues of the '60s Remain," *The New York Times*, May 3, 1989
13. "Affirmative Action Goals, Coupled with Tiny Number of Minority Ph.D.s, Set Off Faculty Recruiting Frenzy," op. cit.
14. Lilla, Elizabeth, "Who's Afraid of Women's Studies," *Commentary*, February 1986
15. See in particular, Sowell, Thomas, "Closed minds in academia," syndicated column, November 1989
16. "SUNY Bids $500,000 For One Prof," *Press and Sun Bulletin*, May 28, 1989
17. Gribben, Alan, "English Departments: Salvaging What Remains," *Academic Questions*, Fall 1989
18. "Prominent Black Poet Refuses UW Offer," *The Badger Herald*, April 20, 1989
19. Abowitz, Richard, "Revolution by search committee," *The New Criterion*, April 1989
20. "June Jordan Lectures at Dartmouth," *Black Praxis*, Summer 1987
21. Abowitz, Richard, op. cit.
22. Ibid.
23. "June Jordan Lectures at Dartmouth," op. cit.
24. Abowitz, Richard, op. cit.
25. "Prof Who Declined UW Position Gives Reading of Poetry, Essay," *The Badger Herald*, April 28, 1989
26. Abowitz, Richard, op. cit.
27. "Student Blasts UW English Department," *The Wisconsin State Journal*, April 16, 1989
28. "Campus Racial Strains Show 2 Perspectives on Inequality," *The New York Times*, May 22, 1989
29. Hollander, Paul, "From Iconoclasm to Conventional Wisdom: The Sixties in the Eighties," *Academic Questions*, Fall 1989
30. "Universities take care," *The Economist*, February 10, 1990
31. Ibid.

32. cited in Hook, Sidney, *Academic Freedom and Academic Anarchy*, op. cit. pp. 174-5
33. "College's Anti-Harassment Policies Bring Controversy Over Free Speech Issues," *Chronicle of Higher Education*, October 4, 1989
34. University Publication on Harassment Policies, 1989
35. "Universities take care," op. cit.
36. Sowell, Thomas, "Free speech is dying on our campuses," *New York Daily News*, July 21, 1989
37. "Universities take care," op. cit.
38. Finn, Chester E., Jr., "The Campus: An Island of Repression in a Sea of Freedom," *Commentary*, September 1989
39. "Colleges' Anti-Harassment Policies Bring Controversy Over Free Speech issues," op. cit.
40. "The Right's Response to Radicalism," *Insight*, December 12, 1988
41. Kors, Alan Charles, "It's Speech, Not Sex, the Dean Bans Now," *The Wall Street Journal*, October 12, 1989
42. "College's Anti-Harassment Policies . . . ," op. cit.
43. "Campus Racial Strains Show 2 Perspectives on Inequality," op. cit.
44. Interview with author, May 29, 1990
45. Finn, Chester, op. cit.
46. Thernstrom, Stephan, Letter to the Editor, *The Chronicle of Higher Education*, May 24, 1989
47. Detlefsen, Robert, "White Like Me," *The New Republic*, April 10, 1989
48. Elshtain, Jean Bethke, "Lessons from Amherst: Dragnet or Agenda for Action," *Commonweal*, March 25, 1988
49. Ibid.

THE ATTACK ON THE WEST

1. Raditsa, Leo, "On Sustenance: Teaching and Learning the Great Works," *Academic Questions*, Spring 1989
2. Barchas, Isaac D., "Stanford After the Fall: An Insider's View," *Academic Questions*, Winter 1989-90
3. Ibid.
4. "Studied Furor in Required Reading," *Insight*, March 7, 1988
5. Grossman, Ron, "Will Stanford Alter the Course of Western Civilization," *The Chicago Tribune*, March 19, 1989
6. Barchas, Isaac D., op. cit.
7. Ibid.
8. "Bennett Says Stanford Was Intimidated Into Changing Course," *The New York Times*, April 18, 1988
9. Photo by James Rucker, *Stanford Daily*, published in *The New York Times Magazine*, July 10, 1988

10. Junkerman, Charles, "Stanford's Philosophy Is An Open Book," *The Wall Street Journal*, January 6, 1989
11. Fanon, Frantz, *The Wretched of the Earth*, New York, Grove Press, 1968, p. 43
12. Ibid., p. 47
13. Ibid., p. 61
14. Ibid., p. 69
15. Bloom, Allan, "Educational Trendiness," *The Wall Street Journal*, January 27, 1989
16. Bell, Daniel, *The Reforming of General Education*, Garden City Anchor/ Doubleday, 1968, p. 58
17. Grossman, Ron, op. cit.
18. Ibid.
19. "A Curriculum of Inclusion, Report of the Commissioner's Task Force on Minorities: Equity and Excellence," July 1989

THE HOLLOW MEN

1. National Endowment for the Humanities, "50 Hours: A Core Curriculum for College Students," Washington, D.C., October 1989
2. Barzun, Jacques, *The Culture We Deserve*, Middletown, Connecticut, Wesleyan University Press, 1989, p. 11
3. General Information Bulletin, Dartmouth College, 1989-90
4. Short, Thomas, "The Curriculum Does Not Have a Core," *Academic Questions*, Summer 1989
5. MacIntyre, Alasdair, *After Virtue* (Second Edition), Notre Dame, Indiana, University of Notre Dame Press, 1984, pp. 1-5

THE HOPKINS ERA

1. Lathem, Edward C., ed., *The Dartmouth Experience*, Hanover, The University Press of New England, 1977, p. vii
2. Wheelock, Eleazer, Letter to English Trustees of Dartmouth College, July 29, 1770
3. Widmayer, Charles E., *Hopkins of Dartmouth*, Hanover, The University Press of New England, p. 3
4. Rudolph, Frederick, *The American College and University*, New York, Vintage Books, 1965, p. 423
5. Widmayer, Charles, op. cit., p. 158
6. Bell, Daniel, op. cit., p. 16
7. Hopkins, Ernest Martin, "The College of the Future," Inaugural Address, October 6, 1916
8. Hopkins, Ernest Martin, *This Our Purpose*, Hanover, Dartmouth College, 1950, p. xviii

9. Choate, Rufus, *A Discourse delivered before the Faculty, Students and Alumni of Dartmouth College on the Day preceding Commencement, July 27, 1853, commemorative of Daniel Webster*, Boston and Cambridge, J. Munroe and Co., 1853

10. Widmayer, Charles, op. cit., p. 83

11. Morse, Stearns, "Hopkins of Dartmouth," *The American Scholar*, Vol. 36, Number 1, Winter 1966-67

12. Widmayer, Charles, op. cit., p. 78

13. Rudolph, Frederick, op. cit., p. 241

14. Ibid. p. 249

15. Ibid., pp. 252-3

16. Ibid., pp. 262-3

17. Ibid., p. 271

18. Ibid., p. 274

19. Ibid., p. 399

20. Pritchett, Henry S., "The Organization of Higher Education," *The Atlantic Monthly*, December 1908

21. Ibid.

22. Newman, John Henry, *The Idea of a University*

23. Milton, John, *On Education*

24. Rudolph, Frederick, op. cit., cf. 291-305

25. Ibid., p. 294

26. Ibid., p. 292

27. Ibid., p. 272

28. Ibid., p. 294

29. Ibid., pp. 304-5

30. Ibid., p. 332

31. Flexner, Abraham, *Universities: American, English, German*, Oxford, Oxford University Press, 1930, p. 3

32. Ibid., p. 44

33. Ibid., p. 55

34. Ibid., p. 72

35. Burgess, John W., *The American University: When Shall it Be? Where Shall it Be? What Shall it Be?*, Boston, 1884, p. 5

36. Bell, Daniel, op. cit., p. 18

37. Lynn, Kenneth, "Son of 'Gen Ed'," *Commentary*, September 1978

38. *Carman Report*, Columbia University, 1946

39. Hopkins, Ernest Martin, "The Critical Period for the College," *Educational Review*, February 1910

40. Hopkins, Ernest Martin, "The Faith of the Historic College," Address, June 24, 1944

41. Bell, Daniel, op. cit., p. 18

42. Hopkins, Ernest Martin, "The College of the Future." op. cit.

43. Ibid.

44. cited in Barzun, Jacques, *The Culture We Deserve*, Middletown, Connecticut, Wesleyan University Press, 1989, p. 114
45. Widmayer, Charles, op. cit., p. 89
46. Ibid., p. 35
47. Hopkins, Ernest Martin, "Dartmouth College: An Interpretation," Address, October 20, 1919
48. Hopkins, Ernest Martin, "Scholastic Colonies," Address, January 30, 1926
49. Schulberg, Budd, "David Lambuth," in *A Dartmouth Reader*, Hanover, Dartmouth Publications, 1969, p. 212
50. Barber, Richard, "Lew Stilwell," *A Dartmouth Reader*, Dartmouth Publications, 1969, pp. 215-18

THE LIBERAL COLLEGE

1. Hopkins, Ernest Martin, Address delivered at the Opening of the 155th Year of Dartmouth College, September 20, 1923
2. Widmayer, Charles, op. cit., p. 106
3. Hopkins, Ernest Martin, *Scribner's Magazine*, February 1928
4. "Freedom of Speech in Colleges Urged," *The New York Times*, November 7, 1925
5. Widmayer, Charles, op. cit., p. 68
6. Lamb, Edward, "Campus Liberal," *A Dartmouth Reader*, Hanover, Dartmouth Publications, 1969
7. Widmayer, Charles, op. cit., p. 109
8. Mecklin, John Moffatt, *My Quest for Freedom*, New York, Scribners, 1945
9. Budd Schulberg quoted in "The End of the Quest," *A Dartmouth Reader*, Hanover, Dartmouth Publications, 1969, p. 189
10. Widmayer, Charles, op. cit., p. 181
11. Ibid.
12. Ibid., p. 182
13. Ibid., p. 183
14. Ibid., p. 184
15. Ibid., p. 221
16. Ibid., p. 222
17. Ibid., pp. 221-2
18. Hopkins, Ernest Martin, "The Goal of Education," Address, September 20, 1923
19. Ringer, Fritz, *The Decline of the German Mandarins: The German Academic Community, 1880-1933*, Harvard University Press, Cambridge, 1969, p. 215
20. cited in Bloom, Allan, *The Closing of the American Mind*, New York, Simon and Schuster, 1987, p. 315
21. Ringer, Fritz, op. cit., p. 218

22. Ibid., p. 228.
23. Steinberg, Michael Stephen, *Sabers and Brown Shirts: The German Student's Path to National Socialism, 1918-1935*, Chicago, 1977
24. Johnson, Paul, *Modern Times*, New York, Harper & Row, 1983, p. 127
25. Hopkins, Ernest Martin, *This Our Purpose*, op. cit., p. xvii
26. Widmayer, Charles, op. cit., p. 59
27. Ibid., p. 95
28. Ibid.
29. Ibid. p. 96
30. Ibid. pp. 97-8
31. "Leaders of New Hampshire," *The New York Times*, January 8, 1924
32. Widmayer, Charles, op. cit., p. 93
33. Ibid., pp. 93-4
34. Ibid., p. 144
35. Ibid., p. 78
36. Ibid., p. 200
37. Ibid., p. 203
38. "Dartmouth's Steady Course," *Alumni Magazine*, March 1990

RENAISSANCE

1. Bell, Daniel, op. cit., p. 19
2. Ibid., p. 21
3. *Carman Report*, Columbia University, 1946
4. Ibid.
5. Ibid.
6. Hart, Jeffrey, "The Case for Western civilization," *The Dartmouth Review*, April 19, 1982
7. Ibid.
8. cited in Ashmore, Harry S., *Unseasonable Truths: The Life of Robert Maynard Hutchins*, Boston, Little Brown, 1989, pp. 69-70
9. Ibid., p. 72
10. Ibid., p. 74
11. Bell, Daniel, op. cit., pp. 35-7
12. Ibid., p. 37
13. Lynn, Kenneth, "Son of 'Gen Ed'," *Commentary*, September 1978
14. Van Doren, Mark, *New York Tribune*, November 8, 1936
15. cited in Ashmore, Harry S., op. cit., p. 166
16. Bell, Daniel, op. cit. p. 51-2
17. Ibid., p. 36
18. Hopkins, Ernest Martin, *This Our Purpose*, op. cit., p. xv
19. Ibid.
20. Widmayer, Charles, op. cit., p. 202-3
21. Hopkins, Ernest Martin, *This Our Purpose*, op. cit, p. xvi

22. Widmayer, Charles, op. cit., p. 229
23. Ibid., p. 230

THE CENTER CANNOT HOLD

1. Rhodes, Richard, *The Making of the Atomic Bomb*, New York, Simon and Schuster, 1986, p. 359
2. *General Education in a Free Society*, Cambridge, Harvard University Press, 1945
3. Ibid.
4. Lynn, Kenneth, "Son of 'Gen Ed'," *Commentary*, September 1978
5. "Higher Education for Democracy; A Report of the Presidential Commission on Higher Education," excerpted in *American Higher Education: A Documentary History*, ed. Hofstadter, Richard and Smith, Wilson, Chicago, University of Chicago Press, 1961, pp. 970-90
6. Ibid., pp. 998-9
7. Hurd, John, "Dartmouth's 'New' Curriculum," *Dartmouth Alumni Magazine*, April 1966
8. "Postwar Change in Dartmouth's Educational Program," *Dartmouth Alumni Magazine*, April 1966
9. "Report of the Committee for the Division of the Social Sciences to Study the Curriculum of the First Two Years."
10. Minutes of "Sixth and Final Joint Meeting of Interdivisional Committees," February 15, 1951
11. "Academic Life Improved During Second Pentad," *The Dartmouth*, February 24, 1970
12. Ibid.
13. "An Education Program for Dartmouth," *Dartmouth Alumni Magazine*, April 1957
14. Ibid.
15. Morrison, Donald, "From Dependence Upon Teaching To Independence in Learning," *Dartmouth Alumni Magazine*, April 1957
16. "An Educational Program for Dartmouth," op. cit.
17. "Dartmouth Cites New Study Plan," *The New York Times*, April 12, 1959
18. "Dartmouth Scans 3-Term Program," *The New York Times*, March 14, 1957
19. "Dartmouth's Revolution in Learning," *The Providence Bulletin*, May 4, 1957
20. Hurd, John, op. cit.
21. Ibid.
22. Ibid.
23. Interview with Author, October 16, 1989
24. "Postwar Change in Dartmouth's Educational Program," op. cit.
25. Bell, Daniel, op. cit., pp. 190-4 and pp. 197-8

26. Barzun, Jacques, "College to University—And After," *The American Scholar*, Spring 1964
27. Trilling, Lionel, *The Last Decade: Essays and Reviews, 1965-75*, ed. by Diana Trilling, New York, Harcourt Brace Jovanovich, 1978, "The Uncertain Future of the Humanistic Educational Ideal."
28. "Action on CEP Report Expected Soon," *The Dartmouth*, November 25, 1964
29. "Freshman-Sophomore Curriculum Revised," *Dartmouth Alumni Magazine*, February 1965
30. "Action on CEP Report Expected Soon," op. cit.
31. "Faculty Committee Proposed Revision of Curriculum for First Two Years," *The Dartmouth*, November 24, 1964
32. Hurd, John, op. cit.
33. Interview with Author, October 18, 1989
34. Dickey, John Sloane, "The Race to Be Human," Convocation Address, 1966
35. Kerr, Clark, *The Uses of the University*, Cambridge, Harvard University Press, 1963
36. Arrowsmith, William, "The Future of Teaching," in *Improving College Teaching*, Washington, D.C., American Council on Education, 1967

REVOLUTION

1. quoted by Spence, Larry D., "Berkeley: What It Demonstrates," in *Revolution at Berkeley*, New York, Dell, 1965, p. 222
2. Hook, Sidney, "Second Thoughts on Berkeley," in *Revolution at Berkeley*, New York, Dell Publishing, 1965, p. 145
3. Glazer, Nathan, "What Happened at Berkeley," *Commentary*, March 1965
4. Glazer, Nathan, "Berkeley: Two Comments," *Commentary*, April 1965
5. Hook, Sidney, "Second Thoughts on Berkeley," op. cit., p. 142
6. Ibid., p. 145
7. Hook, Sidney, *Academic Freedom and Academic Anarchy*, op. cit., p. xi
8. Wilson, James Q., "Liberalism versus Liberal Education," *Commentary*, June 1972
9. Hook, Sidney, *Academic Freedom and Academic Anarchy*, op. cit., p. 177
10. Wilson, James Q., op. cit.
11. cited in Lipset, Seymour Martin and Riesman, David, *Education and Politics at Harvard*, New York, McGraw-Hill, 1975, p. 217
12. Hook, Sidney, *Academic Freedom and Academic Anarchy*, op. cit. pp. 87-8
13. Ibid.
14. Hersey, John, *Letter to The Alumni*, New York, Alfred A. Knopf, 1970, pp. 82-3; also see Brustein, Robert, *Making Scenes*, New York, Limelight Editions, 1984, pp. 107-10

15. Collier, Peter and Horowitz David, op. cit., p. 77
16. Hersey, John, op. cit., p. 27
17. Ibid., p. 77
18. "Paradise Lost at San Francisco State," *Academic Questions*, Spring 1989
19. Bunzel, John, "Black Studies at San Francisco State," in *Confrontation: The Student Rebellion in the Universities*, ed. by Bell, Daniel, and Kristol, Irving, New York, Basic Books, 1970, p. 23
20. Ibid., pp. 28-9
21. Ibid., p. 36
22. Ibid., p. 33
23. Ibid., p. 36
24. Ibid., p. 37
25. Ibid. see footnote, page 38
26. Hook, Sidney, *Academic Freedom and Academic Anarchy*, op. cit., p. 13
27. Ibid., pp. 14-5
28. Ibid.
29. Bunzel, John, "Black Studies at San Francisco State," op. cit., p. 39
30. "Paradise Lost . . . ," op. cit.
31. Bunzel, John, "Black Studies at San Francisco State," op. cit., p. 42
32. "Paradise Lost . . . ," op. cit.
33. Hook, Sidney, *Academic Freedom and Academic Anarchy*, op. cit., p. 100
34. Bloom, Allan, *The Closing of the American Mind*, op. cit., p. 348
35. Horowitz, Irving Louis and Friedland, William H., *The Knowledge Factory: Student Power and Academic Politics in America*, Chicago, Aldine Publishing Company, 1971, pp. 260-2
36. Ibid., p. 267
37. Evans and Novak, *Newsday*, May 2, 1969
38. Hook, Sidney, *Academic Freedom and Academic Anarchy*, op. cit. pp. 82-3
39. Horowitz and Friedland, op. cit., p. 268
40. Ibid., p. 269
41. Ibid., pp. 271-2
42. Hook, Sidney, *Academic Freedom and Academic Anarchy*, op. cit., p. 101
43. Ibid.
44. Ibid., p. 91
45. Ibid., p. 104
46. Ibid., p. 102
47. Lipset and Riesman, op. cit., p. 221
48. Ibid., pp. 217-8
49. Ibid., pp. 223-4
50. Brustein, Robert, *Making Scenes: A Personal History of the Turbulent Years at Yale 1966-1979*, New York, Limelight Editions, 1984, p. 86
51. Ibid., p. 120
52. Hook, Sidney, *Academic Freedom and Academic Anarchy*, op. cit., p. 19

53. Hook, Sidney, *Out of Step*, op. cit., pp. 552-4
54. Ibid., p. 554
55. Ibid., p. 551

1969

1. Fanelli, A. Alexander, memo to Mr. William Meyer, November 13, 1967
2. Kern, Chris, "The Undergraduate Chair," *Dartmouth Alumni Magazine*, December 1968
3. Kern, Chris, "Vox Clamantis 1968," *Dartmouth Alumni Magazine*, June 1968
4. Ibid.
5. Reich, Robert B., "What It's All About," *Dartmouth Alumni Magazine*, February 1968
6. Ibid.
7. Dartmouth Experimental College Catalogue, Spring 1969
8. Ibid.
9. Sevareid, Eric, CBS television newscast of May 4, 1967
10. Hornig, James F., Chairman of the Science Division, memo to Executive Committee of the faculty, May 9, 1968
11. Spritzler, John, "Emergency Bulletin to SDS Faculty and Sympathizers," May 7, 1968
12. Hull, Jonathan, "May 15," typescript, May 1968
13. "College Politics Discussed at Symposium," *The Dartmouth*, January 25, 1972
14. "SDS Prolefeed," newsletter, January 21, 1969
15. Spritzler, John and Van Hoy, John, "Whither SDS?" undated typescript
16. "Special Report," Office of the Vice President, Dartmouth College, November 27, 1968
17. Letter to Colleagues, from Dona Strauss, David Kubrin, Andrew Leddy, and Jonathan Mirsky, January 22, 1969
18. Mirsky, Jonathan, Memo to Dean Leonard Rieser, November 17, 1967; Zinn, Howard, "The Civil Liberties of Napalm or Dow Shalt Not Kill," manuscript, November 1967
19. Kemeny, John G., memo to Dean Thaddeus Seymour, November 26, 1968
20. "Mutual Sensitivity Wins the Day," *Dartmouth Alumni Magazine*, May 1969
21. Ibid.
22. Kern, Chris, "The Undergraduate Chair," op. cit.
23. Interview with author, October 16, 1989
24. "Mutual Sensitivity Wins the Day," op. cit.
25. Ibid.
26. Ibid.

27. Ibid.
28. Ad Hoc Committee on ROTC Affairs, "Chronology and Fact Sheet on ROTC," April 19, 1969
29. "Dickey Fades From Forefront During Recent Years," *The Dartmouth*, February 22, 1970
30. Minutes of the Meeting of the Executive Committee of the Faculty of Arts and Sciences, April 24, 1969
31. Ibid.
32. Minutes of the Faculty of Arts and Sciences meeting, April 25, 1969
33. Ibid.
34. Seymour, Thaddeus, "Memorandum for the file, Re: Events of May 6–7, 1969"
35. Ibid.
36. Dickerson, Albert Inskip, *Selected Writings*, Hanover, Dartmouth College, 1974, p. xi
37. Dickerson, Albert I., memo "To Whom It May Concern, Re: Events in Parkhurst Hall on Tuesday afternoon, May 6, 1969"
38. Ibid.
39. Linda Megantz et. al., v. Herbert W. Ash, U.S. Court of Appeals for the First Circuit, opinion, May 21, 1969
40. "Twelve Hours and Their Aftermath: The Student Seizure of Parkhurst Hall," *Dartmouth Alumni Magazine*, June 1969; See also, "Within Parkhurst: Tension, Debate Over Protest Tactics," *The Valley News*, May 7, 1969
41. "Statement by Thaddeus Seymour, Dean of the College," May 10, 1969
42. Fanelli, A. Alexander, Memo to President Dickey, May 13, 1969
43. Lamperti, John W., Letter to Colleagues, May 10, 1969.
44. McGee, Victor, Letter to Colleagues, May 19, 1969
45. Paul, Kenneth I., "The Senior Valedictory," *Dartmouth Alumni Magazine*, July 1969
46. Petition accompanying letter from Charles T. Wood to Professor William Ballard, May 21, 1969 and May 27, 1969
47. Dartmouth College Office of Information Services, statement, September 16, 1969
48. "Dickey Fades From Forefront . . . ," op. cit.

A CASE OF FREE SPEECH

1. Statement by Carroll Brewster and Leonard Rieser to WDCR Radio, October 7, 1969
2. "Intelligent and Courageous," *The Manchester Union-Leader*, October 10, 1969
3. SDS Flyer, "Demonstrate Against Racism"

4. Mirsky, Jonathan, Letter to NHCLU Free Speech Committee, October 27, 1969
5. NHCLU Free Speech Committee telephone interview with Dean Paul R. Shafer
6. Report of the NHCLU Free Speech Committee, "The Shockley Incident." Other sources include: "Dartmouth Blacks Bar Physicist's Talk," *The New York Times*, October 16, 1969; "Dartmouth Speech 'Cancelled' by SDS," *The Keene Evening Sentinel*, October 16, 1969; and *The Dartmouth*, October 16, 1969
7. Ibid.
8. "Shockley Denied Right to Speak," *The Manchester Union Leader*, October 16, 1969
9. Mirsky, Jonathan, letter to NHCLU Free Speech Committee, October 27, 1969
10. Smith, William, Letter to Dean Leonard Rieser, October 17, 1969
11. Brewster, Carroll, Memo to the File, "Shockley Incident," October 23, 1969
12. Memo from Dartmouth Afro-American Society to The Administrative Offices of Dartmouth College, Re: The Black Judiciary Council, undated
13. "Judgment of the Black Judiciary Committee on 'The Shockley Incident'," November 25, 1969
14. New Hampshire Civil Liberties Union, "NHCLU Report on Shockley Incident," March 3, 1970
15. Report of the College Committee on Standing and Conduct, December 4, 1969
16. "Black Judiciary Members Resign After CCSC Disciplines Blacks," *The Dartmouth*, January 5, 1970
17. "Judgment of the Black Judiciary Committee. . . ." op. cit.

STRIKE

1. "Trustees Name Kemeny to Succeed Dickey as College President March 1," *The Dartmouth*, January 23, 1970
2. "Kemeny Outlines Priorities for His Administration," *The Dartmouth*, January 27, 1970
3. Kemeny, John G., Address to the Annual Meeting of Class Officers, May 2, 1970
4. Masselli, David and Rockwell, Winthrop, "For Want of a Better Word They Called It a Strike," *Dartmouth Alumni Magazine*, June 1970
5. "For a Nationwide Strike," *The Dartmouth*, May 4, 1970
6. Masselli and Rockwell, op. cit.
7. Ibid.
8. Ibid.

9. Kemeny, John, Radio Broadcast, WDCR, May 4, 1970
10. Masselli and Rockwell, op. cit.
11. Report of the Committee Advisory to the President to the Faculty of Dartmouth College, August 18, 1969
12. "Strike Newsletter," Vol. 1, No. 3, May 8, 1970
13. Mirsky, Jonathan, "A Faculty Commentary," *Dartmouth Alumni Magazine*, June 1970
14. Brewster, Carroll, Letter to The Parents of the Students of Dartmouth College, May 12, 1970
15. Davis, James W., "Through the Strike with C.O.P." *Dartmouth Alumni Magazine*, June 1970
16. *The Dartmouth*, May 11, 1970
17. Kemeny, John, Memo to Professor Robin Robinson, May 12, 1970.
18. Congressional Record, May 13, 1970, p. S7099
19. Masselli and Rockwell, op. cit.
20. "Strike Newsletter," Vol. 1, No. 5, May 11, 1970
21. Davis, James, op. cit.
22. "Strike Newsletter," Vol. 1, No. 5, May 11, 1970
23. Penner, Hans, "The Strike: Living As If," *The Dartmouth Review*, May 1970 (NOTE: This publication should not be confused with the later independent *Dartmouth Review*. The above *Review* was an official publication of the College.)
24. Hart, Jeffrey, "What The Strike Means," *The Dartmouth Review*, May 1970 (See above note)

HANGOVER IN HANOVER

1. Kemeny, John G., "The Future of Liberal Arts Education at Dartmouth," May 4, 1972
2. Ibid.
3. Ibid.
4. Ibid.
5. Ibid.
6. Kemeny, John G., "Crossroads for the American Liberal Arts College," October 6, 1977
7. Ibid.
8. Ibid.
9. Ibid.
10. Kemeny, John G., "Challenges to Higher Education," September 1971
11. Ibid.
12. Kemeny, John G., Inaugural Address, March 1, 1970
13. "Kemeny's Leadership Regarded by Some as Too Strong," *The Dartmouth*, March 9, 1971, and "A Call to Leadership," *The Dartmouth*, May 19, 1971

14. Platt, Michael and Chick, Edson, "Liberal Arts Proposal, Dartmouth College, 1971."
15. Valiunas, Algis, "Idea of a University: A Forsaken Ideal?" *The Dartmouth*
16. Kemeny, John, "The Ten-Year Report By the Thirteenth President," 1980
17. Ibid.
18. Ibid.
19. Ibid.
20. "John Kemeny issues a stern defense," *The Dartmouth Review*, October 17, 1980
21. Interview with author, October 1989
22. Kemeny, John, "Ten-Year Report" op. cit.
23. Ibid.

A QUESTION OF RACE

 1. Report of Trustee's Committee on Equal Opportunity, December 1968 (All references to the "McLane Report" are the same as above.)
 2. "Report of the Committee on Diversity," August 1988
 3. Webber, Cleveland, "A Black Student Judges The Strike," *Dartmouth Alumni Magazine*, June 1970
 4. "Addresses Highlight 200th Commencement," *The Dartmouth*, June 14, 1970
 5. Report of the Trustee's Committee on Equal Opportunity—1976, January 7, 1976 (Also known as the Smoyer Report.)
 6. Ibid.
 7. College Board 1987 *Profile of SAT and Achievement Test Takers*
 8. Minority Report, Trustee's Committee on Equal Opportunity, January 7, 1976
 9. Report of the Trustees' Committee on Equal Opportunity, op. cit.
10. Minority Report, op. cit.
11. Ibid.
12. "Paradise Lost at San Francisco State," *Academic Questions*, Spring 1989
13. Ibid.
14. Ibid.
15. Ibid.
16. Wolfman, Brunetta, Memo to Committee on Instruction, RE: Brief Review of Dartmouth Black Studies Program, November 6, 1972
17. "Afro-Am Center Dedicated: Informal White Visits Barred," *The Dartmouth*, November 17, 1970
18. Committee on Instruction, "Recommendation On Black Studies Program: Supporting Statement."
19. Wolfman, Bruneta, op. cit.
20. Committee on Instruction, op. cit.
21. Wolfman, Brunetta, op. cit.

22. Committee on Instruction, op. cit.
23. Ibid.
24. Minutes of Executive Committee of the Faculty, May 14, 1973
25. "AAAS At Dartmouth—An Introduction," brochure, 1977
26. Syllabus, "Introduction to Black Studies," Black Studies 1, Fall 1974
27. Ibid.
28. Ibid.

A CHAMPION OF THE LEFT

1. Davis, James W., op. cit.
2. "Vita, Marysa Navarro"
3. Balch, Stephen H. and London, Herbert, "The Tenured Left," op. cit.
4. Shaktini, Namascar, "Displacing the Phallic Subject: Wittig's Lesbian Writing," *Signs*, Autumn 1982
5. *Signs*, Summer 1984
6. King, Deborah, "Multiple Jeopardy, Multiple Consciousness: The Context of a Black Feminist Ideology," *Signs*, Autumn 1988
7. Hirsch, Marianne, "Mothers and Daughter," *Signs*, Autumn 1981
8. Hirsch, Marianne, "Feminism and Sisterhood," *womyn's re/view*, undated
9. Navarro, Marysa, "Research on Latin American Women," *Signs*, Autumn 1979
10. Ibid.

A QUESTION OF GENDER

1. Navarro, Marysa, "Proposal to the National Endowment for the Humanities for a Pilot Grant in Support of the Women's Studies Program, Dartmouth College"
2. Baer, Elizabeth and Odarenko, Dora Janeway, "The IWY Conference at Houston: Implications for Women's Studies," Women's Studies Newsletter, Winter 1978
3. Navarro, Marysa, "Women's Studies Program: Third Year Review"
4. Ibid.
5. Ibid.
6. Ibid.
7. Ibid.
8. Syllabus, "Women's Studies I: Women in Society," Spring Term, 1981
9. Syllabus, "History and Theory of Feminism," National Endowment for the Humanities Pilot Grant Proposal
10. "Battle Lines on Feminism and Religion," *The New York Times*, May 10, 1989
11. Eisenstein, Zillah R., ed., *Capitalist Patriarchy and the Case for Socialist Feminism*, New York, Monthly Review Press, 1979, pp. 3-4

12. Ibid., p. 357
13. Harstock, Nancy, "Feminist Theory and the Development of Revolutionary Strategy," in *Capitalist Patriarchy and the Case for Socialist Feminism*, op. cit., p. 65
14. Syllabus, "Deconstruction and Reconstruction"
15. Ibid.
16. "Dartmouth's Post-Feminism," *The Dartmouth Review*, May 21, 1984
17. "What To Study, What To Teach," *The Valley News*, October 13, 1988
18. Syllabus, Women's Studies 23, Summer 1989: "Women and Writing"
19. Avenoso, Karen, "Subject: Half of Humanity," *Dartmouth Alumni Magazine*, Summer 1988
20. Ibid.
21. Freccero, Carla, "Angela Davis, *Women, Race, and Class*: One Opinion," *Stet*, 1988
22. Avenoso, Karen, op. cit.
23. Dean of the Faculty, Dartmouth College, Notice of "Gender & War: Roles and Representations," Humanities Research Institute, Dartmouth College, Spring 1990
24. Syllabus, "Women and Social Change in the Third World," Women's Studies 24, Spring Term, 1989
25. Rowbotham, Sheila, *Women, Resistance and Revolution: A History of Women and Revolution in the Modern World*, New York, Pantheon Books, 1971, p. 11
26. Ibid., p. 12
27. Sacks, Karen "Women and Class Struggle in Sembene's *God's Bits of Wood*," *Signs*, Winter 1978
28. Syllabus, "Women and Social Change . . . ," op. cit.
29. Ibid.
30. Ibid.
31. Randall, Margaret, "Introducing the Family Code," in Eisenstein, Zillah, op. cit., p. 296

OF INDIANS AND ART: THE DIVERSITY WARS

1. For a fuller discussion of this incident see Hart, Benjamin, *Poisoned Ivy*, New York, Stein and Day, 1984
2. Report of the Committee on Diversity, August 1988
3. Ibid.
4. Ibid.
5. Ibid.
6. "Native Americans Air Grievances; May Thrash Out Problems Soon," *The Dartmouth*, December 3, 1971
   7. "College Politics Discussed at Symposium," *The Dartmouth*, January 25, 1972

8. Hart, Benjamin, op. cit., p. 217
9. Ibid., pp. 69-70
10. Ibid., p. 72
11. "Cover-up," *Dartmouth Alumni Magazine*, April 1983
12. "Art profs, critics, blast Hovey censorship," *The Dartmouth Review*, May 16, 1983
13. "Dartmouth's Newest Traditions: Censorship and Coercion," *The Dartmouth Review*, April 15, 1987
14. "Dartmouth's Censored Liberal Arts," *The Dartmouth Review*, April 23, 1986

HERETICS: THE RISE OF *THE DARTMOUTH REVIEW*

1. Hart, Benjamin, *Poisoned Ivy*, New York, Stein and Day, 1984, pp. 168-9
2. Ibid., p. 179
3. Ingraham, Edward, "Is the *Dartmouth Review* Good or Bad for Dartmouth?" *Dartmouth Alumni Magazine*, April 1989
4. "Dartmouth College Self-Study Report For Comprehensive Visit By the New England Association of Schools and Colleges," October 23-26, 1988.
5. Directory of Student Activities and Student Organizations, 1987-88
6. *Stet*, 1989
7. Ibid.
8. *womyn's re/view*, undated issue, undoubtedly an oversight by the staff, listed on the masthead as "Sisters (mothers & daughters)"
9. Ibid.
10. Ibid.
11. *womyn's re/view*, Spring 1988
12. These examples are taken from a speech denouncing *The Dartmouth Review* by Professor James Wright to the 156th Meeting of the Alumni Council in June 1988; they are among the most popular quotes used by College administrators and recycled with some frequency.
13. Interviews with author
14. "Dis sho' ain't no jive, bro," *The Dartmouth Review*, March 15, 1982
15. Singh, Harmeet Dhillon, "Shanties, Shakespeare, and Sex Kits," *Policy Review*, Fall 1989
16. O'Brien, Conor Cruise, Introduction to Edmund Burke's *Reflections on the Revolution in France*, Middlesex, England, Penguin Books, 1969
17. Hart, Benjamin, op. cit., pp. 163-4
18. Martz, Larry, "When Dialogue Turns to Diatribe: Is speech at Dartmouth as free as it should be?," *Dartmouth Alumni Magazine*, May 1989
19. Ibid.
20. Hart, Benjamin, op. cit., p. 236
21. Ibid., p. 164
22. Ibid., p. 167

23. Ibid., pp. 168-9
24. Ibid., pp. 152-3
25. Ibid., p. 160
26. Ibid., p. 161
27. Ibid., p. 245
28. Ibid., pp. 172-3
29. "Chronicles of a Dartmouth Conservative," *The Washington Post*, December 5, 1984
30. Hart, Benjamin, op. cit., pp. 213-24
31. Ibid., pp. 15-16
32. Ibid.
33. "Prof. Bill Cole's Song and Dance Routine," *The Dartmouth Review*, January 17, 1983
34. Hart, Benjamin, op. cit., p. 16
35. Ibid., pp. 240-1
36. Ibid., p. 242
37. Interview with Debbie Stone, June 24, 1987

COUP D'ETAT

1. "Portrait of the President as a young man," *The Dartmouth Weekend Magazine*, May 2, 1986
2. Ibid.
3. "Businessman Brings Traditional Views to Presidency," *The Dartmouth Review*, March 2, 1981
4. Churchill, Winston, *The Gathering Storm*, New York, Houghton Mifflin, 1948, p. 238
5. "Toro, Toro," *Forbes*, November 27, 1978
6. "The Toro Team Has a Winning Game Plan," *Nation's Business*, August 1979
7. Ibid.
8. "Toro: Coming to Life After Warm Weather Wilted Its Big Plans," *Business Week*, October 10, 1983
9. "A dry winter stalls Toro's growth plans," *Business Week*, March 2, 1981
10. Ibid. Also see "Toro: Coming to Life . . . ," op. cit.
11. "Toro: Coming to Life . . . ," op. cit.
12. "David McLaughlin's First Five months," *Dartmouth Alumni Magazine*, September 1981
13. "Toro, Toro," op. cit.
14. "David McLaughlin's First Five Months," op. cit.
15. "The Toro Team . . . ," op. cit.
16. "Resigning Blunt official blasts administration," *The Dartmouth*, January 27, 1986
17. McLaughlin, David, "Inaugural Address," March 1, 1981

18. *The Dartmouth*, January 4, 1980
19. "Faculty in Support of Non-Western Requirement," *The Dartmouth*, October 21, 1981
20. *Organization, Regulation and Courses, Dartmouth College*, September 1988
21. "Japanese program still lacking, lack of funds cited," *The Dartmouth*, February 8, 1988
22. Report of the Women's Support Task Force, April 1987
23. "Faculty in Support of Non-Western Requirement," op. cit.
24. Hart, Jeffrey, "The case for Western civilization," *The Dartmouth Review*, September 20, 1982
25. Hart, Jeffrey, *The Dartmouth Review*, October 3, 1980
26. "Faculty committee prepares to debate issue of leadership," *The Dartmouth*, January 7, 1986, also see "Faculty report sharply criticizes Dartmouth president's leadership," *The Boston Globe*, January 7, 1986
27. "Faculty report latest round in Dartmouth clash," *The Boston Globe*, January 12, 1986
28. "Report critical of Dartmouth president is distributed to faculty, staff," *The Boston Globe*, January 8, 1986
29. Ibid.
30. "Shanties, official departures mark fall term," *The Dartmouth*, January 3, 1986
31. Ibid.
32. "Shantytown: 'What's the story?' " *Dartmouth Alumni Magazine*, March 1986
33. "Dismantle the shanties," *The Dartmouth*, January 21, 1986
34. "Mission: Shanty Removal," *The Dartmouth Review*, January 29, 1986
35. Singh, Harmeet Dhillon, op. cit.
36. D'Souza, Dinesh, "Dartmouth guilty of double standard," *The Boston Globe*, February 23, 1986
37. "Taking Action," *The Dartmouth*, January 22, 1986
38. "Protestors draft demands for McLaughlin," *The Dartmouth*, January 23, 1986
39. "Students, faculty gather on the Green to voice protests about shanty town attack," *The Dartmouth*, January 22, 1986
40. "The occupation of President's offices: tears and fears," *The Dartmouth*, January 24, 1986
41. D'Souza, Dinesh, "Dartmouth guilty of double standard," op. cit.
42. D'Souza, Dinesh, "Former Reviewer Examines Shanty Raids at Dartmouth," *The Dartmouth Review*, April 9, 1986
43. "Administration: no action yet against protesters," *The Dartmouth*, January 23, 1986

44. "Professors discuss faculty reaction with rallying students," *The Dartmouth*, January 23, 1986
45. "Shantytown: 'What's the story?'," op. cit.
46. "Classes canceled today: Parkhurst occupation ends," *The Dartmouth*, January 24, 1986
47. Letter from David McLaughlin to the Dartmouth Community, January 23, 1986
48. "College undertakes self-examination at first teach-in," *The Dartmouth*, January 27, 1986
49. "College Symposium Serves Up Hysterical Accusations, Confessions," *The Dartmouth Review*, February 5, 1986
50. "No confidence vote debated by faculty," *The Dartmouth*, January 28, 1986
51. Rafshoon, Scott, "President on the firing line," *The Dartmouth's Weekend Magazine*, January 31, 1986
52. "Sit-in members found guilty but no College action taken," *The Dartmouth*, February 3, 1986
53. Buckley, William F., "Amnesty for the Dartmouth Dozen," syndicated column, March 1986
54. "COS sets penalties for shanty attackers," *The Dartmouth*, February 12, 1986
55. D'Souza, Dinesh, "Former Reviewer Examines Shanty Raids at Dartmouth," op. cit.
56. "Eighteen arrested for obstructing shanty removal," *The Dartmouth*, February 12, 1986
57. "Dartmouth faculty, students petition board on president," *The Boston Globe*, February 15, 1986
58. Ibid.
59. "Sledgehammers at Dartmouth," *The Boston Globe*, March 19, 1986
60. Danziger, Robert A., "An unfair portrayal of life at Dartmouth," *The Boston Globe*, March 26, 1986
61. "College granted new COS hearing to sidestep anticipated legal defeat," *The Dartmouth*, March 7, 1986
62. "Publication's name under fire," *The Dartmouth*, February 25, 1986
63. "College to drop civil charges; will move against Review," *The Dartmouth*, February 25, 1986
64. "Ten attackers found guilty," *The Dartmouth*, March 27, 1986
65. "Simon, Steel, and Sununu Say," *The Dartmouth Review*, April 16, 1986
66. Ibid.
67. Ibid.
68. "Simon blasts McLaughlin," *The Dartmouth*, April 10, 1986
69. "Protests erupt after College commutes sentences," *The Dartmouth*, April 14, 1986

70. "McLaughlin says he won't call re-trial," *The Dartmouth*, May 20, 1986
71. "Administration and Health Service Condone Bizarre Sexual Activities," *The Dartmouth Review*, January 21, 1987
72. Ibid.
73. Hart, Jeffrey, "Safe Sex and the Presence of the Absence," *The Dartmouth Review*, May 10, 1987
74. "Assaults, protests disrupt weekend activities," *The Dartmouth*, October 20, 1986
75. "President calls weekend events an embarrassment," *The Dartmouth*, October 21, 1986
76. "Women getting angry," *The Dartmouth Weekend Magazine*, October 31, 1986
77. Ibid.
78. Ibid.
79. Report of the Women's Support Task Force, April 1987
80. Ibid.
81. Ibid.
82. Ibid.
83. Ibid.
84. Interview with author, October 13, 1989
85. Conversation with author

ONE OF THEIR OWN

1. "The Scholar President," *The Dartmouth Alumni Magazine*, Summer 1987
2. "The Way With Words," *Dartmouth Alumni Magazine*, January/February 1988
3. Dartmouth College, "Affirmative Action Annual Report 1986-1987," November 1987, see pages 25, 39, and 47
4. Freedman, James O., Address to the General Faculty, October 31, 1988
5. "U of I chief no longer considering Texas job," *The Cedar Rapids Gazette*, August 9, 1985
6. "U of I loses Freedman to Dartmouth," *The Cedar Rapids Gazette*, April 14, 1987
7. Ibid.
8. Dartmouth College Self-Study Report for Comprehensive Visit By The New England Association of Schools and Colleges, October 23-26, 1988
9. Report From the Dartmouth College Self-Study Accreditation Committee on Intellectual Environment, p. 4 (Hereafter referred to as "Intellectual Environment.")
10. "Intellectual Environment," pp. 16-17
11. Ibid., p. 11
12. Ibid., pp. 17-18

13. Ibid., p. 15
14. Ibid., pp. 32-4
15. Ibid., p. 19
16. Ibid., p. 16
17. Ibid., p. 40
18. Ibid., p. 42
19. "The Rise of Research," *Dartmouth Alumni Magazine*, February 1989
20. Ibid.
21. Interim Report of the Planning Steering Committee, 1989
22. Interview with author, October 18, 1989
23. Gray, Hanna H., Report to the Faculty, Administration, Trustees, Students of Dartmouth College by an Evaluation Team Representing the Commission on Institutions of Higher Education of the New England Association of Schools and Colleges. Prepared after study of the institution's self-evaluation reports and a visit to the campus October 23-26, 1988. All references to the Gray report are to the above unless otherwise indicated.
24. "Making Ambitious Ends Meet," *Dartmouth Alumni Magazine*, April 1988
25. "Academic Critic to Study Dartmouth curriculum," *The Washington Times*, July 7, 1989 (The "academic critic" is the author of this book.)
26. *The Boston Globe*, October 19, 1987

DIVERSITY TRIUMPHANT

1. I have dealt with this incident previously in *ProfScam: Professors and the Demise of Higher Education*, Washington, D.C., Regnery Gateway, 1988, pp. 253-6
2. "A Dartmouth commitment," *The Boston Globe*, March 29, 1988
3. Lahr, Dwight, "Public Announcement Regarding The Investigation Of The Complaint Against Professor William S. Cole," March 24, 1988
4. "Cole Incident Sparks Racial Strife," *The Dartmouth*, March 1, 1988
5. "Students picket *Review* ad buyers," *The Dartmouth*, March 2, 1988
6. Crovitz, L. Gordon, "Intolerance and *The Dartmouth Review*," *The Wall Street Journal*, December 28, 1988
7. "Rally attracts 400: Speakers address injustice," *The Dartmouth*, March 4, 1988
8. Letter from Black Caucus to President James Freedman, March 3, 1988
9. "The weak in Review," *The Dartmouth*, March 2, 1988
10. Foley, Brian, "The limits of good taste," *The Dartmouth*, March 3, 1988
11. Anderson, Doug, "Examine both principles," *The Dartmouth*, March 3, 1988
12. "Freedman: no place for intolerance here," *The Dartmouth*, March 1, 1988
13. Crovitz, L. Gordon, op. cit.

14. Silberman, Laurence, "Thoughtful Liberals Bear Greatest Responsibility," *The Wall Street Journal*, December 28, 1988 (excerpts from letter to Dartmouth College, declining Daniel Webster Award)
15. Crovitz, L. Gordon, op. cit.
16. Lahr, Dwight, op. cit.
17. Crovitz, L. Gordon, op. cit.
18. "Prof urges faculty to boycott today's meeting," *The Dartmouth*, May 2, 1988
19. Freedman, James O., "Address to Special Faculty Meeting," March 28, 1988
20. "Outsider Who Stirred Emotions at Dartmouth," *The New York Times*, May 11, 1988
21. "The Joys of Hypocrisy," *The Wall Street Journal*, May 4, 1988
22. "Freedman: 'Review' Is 'Cruel, Ugly'," *The Valley News*, March 29, 1988
23. "Dartmouth President Faults Right-Wing Student Journal," *The New York Times*, March 29, 1988
24. "Freedman: 'Review' Is 'Cruel, Ugly'," op. cit.
25. Martz, Larry, op. cit.
26. Gallagher, Margaret Anne, "A Tyranny of Pity," *National Review*, September 26, 1986
27. Ibid.
28. "Yalie Punished for Satiric Posters," *The Dartmouth Review*, October 15, 1986
29. Schmidt, Benno, Inaugural Speech, September 20, 1986
30. "The Joys of Hypocrisy," op. cit.
31. cited in "Dustup at Dartmouth," *Harvard Magazine*, May-June 1989
32. Silber, John, *Straight Shooting: What's Wrong with America and How to Fix It*, New York, Harper & Row, 1989, p. 85
33. "The Dartmouth Dispute," *The Washington Post*, January 10, 1989
34. Washburn, Wilcomb, "Liberalism Versus Free Speech," *National Review*, September 30, 1988 (Adapted from Washburn's speech to the Dartmouth Class of 1948)
35. Silberman, Laurence, op. cit.
36. Ibid.
37. Ibid.
38. Hentoff, Nat, "Rites of Exorcism at Dartmouth," *The Washington Post*, December 23, 1988
39. Schrader, Esther, "Contention is an attractive quality," *The Dartmouth*, February 19, 1988

THE DARTMOUTH MIND

1. Report of the Committee on Diversity, August 1988
2. Ibid., p. 2
3. Ibid.

4. Report of the Committee on Intellectual Environment, p. 16
5. Report of the Committee on Diversity, op. cit., p. 18
6. *Re-Reading America: Cultural Contexts for Critical Thinking and Writing*, New York, St. Martin's Press, 1989
7. Syllabus, Drama 9, "The History of Clothing and the Psychology of Dress," Spring 1989
8. *Organization, Regulations, and Courses, Dartmouth College*, September 1988
9. Syllabus, Sociology 29, "Sport and Society," Spring 1989
10. Syllabus, Education 9, "Humans And Other Animals," Spring 1989
11. Syllabus, Sociology 91, "Corporate and Governmental Deviance," Fall 1989
12. Syllabus, Sociology 31, "Prejudice and Oppression," Fall 1987
13. Strong, Bryan and De Vault, Christine, *The Marriage and Family Experience*, St. Paul, West Publishing Company, 1989, p. 3
14. Ibid., p. 7
15. Ibid., pp. 6-8
16. Ibid., p. 509
17. Ibid., p. 159
18. Wright, James, Speech to Alumni Council, op. cit.
19. quoted in Hart, Jeffrey, "Fascism Returns to Campus," *The Dartmouth Review*, November 8, 1989
20. *National Review*, September 15, 1989
21. "Faculty supports 'minority first' plan," *The Dartmouth*, February 28, 1989
22. "Assembly excludes CIA from College," *The Dartmouth*, November 20, 1986
23. *The Dartmouth Review*, February 7, 1990
24. Gates, Henry Louis, Convocation Speech, Dartmouth College, 1989
25. Fromm, Harold, "The Hegemonic Form of Othering; or The Academic's Burden," *Critical Inquiry 13*, Autumn 1986
26. *Dartmouth Alumni Magazine*, May 1988
27. Smith, John Christopher, "Observations of a Freshman," *The Dartmouth Review*, September 27, 1989
28. Ibid.
29. Grace, William R., "Sex, Lies and Rubber Dams," *The Dartmouth Review*, November 15, 1989
30. "Contradictions," *Stet*, 1989
31. "Divestment announcement expected," *The Dartmouth*, November 13, 1989
32. Ibid.
33. "Dartmouth Decides to Divest," *The Dartmouth*, November 14, 1989
34. Letter to Members of the Dartmouth Community from the Board of Trustees, November 13, 1989

35. McCutcheon, James, "Protestors Occupy Parkhurst: Trustees Cave In To Demands for Divestment," *The Dartmouth Review*, November 22, 1989
36. "Faculty approve Latin A. major," *The Dartmouth*, November 14, 1989

THE FATE OF AN IDEA

1. Ollman, Bertell and Vernoff, Edward, ed. *The Left Academy: Marxist Scholarship on American Campuses*, New York, McGraw-Hill, 1982, pp. 2-3
2. Arrowsmith, William, "The Future of Teaching," in *Improving College Teaching*, Washington, D.C., American Council on Education, 1967
3. Barzun, Jacques, *The Culture We Deserve*, Middletown, Connecticut, Wesleyan University Press, 1989, p. 22

INDEX

DATE DUE

DEMCO 38-296